A Stranger's Knowledge

A Stranger's Knowledge

STATESMANSHIP PHILOSOPHY & LAW in

Plato's *Statesman*

Xavier Márquez

PARMENIDES
PUBLISHING

Las Vegas | Zurich | Athens

PARMENIDES PUBLISHING
Las Vegas | Zurich | Athens

This edition published in 2012 by Parmenides Publishing
in the United States of America

ISBN soft cover: 978-1-930972-79-7
ISBN e-Book: 978-1-930972-80-3

Library of Congress Cataloging-in-Publication Data

Márquez, Xavier.
A stranger's knowledge : statesmanship, philosophy, and law in Plato's Statesman / Xavier Márquez.
p. cm.
Includes bibliographical references and index.
ISBN 978-1-930972-79-7 (pbk. : alk. paper) —
ISBN 978-1-930972-80-3 (ebook)
1. Plato. Statesman. 2. Political science—Philosophy. I. Title.

JC71.P314M37 2012
321'.07—dc23

2012009027

Typeset in Constantia and Gotham Narrow
by 1106 Design | www.1106design.com
Printed digitally by Edwards Brothers, Chicago, IL

1-888-PARMENIDES
www.parmenides.com

To Nancy and Sophia

Contents

List of Figures

Preface

THE *STATESMAN* IS AN UNLOVED (some would say unlovely) dialogue. When I began to work on the *Statesman*, I did not expect to fall in love with it, and indeed at first my interpretation of the dialogue was going to occupy only a small part of a work on Plato's "strangers" that ranged from the *Theaetetus* and the *Sophist* to the *Laws*. But as I began to unravel its many threads, to puzzle together its difficult structure, and to appreciate the subtle artistry of its apparently bizarre surface, I became ever more entranced by its mysteries, to the point where my original project went by the wayside. I eventually came to see the dialogue as a great work of art worthy, if not of love, at least of genuine admiration, capable of holding its place next to Plato's other great artistic and philosophical achievements: the *Republic*, the *Phaedrus*, the *Gorgias*, the *Theaetetus*. If this book achieves nothing else, I would be happy if it at least communicated my sense of the hidden beauty of this much-maligned work.

Though the *Statesman* does possess, I think, a real beauty, this beauty is certainly well hidden: one must arrive, after considerable effort, to the appropriate perspective from which to see that what appeared disproportionate and ugly at the beginning of the journey is in fact the contrary. This book is thus a kind of guidebook; if it succeeds, it should help the reader of the dialogue achieve the proper standpoint for appreciation. Yet the view we gain from this perspective is in some respects bleak: it is a view of the "fall" of the world, ever moving away from the order of things, and of the absence of genuine political order. In depicting the statesman, the *Statesman* tells us how far we are from statesmanship; and in depicting the cosmos, the *Statesman* tells us how slender our connection to the divine order is. As a stranger—a foreigner to Athens—discourses about statesmanship with a young mathematician named Socrates, the dialogue reveals that statesmanship remains, and in some respects must remain, foreign to politics. Such order as political life retains depends on a mere remedy, the *pharmakon* of law, an imperfect and in some respects poisonous drug that, when it does not kill the patient, hardly helps it thrive. Nevertheless the dialogue keeps the spirit of the fundamental Platonic project alive: that we must try to embed reason as far as possible in politics. I have tried to bring out this message in its fullness through as sympathetic an interpretation of the dialogue as I could manage. We can still learn from Plato's vision.

This book has taken a long time to travel from conception to publication. It originated in my doctoral dissertation of 2006, and has benefitted throughout from the comments and criticisms of a large number of people. My dissertation supervisor, Catherine Zuckert, was always encouraging and gave me sharp and challenging feedback. Walter Nicgorski, David O'Connor and Fred Dallmayr helped me find my focus. Kevin Cherry and Emma Cohen de Lara made very useful comments on various pieces extracted from the book. Bits and pieces of the manuscript were presented at various conferences, where I benefited from the comments of colleagues whose names I no longer remember, but whom I would wish to thank; some of these bits and pieces eventually grew and became papers published in the journals *Ancient Philosophy* and *Political Studies*, where they in turn benefitted from anonymous peer review, which eventually improved this book as well. I was inspired in my efforts by Mitchell Miller's and Seth Bernardete's books on the *Statesman*, which greatly influenced my overall interpretation of the dialogue, and I also learned much from disagreeing with two scholars of Plato's political thought, Christopher Rowe and George Klosko, who, though they may not know it, provided the spur for some of my ideas and corrected some of my persistent misconceptions. If I in turn criticize their views severely here, I hope they do not consider me guilty of parricide; I plead the Eleatic's own defense. Several anonymous reviewers of earlier versions of the manuscript also provided fair and challenging criticism. The Political Science and International Relations Programme at Victoria University of Wellington provided a congenial space to work and enough time for me to rethink my first draft. My head of school, Ken Perszyk, generously made resources available at short notice to support the completion of the book. My editor at Parmenides, Eliza Tutellier, expertly guided me through the publication process. My parents Axel and Marisabel, and my sister Maya, were always supportive. And, most importantly of all, my wife Nancy and my daughter Sophia encouraged my writing, helped me complete and proofread the manuscript, and kept up my hopes that this work would eventually see the light.

Wellington, 7 December 2011

Introduction

THIS BOOK IS PRIMARILY A STUDY of Plato's *Statesman*. A new book on Plato's political thought always requires some justification. People have been writing about, and arguing with, Plato for over two millennia, so it is no wonder that there is a surfeit of books and articles on all aspects of Plato's thought. Though the *Statesman* is relatively neglected among commentators, a large number of monographs and articles on various aspects of the work still exist, and interest in the dialogue has picked up in the last two decades. And though there is no consensus regarding the interpretation of the work—scholars disagree about such fundamental matters as whether the dialogue is actually about politics, despite its title—the very variety of positions that have been taken about its meaning indicate that the *space* of alternative interpretations is already well mapped. Worse, a commentator cannot hope to support a novel interpretation of the dialogue with truly "new" evidence, since the text of the dialogue has not changed, and no new independent information about Plato or his context has emerged for many years; the last important new "fact" to be discovered about Plato's work was the relative dating of the three main groups of dialogues by means of stylometric analysis, and even this "fact" is highly contested. The interpreter proposing a novel reading must use the very same text used by those who have plausibly argued for very different interpretations; and if his interpretation is indeed better than theirs, it can only be because it organizes the existing evidence in ways that have the effect of correcting some earlier misconceptions and errors, of making a few overlooked connections, and of making Plato speak in clearer, more interesting, and more relevant ways than earlier commentators have made him speak. But since the text (and the associated historical information we know about Plato) underdetermines the *space* of possible interpretations, a novel reading faces an uphill struggle to convince. There can be no Platonic knowledge of a Platonic dialogue.

The task is further complicated for a political theorist by the problem of Plato's relevance for current political thought. Plato was a participant in a different conversation than ours; he was not speaking *to* us and our problems, even if some of the things he (or rather his characters) says resonate with our concerns. He is not "our contemporary" in any straightforward way,[1] and any attempt to translate his thought so that it will become "contemporary" risks falsifying it.

Indeed, many aspects of Plato's political thought, with its insistence that the purpose of politics is the inculcation of virtue and its claim that only those with knowledge should rule, no longer seem to provide compelling alternatives to currently dominant ideas, or even to speak to the dominant concerns of modern life, however great his dialogues may still seem as works of art. Few people today, or at least few political philosophers, would defend the classic Platonic thesis that only those with knowledge should rule, and most would defend some version of democracy, that is, the idea that the many should rule, a thesis which Plato strenuously criticized throughout his life.[2] There is today an immense literature dedicated to arguing the

---

1 Cf. Schofield (2006, 1): "Is Plato our contemporary? Well, yes and no."

2 For an overview of Plato's opposition to democracy, see Schofield (2006, ch. 2). To be sure, Plato criticized Athenian democracy, which was quite different from what we today would call democracy, but many of his criticisms would seem to apply to modern democracies as well, even if these do avoid some of Plato's most important arguments.

case for democracy,[3] and an even larger literature that simply assumes that this case is conclusive and moves on to critique various aspects of modern politics on the grounds that it is inadequately democratic; there is hardly anyone arguing for expert rulers.[4] Most philosophers today do not want to be kings; indeed, many go out of their way to argue that philosophers, *qua* philosophers, lack both right and qualifications to rule.

Yet few propose that rule should be thoughtless, that expertise is unnecessary in modern, complex societies, or that collectively binding decisions cannot be better or worse according to criteria that are independent of the particular preferences or views of the current majority. Many modern defenders of democracy in fact emphasize that a properly structured public sphere in a representative system should refine the views of the people and incorporate the insights of experts as far as possible, even if they argue that knowledge cannot directly justify political authority and that the knowledge of experts is not the only knowledge that matters. Indeed, one could argue that insofar as philosophy intends to be *political,* it is necessarily the attempt to embed reason in politics in some form, whether in people or in institutions; and this is, at bottom, the essence of the Platonic program. The claim of knowledge to rule has thus not entirely vanished from our consciousness, even if it has been sometimes banished to obscure corners of the philosophical conversation.[5]

3 See, e.g., Dahl (1989) for one influential example.

4 Moreover, those who are skeptical of democracy tend to be skeptical of politics as such, like philosophical libertarians or anarchists, and hence to reject the Platonic concern with expert rulers, even if they criticize democracy for lacking sufficient expertise to make wise collectively binding decisions. See, e.g., Caplan (2007).

5 There has been some recent interest, for example, in "epistemic" defenses of democracy (see, e.g., Estlund [2008]; Goodin [2003]), that is, defenses of democracy that ground the legitimacy of democratic procedures partly in their ability to get the "right" answer to the questions faced by a people. Yet epistemic democrats are few and far between, and at any rate they defend *democracy,* not some form of expert rule, unlike Plato.

To be sure, if politics should be based on the twin ideas of consent and rights, as it is often argued or assumed today, then political expertise can only play a subordinate role. Yet in order to understand what this subordinate role may be, or even to understand the critical function that the ideal of political expertise can play in a democratic age, we need to understand more clearly what political knowledge could be and how it may be connected with other forms of knowledge.

This is reason enough to turn to Plato, whose thought remains the most serious and complete philosophical challenge to current ideas about the possibility and limits of reason in politics. His work would be worth exploring even if, on examination, we found his arguments wanting and his solutions problematic. But I contend in this work that Plato's conception of political knowledge or "statesmanship"—its nature, its relationship to other forms of knowledge, and its implications for the construction and justification of political institutions—still provides powerful resources for thinking about the fundamental problems of politics; and the most complete treatment of the meaning and limits of political knowledge in Plato is not to be found in the *Republic* or the *Laws,* two well-studied and well-known dialogues, but in the less familiar *Statesman.*

Why study the Statesman?

The *Statesman* depicts a conversation about the nature of statesmanship or political knowledge between an unnamed Stranger from Elea and a young mathematician named Socrates, in front of an audience consisting of the elder Socrates, an established mathematician named Theodorus, and Theaetetus, another young mathematician. The conversation takes place on the eve of the elder Socrates' trial, and is located in fictional continuity with the conversations depicted in the *Theaetetus* (where the elder Socrates talks with Theodorus and Theaetetus about the nature of knowledge) and the *Sophist* (where the Eleatic Stranger first appears and discusses the nature of sophistry with Theaetetus). As in the *Sophist,* the elder Socrates speaks only in a short prologue, and the remainder of the discussion takes place between the Eleatic Stranger and Young Socrates.

The actual conversation between Young Socrates and the Stranger attempts to isolate the nature of statesmanship by means of a series of sometimes bizarre "divisions" that contrast statesmanship with other forms of knowledge. These contrasts, which are only sometimes justified by argument rather than appeals to intuition, initially culminate in the identification of statesmanship with the "theoretical" and collective "nurture" of human beings understood either as two-footed pigs or as featherless bipeds (258b–267e). But this identification is found to be partially defective, and the Stranger resorts to telling a great and puzzling myth in order to determine the source of the problem (267e–274e). Using the myth, the Stranger argues that their initial identification was flawed primarily due to a mistaken conflation of "nurture" with all forms of care and of "divine" with "human" care (as well as, less clearly, to a confusion between tyranny and genuine kingship).

The initial division is then corrected, but the Stranger remains unsatisfied with the results attained (to 277b) and leads Young Socrates through a series of difficult methodological reflections on the need for, and the proper use of, paradigms, including a discussion of weaving, as well as a discussion of the art of due measure (to 287b), all of which are put to use in order to refine the original identification of statesmanship, which is now characterized as the integrating art in the network of arts that constitute the city and enable the care of human beings by human beings. Along the way, however, the discussion is sidetracked by the need to distinguish the statesman from the false rulers of cities, who are said to be sophists (beginning at 291a), a task which in turn leads to an examination of the nature and limits of law *vis-à-vis* genuine political knowledge (to 303c). This section, which in a sense constitutes the core of the political theory of the dialogue, makes a complex argument both for the superiority of political knowledge to law and for the superiority of law to the rule of the ignorant, but does not affect the identification of statesmanship as the art that gives the other arts for the care of human beings their point and whose work completes theirs. At any rate, after this discussion the Stranger completes the characterization of statesmanship by describing the statesman's task as the "weaving" of the conflicting dispositions of human beings towards the timing of action, that is, the dispositions belonging to those normally thought of as "courageous" and "moderate." This weaving is ultimately accomplished by inducing stable true opinions concerning the just, the good, and the noble among the citizens, and through the establishment of a marriage system that mixes these conflicting dispositions as much as possible; with these considerations, the dialogue ends.

As is the case for many other Platonic dialogues, a number of prejudices surround the *Statesman*, like barnacles covering a ship, which prevent the first-time reader from taking the dialogue very seriously. The *Statesman*, it is said, compares poorly in purely literary respects with earlier works of Plato.[6] Its dramatic features have been derided as a mere façade,[7] its humor damned as "professorial,"[8] its structure indicted as hard to discern.[9] The dialogue, we are told, is mostly an exercise

6 See, e.g., Campbell (1867, xxii): "the loss of conversational freedom and liveliness is accompanied by a corresponding decline of poetical grace and power."

7 See, e.g., Rowe (1996, 171–178); Skemp (1987, 8); Schofield (2006, 166), with some caveats.

8 See Skemp (1987, 24).

9 See, e.g., Annas and Waterfield (1995, xii). Klosko (1986, 188), is even more lapidary: "the *Statesman* discusses a bewildering variety of topics in a rambling, at times almost arbitrary manner." It is no wonder that scholars have occasionally argued that the *Statesman* was not written by Plato. Grote (1875, II.396) discusses some early attempts to deny the Platonic authorship of the *Statesman*, but as late as 1977, some scholars still maintained the implausible view that Plato did not write the dialogue; see, e.g., Masters (1977) who later changed his view. Other writers have dealt with what they see as the inadequacies of the dialogue by reading it ironically, arguing that perhaps the Eleatic Stranger should be seen as a sophist of sorts rather than a real philosopher; see, for example, Tejera (1999), Scodel (1987).

in method,[10] its political content merely an afterthought; and whatever political content the dialogue is allowed to have, it is thought to reflect an unstable transitional view between the great ideas of the *Republic* and Plato's final mature thoughts on politics in the *Laws*, having interest only as evidence of the development of Plato's thought.[11] The dialogue's political thought is praised, if at all, as showing Plato's increasing "realism," though still not sufficient realism to purge him of his fascination with the autocratic rule of knowledge: the lessons of Sicily have barely begun to sink in.[12]

There is truth in some of these prejudices. The *Statesman* lacks the accessible charm and obvious dramatic give-and-take of many other Platonic dialogues, and there is no question that its structure is sometimes difficult to discern. A reader interested in Plato's political theory has to trudge through much discussion of apparently only methodological interest, and the dialogue's political conclusions do not seem especially earth-shattering when considered in isolation. But there have always been some who reject the view that the *Statesman* is a "weary dialogue";[13] and, as Elizabeth Rawson once wrote of Cicero, "closer knowledge . . . tends to breed greater appreciation."[14] Like many a difficult work of art, a bit of study is often sufficient to enhance one's appreciation of the dialogue's complex artistry and even drama.[15] Moreover, in recent years a number of studies have more forcibly challenged the idea that the key interest of the dialogue lies in its methodological reflections,

---

[10] Barker (1918, 271); Diès (1935, ix); Skemp (1987, 66); White (2007); for a more sophisticated statement of this view, emphasizing that the dialogue is primarily an education in dialectics, see Delcomminette (2000).

[11] Cf. Kahn (1995, 51).

[12] See, e.g., Annas and Waterfield (1995, xviii); Klosko (1986, 191), who follows in the footsteps of Barker (1918, 279–287).

[13] So Guthrie (1978, 164), who suggested that the dialogue does not feel "weary" to "those who enjoy Plato's mastery of the art of weaving."

[14] Rawson (1975, vi).

[15] On the dramatic complexity of the dialogue, see, e.g., the studies of Miller Jr. (1980) and Blondell (2002).

or that its political doctrines are of interest merely as evidence for the development of Plato's views.[16] Platonic scholarship is a slow enterprise, however, and entrenched views take a long time to change; and when they change, they usually do so through the efforts of many scholars. A key aim of this book is to continue the process of hacking away at the barnacles, so to speak, so as to reveal a bit more of the beauty and power of this most peculiar dialogue.

To this end, this book offers a novel interpretation of the *Statesman* that argues for its coherence and interest as a work specifically of *political theory*, not just as a methodological discussion or even as an education in dialectics. My hope is to help recover the *Statesman* not merely as an object of antiquarian study but as a work that awakens thought about the problematic place of knowledge in political life. Indeed, my interpretation of the *Statesman* suggests that political knowledge has and can have no permanent place in the political community: it is always a "stranger's knowledge," whose need is always felt but whose presence cannot be ensured.

This concern with the "recovery" of what is valuable for political theory in the *Statesman* means that I therefore tend to present the various claims and arguments of the dialogue in the most charitable light possible and defend them against potential objections at key points. This does not mean that I believe the dialogue's account of political knowledge is simply true; only that there is more profit, in a democratic and anti-Platonic age, in attempting to sympathetically recover the *Statesman's* views than in rehashing, once again, easy dismissals that no longer illuminate. There is some critical engagement with the work along the way (especially in the final, concluding, chapter) but it is muted; the dominant interpretive mode of this study is rather one of critical rehabilitation. Moreover, since my purpose is to

[16] See, e.g., Lane (1998). Many scholars influenced by Leo Strauss of course never thought that the dialogue's key interest lay in its methodological reflections; see, for example, Benardete (1984b).

bring out the key features of the *Statesman,* I neglect in what follows detailed comparisons to other Platonic dialogues except in a few cases. My lack of attention to other dialogues should not be understood as a denial of continuity between the *Statesman* and other works in the *corpus*; indeed, as I argue at several key points, there are deep continuities between the political theory of the *Statesman* and that of other Platonic dialogues, especially the *Laws*. But I am not primarily concerned with demonstrating either development or continuity in Plato's political thought. Finally, since my concern is with the dialogue as a work of *political* theory, I tend to neglect detailed consideration of the methodological discussions it contains, except insofar as they bear on the determination of the nature and limits of political knowledge. This does not mean that I deny that the dialogue has any methodological content, but I do argue at several points that any purely "dialectical" reading of the dialogue is insufficient.

The themes of this book

The *Statesman* is a book about political knowledge or "statesmanship." To a first approximation, this is the knowledge that political rulers *should,* but do not normally, have. Most of the dialogue is concerned with investigating the nature and limits of this knowledge: its object, the role it plays in the web of knowledge that sustains and to some extent constitutes human society, and the specific activities that it makes possible. It is not concerned, except in passing, with the question of whether the knowledge so described is actually the kind of knowledge that a human being may acquire after an appropriate process of learning, or with the nature of the process of learning that might lead to such knowledge; and it also bypasses the apparently more fundamental question of whether "knowledge" has any place in politics (a question, at any rate, that is treated in other Platonic dialogues, including the *Gorgias,* the *Republic,* and the *Protagoras*). Yet the dialogue's answer to the question of the nature of political knowledge implicitly contains answers to some of those other questions as well.

The view of the nature and limits of political knowledge that emerges from the *Statesman* may at first glance appear unfamiliar to those accustomed to the standard interpretation of Plato's political thought. For the dialogue invites us to consider political knowledge in isolation from philosophy: the statesman is not presented, or not simply, as the philosopher-king (whose knowledge is simply the knowledge of the good, and who aims to make the city as happy as possible), but as the possessor of a specialist expertise that enables a legislator to structure the city's institutions so that they will be resilient against external and internal conflicts for as long as possible.

One important implication of this conception of statesmanship is that the statesman is not understood as a day-to-day ruler (as the philosopher-king seems to be understood in the *Republic*) but as a founder whose task turns out to be, paradoxically, to prepare the city for his absence.[17] The statesman, like the dialogue's main character, turns out to be a perpetual "stranger" to the city, someone who produces the city but cannot be produced by it or integrated into its structure. As we shall see, in the *Statesman* the best possible regime thus turns out not to be a regime that is presided over by someone with knowledge for an indefinite period of time, but a regime whose laws and mores approximate genuine knowledge as far as possible. Hence the conception of political knowledge developed in the *Statesman* elevates the role of the law as the repository of the city's imperfect cognitive capital and makes the statesman into a self-limiting figure.

I develop this argument in detail in the chapters that follow. But it is perhaps useful to explain some of these claims briefly beforehand and to situate them in the context of entrenched views of the dialogue and of Plato's political philosophy before I provide any real evidence for them.

---

[17] Yet even in the *Republic*, it is worth remembering, the figure of the philosopher-king is initially introduced as the founder of the perfected city (473b).

The distinction between statesman and philosopher

One key assumption of this study is that in the *Statesman*, at least, Plato is not committed to any straightforward identification of the statesman with the philosopher, much less with the paradigmatic philosopher in the Platonic corpus, namely Socrates. On this reading, the *Statesman* either abandons or qualifies the idea, prominent in the *Republic*, that the philosopher, *qua* philosopher, is qualified to rule. One needs a special kind of knowledge, described in the dialogue, and which is not identical with the mere practice of philosophy or even with the result of philosophical inquiry, in order to rule.

I do not deny, to be sure, that the philosopher and the statesman are closely related. For one thing, the philosopher, as a seeker of wisdom, is always on the way to the knowledge of the statesman, since that knowledge must always necessarily include in some form the knowledge of the good, the just, and the noble which the philosopher seeks, as we shall see. A potential statesman is thus always first of all a kind of philosopher. Moreover, as I shall argue in some detail (especially in chapter 5), the Socratic philosopher *qua* philosopher retains a political role as the most qualified ruler of the imperfect or law-abiding regimes, since only such philosophers could ultimately have the cognitive self-restraint necessary to abide by the law while retaining an interest in inquiry into the just, the noble, and the good that is necessary to avoid the most lethal consequences of legal conservatism. Only the (Socratic) philosopher, in other words, knows that he does not know, and hence knows that he does not know better than what the law declares is just or good or noble, even though he realizes that the law does not know this either. In a sense, therefore, the distinction between philosopher and statesman sketched in the *Statesman* is a vindication of the idea of a sort of philosopher-king, not because the philosopher should be understood to be identical to the statesman, but because only philosophically-minded rulers, and in particular rulers with a properly Socratic attitude towards the law, could be truly qualified to rule in the absence of genuine political knowledge, an absence that the dialogue suggests is necessarily nearly total.

But even if we do not identify the Socratic philosopher with the philosopher *tout court* in Plato, it is still clear that the statesman is not *simply* a philosopher, Socratic or otherwise. In particular, as we shall see in some detail, whereas philosophy is described in the dialogue as a practice essentially open to everyone, statesmanship is not, being a scarce expertise that depends on the acquisition of a difficult form of knowledge; whereas philosophy is understood as a key component in a happy life for an individual, statesmanship makes possible life for groups of people, but it cannot ensure the fullness of human happiness either for the statesman or for the members of the group; and whereas philosophy is ultimately concerned with the contemplation of eternal forms, statesmanship must be an expertise capable of mediating between such forms and the flux of particulars in given circumstances. In sum, statesmanship, as conceived in the *Statesman,* plays a different role in Plato's thought than philosophy.[18]

[18] It is tempting to suggest (as an anonymous reviewer of an earlier version of this manuscript did) that the Platonic statesman in the *Statesman* plays a role closer to the Aristotelian *phronimos* (*Nicomachean Ethics* 1107a1, 1140a25ff.), who determines the mean between the extremes to serve as the measure of virtue, than to the philosopher-king of the *Republic*. Yet, though there are some obvious similarities between both (the Platonic statesman deals with what is good or bad for a population in particular circumstances, for example, and determines the mean of the "quick" and the "slow" dispositions as the measure of genuine virtuous action), it is necessary to stress, as we shall see, that the knowledge of the statesman depends in a crucial way on a theoretical grasp of the forms of order that is absent from the Aristotelian discussion of *phronēsis*. In fact, Aristotle stresses that the man of *phronēsis* has a virtue that ought to be distinguished both from the kind of knowledge that grasps unchanging things and from *technē* (*Nicomachean Ethics* 1140a25–b7), whereas, as we shall see, statesmanship is linked both with craft-knowledge (as a kind of production) and with the grasp of unchanging forms of order (the equivalent of what Aristotle calls *nous*). Whether or not Aristotle nevertheless modeled the *phronimos* on the Platonic statesman of the *Statesman* is an interesting question which I am inclined to answer in the affirmative; but a full demonstration would be beyond the scope of this study.

The dissociation of the statesman from the philosopher is announced at the very beginning of the *Sophist*, where the Eleatic Stranger unhesitatingly tells Socrates that he believes that "sophist, statesman, and philosopher" are "three," rather than two or one (217a–b), despite the fact that the elder Socrates had just indicated that philosophers sometimes appear as statesmen. And this is not an accidental slip, or a loose way of speaking; both the dramatic context of the *Statesman* (a context which of course includes the *Sophist*) and much other evidence supports the view that the statesman must be at least *prima facie* distinguished from the philosopher. Indeed, neither the elder Socrates nor the Eleatic Stranger, both paradigmatic if perhaps not entirely unproblematic exemplars of "philosophers" in the Platonic universe, turn out to resemble the statesman described by the Eleatic.

This view of the relationship between the philosopher and the statesman contradicts the common view, asserted often without argument, that in the *Statesman*, as in the *Republic*, the philosopher and the statesman are one, or are at least straightforwardly related, as if the statesman were simply an older or better philosopher.[19] It is only recently that this unproblematic identification of the philosopher and the statesman has begun to be questioned, though the implications of not identifying them have not yet been fully explored.[20]

The most comprehensive attempt to make the case for the distinction between the philosopher and the statesman in the dialogue is due to Malcolm Schofield, who has argued (2006, chapter 4) that the view of statesmanship developed in the *Statesman* is at least in tension with the conception of the philosopher-king prominent in the *Republic*, and that in fact Plato's later thought seems to be characterized by what he elsewhere

[19] See, among others, Skemp (1987, 21); Klein (1977, 200); Rowe (1995b), note to *Statesman* 257b3–4; Samaras (2002, ch. 8, especially 146); Voegelin (1987/1956, 150); White (2007, 12); Delcomminette (2000).

[20] See, with varying degrees of explicitness, Lane (1998, 7n19); Griswold Jr. (1989, 263n13); Notomi (1999, 25, especially note 82); Schofield (2006, 176–180); and Benardete (1984a, 73–74).

calls the "disappearance of the philosopher-king."[21] Schofield provides at least four distinct arguments for this thesis. First, he shows that the statesman of the *Statesman*, characterized as the possessor of an "architectonic" knowledge that "uses" other arts, traces its ancestry to views that Plato had portrayed Socrates as rejecting in dialogues like the *Charmides* and the *Euthydemus*, and which Plato is always careful not to attribute to Socrates.[22] Second, he argues that the philosopher-king of the *Republic* is not somebody who "uses" the knowledge of other arts in order to weave the web of politics, and his knowledge is not understood there to involve a relationship to the world of becoming as well as to the forms of order (the good, the just, and the noble), unlike the statesman of the *Statesman*, whose knowledge is directly related to the flux of human affairs. Third, he claims that the philosopher-king is somebody whose education makes him reluctant to rule, and unlikely to have the kinds of "political skills" we normally associate with politicians, whereas the statesman is somebody whose *raison d'être* is to rule, and whose expertise is described as a kind of infallible capacity for making political decisions. Even though the philosopher-king of the *Republic* is not necessarily bereft of experience of practical affairs, this experience is not itself characterized as a kind of knowledge, and the need for such experience is at any rate minimized, as Schofield also notes, by the *abolition* of politics in the ideal city of the *Republic* through the radical restructuring of social relations. By contrast, the knowledge of the statesman, for the Eleatic Stranger, is directly related to his ability to make political decisions without the need for an antecedent restructuring of social relations. Finally, Schofield notes that though the philosopher-king is supposed to have a kind of knowledge of the good that Socrates never claims to possess, there is an essential "continuity between

21 See Schofield (1997), as well as Samaras (2002) for another version of this thesis.

22 Schofield (2006, 144–155).

Socrates' philosophical project and (different though it is) the *Republic*'s vision of the ideal philosopher shaping the good city" (163), whereas the kind of judgment of timing that the Eleatic Stranger ultimately claims constitutes the specific expertise of the statesman is not something that either Socrates (or the Eleatic Stranger, for that matter) ever appear to cultivate.

Schofield's view receives support from other considerations as well. Many claims that the Stranger makes about statesmanship and sophistry are in apparent conflict with some explicit claims that Socrates makes elsewhere in the Platonic *corpus*. For example, the Stranger argues for the distinctiveness of sophist and statesman on the basis of the specific forms of expertise (*technē*) that each can be said to have, and more generally suggests that the proper way of answering Socrates' question about whether the statesman, sophist and philosopher are one, two, or three is to identify their respective "capacities" (*dunamin* 219a5). So we should expect that the Stranger believes that sophist, statesman, and philosopher differ insofar as each of them is the possessor of a specific capacity, indeed a specific form of knowledge or art. To the extent that the Stranger attributes a *technē* to the sophist, his account of the differences among these three figures is already in conflict with some very explicit claims of the elder Socrates elsewhere concerning the lack of expertise of sophists;[23] yet the Stranger appears quite willing to suggest that all three figures have a particular specialized expertise, and are not simply related to one another insofar as one or more of them is an "image" or "aspect" of one or more of the others (as would be the case if, for example, the sophist simply imitated the philosopher or the sophist without having an art of his own, or the statesman were simply an aspect of the philosopher).[24]

---

23 Cf. especially *Gorgias* 463a6–463b6. For further discussion, see Ambuel (2007, 42–45), who makes much of this point.

24 Ambuel (2007), like other commentators, has suggested that *Sophist* 268b–c implies that the sophist imitates the philosopher. Yet the passage at best implies that the sophist imitates the statesman, and at any rate does not imply that the sophist does not have his own particular art.

More generally, Socrates' conception of the statesman in both the *Republic* and the *Gorgias* can be distinguished from the Stranger's conception of the statesman along a number of other dimensions. Socrates tends to emphasize that the statesman is first and foremost the supremely virtuous individual, not a technical specialist, his knowledge primarily a knowledge of the form of the good; that the purpose of political rule and political knowledge is not just to preserve the citizens physically or even make them wealthy (*Gorgias* 502ff., 515c, 517b), but to improve the citizens, to make them better rather than worse (*Gorgias* 464b); and that the political art is ultimately best expressed in the private conversations that Socrates had with individual Athenians, not in the collective business of making laws or ruling groups (*Apology* 31d–e, *Gorgias* 521d). By contrast, the Stranger downplays the virtue of the statesman (even though he nowhere denies that the statesman is supremely virtuous), and stresses that the statesman's knowledge is a specialist knowledge tied to a concrete consideration of the city's circumstances, not just a knowledge of the good (the statesman, for one thing, needs an art of measurement that is never discussed by Socrates); that the role of the statesman is less making citizens better (though he does not deny this) than protecting them in a hostile universe;[25] and that political care is always directed at groups, not at individuals. The Stranger would presumably disagree with Socrates when he says, in the *Gorgias*, that he is the only person in Athens to practice the "true political art" (521d7), that is, the only person in Athens concerned with making citizens better rather than worse. Moreover, while the focus of Socrates' reflections on politics is on what we may call moral education—the education of the statesman as much as the citizen—rather than on a specialist knowledge or even legislative activity, which is disparaged by Socrates in the *Republic* (425e–427a) as something that properly

[25] See, for example, Arends (1993), Kochin (1999), Griswold Jr. (1989), Rosen (1995), Zuckert (2005).

educated citizens could do quite well on their own, the Stranger seems to dismiss the possibility of a complete moral education, capable of reproducing the knowledge of the statesman in the city, and reintroduces a concern for law that seems not to be present in the dialogues where Socrates talks about politics.

Not only is the Stranger's conception of statesmanship *prima facie* different from that of Socrates, but he appears to go out of his way to *distance* philosophy from statesmanship. His few explicit comments about philosophy in the *Sophist* identify it with the "science of the free," dialectics (*Sophist* 253c–d), which is further characterized as the science of dividing according to kinds. But the Stranger nowhere identifies statesmanship simply with the science of division according to kinds, even if there is a sense in which the statesman must have a part of this dialectical science; indeed the search for the statesman is said to be *more* for the sake of becoming better at dialectics (*Statesman* 285d5–8) than for the sake of learning about statesmanship, which indicates that the Stranger understands dialectics (philosophy) to be at least broader than statesmanship. And to the extent that the Stranger suggests that philosophy may be (but isn't necessarily) both possible and necessary in the "age of Cronos" (*Statesman* 272c) even though statesmanship is neither possible nor necessary at that time (as we shall see in more detail in chapter 3), we are prompted to draw the conclusion that statesmanship is a specialist expertise, made necessary by the conditions of scarcity and imperfect cooperation of the current age, and significantly different from "pure" philosophy. Thus, if we take the Socratic view to be that the statesman and the philosopher are one, then the fact that the Stranger seems to present a quite different picture of statesmanship and to distance statesmanship from dialectics suggests that he rejects a simple Socratic identification of philosophy and statesmanship.

Some of these differences between Socrates and the Stranger are merely apparent, to be sure; Socrates' focus on private conversations rather than public legislation can be understood, for example, as a second best response to the corruption of Athens. And others could be explained as differences in emphasis rather than as substantive disagreements, such as the Stranger's lack of attention to the statesman's virtue. But there can be no denying that the Stranger invites us to consider statesmanship as a form of knowledge that is different from philosophy, resulting in conclusions that are not obviously compatible with the more "Socratic" views of statesmanship expressed elsewhere in the *corpus*.

It should be stressed that to say that the Stranger's conceptions of statesmanship and philosophy are *prima facie* different from those of Socrates is not *eo ipso* a reason to prefer one to the other, or even to attribute one or the other to Plato. Socrates' meager remarks at the beginning, and his silence in the bulk of both dialogues, can be interpreted as either a positive or a negative judgment on the Stranger's performance;[26] and the fact that the *Philosopher* dialogue, apparently foreseen at *Sophist* 217a7–9, is missing, can be understood as either an invitation to construct the missing account from the material in the existing dialogues, an admission that the philosopher is the statesman, despite the *prima facie* differences between Socrates and the Stranger, or even a purely contingent failure on Plato's part to complete the Eleatic's declared project.[27] These facts have not prevented scholars from occasionally "taking sides," as it were, attempting to either uphold the Eleatic's views on sophistry and statesmanship as distinct improvements on Socrates' views on these matters,[28] or condemning the Stranger's argu-

---

[26] For an example of the "negative" interpretation, see Scodel (1987, 15); for an example of the "positive" interpretation, see Miller Jr. (1980).

[27] Similar possibilities with respect to the other unfinished Platonic sequence of dialogues (the *Republic-Timaeus-Critias-Hermocrates*) are surveyed in Ausland (2000).

[28] Much scholarship on the *Sophist* argues that the Eleatic's views represent an improvement over Plato's "middle period" theory of ideas, and interpret Plato's use of the Eleatic as a spokesman as a way for Plato to signal his awareness of this fact, and the standard interpretation of the *Statesman* emphasizes that the Stranger's view of politics is more "realistic" than Socrates' view; see, for example, Kahn (1995).

ments as failures, even going so far as to accuse the Stranger of being a kind of sophist himself.[29] For our purposes all that matters is that Plato explicitly presents a view of sophistry and statesmanship that he takes some pains to distinguish from the view normally associated with Socrates, and that he gives no obvious signs that he thinks that this view is clearly or systematically wrong.[30]

Schofield again provides a fruitful approach to the question of how to evaluate the differences between the Socratic philosopher-king and the Eleatic statesman. He argues that these differences should be taken as symptoms of an unresolved tension in Plato's own views, rather than as indications of Plato's development or change of mind. But he also argues that Plato never fully recommends the Eleatic vision of statesmanship as architectonic knowledge, whereas he seems to be committed to the "Socratic" view of the philosopher-king. On his reading, the *Statesman* represents a kind of thought experiment:

> It is as though Plato is engaged in the *Statesman* on an essentially exploratory exercise. Let's take the idea of political knowledge as the key to a proper politics, it says. Let's see how far the attempt to analyse it can take us in our exploration of what sound dialectical method consists in. And let's find out how far it really opens the door to an understanding of politics. In the course of the enterprise some false moves are subsequently flagged up as such. The *Statesman* is a lesson in method and in politics. But (as elsewhere in Plato) there are some false moves we are left to spot for ourselves—that is part of the lesson.[31]

[29] For some of the more extreme examples of this position, see Scodel (1987), Ambuel (2007), and Tejera (1999).

[30] This does not mean that Plato agreed with the Stranger's view of sophistry and statesmanship, but it also does not mean that he disagreed with it in the absence of *internal* indications of disagreement.

[31] Schofield (2006, 183).

This view is quite attractive as a reconstruction of Plato's purposes in writing the *Statesman*, and indeed my own interpretation of the dialogue can be seen to support it. But I think it can be pushed further. We might say that Plato in the *Statesman* is exploring the possibility of divorcing philosophy from politics. Statesmanship then appears as a kind of godlike expertise, and the statesman is likened to the absent god who has not yet returned to save the city, while the paradigmatic philosopher is no longer the *engagé* Socrates, but the more theoretical and resolutely "private" Eleatic Stranger. Philosophy is no longer the wisdom that can resolve the problems of cities, even if it may be a necessary step in that direction; what is required is the supreme (yet still human rather than divine) expertise of the statesman, who can "weave" characters and "orchestrate" arts so as to minimize internal conflict and make the city resilient in the face of external conflict. This leads to a reevaluation of law as a repository of political experience that, though by no means adequate as *knowledge*, constitutes a real, if limited, sort of cognitive capital on which the city can often successfully draw in the absence of the statesman.

Whether, and to what degree, such an exploration would also represent a shift in Plato's own "position" is not, philosophically, a very important question, even if it is a historically interesting one. I am at any rate unconvinced, *pace* Schofield, that Plato is not committed, by this point in his life, to a non-Socratic view of statesmanship as a special expertise. Indeed, it is perhaps evidence of a shift in his views that the Socrates of the dialogues that are more or less contemporary with the *Statesman* (the *Theaetetus* and the *Philebus*) also appears to accept a diminished political role for philosophy: the digression of the *Theaetetus* depicts a philosopher who is uninterested in politics and perhaps incapable of ruling well, since he thinks of ruling as a kind of herding (*Theaetetus* 175d–e), a view of ruling that is decisively rejected in the *Statesman*; and the discussion of the good life in the *Philebus* is nowhere connected with politics and political life. Moreover, as Schofield notes, even the Athenian Stranger of Plato's last dialogue, the *Laws*, is not presented as a (Socratic) philosopher, but as a wise man of Solonian stamp and wide "empirical" knowledge of constitutions.[32] These are suggestive indications that Plato no longer believed (if he ever did) that "mere" philosophy was sufficient to solve the primary political problem facing human beings, namely, the problem of conflict; a different kind of expertise, for which philosophical activity is merely a preparatory stage, seems to be required. Perhaps the lessons of Sicily did play a role here;[33] but if so, they did not do so merely because Plato suddenly noticed the commonplace that power corrupts or that the moral virtues of a philosopher-king are unlikely to be found in actual human beings, but because he came to understand differently the kind of knowledge required to achieve lasting political stability and justice, and perhaps came to think that his own knowledge was inadequate to the task.

More modestly, we can perhaps say that while Plato's political philosophy remains overwhelmingly concerned throughout his life with the evident scarcity of political knowledge, his preferred solution to this problem shifts over time in response to changes in his conception of the nature of this knowledge. The Plato of the *Republic* conceives of political knowledge as simply the knowledge of the good, and believes that the problematic scarcity of this knowledge is best ameliorated through the *production* of philosopher-kings (statesmen) via the right sort of educational system and the restructuring of social relations so that the knowledge of the good can become effective in the city; the Plato of the *Laws* and the *Statesman* conceives of political knowledge as a specialist knowledge that demands

---

32 Schofield (2006, 75–76) suggests that the very designation "Athenian Visitor" recalls Herodotus 1.30, where Croesus greets Solon as follows: "Athenian Visitor, a great deal of talk has reached us about you, on account of your wisdom and your traveling. You have traversed much of the earth in your philosophical efforts to contemplate things" (76).

33 As many scholars have consistently claimed over the years; see, e.g., Barker (1918) and Klosko (1986).

more than the knowledge of the good, and thus believes that the very same scarcity is best tackled through a revaluation of the rule of law, as we shall see in this study. What changes is not Plato's estimate of the degree of scarcity of political knowledge (which was always high) but his estimate of the best means for ameliorating the effects of such scarcity in light of his changing conception of political knowledge.

To be sure, education and law are not mutually exclusive responses, but they are *contrasting* responses: perfectly effective education would render law more or less unnecessary, whereas law is most needed in the absence of effective education. We might then say that if Plato lost faith in anything, it was in the possibility of producing genuine statesmen through education; what was left was the more modest aim of integrating the rule of law with the few fruits that philosophical inquiry could actually produce, and which did not necessarily include genuine knowledge to any significant degree. To the extent that this study has conclusions relevant to the characterization of the development of Plato's political thought, I thus want to emphasize that the important question is not whether or not Plato "lost faith" in the ability of the philosopher-king or genuine statesman to solve the fundamental political problems, but whether or not Plato continued to think that education could generally produce people with real political knowledge.

Statesmanship and the stability of the city

For Plato, the preeminent political problem is the problem of conflict. Not, perhaps, all conflict, except insofar as all conflict has the potential to escalate to the point where it tears apart the city; but nevertheless conflict and its sources play a central role in Plato's political thought, to the point that the best political community is consistently characterized as a community where conflict is either absent or at least not threatening to the community's common life. The *Statesman* is no exception; indeed, as I shall argue, statesmanship is a specific expertise, distinct from philosophy, precisely because it is the knowledge that enables the statesman to structure the city's institutions so that the city can be maximally stable, that is, to mitigate internal and external conflict. And as we shall see in chapter 1, statesmanship is necessary for human beings not because they are rational beings (as philosophy may in general understand them), but because they are imperfectly "tame," that is, imperfectly cooperative.

Yet I say "mitigate" rather than "eliminate" conflict, for, as we shall see in detail in chapters 3 and 6, the *Statesman*'s political theory is premised on the impossibility of eliminating the ultimate sources of human conflict. Human beings are only imperfectly cooperative, partly because their reason is normally articulated into distinct arts that cannot each care for the whole of human existence and cannot each consider the whole of the human good, and partly because the politically relevant judgments of different individuals must always be biased in conflicting ways so long as their having specific arts of their own precludes their having the art of the statesman. The task of the statesman can only be to make the city *resilient* to conflict, so that the disagreements among its citizens do not escalate to the point of tearing it apart or allowing it to be destroyed by other political communities.

More specifically, the Stranger identifies the expertise of the statesman with the ability to determine whether quickness or slowness, violence or deliberation, action or inaction, is the appropriate quality of the policy necessary to preserve the city at a specific time. This is so in two different ways. First, the statesman must know the appropriate time, in moments of crisis, to either use the art of rhetorical persuasion to change laws or negotiate advantageously with other cities, or to use force to eliminate existential threats to the city. But second, and most importantly, the statesman must also be able to structure the city's institutions so as to diminish the biases that ordinary people have towards action or inaction, violence or deliberation, and which can tear the city apart and endanger its survival in the face of external enemies. In both cases the statesman confronts the possibility that conflict will destroy the city, but in neither case can he fully eliminate its sources. In other words, in the *Statesman* the Eleatic Stranger implicitly argues that even the kind of communism contemplated in the *Republic* could not fully eliminate the human biases towards quickness or slowness in action that are at the root of the city's vulnerability to conflict, though it could perhaps diminish them substantially.

The absence of the statesman

If the statesman's key task is the creation of a resilient community, then it is evident that we cannot conceive of his role merely in terms of day-to-day ruling. He is not simply an "absolute monarch," as many have often viewed him.[34] On the contrary, in his concern for the long term, including the time when he will not be there, he must be viewed primarily as a founder and legislator, even if he also sometimes rules. Indeed, as we shall see, most of the detailed description of the statesman's role in the city in the later part of the dialogue simply does not make sense on the assumption that he is merely its ruler, for then he would have no concern to mitigate the biases in the citizens' judgment.

Similar arguments about the role of the statesman have been advanced by others,[35] but I stress in this work the essential *incompatibility* between the statesman and the city. As we shall see especially in chapter 6, the statesman must produce stable and shared true opinions among the citizens in order to make the city resilient to conflict. But given the conception of knowledge with which the Stranger operates (a conception I explore in some detail in chapter 4), and the likely means by which the statesman must produce these opinions, his very presence is incompatible with their stability. Moreover,

34 See, e.g., Grote (1875), Barker (1918), and Skemp (1987).

35 See, e.g., Arends (1993), Lane (1995), though she partially retracts this position in her later work, Lane (1998), and Stern (1997).

the nature of his knowledge is also such that it cannot be properly reproduced through the institutions of the city, and it cannot be expected to emerge naturally; it can at best be approximated in laws and institutions. The statesman turns out to be a kind of stranger, someone like the Athenian of the *Laws*, who might grow by chance in one or another city but who cannot be produced on demand. The evidence for these points is sometimes indirect, and some of it is to be found not in the *Statesman* but in the *Laws*. But as I shall argue in some detail, the Stranger's presuppositions commit him to some such view of the relationship between the genuine statesman and the city, and hence to the conclusion that the long-term rule of the genuine statesman is in a sense incompatible with the conditions of the city's stability.

Moreover, the key metaphors and analogies that the Stranger uses throughout the work all point to a conception of statesmanship as an essentially temporary activity, undertaken in times of crisis and incompatible with the city's regular institutions. As we shall see in chapter 3, there is a deep analogy between the god's care for the cosmos and the statesman's care for the city, an analogy that extends to the compulsion that the god experiences to let go of the cosmos and of the consequent need for the cosmos to rule itself in its absence, "remembering [the god's] instruction" (273b): just as the god must let go of the cosmos so as to preserve its essential nature, and can return only when disorder becomes again an existential threat to the universe, so the statesman's care for the city must also end in the establishment of law, his return merely hoped for when disorder again appears as an existential threat to the city. Moreover, the metaphor of the statesman as the weaver of a cloak for the city also indicates the temporary role of the statesman in the city as the craftsman who constructs an artifact (the web of politics) meant to protect the city even in the stormy times that are sure to come in his absence, but who cannot make himself a part of this artifact, just as the weaver cannot make himself a part of the web.

Law as cognitive capital

The conception of statesmanship sketched in the *Statesman* goes together with a certain conception of law. Since statesmanship cannot be produced or reproduced at will, it must often be at least approximated; and the dialogue claims that only law can approximate it. As we shall see in detail in chapter 5, the law can approximate the knowledge of the statesman only by being a kind of cognitive capital, a repository of the collective experience of the city concerning those policies or institutions that have helped it survive in the past (mainly by helping it triumph over external enemies and limiting internal conflict). By themselves, neither the law nor the people can provide an account of why these policies or institutions actually did help the city in the past, or why conditions will (or will not) remain the same in the future, but so long as these conditions do not change, the policies and institutions thus embodied in the law can actually help the city survive. The law, or rather, proper law (for not all law will be such a repository of the city's experience) thus stands to the rule of the statesman in some ways as true opinion in Plato's thought stands to genuine knowledge. The analogy between law and opinion is, to be sure, imperfect; unlike opinion, for example, law is always general,[36] even if opinion can also be about general matters. But in an important sense, in making laws, the city opines rather than knows, and the law is simply the city's (sometimes true) opinion about important matters, rather than its knowledge.

The disadvantages of law are therefore the disadvantages of true opinion *vis-à-vis* knowledge, or rather, of opinions that happen to be true at some point in time: changes in circumstances might falsify them, making things that used to preserve the city into things that do not; the lack of insight into the regularity that made a law effective in the past (the inability

---

36 There are exceptions, such as the *psephismos*, a decree of the assembly, but the *Statesman* typically conceives of laws as general rules, not particularized judgments.

to give a sufficient account of it) makes it impossible for the people to reliably adapt it to changing circumstances. We might say that law-governed regimes are like regimes based on correlation rather than causation, to use modern terminology. But since the practices they enshrine did prove to be useful in preserving the political community in the past, then so long as conditions do not change too drastically, they can continue to work and hence make the city endure. By contrast, regimes that depart from established laws by enabling some people to change them by following their private interests cannot guarantee, in the absence of knowledge, that the policies they enact will preserve the city, except by chance.

This conception of (genuine) law as a kind of cognitive capital is the key to understanding the Stranger's defense of the rule of law against possible alternatives, and indeed to understanding the particularly conservative view of the rule of law which the Stranger recommends, which is apt to strike modern readers as overly rigid or even incoherent.[37] The Stranger claims that even laws that have been created without the benefit of knowledge (that is, not by genuine statesmen) are worth holding on to, unless and until those with knowledge change them, insofar as such laws embody the real experience of a city. Interpreters have been particularly puzzled by this claim, since the Stranger's arguments about the superiority of knowledge to law seem to rule out the possibility that laws created without knowledge would have any real value.[38] Moreover,

---

37 So, e.g., Annas and Waterfield (1995, 68) and Klosko (2008).

38 This puzzlement has given rise to at least two divergent responses. Klosko (2008), for example, argues that there is a real tension, amounting to a contradiction, between the "positive" and the "negative" views of the law in the dialogue, due primarily to the slow development of Plato's views. Rowe (2005), by contrast, has argued that the Stranger cannot be conflating the laws that genuine knowledge could create with the laws that an untutored people might enact; in his view, which I also reject in this work, the Stranger's defense of the rule of law does not depend on any cognitive content they might have, since the laws that a people might make cannot have any cognitive value.

the rigidity of this prescription is paradoxically combined with the view that the statesman ought not to be bound by law. The difficulty of combining the statesman's disregard for law with effective norms ensuring respect for law in his absence is plain enough, even before we consider the complication introduced by the Stranger's view that the people ought to be open to the arrival of a genuine statesman and accept the latter's disregard of their laws when he is present.

Yet, as I shall argue in chapter 5, the Stranger's position is both more justified and less rigid than it has appeared to some. His position is more justified than it appears because of the large risks threatening the *polis* from bad changes to the law, which make a great degree of loss-aversion "rational," to use modern terminology. On the assumption that conditions do not change radically, the political experience of a city, as embodied in its laws, is likely to be a good guide to action, though of course it cannot produce an account of itself. Moreover, given the people's inability to distinguish between sophists and genuine statesmen, it makes a great deal of sense for them to err on the side of conservatism. And, contrary to appearances, this conception of law as the cognitive capital of the city does not necessarily prevent all inquiry and change, and at points prefigures the more overtly flexible view of law in the *Laws,* where (slow) change in the laws is made possible through the accumulation of experience in the special institution of the Nocturnal Council.[39] As we shall see, the apparent rigidity of the Stranger's position is to be explained by the purposes of the argument, and in its more extreme form it cannot be a position that Plato himself endorsed. Plato's project throughout his life remains the attempt to embed knowledge and reason in the city, and the rule of law, properly conceived, is the best substitute that he can find for the embodied knowledge of the

[39] Contrary to a recent argument of Klosko (see previous note), and in keeping with the earlier views of Morrow (1960a, b), as I have argued in Márquez (2011).

statesman; but it is a rule of law that is tempered by inquiry, not an unthinking and irrational attachment to dead opinions.

The structure of this book

The *Statesman* is a complex work of art, weaving together many threads in subtle ways, and offering many aesthetic and philosophical rewards for the student willing to look past its uninviting façade, with its many discussions that are apparently irrelevant to its political theory. In order to fully understand what the dialogue says about statesmanship, it is thus necessary to understand all of its parts; and to this end, this work is organized in six chapters, each of which discusses some particular aspect of the dialogue's conception of statesmanship and its place in the city, and which loosely follow the order of the argument in the dialogue, plus this introduction and a concluding chapter that discusses the problem of knowledge in politics more broadly.

In chapter 1, I argue that the discussion of weaving starting at 279b provides the most important clue to the structure of the dialogue as a whole. Not only is the art of weaving a paradigm of statesmanship (reflecting its formal structure to a significant degree), the *discussion* of weaving is itself a paradigm of the discussion of statesmanship. The discussion of weaving, like the discussion of statesmanship, proceeds in two parts, interrupted by a methodological interlude: one part that identifies weaving as the art that is concerned with woolen cloaks, that is, the art that produces an artifact that protects human beings from the harshness of winter, and another part that articulates the relationships between weaving so conceived and all the other arts that contribute to the production of cloaks. The first part separates weaving from the arts insofar as these are not concerned with the production of cloaks as protective artifacts, and the second separates weaving from the arts that are in fact partially concerned with the production of cloaks. Similarly, the first part of the division of statesmanship identifies statesmanship as the art that cares for human beings, and, as we learn later, does so by producing and putting in order a protective artifact against the unsocial tendencies of human beings, namely, the city. But other arts also contribute to the creation of the city, and hence the Stranger (in the second part of the division) must articulate the relationships between statesmanship and all these other arts. The first part of the division thus separates statesmanship from other arts insofar as they do not contribute to the care of human beings, whereas the second part of the division separates statesmanship from other arts insofar as they do contribute to that care. Together, both parts of the division articulate a specific conception of what it means to care for human beings. Contrary to some widespread views, I thus stress that there is a single, continuous division running throughout the dialogue that is never discarded, though it is modified slightly at key points.[40]

In chapter 2, I continue the argument for the unity of the *Statesman* by showing that the early part of the dialogue, long considered more or less irrelevant to the final determination of the statesman's knowledge due to its apparent methodological errors and bizarre conclusions,[41] substantially contributes to this endeavor. More specifically, I argue that the problematic features of this division (especially the denial of human rationality implicit in the identification of human beings as featherless bipeds or two-footed pigs) can be best understood in the light of the Stranger's attempt to show Young Socrates that the most relevant characteristic of human beings from the point of view of statesmanship is not their rationality but their imperfect "tameness," that is, their imperfect sociality or unwillingness to fully cooperate with one another. Accordingly, these early divisions show (in connection with the myth) how statesmanship must be the collective care of imperfectly tame beings who can partially care for themselves, that is, must be

[40] As Delcomminette (2000), Rowe (1995a), and Rowe (1996) have argued, though my interpretation is importantly different from theirs at key points.
[41] For an extreme version of this view, see Scodel (1987).

the science of organizing their cooperation. Throughout, we see how merely "methodological" problems thus have political implications; in particular, how one understands human beings is seen to matter enormously for how one understands political knowledge.

In chapter 3, I present a full interpretation of the memorable myth of the "reversed cosmos" (268e–274d). I argue that the myth serves three basic purposes within the overall economy of the dialogue. First, the myth describes those essential features of the cosmos that affect the way in which we should conceive of the knowledge of the statesman and its ability to shape the city. These features include a lack of direct divine guidance, the hostility of nature and the scarcity of the means of life, the division of human rationality among a number of different arts, and the "entropy" of the cosmos in its present age (its partial tendency towards disorder). Second, and relatedly, the myth serves to correct the earlier division by pinpointing the specific conditions of the cosmos that would make its various features relevant to the determination of the knowledge of the statesman, and in particular it shows the way in which the human possession of reason or *phronēsis*, which had been deemphasized in the earlier division, is in fact relevant for the determination of the knowledge of the statesman. Finally, and most importantly, as I have already mentioned, the myth also articulates a number of parallels between the rule of the god over the cosmos and the rule of the human statesman over the city which turn out to be of great importance for understanding the nature and limits of human statesmanship. In particular, the myth suggests that the statesman is and can be at best a temporary savior of the city, whereas philosophy and philosophical activity are permanent possibilities of human life, just as the god of the myth can be at best a temporary savior of the cosmos, concerned with putting it in order so that it will endure independently for as long as possible. Throughout this chapter, I take aim at a recent interpretation of the myth, put forward especially by Christopher Rowe, Luc Brisson, and

Gabriela Roxana Carone, that claims that the myth describes three rather than two cosmic ages, showing that such an interpretation misses the most important political implications of the myth.[42]

In chapter 4, I explore the conception of knowledge that the Stranger implicitly uses in his discussion of statesmanship. Drawing on the *Republic*, the *Meno*, the *Gorgias*, the *Theaetetus*, the *Sophist*, and the *Statesman*, I examine some of the links between knowledge and correct judgment in the Platonic *corpus*, and argue that in the *Statesman* more than in earlier dialogues Plato articulates how an expertise enables knowledge of invariant form to secure the reliability of judgments about particular actions via the practice of "measurement." The statesman's knowledge is thus not exhausted in the contemplation of eternal forms, but is instead conceived as the ability to make use of a grasp of the invariant structure of reality to order the unstable world in which he must operate. Moreover, I show that in order to come to terms with the idea of "false judgment" in the *Sophist*, the Stranger develops a distinctive and original conception of imitation as the reproduction of formal relationships in different media that will enable him to explain how laws can imitate the knowledge of the statesman while still retaining some epistemic value.

In chapter 5, I show how the scarcity of statesmanship leads the Stranger to develop an argument for the rule of law that values it insofar as the law can be said to "imitate" the knowledge of the statesman. The law imitates the knowledge of the statesman whenever it is so constructed that it embodies those policies that have served it well in the past to confront external aggression and prevent or limit internal conflict; and it can be constructed in this way whenever the city produces it by looking to its experience and that of other cities. The law so conceived cannot be a substitute for the knowledge of the statesman (since it is a mere opinion, though one that has a

42 See Rowe (1995a, b), Rowe (2001b), Brisson (1995), and Carone (2005).

good chance of being true in a variety of circumstances), but it does have a limited value in the absence of the knowledge of the statesman. Moreover, contrary to some recent interpretations of these passages, I show that the Stranger cannot be committing himself to a conception of law that is wholly unrevisable and unchangeable in the absence of secure knowledge; political regimes must leave open a *space* for philosophical inquiry, even if such inquiry is partially sheltered from the political community as a whole (as in the Nocturnal Council of the *Laws*). In fact, the argument of this chapter shows that the best rulers of the best non-ideal regimes will be, in a sense, "philosopher-kings," rulers who have the knowledge that they do not know better than the laws and hence are not tempted to overstep it and yet are committed to inquiry into the law.

In chapter 6, finally, I explore the conception of the statesman to which the Stranger finally arrives, that is, the statesman as the weaver of the "courageous" and "moderate" dispositions, and show how this conception fits within the earlier idea of statesmanship as the integrative care of imperfectly tamable beings. This chapter also concludes the argument for the incompatibility of statesmanship and the city, showing that the "weaving" of the statesman, given the conception of political knowledge that the Stranger has used and the conception of law that derives from it, necessitates his ultimate departure from the city, on pain of "unweaving" his own workmanship.

As I have already mentioned, the main critical mode of this study may be characterized as one of "critical rehabilitation." Though I occasionally criticize the Eleatic Stranger's views, I am more interested in interpreting them in ways that are productive for further thought than in refuting them in ways that close off further reflection. Or, to return to the earlier metaphor of barnacles: the ship of the *Statesman*, like a fragile and neglected Athenian trireme, may still be seaworthy once we scrape those barnacles. One may still ask, however, why any Platonic views about the nature and limits of political knowledge deserve any kind of critical rehabilitation. I devote the concluding chapter to two tasks related to this question. First, I try to refute some common objections to the very idea of political knowledge and its authority. And second, I try to show how the idea of political knowledge, suitably rehabilitated, can still be very fruitful even for democratic theorists.

Objections to the possibility of political knowledge are of three sorts, which we might call "ontological," "epistemological," and "political." Ontological objections deny that there can be an object of political knowledge; epistemological objections deny that any individual can have systematically better access than others to this object; political objections claim that even if political experts existed they could not have a justified claim to rule on the basis of their expertise. I argue in all three cases that the objection has either less force than is normally supposed, or that the view of political knowledge developed in the *Statesman* circumvents it.

The view of political knowledge presented in the *Statesman* can prompt a renewed appreciation of both the rule of law and of the importance of a proper relationship between philosophical inquiry and political life. But the more important use of the ideal of political expertise is critical. The *Statesman*, as we shall see, reminds us of the shabbiness and inadequacies of our institutions, and of the great distance between our current practices and the genuine care of human beings. From this point of view, the knowledge described in the *Statesman* is a stranger's knowledge, out of place everywhere and yet everywhere needed.

Some remarks on reading Plato

A few methodological remarks are in order before beginning the interpretive task. As I have already indicated, this study proceeds by means of a very close reading of the *Statesman*, as well as of selected passages of other dialogues. But the study of the Platonic dialogues has always been riven by controversies concerning their proper interpretation. This is not surprising, since the dialogues are open-ended and opaque about the intentions of their author to a degree that few other texts in the history of thought ever are. Major schools of interpreting Plato can trace their roots almost to the beginnings of the Academy,[43] and the passage of time has multiplied, rather than reduced, the number of approaches.[44]

Much of the twentieth century was nevertheless dominated by the so-called "developmentalist" approach, though there were always variations in emphasis and dissenting voices, including the Tübingen School and those interpreters influenced by the work of Leo Strauss. Developmentalist interpreters tended to approach the dialogues as systematic expositions of doctrine, and explained the differences in the views expressed by the main characters of different dialogues as the result of the gradual development of Plato's views. This approach seemed particularly useful for interpreting the *Statesman*, which lacks much of the obvious dramatic depth of a dialogue like the *Republic*. It certainly *seems* plausible to interpret the *Statesman* as a straightforward exposition of Platonic doctrine, even if, as Skemp vaguely put it, "something of the general meaning is lost if the outward shape is broken."[45]

Yet in the last decade or two the scholarly consensus over this approach has vanished. Scholars are perhaps more divided than ever over whether the dialogues should be taken to be expositions of Platonic doctrine, whether Platonic characters should be taken to express Plato's views or how seriously to take the dramatic elements of the dialogues.[46] I will not rehearse here all of the arguments concerning the proper way of interpreting the dialogues, which have been well explored elsewhere. I only stress that it seems obvious to me that the dramatic elements of the Platonic dialogues are of genuine importance for our understanding of the arguments in them, or else Plato

43 See Annas (1992), Tarrant (2000a), Tarrant (2000b), and Sedley (2002).

44 See Annas and Rowe (2002), Tigerstedt (1977).

45 Skemp (1987, 8).

46 For a good survey of these disputes, see Ausland (1997).

would not have written dialogues, though of course there can be genuine disagreement regarding *how much* they actually matter, especially in a dialogue like the *Statesman*. Thus, in general I shall refuse to read the arguments in the dialogues as if they were the straightforward expressions of Plato's beliefs. Methodologically, this means that I prefer such locutions as "the Stranger argues," or "Socrates says," rather than "Plato argues" or "Plato says." Whatever Plato says is filtered through his characters; and it is simply good interpretive practice to avoid attributing to Plato the beliefs that are expressed by them, even when the evidence suggests that Plato would have shared such beliefs, since he chose (for whatever reasons) to distance himself from them by using the dialogue form.

This is not to say that I deny that Plato "says" anything or has doctrines or beliefs, or that there is development in Plato's views; as mentioned above, I take it that there are some identifiable developments in his views. But I also take it that the dialogues, including the *Statesman*, are portrayals of philosophy in action, and in particular of philosophers as teachers, not merely convenient fictions for presenting the pro- and con- sides of arbitrary arguments, or window-dressing for the presentation of doctrine. At any rate, the dialogues clearly have multiple purposes, and these need not always (or ever) include the straightforward presentation of Plato's "views," and the *Statesman* is no exception. Indeed, it seems to me that often the search for Plato's real doctrines is of little philosophical value;[47] to echo Socrates in the *Phaedrus*, it hardly matters if the arguments depicted in Plato come "from an oak or a rock" (275b5–c2) if they happen to lead to true conclusions and to foster the development of knowledge (which, we do well to remember, is not identical with true beliefs or opinions, as the *Theaetetus* shows). We do just as well if we merely evaluate the arguments and the actions of "Socrates"

47 Cf. Nails (2000, 20ff.)

or "the Eleatic Stranger" than if we make unsupported claims about the arguments of "Plato" (who is at any rate unavoidably responsible for all the arguments he puts into the mouths of his characters, no matter how mutually contradictory). This should not be taken as an excuse not to attend to what the dialogues actually *say*, but rather as an argument for taking their arguments seriously rather than merely as objects of antiquarian scholarship. What Plato *means* in the dialogues is what the arguments and actions of his characters entail; and it is precisely such arguments and actions that we must interpret and evaluate if we are to understand what makes the *Statesman* philosophically valuable.

Yet the arguments of the dialogues are not thereby to be evaluated in a vacuum. The dialogues are generally portrayals of philosophy in action that reflect on philosophy itself. This element of self-reference is, I submit, key to understanding them, for it makes the relationship between form and argument reciprocal. To take a simple example, if Socrates is an image of a philosopher, then what is said about philosophy in the dialogues must in some way refer (perhaps ironically) to Socrates' own activity. Methodologically, this means that no immediate preference is to be given to claims about philosophy put into the mouths of characters over the activities of the philosophical characters themselves; to put the point more generally, either the drama or the argument of the dialogue may take precedence, and either one may indicate a deficiency in the other.

Furthermore, the action of every dialogue, including the so-called "late" dialogues, depends to a great extent on the interactions of a main philosophical character with one or more non-philosophical interlocutors. The reactions of these minor characters reveal much about the deep meaning and limits of the arguments presented by the main philosophical spokesmen in each work. The *Statesman* is no exception, insofar as it depicts a peculiar pedagogical encounter between a philosopher and a young mathematician whose pliant responses and occasional confusions and enthusiasms provide important indications about the proper way of interpreting the Eleatic Stranger's account of statesmanship.[48]

One might argue that the interactions between philosophical spokesmen and minor characters might be important in some of the "earlier" Socratic dialogues, but that by the time Plato wrote the *Statesman* the dialogue form had become a mere formality; after all, one might say, it is hard to imagine a more pliant and characterless interlocutor than Young Socrates. Yet the dialogue itself draws our attention to the importance of the interaction between the Eleatic and Young Socrates. At the very beginning of the conversation the elder Socrates explicitly indicates (257d1–258a6) that he would prefer that the Eleatic Stranger choose as his interlocutor the younger Socrates, because he (the elder Socrates) has already conversed with Theatetus and seen him in conversation with the Eleatic Stranger, whereas he has not yet seen Young Socrates in action, and it is necessary for him to see both in action in order to discover their "kinship" with him. Both young men are similar to the elder Socrates in some superficial respect—Theaetetus has similar looks and Young Socrates has the same name—but he wants to discover whether or not they have a philosophical nature. This comment suggests that the dialogue is to be read, at least in part, as a "test" of Young Socrates' character, as Mitchell Miller Jr. (1980) has argued, a character which in turn appears to have been chosen as representative of certain young men with theoretical inclinations, like the young men who flocked to the Academy.[49]

This "test" reveals that Young Socrates' theoretical inclinations lead him to make certain characteristic mistakes concerning the nature of statesmanship; and these mistakes in turn shape the pedagogical movement of the conversation, with

---

48 In this I follow Benardete (1984b), Blondell (2002), Gill (1995), and Miller Jr. (1980), among others.

49 See Miller Jr. (1980, 5–8), for further discussion.

its many digressions and apparently bizarre outcomes. Young Socrates' mistakes are those of the excessively theoretical mathematician; if the *Republic* is intended to lead a spirited Glaucon away from the particular and to pay more consideration to eternal forms, in part by praising a training in mathematics, the *Statesman* may be read as doing the opposite, leading away Young Socrates from the contemplation of the eternal verities of mathematics and towards the business of thinking properly about politics. The apparent errors and problems that are so evident to modern commentators on the dialogue constitute a veritable presentation of the "vices" that theoreticians are particularly prone to when thinking about politics, and illustrate the difficulties in bridging theory and practice. These vices are multiple and contradictory, sometimes inclining the theoretician towards what, following Foucault,[50] we might call pastoral tyranny, sometimes towards the rigidity of law, and sometimes towards its revolutionary opposite, but they are all born of the self-confidence of a "theoretical" knowledge that does not know its limits. We might then say that the drama of the dialogue is intended as a corrective to such vices.

With these considerations about methodology out of the way, we can now turn to the dialogues themselves.

50 Foucault (2000 [1979]).

1. Weaving

MANY SCHOLARS HAVE EXPRESSED the view that the *Statesman* is a disjointed dialogue, full of dead ends;[51] and it is true that the early parts of the Stranger's discussion, especially, seem immaterial to the final characterization of statesmanship, or else appear to be superseded by later parts. For example, a number of commentators have argued that the classification of statesmanship as a "theoretical" form of knowledge early in the dialogue (259d) must either be tacitly put aside later in the dialogue, even though the Stranger nowhere disavows it, or else that Plato is guilty of inconsistency.[52] Many scholars similarly ignore the divisions that characterize human beings as featherless bipeds or two-footed pigs, implicitly claiming that, coming before the myth, they necessarily form part of the "discarded" characterization of the statesman as a shepherd of human beings (a conception that is corrected after the myth), even though the Stranger explicitly reasserts the validity of these divisions *after* the myth (276a3–7). At any rate it is not altogether clear that all the different characterizations of the statesman fully cohere with one another, or that the

[51] See, e.g., Annas and Waterfield (1995, xii), and Klosko (1986, 188).

[52] See, e.g., Benardete (1984b, 79); Gill (2005); Griswold Jr. (1989, 152); Hemmenway (1994, 257); Rosen (1995, viii); Scodel (1987, 27–30); Skemp (1987, 122–123n1); Sprague (1976, 101); Stern (1997, 267); Strauss (1989, 221); and White (2007, 119). These scholars do not necessarily agree, however, on the *grounds* for thinking that the Stranger puts aside the classification of the statesman's knowledge as theoretical.

Stranger consistently applies the same method to the search for the statesman: so, for example, the idea that the statesman is to be distinguished from the tyrant by the consent of his subjects (276e) seems to be in tension with the later arguments in the dialogue that establish that the criterion of consent is of no validity in identifying the genuine statesman (293a–e);[53] and the Stranger appears to abandon the dichotomous method of division he had used early in the dialogue after the discussion of measure, perhaps indicating that these early divisions were methodologically problematic.[54]

The key interpretive question for our purposes is the extent to which the Stranger's revisions of the initial account of the statesman (258b–267e) imply that earlier divisions are superseded by later divisions, and thus the degree to which we can speak of a "single" account of the statesman, rather than of a number of such accounts, some of which turn out to be erroneous and are therefore discarded, or even the degree to which the various divisions are consistent with one another. I argue here and in the next chapter that the Stranger and Young Socrates produce a *single* account of statesmanship embodied in a single long division, variously corrected and interrupted at several points, but never altogether abandoned, as Christopher Rowe (1995a) and Sylvain Delcomminette (2000) have rightly seen. Earlier steps in the division are never simply discarded except when the Stranger explicitly revises them, and the problems mentioned above are merely apparent, including the problem of the classification of statesmanship as a sort of "theoretical" knowledge. But this division has two major parts, and the nature of the connection between these two parts has been a primary cause of the scholarly confusions over the structure of the dialogue. In this chapter I suggest that the discussion of weaving provides the best clue as to how these two parts are to be connected; in the next chapter

53 See Annas and Waterfield (1995, xvi), and Skemp (1987, 16–17).

54 See Scodel (1987, 151ff.).

I show how the more bizarre features of this division are in fact tightly integrated into the overall view of statesmanship that the Stranger develops.

The argument, briefly, is this. Weaving is a paradigm of statesmanship: it reflects its formal structure to a significant degree. But weaving is not only a paradigm of statesmanship; the discussion of weaving is also a paradigm of the discussion of statesmanship. The discussion of weaving, like the discussion of statesmanship, proceeds in two parts, interrupted by a methodological interlude: one part that identifies weaving as the art that is concerned with woolen cloaks, that is, the art that produces an artifact that protects human beings from the harshness of winter, and another part that articulates the relationships between weaving so conceived and all the other arts that contribute to the production of cloaks. The first part separates weaving from the arts insofar as these are not concerned with the production of woolen cloaks as protective artifacts, and the second separates weaving from the arts that are in fact partially concerned with the production of woolen cloaks. Similarly, the first part of the division of statesmanship identifies statesmanship as the art that cares for human beings, and, as we learn later, does so by producing a protective artifact against the unsocial tendencies of human beings, the city. But other arts also contribute to the creation of the city, and hence the Stranger (in the second part of the division) must articulate the relationships between statesmanship and all these other arts. The first part of the division thus separates statesmanship from other arts insofar as they do not contribute to the care of human beings, whereas the second part of the division separates statesmanship from other arts insofar as they do contribute to that care. Together, both parts of the division articulate a specific conception of what it means to care for human beings.[55]

[55] My view thus differs from that of Delcomminette, in particular, in that I do not see the connection between these two parts of the division as one between "ideal" and "application."

I begin by briefly considering the operation of the "method of division" the Stranger uses. I then examine how the section on weaving gives us clues about the structure of the long division in the *Statesman,* and in particular about the connection between its two main parts.

Divisions

Unlike the elder Socrates elsewhere in the Platonic *corpus,* the Eleatic Stranger does not begin the discussion by asking Young Socrates the typical "what is X" question—e.g., "what is statesmanship?" One senses that such a question would be unlikely to lead to a productive answer from Young Socrates, and at any rate the elder Socrates had asked for *his* view about statesmanship, not that of Young Socrates (even as he had also expressed an interest in testing Young Socrates, 258a). Instead, the Stranger, in cooperation with Young Socrates, provides his own answer to the question of the nature of statesmanship, which takes the form of a long and sometimes puzzling "division," interrupted by a myth and other methodological interludes, locating statesmanship among the many possible forms of knowledge. This division is supplemented at the very end of the dialogue by a more positive characterization of the specific activity of statesmanship (in contrast to the specific activity of other arts and forms of knowledge) as a kind of weaving of human dispositions. Yet the method of division in general, and the structure of the long division that the Stranger uses to define statesmanship in particular, have been much misunderstood; some words are therefore necessary to clarify how the method is intended to work.

In the *Statesman* "division" works very roughly as follows.[56] First, an initial *dividendum* is established. In the

[56] The best and most detailed account of the method of division in the *Statesman* that I know of is in Delcomminette (2000), though Delcomminette assumes more Platonic metaphysics than is perhaps necessary for a consistent account of it.

Statesman this class is quickly assumed to be knowledge (*epistēmē,* 258b4–5).[57] Then the Stranger proposes a potential division of this class into two or more sections, and asks Young Socrates in which section the statesman's knowledge is to be found. If Young Socrates is uncertain or confused, the Stranger will offer an argument for why the statesman belongs in one section of the division rather than in the other. The process is then repeated, until the division yields as one of its classes the knowledge of the statesman, that is, until the division allows them to agree that some particular form of knowledge (qualified by all the contrasts implied by the earlier divisions) is statesmanship. Note that the method appeals to intuition at every step, and thus requires at least a dim awareness of the thing to be identified if it is to work at all; without such an awareness division is very much apt to mislead, as we soon see in the early part of the dialogue. But it also disciplines intuition. Rather than asking Young Socrates the—too broad—Socratic question "what is statesmanship?" he always asks the much easier question of whether the statesman is A or B, and if B, whether he is also C or D, and so on, until they arrive at a definition that says that the statesman is B *and* D *and* F (and so on). The final definition of the statesman lies at the *intersection* of A through N, which reflects what we might call the "formal structure" of statesmanship or (to put the point in more Platonic terms) *one* set

---

57 The choice of words is significant, even though later in the dialogue the Stranger appears to use the Greek terms *technē* (art or expertise) and *epistēmē* (knowledge or science) interchangeably. For more on the question of the difference between the words "art" and "knowledge or science" in the dialogue, see ch. 4, pp. 178–183. I usually translate *epistēmē* as "knowledge" or "form of knowledge," since the word indicates something broader than *technē* yet inclusive of it, but "science" is also a possible translation, pointing to the fact that what the Stranger usually means by the word something like a *capacity* to gain access to certain forms of order, not merely the possession of factual information, as we shall see.

of the forms in which statesmanship participates and which uniquely identify it.[58]

A "division" is thus a kind of *genealogy*. Indeed, insofar as the Stranger's divisions operate by separating "classes" of things (*genē*, cf. 263a3; the word also means family or race) from one another the resulting account (*logos*) is a kind of family lineage, as the Stranger playfully indicates at the end of the *Sophist* (268d3: the Stranger says that the sophist is "of this lineage and bloodline" when recapitulating the final division of sophistry). Such genealogies were the preeminent means of "identification" in the ancient world: distinguishing one stranger from another often required paying close attention to their parentage. But the conceit of genealogy is put to work here for the theoretical purpose of distinguishing one capacity, and in particular one form of knowledge, from another, as well as, like any other genealogy, the kinship and relatedness of these forms of knowledge. The Stranger's genealogies identify a target capacity while articulating its relationships to forms of knowledge that are "kin" to it. Whether the resulting account represents *knowledge* of (about) the target capacity is a complex question that we are not yet in a position to answer (for more on this question, see chapter 4).

The structure of the statesman's genealogy

The specific genealogy of statesmanship that the Stranger and Young Socrates produce has two main parts. The first of these parts, which ends at 277a, characterizes statesmanship, very roughly, as the art of the collective care of human beings, and distinguishes it from all the other arts and aspects of knowledge that are not directly related to such care (see figure 1). The second of these parts locates statesmanship

---

[58] "One" set of such forms, because, depending on our starting point, we can uniquely identify statesmanship through a different sequence of forms, as we shall see. No single sequence lists *all* of the forms in which statesmanship participates.

within the social division of expertise that jointly achieves the collective care of human beings, and identifies it with the art which completes or coordinates the work of all the other

Power or capacity (*dunamis*, *Sophist* 219a6)

0.	Other capacities	Knowledge or expertise	*Statesman* 258b4
1.	Practical	Theoretical or cognitive	258b6-259d6
2.	Critical	Commanding or directive	259d7-260b6
3.	Mediating	Autonomous	260c6-261a1
4.	Concerned with inanimate beings	Concerned with ensouled beings (=care of animals)	261a1-c3; an extra step seems required to separate plants from animals
5.	Of wild animals	Of tame animals	264a1-4; not strictly speaking a division of knowledge
6.	Individual care	Collective care	261c4-e4, 264a5-6
7.	Of water-dwelling animals	Of land-dwelling animals	264b7-e2
8.	Of users of wings for locomotion	Of users of feet for locomotion	264e2-11
9.	Of animals with horns	Of animals lacking horns	265b8-d5
10.	Of interbreeding animals (=smooth hooves)	Of non-interbreeding animals (=split hooves)	265d6-e9
11.	Four-footed (=pig)	Two-footed (=man)	265e10-c7
12.	Divine care	Human care	276c12-d7
13?	Unwilling (=tyranny)	Willing	276d8-276e14; dubious (recapitulated later)

Figure 1: Statesmanship as the care of human beings by human beings

arts directly involved in such care (see figure 2). Here the Stranger identifies the specific *role* of statesmanship within this network of expertises that produce the city, namely, the weaving of the dispositions of the citizens who have been "produced" by all the other arts of the city. The first part of the genealogy identifies statesmanship among the many possible modalities of care and the many possible objects of care (of which human beings are only one), distinguishing it from such modalities and objects of care while showing its relatedness to other modalities of care (in particular, the care of the good for human beings); the second part brings to light those forms of knowledge that, in contributing to

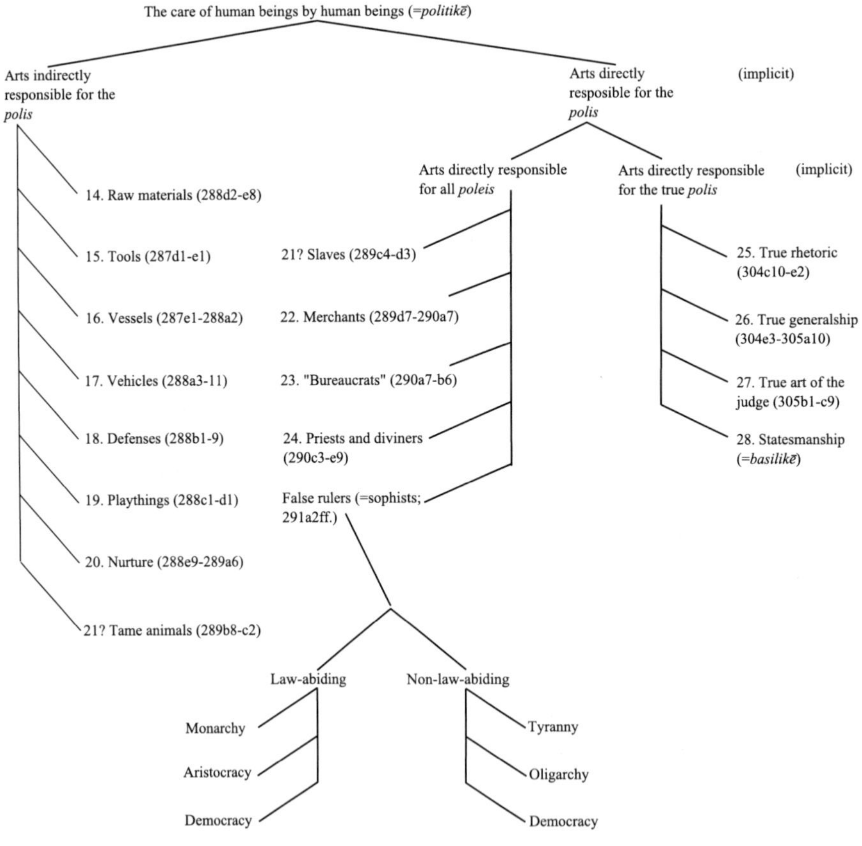

Figure 2: Statesmanship in the network of arts that care for human beings

the care of human beings under the statesman's direction, are kin to it to a greater or lesser extent. The dialogue thus depicts statesmanship as the "keystone" art which ultimately regulates, directly or indirectly, the contributions of all the other arts to the care of human beings.

This basic structure is complicated by two features of the discussion. The first is Young Socrates' inability to tell when the genealogy is actually complete. Twice the Stranger invites Young Socrates to say whether he thinks they have fully identified the statesman, and twice Young Socrates incorrectly suggests that he thinks they have (267c4ff., 277a1ff.), which forces the Stranger to introduce lengthy methodological considerations designed to show Young Socrates what is missing in the division. This may give the impression that the initial division is somehow incorrect, when it is not so; the Stranger in fact emphasizes that their account of statesmanship is "insufficient" or "incomplete" but true (267c8, 277a–c, especially 277a5). The second is the explicit "revision" of the initial division after the myth (274e–277a). This revision does in fact correct one significant error in the initial division, which might give one the impression that other, bizarre-seeming parts of the division (e.g., the identification of man with the featherless biped) are also implicitly corrected even though they are not. Young Socrates' mistakes are in fact significant for understanding the dialogue, since they are the mistakes of a theoretician; but we shall postpone their discussion for the moment to focus on the overall structure of the division.

We can better understand the structure of the long division of statesmanship by starting, not with statesmanship itself (which is a complex and difficult being to exhibit properly, as the Stranger says, 285d–286a), but with weaving, which the Stranger uses as a paradigm of statesmanship after they have run into trouble with the division of statesmanship (279a–283a), being unable to fully distinguish the statesman from all his competitors. The Stranger had started the

Sophist with a division of "angling," which he used as a small paradigm of sophistry (*Sophist* 218d8–e5), that is, an example that preserved enough of the formal structure of sophistry to be useful as a guide to the structure of the latter; his decision to forgo the use of a small example at the beginning of the *Statesman* perhaps accounts for some of the difficulties they run into with the division of statesmanship, as the Stranger himself indirectly acknowledges (cf. 277b1–6). In fact, the *Statesman* as a whole is built on the basis of large analogies or paradigms—between statesmanship and weaving, as we shall see here, but also between the statesman and the shepherd, the statesman and the god, and the statesman and the doctor and the ship captain. A fuller discussion of paradigms in the dialogue will have to wait until chapter 4; for the moment we shall simply show how the discussion of weaving can illuminate the structure of the dialogue and ultimately of statesmanship itself.

Weaving can serve as a paradigm for statesmanship because, in the Stranger's view, it has the "same business" as statesmanship (279a8). The exact business of weaving is detailed in what I will call the first division or genealogy of weaving (279c7–280a6, see figure 3), and summarized as "caring the most for cloaks,"[59] a puzzling phrase that echoes the idea of statesmanship as "caring" for human beings at 276b. Otherwise translated, this simply means that weaving's main objects of "concern" *(epimeleia)* are cloaks: weaving is the art that is most concerned with (the making of) cloaks. Statesmanship, of course, is not concerned with cloaks, yet we might also say that weaving *indirectly* cares for human beings through the production of woolen cloaks that will help protect them from the rigors of winter (a symbolically significant characterization, as we shall see in chapter 3). The identity of the business of statesmanship and that of weaving thus

59 Cf. τὴν δὲ τῶν ἱματίων μάλιστα ἐπιμελουμένην τέχνην, 279e6.

consists in the fact that both can be characterized as ways of *caring* (*epimeleia,* cf. 276a9–c2, 279a1–5, 279e6), indeed caring for human beings: they exemplify or instantiate the formal structure of care.

But the analogy goes deeper: for the paradigm of weaving implies that the task of statesmanship (along with the arts that contribute to the care of human beings) is the production of the *city,* understood as the artifact that protects us from the conflicts that result from our imperfect "tameness" or "sociality." As we shall see in more detail below and in the following chapters, just as weaving produces (with the cooperation of other arts under its ultimate direction) an artifact that, in protecting human beings from the inclemency of winter weather, contributes to their care, statesmanship similarly produces (with the cooperation of other arts under its ultimate direction) the city (or rather, the political regime or *politeia* of the city), which is an artifact that protects human beings from each other.

I have not yet shown, to be sure, that the Stranger thinks that the business of statesmanship is the production of this protective artifact against the conflicts generated by the imperfect tameness of human beings; at best, I have only suggested that his use of the paradigm of weaving points in this direction. A detailed examination of the parts of the division that define the main characteristics of human beings from the point of view of the search for statesmanship (chapter 2) and of the conditions that make necessary such protection (discussed in the myth; see chapter 3) will be needed to fully establish that the imperfect tameness of human beings is the problem, and the production of the (ordered) city the solution. At any rate, the Stranger introduces the paradigm of weaving only after he has established those ideas. For the moment, however, we will get a better sense of the "macro-structure" of the dialogue if we simply take it for granted that the statesman's task is the production of the city understood as a particular kind of protective artifact, as the paradigm of weaving indicates.

Weaving is not only used as a paradigm of statesmanship; the presentation of the example of weaving is *itself* paradigmatic of both their difficulties with the division of statesmanship, and of the way out of these difficulties. The Stranger first reenacts in a "small" case their own difficulties with the first account of statesmanship, producing a first division or genealogy of weaving (*Statesman* 279c7–280e7, see the first ten steps in figure 3) that separates weaving from all other arts that are not concerned with the making of woolen cloaks. But this division suffers from the same problem as their first account of statesmanship,[60] namely, that it says something true but incomplete (280e6, 281c7–d3), because it identifies "weaving" or "cloaking" (*himatiourgikē*, 280a2) with the entire set of arts that are concerned with the production of a woolen cloak (properly understood as a kind of protective artifact for human use, as the division makes clear), and hence is unable to fully describe weaving (*huphantikē*, 280a3, 281c7) as the art that has the "biggest part" in this productive process.[61] Similarly, the first division of statesmanship identifies political knowledge (*politikē*) with the art or set of arts that cares for human beings (by producing a city, as the remainder of the dialogue makes clear), but is not able to fully characterize the

[60] Indeed, this first division has the same number of steps (ten) as the first division of statesmanship (before the myth or the post-myth corrections), and also the same number of steps as the division of the angler in the *Sophist*.

[61] Campbell (1867, note to 281e), notes nicely how the characterization of weaving as the "biggest art" but not the sole art among those making the web, and thus by implication of statesmanship as the biggest form of care, but not the sole one, recalls *Theaetetus* 207dff., where Socrates' third hypothesis concerning knowledge is put to the test and found wanting, namely, that to have knowledge of something is to have a distinguishing sign, a superlative characteristic.

science of the king (*basilikē*, 280a5) as the art that makes the biggest contribution to this care (cf. 279a1–5).[62]

The Stranger then shows why this account of weaving was incomplete (280e8–281d4), and introduces the tools that allow them to surmount this difficulty, modeling their use until he finally produces a complete account of weaving (*Statesman* 281d5–283a9) that describes its relationships to all the other arts that contribute to the production of woolen cloaks, just as he will later use the conceptual distinctions introduced here to produce a full account of the relationships between statesmanship and all the other arts that contribute to the care of human beings. In particular, the Stranger introduces a number of conceptual distinctions that allow him to distinguish among the various forms of expertise that contribute to a productive process according to whether they do so indirectly (by providing tools used by other forms of expertise involved in the process, 281d9–e4), directly (by creating or refining the "materials" used in the process, like the arts of warp and woof making), or actually complete it (by putting these materials together to create the final product, like weaving itself, which puts together warp and woof). The result is a secondary division of weaving (see figure 3, steps 11–14), or rather, a division of the set of arts that contribute to the making of cloaks that hierarchically organizes these arts according to their role in the production of cloaks, and hence characterizes weaving properly as the art that completes the productive process, that is, as its most important part. Similarly, when these distinctions

[62] The Stranger does not make a consistent distinction between *himatiourgikē* and *huphantikē*, or between *politikē* and *basilikē*; indeed he says that the arts in both pairs they differ "only in name." Nevertheless he does indicate that the first division of statesmanship, like the first division of weaving, insufficiently identifies the art of the statesman properly speaking, pointing indiscriminately to the set of arts that together care for human beings (i.e., produce a city), just as the first division of weaving insufficiently identifies the art of the weaver properly speaking, pointing instead to the entire set of arts that together produce woolen cloaks.

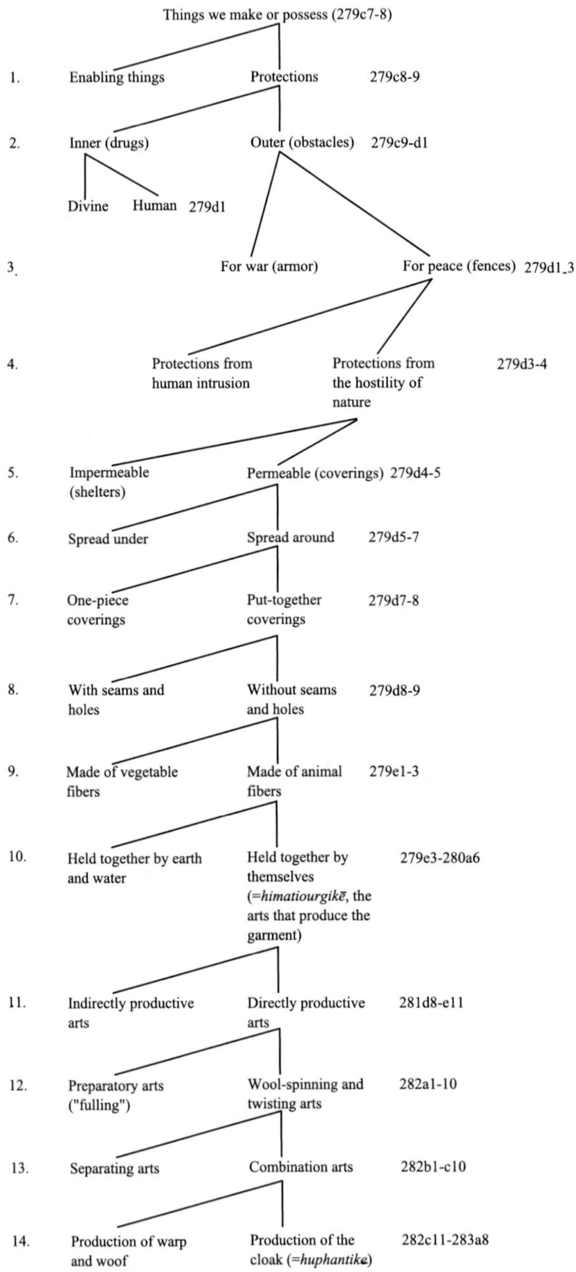

Figure 3: The complete genealogy of weaving

between indirectly contributory and directly contributory arts are applied to the set of arts that care for human beings, the result is a secondary division of statesmanship that hierarchically organizes the arts that contribute to the care of human beings according to their role in the production of the "web of politics," that is, the city (287b3 to end, with many interruptions). Statesmanship completes the work of creating the city as a protective artifact by taking the men that the other arts have "produced" (with their possessions and dispositions) and "weaving" them together into a lasting community.

Just as the second division of weaving (which identifies it with the art that makes a web by putting together warp and woof well) completes, but does not supersede, the first division of weaving (which identifies it with the art that makes woolen garments, and describes these woolen garments in terms of their function in the care of human beings), so the secondary division of statesmanship after 287b (see figure 1) completes, but does not supersede, the first (corrected) division of statesmanship that concludes at 277a (see figure 2). Indeed, though the first division of weaving seems at first glance tautological (*himatiourgikē*, cloak-making, is defined as the art that is concerned with [making] woolen cloaks), its value as a paradigm of statesmanship lies in the way in which it defines both the manner of the concern of the weaver (as a form of production) and its key object of concern (as a specific kind of protective artifact against the hostility of nature, useful to the care of human beings) while separating weaving from other forms of knowledge that are not concerned with the making of cloaks. Similarly, as we shall see in greater detail shortly, the first division or genealogy of statesmanship determines both the overall manner of the care of the statesman (as a "theoretical" or "cognitive," "directive," "autonomous," and "collective" form of care) and the nature of its key object of concern (human beings conceived as imperfectly "tame" beings, as we shall see), while separating statesmanship from arts that are not concerned with human beings in the same manner or which have a different object. And just as the second division of weaving is necessary to fully characterize the relationships between weaving and all the other arts that contribute to the making of cloaks as protective artifacts against the hostility of nature, the second division of statesmanship supplements the first with an understanding of statesmanship as an art that organizes and renders meaningful the activity of all the other arts involved in the creation of the city as a protective artifact against the hostility of other human beings.

It is also worth noting that though both the results of the division of weaving and of the final division of statesmanship can be put in the form of a long dichotomous division—as I do in figure 3 for weaving, and Goldschmidt (1947) does for statesmanship—even if the Stranger does not do so, both "secondary" divisions are fundamentally different from the primary dichotomous divisions that identify weaving and statesmanship as forms of care. In the first divisions the "rejected" sections of the division contribute nothing to the task of the particular form of knowledge being investigated; the care of cranes, considered only *qua* care of cranes (and not as contributing to the provision of meat for human beings, for example), does not contribute to the care of human beings, just as the production of drugs does not contribute anything to the production of woolen cloaks. Pure dichotomous division was thus sufficient for this first part of the process of identifying an art, since we did not need to keep in mind a single whole to which all the separated arts belonged in order to disclose the sought-for art. The separated arts could be simply discarded without prejudice to our understanding: we do not need to understand the art of the tanner to understand the art of the weaver.

But dichotomy is no longer very appropriate when the art to be discovered is the guiding core of a productive process that involves other arts, organizing their activity and/or rendering it meaningful: there the parts to be divided stand to one another in an "organic" relationship, and hence their separation must pay attention to the "natural joints" if we are to gain understanding from the division. For example, since the weaver is not independent of the carder and the fuller and warp-maker, but depends on them to complete the task of weaving the web, we must understand the arts of the carder and the fuller and the warp-maker in order to understand the art of the weaver, or rather, we must understand the place of these arts *vis-à-vis* the art of the weaver. Hence we cannot discard them by splitting them off from weaving through some general dichotomous division (e.g., the division of diacritic and synthetic arts), but must list them along with all the other arts that contribute to the creation of the web; and similarly for statesmanship, which is not independent of the arts that produce the city.[63] The Stranger will, accordingly, abandon dichotomous division in his search for the statesman (287b10ff.) as it becomes clear that they are looking not for an art in isolation from all other arts but for an art in a specific relation to other arts, and in particular an art whose work can only be achieved with the help of other arts; but his abandonment of dichotomous division at that point in the dialogue does not imply a criticism of his earlier methodological stance, as has sometimes been argued, since dichotomous division was perfectly adequate for the first stage of the division.[64]

Theory and Practice

The relationship between weaving as the central art that coordinates and renders meaningful the activities of other arts that contribute to the production of a cloak is, however, different from the relationship between statesmanship and the arts that contribute to the care of human beings. Weaving is characterized as a productive and practical art from the beginning, which is plausible since weaving is physically involved in

---

63 It should be noted that some of these arts appear twice, as it were (e.g., carpentry, which is separated first as a practical art, and second as the art that makes particular vehicles or seats): first considered in relationship to their own "intrinsic" purpose (in which light they have nothing to contribute to the care of human beings) and second considered in relationship to their contribution to such care.

64 By, e.g., Scodel (1987).

the production of a cloak, whereas statesmanship is identified, less plausibly, as a "theoretical" or "cognitive" (*gnōstikē*) art of sorts,[65] not as a productive art, though the productive character of statesmanship is more or less explicitly, if at first unclearly, asserted later (261b), as we shall see in more detail in the next chapter. Nevertheless, the nature of the relationship between statesmanship and the other arts that contribute to the care of human beings (and which only appear much later in the dialogue) needs to be clarified; and for that task, we need to understand the very beginnings of the division, in particular the first three steps of the genealogy of statesmanship.

These first steps characterize the "mode" in which statesmanship relates to other arts. Statesmanship is first said to be located (mostly) among the *gnōstikai*, "theoretical" or "cognitive" forms of knowledge (259c10–d6), rather than among the "practical" ones; within the theoretical forms of knowledge, statesmanship is characterized as a "directive" or "commanding" (*epitaktikē*, 260c1–5) rather than a merely "critical" or "judgmental" (*kritikē*) form of knowledge; and within the "directive" forms of knowledge, statesmanship is a "self-ruling" or "autonomous" form of knowledge rather than a form of

[65] I follow tradition in translating *gnōstikē* as "theoretical" form of knowledge. See, for example, Annas and Waterfield (1995), Diès (1935), and Rowe (1999). This translation is not fully satisfactory, however, since it gives the impression that the "theoretical" character of statesmanship has something to do with *theōrein*, to see or contemplate, rather than with *gnōnai*, to know, and hence may mislead about the actual character of the contrast between *gnōstikē* and *praktikē*. Furthermore, other translations are possible: for example, Benardete (1984b) uses "cognitive" (which I also like), Skemp (1987) prefers "pure" science (and "applied" science for *praktikē*), and Taylor (1961) opts for "science of knowing" (and "science of action" for *praktikē*). Nevertheless, as I argued in Márquez (2007) and as we shall see below, the contrast between *gnōstikē* and *praktikē* that the Stranger introduces does resemble somewhat the contrast between "theory" and "practice" for us, insofar as *gnōstikē* refers to forms of knowledge that are not directly "physical," whereas *praktikē* refers to forms of knowledge that are directly embodied in physical activities. Hence I have opted to retain the translation of *gnōstikē* as "theoretical," with the caveat that "cognitive" is also a useful translation.

knowledge whose use is directed or ruled by others (260d11–e9). The discussion of the statesman's object of concern (human beings) before and after the myth will bring further qualifications to this characterization of the mode of the statesman's knowledge (statesmanship will eventually be identified as a form of collective care, and indeed as a form of collective care that is "voluntarily accepted"), but let us focus for the moment on these first three steps, and in particular the first one, which characterizes statesmanship as a "theoretical" or "cognitive" form of knowledge.

As I have already indicated, this step has encountered a certain amount of skepticism among commentators, most of whom believe either that statesmanship is later implicitly said to be "practical" or else that this step is inconsistent with the overall characterization of statesmanship in the dialogue.[66] But this inference rests on an implicit notion of "theory" and "practice" that goes beyond what the Stranger has in mind when he says that statesmanship is *gnōstikē* rather than *praktikē*. Indeed, as I have argued in detail elsewhere—Márquez (2007)—all that the Stranger means by a "theoretical" or "cognitive" (*gnōstikē*) form of knowledge is a form of knowledge that does not require any characteristic physical performance (does not require any specific form of *praxis*) and is not embodied in any "physical" skill, and hence is not a science of the performance of those actions (is not *praktikē*); as he says, such forms of knowledge are "bare" of actions (*psilai tōn praxeōn*, 258d5). Practical forms of knowledge, by contrast, are either intrinsically dependent on embodied skills (consider, for example, the arts of wrestling, carpentry, or basketball), or else tied to the skillful performance of specifiable actions (as the office of a king may be tied to the skillful performance of court ceremonial); they are not "bare" of actions, but rather considerably encumbered by them.

To the extent that we agree, with Young Socrates, that the true king can be someone who can give knowledgeable

[66] See note 52.

advice to a "formal" ruler (259a6–8), that is, that what is essential in the statesman is that he have the knowledge of rule, we divest him of associations with any specific set of (physical) actions: we make his knowledge "bare" of actions. Moreover, insofar as the statesman need not be someone who plays a specific public role, he can be identified with a private individual, that is, a head of household, whose rule over his slaves (in the Greek context) is also not manifested in the performance of any specific physical actions. The household head only needs to *order* properly what his slaves are to *do* for the household to be ruled properly, so that the *actions* are associated with the slaves, not with the head of the household.[67] Such "orders" need not follow any specific pattern except the good of the household; and so the head of the household can be indifferently described both as a *despotēs* and an *oikonomos* (259b7), words that resonate with connotations of lawlessness and lawfulness respectively, and which prefigure the later description of statesmanship as a form of knowledge that can go beyond the law.

For the Stranger, then, the distinction between the head of household and the king cannot be a distinction between a public role, whose potential "actions" are both limited and partially specified by constitutional arrangements, and a private individual whose expertise is both potentially "lawless" and not manifested in the performance of any specific physical actions. And so from this point of view, the distinction between a large household and a small city appears insignificant. Yet the Stranger does not altogether abolish all distinctions between household and city, contrary to appearances; for the household is merely a two-dimensional version (a *schēma*, 259b9, a figure) of the three-dimensional city (which has bulk, *onkos*, 259b10), and hence the statesman's knowledge subsumes the knowledge of the household head, but is not subsumed by it

[67] See Rowe (1995b, note to 258e11).

in return.[68] Statesmanship, like the expertise of the ruler of a household, is ultimately not "practical" in the relevant sense because in both cases the achievements of expertise depend less on physical activity (exemplified in the idea of the work of the *hands*) than on the "strength" of the soul of the possessors of expertise (259c8).

Yet as the unusual phrase "wit and strength of the soul" (*tēn tēs psuchēs sunesin kai rōmēn*) suggests, the "effectiveness" of king and household head as *rulers* (and hence not merely as advisors, who may be ignored) may depend partly on factors other than their knowledge (their "charisma," for example); and the Stranger further recognizes that there may be some residual need to engage in physical activity on the part of the king by saying that statesmanship belongs "more" among the theoretical forms of knowledge than among the practical ones (259c10–d2). These two qualifications do not affect the overall point the Stranger is making as much as they suggest that the true statesman's place in the city cannot be made secure, a point to which we shall have occasion to return repeatedly.

It is worth emphasizing that in saying that the statesman's knowledge is bare of actions (and hence not "practical," that is, not a science of *praxeis*), the Stranger is not saying that the statesman's knowledge is not "practical" in *some* sense of the term, only that it is not practical in the specific sense in which the Stranger uses the term *praktikē*. To the extent that statesmanship is a "practical" form of knowledge (in our sense of the term, not the Stranger's), it is because statesmanship is the kind of knowledge that cannot complete its work

[68] Contrast this with the argument in Xenophon's *Memorabilia* III.4, the effect of which in identifying the knowledge of the household head and the knowledge of the statesman is to legitimize the knowledge of actual managers of households and economic enterprises. Aristotle's critique of the idea that city and household differ only in degree would apply much more clearly to this argument of Xenophon than to Plato's argument here, though the first book of the *Politics* has often been read as a critique of the latter rather than the former. For further discussion, see my "Theory and Practice in Plato's *Statesman*," Márquez (2007).

"internally," as it were; it requires the cooperation of other arts, including the cooperation of arts embodied in specific physical skills, in order to complete its work, which involves the bringing into being of something external to the soul of the statesman. This is the point of the distinction between "directive" or "commanding" arts and "critical" or "judgment" arts. While the latter can complete their work (*ergon*, 259e5) without the cooperation of any other arts, since their work is only a "judgment" that happens internally (inside the soul of the knower), the former require the cooperation of other arts in order to complete an external "handiwork" (cf. *cheirourgian*, 259e12), since they themselves do not engage in or produce any such "handiwork." From this point of view, statesmanship is already importantly different from philosophy, as the Stranger signals in characterizing their own inquiry as part of a "critical" activity (cf. 260c1–4: the Stranger and Young Socrates are merely "observers" rather than "masters").

Moreover, statesmanship is not merely a theoretical-directive art; it is also identified as an "autonomous" or "self-directing" art. That is, statesmanship, as a directive art, generates its own "orders," rather than merely applying or interpreting the "orders" generated by other forms of knowledge, and hence always stands at the apex of some hierarchy of arts (which include the arts of heralds, diviners, and the like, including some arts that the Stranger will only name later) that contribute to the care of human beings. This hierarchy of arts is a *productive* hierarchy, as in the example of weaving, and what is produced through the different contributions of various arts is the *city* conceived as the protective artifact through which human care is mediated. Statesmanship is, like weaving, the keystone art that ensures that the production of this artifact can be satisfactorily completed. This hierarchy of arts is only sketched out beginning at 287a, after various methodological interludes and corrections have finally succeeded in firmly identifying statesmanship as the art of caring collectively for human beings and clarifying the meaning of and reasons for such care (in particular, identifying the imperfect sociality or tameness of human beings as the reason why they need statesmanship, as we shall see in the next chapter). Yet a brief consideration at this point of the relationships between these arts and the theoretical-directive-autonomous (or "cognitive-directive-ruling") knowledge of the statesman can clarify both the connection between the earlier and later parts of the dialogue and the overall picture of statesmanship as the knowledge that "produces" the city.

The set of arts that contribute to the care of human beings (either directly or indirectly) is divided into two parts, the arts that produce the "possessions" of the city (287a–289c), and the arts of the "servants" of the city (289cff.). Each of these sets of arts contributes in distinct ways to the care of human beings, with (in general, as we shall see) the arts that produce the possessions of the city being less dependent on the knowledge of the statesman as they contribute to this care (and hence less "regulated" by such knowledge) than the arts of the "servants" of the city (which are more directly regulated, and in some cases controlled, by such knowledge).

The "possessions" of the city (cf. 289a7) are all those things (raw materials, tools, vessels, vehicles, defenses, and playthings) that are necessary for the production and reproduction of human beings as physical creatures or animals who must be "nurtured" (*thremma*, 289b2); indeed, human beings as bare creatures constitute the final possession of the city. The arts that produce these things make possible what in the *Republic* Glaucon called the "city of pigs," or, in modern terminology, they make possible "society" (or even the "economy") but not the *polis* properly speaking. In the Stranger's technical terminology (introduced during the discussion of weaving, 281eff.), these arts are only "indirect causes" of the city (*sunaitioi*, 289c9), rather than its "direct causes," where the city must be understood as the protective artifact produced jointly by the many arts that contribute to the care of human beings. As such, though these arts are all to some degree "practical" arts in the sense of

259d–e, they are not necessarily directly regulated by statesmanship; in fact, most of them retain some degree of autonomy from statesmanship, since the producers of these "possessions" can contribute to the care of human beings without requiring a statesman to regulate their work. In modern terms, "society" is prior to the *polis*; the statesman is not, in the Platonic view, directly concerned with what we may call the management of the economy. But while the statesman need not necessarily regulate them directly, they get their *point* from statesmanship, just as the activity of the maker of looms gets its point from weaving: without weaving, there is just no good *reason* to make looms.

This is not to say that these arts are *entirely* exempt from regulation by the statesman's knowledge, as the Stranger indicates by his careful choice of words. Only some of the possessions they produce are "not at all" the business of statesmanship (e.g., the production of raw materials), whereas in other cases the Stranger is content to say that it is "more correct" to say that these possessions are not the business of statesmanship (e.g., the nurture of human beings) and in one case he completely fails to say that statesmanship is not concerned with them (playthings, which presumably can be used in education, and hence must be tightly regulated by the statesman).[69] The key point is that some of the arts that produce the possessions of

[69] Each of the arts that produce the possessions of the city is separated from statesmanship with a phrase expressing the lack of involvement of *politikē* (in the narrow sense of the word) or *basilikē* in their work: thus, raw materials are said to be "in no wise" the province of *basilikē* (288e7), tools are separated from statesmanship with the decisive "not at all" (287d4–5), vessels with the slightly less decisive "simply not" (*ouden atechnōs* 288a1), vehicles with the even less decisive but still quite categorical "not very . . . but much more" (*ou panu . . . alla māllon polu* 288a8–10), defenses with the softer "more by much [the province of other arts]" (*pollōi mallon* 288b6), playthings are not separated explicitly, and the forms of nurture are separated from statesmanship with the mild expression that it is "more correct," *orthoteron*, for the arts of nurture to deal with them than for statesmanship (289a5).

the city have "political" implications, in the sense that they impinge either on the sources of conflict among human beings (e.g., by affecting "honor" and "dishonor"; cf. 288a5 on how "vehicles" are sometimes honorable and sometimes dishonorable) or on the education and character of citizens (playthings, the arts of nurture), and to that extent their work will not fully contribute to the care of human beings except under the guidance of a genuine statesman. But their degree of dependence on the statesman's knowledge for their ability to contribute to the care of human beings is generally (though not always) less than the degree of dependence of the "service" arts on this knowledge, as we shall see, just as the degree of dependence of the toolmaker on the weaver's knowledge for his ability to contribute to the making of a woolen garment is much less than the degree of dependence of the carder or warp-maker; the latter's knowledge needs the guidance of a weaver in order to properly contribute to the making of a garment in ways that the former's knowledge does not.

The "service" arts (cf. *hupēretas*, 289c4, 289d7; the practitioners of those arts are "servants") are those arts that make use of the "possessions" of the city (produced by the first set of arts) in order to contribute to the care of human beings *directly* rather than indirectly. These arts are in turn implicitly divided into two groups. In the first group (289c–291c, 303c), we find the arts of the slave, the wage laborer, the wealthy merchant, the "bureaucrat," the priests and diviners, and the rulers of the city without knowledge, that is, the sophists. The first two of these categories of service merely recapitulate the arts that produce the possessions of the city on the assumption that the productive arts are stripped of all autonomy: slaves and wage laborers merely are the producers of the possessions of the city, but *qua* slaves or wage laborers they cannot produce anything on their own initiative. At any rate, all of these six arts together are understood to give rise, via their use of the possessions of the city, to the "imperfect" or "actual" city, that is, the city as an imperfect artifact for the protection of human beings that is spontaneously created in the absence of the true statesman. This kind of city (as we shall see in more detail in chapter 5) cannot be expected to reliably serve as an artifact for protecting human beings from conflict.[70] In the second group, we find the arts of the genuine general, rhetor, and judge, which, when joined with the art of the true statesman (and only when so joined!), give rise to the true polity, that is, to the city understood as an ordered artifact (a city with a constitution or *politeia*) that can reliably protect human beings from the conflicts generated by their imperfect sociality.

The key point to note here is that without the regulation of statesmanship, these arts are incapable of truly managing the conflicts endemic to human existence: the general may prefer war at the wrong time, or the rhetor may persuade people of the wrong thing. A general who decides on his own whether to wage war (without having the knowledge of the statesman) does not contribute to the care of human beings but undermines it. Like a woolen cloak produced by someone without knowledge of weaving, which may "work" in normal times but fall apart in more extreme weather, the cities produced by the "servants" of the city in the absence of the statesman may provide for the care of human beings (more or less) in normal circumstances, for reasons that are explored in the arguments about law that begin around 291d (see chapter 5), but they are unlikely to protect them in more trying times. And to the extent that the statesman is absent from the city, some of the practitioners of these arts will take his place to produce "normal" cities (and hence will become sophistic rulers of cities). Statesmanship must constantly police the boundaries of these arts (excluding, perhaps, slaves and wage earners), keeping them within their assigned roles within the process of caring for human beings, as the Stranger indicates by commenting on the "arrogance" (290d–e) of priests and diviners. Though we shall say more

[70] The "actual" city is, in the terminology of the *Republic* (and with rather less dramatic flair in the *Statesman*) the "feverish" city.

about these arts in chapter 6, it is thus worth noting that this means that the position of the statesman, *qua* statesman, at the top of this hierarchy of arts is always precarious, and his autonomy a normative ideal more than a realistic possibility. The care of human beings demands that the arts of the general, the rhetor, the priest, the merchant and the judge submit to the judgment of the statesman regarding the proper scope of their contributions to this care, but their internal sense of their own autonomy makes it difficult for them to recognize the true statesman.

The characterization of statesmanship as a form of knowledge that is theoretical, directive, and autonomous, (or cognitive, directive, and regulatory) in conjunction with the later discussion of the other arts that, in producing the city, contribute to the care of human beings, thus describes what we might call the statesman's relationship to practice, the world of *praxis*. Statesmanship is not a physically embodied skill, but it requires the cooperation of such physically embodied arts in order to achieve its work, and indeed it should direct these other arts to a greater or lesser extent, depending on the particular art in question and its place within the process of production and reproduction of the city as a protective artifact through which human beings care for themselves. The social division of knowledge in the city is organized as a productive process, where the knowledge of the statesman is the kind of knowledge that can ensure that this productive process does not miscarry. Yet this characterization can only carry conviction if we can understand what the Stranger means by "care" and why such care is necessary; and for this, we need to turn to the parts of the division we have not yet examined, starting at 261a, that discuss the statesman's immediate object of concern and culminate in the notorious characterization of human beings as "featherless bipeds" or "two-footed pigs" and of statesmanship as the art of taking care of such beings.

2. Human Beings

THE PART OF THE DIVISION from 261b to 267c, and its apparent correction after the myth (274e–277e), is one of the most puzzling parts of a puzzling dialogue. It is here that the Stranger arrives at the striking conclusion that man is the "featherless biped" rather than the "rational animal"; indeed, the idea that man is a rational animal is apparently rejected by the Stranger when he corrects Young Socrates' hasty attempt at separating man from the other animals at 262aff., and this rejection is never explicitly retracted. It is not surprising that scholars have long neglected this part of the division; even in the ancient world the idea that man was a featherless biped was taken to be some kind of elaborate joke, if the anecdote about Diogenes the Cynic recounted by Diogenes Laertius (VI.40) is anything to go by.[71] Modern commentators concur; Campbell (1867) suggested that this part of the division was worthy of Swift, but not an especially important part of the political theory of the dialogue, and later scholars have tended to see the value of the division in terms of the meager methodological insights it generates, such as the idea that one should divide classes of things only into other real classes ("eidetic" parts),

---

[71] Diogenes the Cynic is told that Plato defined human beings as featherless bipeds, and was "much applauded" for that, so he came into the academy with a plucked chicken and said, "here is your Platonic man." So the school had to add the qualification "with broad nails" (*to platuōnuchon* [τὸ πλατυώνυχον]) to the definition, which is obviously a pun on *to platōnikon* (τὸ πλατώνικον).

and not just mere parts (263a–b).[72] Moreover, it is in this part of the division that we find all the "mistakes" that the dialogue spends so much time correcting later (e.g., the confusion of "care" and "nurture"), so it is not surprising that most scholars assume that its main results must all be discarded later in the dialogue.

There is, to be sure, more to this part of the division than the idea that man is a featherless biped (or a two-legged pig). In fact, throughout this part of the division the Stranger and Young Socrates struggle to come up with an adequate description of the kind of relationship that should hold between the statesman and the key object of his concern, namely human beings, and settle on a model of this relationship as a form of collective care for tame (or tamable) animals. But I want to suggest here that understanding properly this model of care we need to take more seriously than has hitherto been the case the strange idea that man is not, for the purposes of understanding statesmanship, the rational animal. A correct characterization of the proper relationship between the statesman and human beings needs to de-emphasize human rationality and (as we shall see) emphasize human sociality and its deficiencies. But in order to understand how the Stranger gets there, we need to pay especially close attention to the dramatic and literary details of the conversation from 261a to 266d, and then from 274e to 277e.

Young Socrates' mistakes

As we just noted, a salient characteristic of the part of the dialogue with which we are currently concerned is the prominence of Young Socrates' errors and confusions and of the Stranger's explicit attempts to correct him. In particular, Young Socrates is depicted as erring in separating man from the animals without checking whether the two "sides" of the

---

72 See, e.g., Annas and Waterfield (1995, x); Lane (1998, 44). There are some exceptions, especially Benardete (1984b) and Clark (1995).

division are genuine forms (262a) on the basis of the criterion of rationality. Yet it is not clear why Plato wanted to depict Young Socrates erring at precisely this point in the division, and moreover erring in such a way that the "correction" of his error would lead to a conclusion that seems even more bizarre than the error, namely, the characterization of human beings as two-footed pigs or featherless bipeds and of statesmanship as the art of "shepherding" such creatures. If Plato had simply wanted to make some points about the proper use of the method of division, he could have introduced Young Socrates' errors elsewhere in the dialogue, or at the very least not used the corrections of the error as a way to arrive at such apparently bizarre conclusions.

Before we rush to dismiss this whole section as some kind of academic joke that makes some purely methodological points, however, it is worth noting that there are a number of reasons for thinking that the method of division (and the disciplining of intuition on which it depends) would experience some difficulties in articulating the exact nature of the relationship between the statesman and other human beings. The Stranger assumes (261b) that there is a broad sense in which statesmanship is involved in the "production" of human beings, that is, it participates (in some capacity) in the process which ensures the continuing existence and development of human beings; and from this point of view, statesmanship can be fairly characterized as a form of *care, epimeleia* (261d6). But the exact role that statesmanship plays in this process, and hence the exact nature of this "care" is much more difficult to determine, depending on how we evaluate the centrality of its role (how badly the process of producing human beings would be impaired without the contribution of statesmanship), the specific nature of its contribution (exactly what statesmanship contributes to the existence and development of human beings), and the nature of the thing produced (human beings). Indeed, the initial characterization of this care on the model of the "nurture" (or, perhaps more accurately, "feeding," *trophē*

261d4, as we shall see in more detail below) of animals collected in a herd turns out later to be erroneous because it hides the dependence of statesmanship on a social division of expertise which contributes to the overall care of human beings (their "production" in the broadest sense) and in which he plays only a limited role. Whereas without "nurture" the herd dies, since the shepherd monopolizes all the capacities necessary to keep the herd in existence, without statesmanship human beings simply do worse, depending on the other capacities and forms of expertise available to them and on their ability to cooperate with one another. Hence the idea that statesmanship is a form of "nurture" needs to be eventually corrected by returning to the more abstract idea of "care" (275d–e), but this is of course not enough to fully characterize the true relationship between the statesman and human beings; for that, we have to wait until the identification of the statesman as the "weaver" of the city (discussed in chapter 6), which properly describes both the importance of the statesman's role and the specific nature of his contribution to the process of "producing" human beings.

More generally, the proper determination of the correct model of care describing the relationship between the statesman and human beings is not independent of the determination of the politically relevant features and capacities of both statesman and human beings more generally, or of the conditions under which they relate to one another. This part of the division would thus need to simultaneously determine the characteristics of human beings that are politically relevant as well as the model of care that is appropriate to such characteristics, something that cannot be easily done without first assuming some important things about the statesman and the conditions of his care. Thus, as we shall see in greater detail below, the "shepherd" model of care makes sense on the assumption of a godlike shepherd and conditions of perfect abundance obtaining in what the myth will call the "age of Cronos," but it does not make sense otherwise. Conversely, many features of human beings that are "politically irrelevant" from the point of view of current conditions (e.g., whether an animal has split horns or not) become relevant on the assumption of a "shepherding" model of care, whereas features that one might have thought important, like human rationality, become irrelevant on that same assumption: one cannot properly hold both that human beings are primarily rational beings and that their care is a form of "nurture," as Young Socrates implicitly holds. The Stranger and Young Socrates would thus have required a full awareness of the conditions described in the myth *before* attempting to discuss the proper model of care for the relationship between the statesman and human beings.

That the Stranger does not start by describing the conditions that constrain the possibility of political care indicates that Plato thinks that the pedagogical value of exploring the errors the Stranger and Young Socrates make as they stumble about under the erroneous assumption that statesmanship is a kind of "nurture of herd animals" outweighs the value of having the Stranger simply lead the discussion towards the right answer; but it would be incorrect to assume that this value is to be found entirely in the few purely methodological points concerning the correct application of the method of division the Stranger makes in this section. In fact, though the Stranger allows Young Socrates to err in the identification of the proper model for the statesman's care, he guides him through his mistakes towards a potent insight: that the key feature of human beings from the point of view of statesmanship (the "political" point of view, we might say) is not their rationality, as Young Socrates, with all the pride of a mathematician, blithely assumes, but what I shall call their "imperfect tameness" or their incapacity to cooperate fully with one another. We might say that the Stranger argues here that statesmanship, unlike philosophy or mathematics, is not concerned with human beings as primarily rational animals, but with human beings as featherless, imperfectly cooperative birdbrains. Or, in more modern and sober terminology, the Stranger is arguing that the most significant feature of human beings from the point of view of identifying the knowledge of the statesman is that human beings are social, but not *eusocial*, beings.

In order to understand the dramatic movement of this section, and hence the thrust of the Stranger's implicit pedagogy, the main thing to notice is that there are three methodological mistakes in it, though only one is normally noted by commentators and explicitly flagged by the Stranger, namely, Young Socrates' division of living beings into human beings and all other animals at 262a, which exemplifies the mistake of dividing without keeping track of whether all parts of the division constitute real classes of things. But Young Socrates' mistake is preceded and facilitated by two earlier mistakes for which the Stranger himself is responsible: first, the use of the criterion of worth or nobility to identify the branch of the division in which the statesman is to be found (261c7–d2), a criterion he had explicitly condemned at *Sophist* 227a7–c6, and which he will later condemn again (*Statesman* 266d4–11), and second, a studied inattention to the conceptual implications of names (261e5–7), which he will later rue (275d4–6). These two mistakes predispose Young Socrates to believe (erroneously) that what is valuable about human beings (their rationality) is *eo ipso* their most relevant feature from the perspective of identifying statesmanship; and to believe (again erroneously) that it does not matter much whether we characterize statesmanship as a form of "nurture" or as a form of "care."

The first mistake

Let us begin with the first mistake. As noted above, this section of the division begins with the claim that the statesman's knowledge, which is directive and autonomous, issues commands "for the sake of" some process of generation (261a10–b2). The Stranger is here simply drawing the logical inference from the characterization of statesmanship as directive and autonomous: such knowledge organizes the work of other arts so as to produce something that did not exist before or could not continue to exist properly without its instructions, or, in the terminology of the *Sophist*, that his knowledge is *productive* (219a11–12), like the weaver's knowledge.[73] The Stranger then tells Young Socrates to consider a division of generated things into "ensouled" (living) and "inanimate," and asks whether the statesman's knowledge organizes the production of the first or the second kind of thing. However, like Theaetetus in the earlier conversation about the sophist (*Sophist* 226e1–227c9), Young Socrates has trouble deciding whether the activity of the statesman is geared towards the generation or production of ensouled or inanimate beings.

His confusion is understandable: not only is he, as a mathematician, rarely concerned with the generation of things, but the Stranger's previous divisions had not specifically stressed the productive aspects of the statesman's knowledge, or

73 As I have argued at more length in Márquez (2007), the fact that the knowledge of the statesman can be characterized as "productive" is not in contradiction with the earlier characterization of the statesman's knowledge as "theoretical," *pace* Roochnik (2005). The idea that the statesman's knowledge is productive can in fact be analyzed in terms of the complex of ideas describing the statesman's knowledge as theoretical-directive-autonomous (or cognitive-directive-ruling): statesmanship produces beings that did not exist before (the city, or rather, the city's constitution) insofar as it uses its theoretical insight into the forms of order (the just, the noble, and the good) to issue *orders* to other arts that in turn *direct* them to order pre-existing materials (human and non-human) in accordance with the order intuited by the statesman (i.e., the statesman's grasp of the just, the good, and the noble), just as a master artisan uses his grasp of the form of an artifact to issue orders to subordinate arts to order (arrange and put in proper relation) raw materials so as to bring into being an object that did not exist before. To be sure, other forms of productive knowledge are imaginable, including what we might call practical-autonomous and practical-non-self-directed forms, which would comprise the forms of knowledge of most artisans, but statesmanship as such would still be classified as a productive art.

indicated whether such production as the statesman directs is to be likened more to the activity of the master carpenter, the animal breeder, or the educator (who produces opinions in the souls of human beings). For all we know at this point, statesmanship may be specifically concerned with the production of defensive fortifications. Moreover, without the idea of a social division of knowledge (which will only be introduced with the discussion of weaving), the idea that the statesman *produces* human beings (which is what the Stranger is aiming at) seems distinctly odd, implying that the statesman is a sort of breeder of men, a "shepherd." But because Young Socrates and the Stranger proceed without having clarified the distinction between a form of knowledge that *produces* living beings by itself and a form of knowledge that *organizes* a social division of expertise whose final end is the production of social relations that preserve and develop distinctively human beings, that is, "generate" them in the broadest possible sense, they are helping to pave the way for the (erroneous) identification of the statesman with the shepherd of man.

In order to help Young Socrates see that the statesman is concerned with the production of living beings, the Stranger introduces a criterion that he had earlier disparaged, namely, the criterion of worth or nobility (*Sophist* 227a7–c6; *Statesman* 266d4–11). By pointing to the worth of statesmanship, he indicates (261c7–d2) that it could not possibly be in charge of producing inanimate things, like the art of a master carpenter; hence (he says) statesmanship must be concerned with the generation of living (ensouled) beings, which are of higher worth or nobility. The Stranger thus has recourse to common, non-mathematical opinion: what is alive is nobler than what is not alive; kingship is nobler than carpentry; hence kingship must be concerned with things that are alive. But the Stranger pays a price for breaking his methodological commitments, insofar as he suggests that what is *valuable* or *noble* about human beings (e.g., their rationality), and hence what they can take *pride* in (cf. 262a5), is always what is *relevant* for defining statesmanship; and as we shall see shortly it is precisely this suggestion that leads Young Socrates to make a mistake at 262a3ff., dividing all herd animals into human beings (rational animals) and the rest of the animals. Statesmanship is indeed concerned with nobler beings than carpentry, but it is not *primarily* concerned with the features that *make* such beings noble, except insofar as such features make them imperfectly governable (by, e.g., making them presume to be wise when they are not).

The second mistake

The second methodological mistake, lack of attention to names, follows closely on the first. The Stranger now claims (261d) that this theoretical-directive-autonomous knowledge that is concerned with the generation of living beings must be divided according to whether it operates on a single individual or on a group, and suggests that the statesman's knowledge is of the latter kind. But in the process he now gives a name, or rather, a series of names, to the kind of knowledge that is to be so divided; and the names are not innocent of theoretical implications, as the Stranger will acknowledge later on in the dialogue (275d4–6). Thus the theoretical-directive-autonomous knowledge that is concerned with the generation of a *single* being is called first a form of *monotrophia*, "singular" nurture, and its practitioner is said to be an *idiotrophos*, a "private" nurturer, among which we find the ox-driver (*boēlatēs*) and the horse-groom (*hippokomos*), whereas the knowledge that is concerned with the generation of a *group* of beings is called a form of *care* (*epimeleia*) in common of creatures (*thremmatōn*) in herds, among which we find the horse-feeder (*hippophorbos*) and the ox-feeder (*bouphorbos*). The statesman is said to be *more akin* to the horse-feeder and the ox-feeder than to the ox-driver and the horse-groom; but his apparent kinship with these two figures blurs other important similarities with the other two.

Note that the division does not rest on horses or oxen being naturally gregarious or naturally solitary, only on the kind of activity that tends to them. After all, if the purpose of the comparison were to show that the living beings with which the statesman is concerned are naturally gregarious, the Stranger would not have used a comparison that refers to the same animal in both "sides" of the cut (horse-feeder versus horse-groom; the horse can hardly be a herd animal and a non-herd animal at the same time!). If this is so, the point of the division cannot be simply that some living beings form "herds" whereas some other living beings do not; it is not, in other words, a division of animals into "social" and "non-social" animals.[74] The herd terminology, to the extent that it has philosophical significance, serves to suggest an undifferentiated multitude of functionally identical animals who are different in kind from the person who cares for them, do not contribute meaningfully to own their care, and do not come into conflict with one another, not a society bound together by ties of affection or need whose members can come into conflict with one another. Indeed, most of the appearances of the word *agelē* occur before the discussion of weaving, that is, before the introduction of the notion that the *polis* is not an agglomeration of undifferentiated animals but a structured group of people with diverse functional specializations; afterwards the Stranger prefers to speak of a *polis* rather than a herd, and does not suggest again that human beings are by nature herd animals.[75]

---

74 Scholars sometimes ignore this point: see Scodel (1987, 47) and Clark (1995, 238) for two examples of this error. It is only later, with the division of animals into tame and wild, that—retrospectively—the Stranger takes the point as one about the nature of human beings as herd animals rather than about the nature of the activity of the statesman (cf. 264a1ff.).

75 The word *agelē* (and a synonym, *poimnē*) occurs twelve times before the myth, once in the myth, three times in the discussion of the mistakes they made in the original division, and only three times in the rest of the dialogue, after the mistake has been corrected: at 287b5, after the statesman

The point of the division thus concerns not the differences between herd and non-herd animals but the differences between "feeding" and "grooming" or "driving." The ox-feeder or horse-feeder puts the feed in a trough or some other appropriate place and lets a number of horses or oxen feed themselves, without paying attention to any particular horse or ox. So long as the horses or oxen are in general well fed, the horse-feeder or ox-feeder has done his task. The horses or oxen are then free to do as they wish. The horse- or ox-feeder does not attend to sickness or individual problems or talents; for that, you need a horse-groom. More generally, the horse-feeder's care of living beings (horses) extends only to their bodies, not to their souls, a fact that minimizes the importance of the ensouled/inanimate division. And insofar as he takes care of their bodies, the horse-feeder does not attend to the peculiar dietary needs of each horse, but provides a single sort of food for all.

has been separated from the other arts that take care of herds, at 294e10, establishing the similarity of the legislator to other mass trainers, who are concerned with the care of the body, and at 295e6, establishing the similarity of the legislator to the doctor who writes down his prescriptions in order to care for the patient's body. In all three cases after the corrections the word is used only to denote a similarity between statesmanship and activities that care for *bodies* in common, and in particular between lawgiving as the kind of care in common that does not concern itself with individuals and the care of herds, not to suggest that the statesman should be considered a herder. It should also be noted that the word is relatively infrequent in Plato: it occurs also at *Minos* 318a (twice), once in a non-political context at *Theaetetus* 197d (though the general image of the king as a shepherd also occurs, with some irony, in the digression, 174d3ff.), twice in the *Republic* (459d, 451c; *poimnē* occurs at 415d) and seven times in the *Laws*, relatively few times for a dialogue of that size. As we can see, the characterization of human beings as living in herds, though marginally more common for the two "Strangers," is rather unusual, and Socrates hardly uses it, especially if we except the *Minos*, which may not be by Plato. The two times he uses it are clearly metaphorical usages, and his ironic use of the "shepherd of the people" image in the digression of the *Theaetetus* suggests that Socrates does not think human beings are merely a herd or should be treated as such. Moreover, as Weiss (1995, 215), points out, the shepherd analogy in the *Republic* is not itself Socratic, but is taken over from Thrasymachus.

He does not transform his charges into *idiotrophoi*, eaters of a personalized diet,[76] as the horse-groom may do, but keeps them as **koinotrophoi*,[77] eaters of a common diet, eaters in common out of a common trough or feeding-place. This is what makes his activity a care "in common," insofar as he need not, and *qua* feeder does not, pay attention to the individual horse or ox but only to the stud of horses or the herd of cattle.

Both the horse-groom and the ox-driver, on the other hand, must pay attention to individual horses or oxen, though in different ways. The horse-groom grooms a particular horse to make him the best he can be, not in relation to any common endeavor with other horses, but merely for the sake of its individual potential. The ox-driver must also pay attention to each ox individually, even when more than one is yoked to a harness, but not for the sake of each ox's particular potential, but rather for the cart to move in the right direction or the plow to plough correctly, that is, for the sake of a common endeavor whose goal is set by the ox-driver. Ox-driving for plowing in fact requires choosing or training each individual ox with a view to their work together with the others in the team (e.g., making turns together, a difficult matter, since the "exterior" ox must start to turn before the "interior" ox). An ox-driver who does not pay attention to the "character" of each of his oxen will often find that they do not "work" together very well; that is why they must often be trained together from a very early age. So in *Works and Days* 436ff., the poet tells his brother Perses to get "[t]wo nine-year-old bull oxen. In their prime / They have full strength, and work the best, nor will / They quarrel in the furrows, break the plough, / And leave the work unfinished" (Dorothea Wender translation), clearly implying that these oxen would have been trained together from an

[76] See LSJ, s.v. *idiotrophos*, second meaning.

[77] This word does not occur in classical Greek, according to LSJ, though the Stranger coins *koinotrophikē* as one possible description of the art of the statesman at 261e2.

early age.[78] One could also note here the image of the chariot in the *Phaedrus*, drawn by a team of a white and a black horse, each of which has its own nature and each of which must be individually attended to for the sake of the common task of reaching the beautiful (cf. *Phaedrus* 253c7ff.). Thus, whereas the horse-groom attends to each horse individually for the sake of the horses' individual good, the ox-driver attends to each ox individually in order to ensure the harmonious performance of a common task. We might say that the horse-groom is purely "idiotrophic"—in that his activity is not essentially concerned with any group of horses or any common activity that any group of horses may accomplish on their own, but that the ox-driver must be both *idiotrophos* and *koinotrophos*; he is not a pure example of either side of the division.

We now begin to see that it is by no means obvious that the statesman should be likened more to the ox- or horse-feeder than to the ox-driver or the horse-groom. In fact, the three basic analogies the Stranger uses (horse-feeder, horse-groom, and ox-driver) each yield three plausible "models" of statesmanship: the statesman as legislator, the Socratic statesman, and the statesman as the "captain" of the city, respectively. Let us look at these "models" more closely.

If the statesman's art were like that of a common "feeder," (as in fact the Stranger forcefully suggests it is, for reasons that are not entirely clear at this point) then he would be in charge of a relatively small part of the care of human beings; once they are fed, horses are entrusted to the care of other arts or remain free to do as they wish. The stranger of course takes quite literally the notion of a "feeder" (*trophos*) of human beings (cf. 267e7–268a4 and chapter 3 below), with quite comical results. The more important point, however, concerns the idea of feeding in common: e.g., from a common trough or pasture,

---

[78] This is also the reason why ox-drivers in English are often called "teamsters": plowing and pulling carts are done with "teams" of oxen who must be properly coordinated. For more on training oxen, see, e.g., Conroy (1999).

as described above, without regard for differences within the "herd." In this horse- or ox-feeding can be seen as images of the rule of law, in that common feeding and the rule of law are both unable or unwilling to come to terms with particular needs or problems, a critical point in the Stranger's argument against the latter (cf. 294a10ff.). The statesman as horse-feeder, then, is purely "koinotrophic"; we may call this the "legislative" model of the statesman.

If, by contrast, the statesman's art were like that of a horse-groom (which the Stranger suggests it is not), then he would be a kind of private educator. The word *hippokomos* (horse-groom) recalls *Laws* 666e1ff., where the Athenian Stranger criticizes the Dorian regimes for treating their young as if they were young horses grazing (*nemomenous phorbadas* 666e3; compare with the term the Eleatic Stranger uses, the *hippo-phorbos* or horse-feeder, the one who provides *phorbas,* feed, to the horses) as a herd, and not appointing private grooms (cf. *hippokomon* 666e5) to soften and educate the savage and harsh nature the youths acquire when so treated, that is, to instill moderation alongside courage, or, to use the Eleatic Stranger's categories from later in the dialogue, to moderate their courageous tendency and thus instill justice in them (cf. *Statesman* 308d–e). The statesman's art, for the Athenian Stranger, thus appears to consist in being able to provide just that kind of individual grooming alongside the laws, or at least not against them, which the Stranger more or less forces Young Socrates to reject at this point in the dialogue (though note that the Stranger is careful to say that the statesman is "more akin" to the horse-feeder than to the horse-groom, not that his activity is "identical" to that of the horse-feeder). The statesman's activity would consist, on this model, in grooming each particular individual—making each individual good as far as possible—on the assumption that the good of each individual adds up to the common good. We may call this the "Socratic" model of the statesman, as it is also close to Socrates' own practice of speaking to and caring for individuals, which he suggests in the *Gorgias* constitutes the true political art (cf. *Gorgias* 521d). In fact, the Stranger's "correction" later on in the dialogue will partially reintroduce "grooming" into the conceptual vocabulary of statesmanship, since one of his suggested terms for the art from which the art of the statesman descends is *agelaiokomikē* (275e6), the grooming of herds.

Finally, if the statesman's art were like that of the ox-driver, then he would be a kind of captain supervising the completion of a common task, or leading the city to its appointed destination. In this case, the statesman would have to be both an *idiotrophos* (giving private attention to particular individuals) and a *koinotrophos* (coordinating their activities for the sake of a common task); if he were only one or the other, the common task could not be properly completed. This common task can be conceptualized as the common care of human beings as ensouled beings, and indeed this appears to be the model of statesmanship that eventually emerges from the Stranger's argument, in spite of the identification of the statesman with the horse-feeder at this point. At the same time this model of statesmanship turns out to be strictly speaking impossible, leading the Stranger to articulate statesmanship on the model of the legislator, with all its disadvantages. So in a certain sense the "horse-feeder" model of the statesman is never quite abandoned, even if it is clearly found to be suboptimal.

Young Socrates was somewhat non-committal when asked whether the statesman should be likened to a horse-feeder or to an ox-driver or horse-groom: now that it has been said, he replied, it does appear so, namely, that the statesman is like the horse- or ox-feeder (261d11). The Stranger more or less forced Young Socrates to say that the statesman is more like the horse-feeder than like an ox-driver (a much more promising image in some ways) or a horse-groom. But now the Stranger offers Young Socrates the choice between calling the statesman's art *koinotrophikē* (nurture in common) and *agelaiotrophia* (nurture of herds; 261e1–3). Young Socrates is indifferent: he suggests that either name is fine by him. The Stranger praises him for this answer, with a great deal of irony, saying that if he guards against taking names too seriously, he will reach old age richer in *phronēsis* (261e4–7). What he does not say is that inattention to names should be accompanied by attention to the implications of the concepts the names refer to, if the promised wealth is to materialize; and it is the Stranger, more than Young Socrates, who has in this section been inattentive to the conceptual implications of the names he uses, an inattention that he will acknowledge as the cause of their key mistake (275d1–e9). Indeed, had the Stranger paid more attention to his own terminology, they could have avoided this error completely, since earlier they did describe the statesman's knowledge as a form of care, *epimeleia* (261d6). Yet it must be said that without the idea, introduced in the section on weaving, of a productive process, the distinction between the care and the nurture of a living being is difficult to sustain; and there is no point in introducing that distinction at his point without needlessly complicating the division, or missing much that Young Socrates still needs to learn about human beings.

The third mistake

These two methodological errors of the Stranger (the use of the criterion of value and his inattention to the conceptual implications of names) make Young Socrates' explicit mistake, the third in the division, possible. After the Stranger praises him for his inattention to names, he asks him to divide *agelaiotrophikē*, and Young Socrates "eagerly" obliges, dividing man from all the "beasts" (*thēriōn*, 262a3–4), on the basis of the criterion (explicitly identified by the Stranger only at 263d) that human beings possess *phronēsis*, intelligence, whereas the beasts do not. As noted above, the Stranger's use of the criterion of value for separating living from inanimate beings encourage Young Socrates to think that what is uniquely valuable about human beings (their—fallible, as his own contribution shows—rationality) is precisely what is relevant for identifying statesmanship. Yet if Young Socrates had understood the implications of the idea of nurture as a model for statesmanship, he would not have so quickly separated human beings from the beasts; for nurture does not require that the beings nurtured be rational, or vary much from each other. Young Socrates is in danger of thinking, we might say, that beings with *phronēsis* can or should be ruled or cared for as if all they needed was sufficient feeding, without regard for their virtue and freedom.

Young Socrates' (dimly implied) idea is not silly. The conception of the statesman as the shepherd of man to which it points has a long and distinguished history up to the present, as Foucault argued (2000 [1979]). Though we may not say today that the statesman is the shepherd of man, we often do suggest that the statesman's business is to care for the material prosperity of the ruled, even to the extent (as in the great communist experiments) of placing all responsibility for such prosperity in the state; and the idea that politics should be replaced by the technocratic administration of things, so prominent in some versions of Marxism, is simply another version of the idea that statesmanship is the art of shepherding men. But, as the Stranger's divisions will show, it cannot be the truth about statesmanship. The division of living beings into men and beasts cannot capture the specific features of human beings that make statesmanship both possible and necessary. In fact, such a division merely suggests a dilemma: on the one hand, if statesmanship is merely a form of "feeding" or "nurture," presided over in its entirety by the statesman, then the rationality of human beings cannot make any difference to their care; but if, on the other hand, statesmanship is *not* a form of feeding or nurture, human rationality should make the statesman's care unnecessary, as human beings should be able to take care of themselves without his help (they would be "ruled by reason," in standard Platonic terms). Hence rationality cannot be the feature of human beings that makes statesmanship necessary.

Young Socrates had expressed a special eagerness (cf. *prothumēsomai* 262a3) in answering the Stranger's prompt, and the Stranger had in turn emphasized Young Socrates' eagerness and "manliness" (262a5). But *thumos* is precisely one of the characteristics of human beings that are overlooked in thinking of the care of man as a form of feeding. If human beings were entirely dominated by the appetites that make it necessary for them to eat or sleep, then statesmanship would certainly be a kind of nurture; but human beings also have spiritedness, which makes them proud and sometimes quarrelsome. Indeed, it is the combination of *thumos* and the capacity for *phronēsis* (though not necessarily the actual exercise of this capacity) that makes human beings think that they are able to rule themselves even if they are not. Thus Young Socrates' rash distinction threatens, one the one hand, to render the statesman irrelevant or even impossible, since human beings would think that they are able to rule themselves without his help; and on the other hand, to render human beings intractable and disobedient, since an animal who believes that he can rule himself would not accept a shepherd-like ruler.

The problem with Young Socrates' use of *phronēsis* to separate human beings from beasts can also be characterized in a slightly different way. As the Stranger puts it, Young Socrates acts like the cranes, who, believing themselves to be in possession of *phronēsis*, raise themselves above all other creatures, or, more precisely, make themselves holy (cf. *semnunon auto heauto*, 263d7), like gods. Young Socrates' division of living beings into human beings and beasts did not make *space* for the gods, after all; he restricted all *phronēsis* to human beings. But if human beings think of themselves as gods, they become unruly and disobedient, hubristic even. Either, then, a statesman is not needed and cannot exist (because human beings, possessing *phronēsis*, can rule themselves), or he is needed but is unable to make his rule effective (because human beings who "make themselves holy" are unable to accept the rule of other human beings).

The Stranger's corrections

I will not discuss here the Stranger's methodological remarks in response to Young Socrates *per se*, since they have no real bearing on the kind of knowledge that the statesman is supposed to have, and at any rate the topic has already generated a great deal of commentary,[79] whereas the division up to this point and after the methodological remarks tends to be dismissed as a whimsical exercise. The basic methodological point, at any rate, is quite simple: division should distinguish among eidetic or what we might call "look-yielding" parts of a whole (parts with their own internal unity) rather than among mere arbitrary parts (parts without an internal principle of unity, and hence without a characteristic look or *eidos*), which is the same as to say that it should arrive at true families (*genē*) that have members on both sides that bear family "looks."[80] I will thus use the phrase "eidetic part" to refer to those parts of a whole that have an internal principle of unity and thus a characteristic look (an *eidos*), in contrast to mere parts, which do not have such an internal principle of unity and hence do not have a distinctive look.[81] I take it that *eidos* means the same

---

79 The commentary ranges from the exceedingly banal to the highly sophisticated. I find the discussion in Miller Jr. (1980, 20–22), fairly useful; Delcomminette (2000) is excellent; and Scodel (1987, 50–52), also raises many interesting questions, though his interpretation is marred by a belief that the Stranger does not represent a genuine Platonic position. For more mainstream views, one could consult Diès (1935, xviii–xx); de Pinotti (1995); Chiesa (1995), and many others.

80 It has been noted by, e.g., Rowe (1995b, note to 262e7) that *eidos* and *genos* seem to be indistinguishable in the *Statesman*. By *genos*, however, it seems to me that the Stranger usually means the *eidos* in its genetic connection to other *eidē*, i.e., in genealogy or division, whereas by *eidos* he means the form or whole by itself, independently of any connection it might have to other *eidē*.

81 A non-Platonic example may be useful to understand the difference. A book can be said to be composed of *eidetic* parts (like pages, words, letters, paragraphs, etc.) that stand in some relation to each other to constitute the whole, and each of which displays some internal unity and hence a particular "look" as a thing; or *non-eidetic* parts, as, e.g., the parts that result when we chop it to pieces, which merely aggregate together to form the whole without themselves displaying any particular "look."

thing in this dialogue as in other Platonic dialogues, that is, "form," though this point hardly affects anything of importance in my argument and may be bracketed off.

The problematic "interbreeding" of men

Two substantive points about the Stranger's correction of Young Socrates need to be noted, however. The first concerns the ambiguous status of the *genos* or *genē* of human beings in the Stranger's methodological examples. The second concerns the possibility of a correct division using Young Socrates' criterion of *phronēsis*. Let us examine each of these points in turn.

In order to explain to Young Socrates the difference between an eidetic part and a non-eidetic part of something, the Stranger uses two examples that show two different possible divisions of the *genos* of human beings (the human "race"), one of them resulting in eidetic parts and another in non-eidetic parts. In the first example, the Stranger suggests that there are different *genē* of human beings, peoples (cf. 262d1–6), each one potentially in need of a statesman, and each one displaying its own principle of unity (that is, each one an eidetic part of the *genos* of human beings). The Greeks form a *genos* because they marry each other and speak the same languages, the Stranger says; the Barbarians, by contrast, do not form a single *genos* (they are merely the "non-Greeks"), but rather a large number of *genē*, each of which yields, for itself, just as much a true "look" as the Greeks do for themselves. All these *genē* can be identified due to their lack of interbreeding and their inability to communicate with each other; they are, as it were, different animal species. In this view, each particular people would require a statesman whose knowledge is geared to its particular characteristics as a people, though no single people is more important than any other.

In the second example (262e6–263a1), the Stranger suggests by contrast that Lydians and Phrygians (two *genē* of human beings, and two parts of the *genos* of human beings) are not eidetic parts of the *genos* of human beings. The division of this *genos* into Lydians and Phrygians can only be accomplished, according to the Stranger, once *genos* and *meros* can no longer be found together, that is, once further division no longer yields parts with an internal unity; hence neither Lydians nor Phrygians constitute true eidetic parts of the human race, even though there is a look or *eidos* of the human herd, or rather, of the whole human species considered as the aggregate of its members, that is, as a universal herd. The Stranger admits, after all, that Young Socrates hit upon the proper "herd" of the statesman (262b5), that is, the human herd, and they are evidently not looking for Greek or Lydian statesmen, but for the statesman as such. In this view, only the universal human herd—the entire human race (*genos*) exists from the perspective of political science.

Thus we have two examples whose *political* implications seem to be in tension: if we look at the Lydians and Phrygians, the despised "barbarians" from the Greek perspective,[82] we find that there is only a single *genos* of human beings, a universal human family, of which the particular peoples are mere parts (that is, herds), though not eidetic ("look-yielding") parts; but if we look at the Greeks and the Barbarians as a whole, we find that there are innumerable *genē* of human beings, true eidetic parts, which neither mix nor communicate with each other, and which require particular rulers. Both examples imply that "barbarian" is not an eidetic part of the human species (there is no single "look" corresponding to the term "barbarian") but for different reasons: in the first case, there is a universal human family, and thus no specifically Barbarian *genos* (nor, for that matter, a Greek *genos*); in the second, there are only particular peoples, and thus, again, no specifically Barbarian *genos*, but there is a Greek *genos*.

From the first point of view, the appearance of nations and peoples is deceptive; to put the matter somewhat bluntly,

[82] Cf. Campbell (1867, note to 262e), and Rowe (1995b, note to 262e6), for discussion and references.

a political rule according to nature would have no use for them. From the second point of view, on the contrary, Greeks and the various peoples that form the (apparent, but not real) Barbarian *genos* do exist, and a political rule according to nature would have to take them into account, though without raising one above the others merely *qua* nation. The first case points to the universal rule of the god in the age of Cronos as the only form of rule consonant with the nature of things; the second case points to the multiplicity of *poleis* and other political communities, both Greek and non-Greek, of the age of Zeus. Political knowledge needs both perspectives, as the ambiguity of the treatment of the human *genos* shows.

The legitimacy of rationality as a criterion of division

The second substantive point that must be noted about Young Socrates' mistake is that the criterion he used in making the distinction between human beings and beasts could in fact have served to divide *agelaiotrophikē*, the Stranger's methodological protestations notwithstanding. The Stranger could have corrected Young Socrates' division of *agelaiotrophikē* by saying that there is a form of *koinotrophikē* that is concerned with creatures that have *phronēsis*, and another that is concerned with creatures that are not so capable, a division that yields two perfectly acceptable *eidē*, at least if the division of the creatures into interbreeding and non-interbreeding, or horned and lacking horns, or winged and unwinged, which the Stranger accepts as proper divisions later on, does. One can easily imagine the rest: of creatures having *phronēsis*, some are divine, some are mortal; of those that are not divine, some are winged (like, fancifully, the crane: cf. 263d4), some are unwinged; of those unwinged, some have four feet (like, fancifully, the centaur), some have two; and so on, until one reaches human beings. In other words, Young Socrates' methodologically dubious division of animals into non-human and human could have been transformed into a more methodologically respectable division of animals into non-rational and rational, of which human beings would have been only one kind.

There is thus no reason to drop the criterion of *phronēsis* from the division, as the Stranger does in the sequel, unless one has an interest in showing that the possession of *phronēsis* by human beings is of limited relevance to the possibility and necessity of statesmanship for human beings, which is precisely what the Stranger wants to show Young Socrates. In particular, as we shall see, Young Socrates is unable to see what we might call the problem of obedience, namely the need for the statesman precisely on the assumption that beings have not only a capacity for *phronēsis* but also spiritedness, and are hence capable of both rebellion and consent.

Tameness and conflict

The Stranger thus suggests (263e1–264a3) that instead of dividing all animals into rational and non-rational animals, they should start with a division of animals into tame or at least animals willing to be tamed, and animals that are wild or not so willing (cf. *thelonta* 264a3); and, he says (using "hunting" language, perhaps ironically, 264a5) statesmanship concerns only the "tamable" animals. The division of animals into tamable and not tamable (or tame and wild) takes priority, indeed substitutes for, the division of animals into those capable of *phronēsis* and those incapable of it. Yet, as the Stranger's language signals, this division is still problematic; for it is not clear that human beings are fully tame. If by "tame" we mean something like an animal that can be ruled, and who recognizes its need to be ruled, human beings are not fully tame; and neither are they fully tame if by tameness we mean something like a fully cooperative nature, that is, one that does not naturally generate conflict with other beings of the same kind, especially not with its rulers, as we can infer from the Stranger's somewhat outlandish choice of examples of tame animals (certain flocks of geese in Thessaly and certain schools of fish in the Nile or the ponds of the Great King, 264c). Moreover, to have a nature that is merely open to the possibility of being tame is not the same as actually being tame (that is, obeying the statesman's commands or cooperating with one another in non-conflictual ways), as we also saw, indirectly, at a similar point in the *Sophist* (222b2–d2).[83]

The fact that animals are not already tame, but must be tamed, raises the question of whether statesmanship is partly the science of taming human beings, that is, of making them obedient, willing subjects to the king instead of unwilling, difficult ones. We could thus perhaps think of statesmanship as (partially) the knowledge that the statesman uses to make the (potentially) tame herd of human beings into a fully tame herd, that is, as the science of taming human beings, presumably continuously, by means of *logoi* (such as laws, educational speeches, and arguments). This is a plausible idea, echoed by the Athenian Stranger in the *Laws*,[84] and indeed there is a sense in which the task of the statesman turns out to be to reduce the human propensity for conflict, that is, to make human beings tame. But the statesman's "taming" of human beings will not turn out to be much like the taming of pigs or other domestic animals, for it does not operate through purely "eugenic" operations (even though there is something of the sort in the later description of the "human bond," 310d), or render

---

83 There, the Stranger also made a distinction between tame and wild animals, and claimed that the sophist would be a hunter of tame animals, but Theaetetus had a hard time imagining that there could be such a hunting. The Stranger replied that, if human beings are tame, then there is such a hunting. Nevertheless, immediately afterwards he spoke of such human activities as piracy, slave-dealing, tyranny, and all the arts of war, which suggested that, if human beings are tame, they have to be made tame, i.e., their nature is merely open to domestication, but is not necessarily tame in actuality. Cf. also Benardete (1984b, 90): the tame are the "law-abiding," whereas the wild are those whom "man cannot subjugate."

84 Cf. *Laws* 766a1–4, where the Athenian Stranger asserts that "man is the most tame (*hēmerōtaton*) and divine of animals when educated properly [or rather, he loves to become such, *gignesthai philei*; he does not always do so, apparently, even when educated properly], but the most savage (*agriōtaton*) when not."

human beings permanently willing to be ruled, or permanently devoid of propensities for conflict.[85] In a sense, therefore, even if the statesman's art is conceived as an art of "taming" (or, perhaps more accurately, actualizing their "tamable" potential and so rendering them less conflictive) there always remains something wild in human beings, namely, that aspect of man's nature that the Stranger will later identify with the "courageous" disposition (cf. 308e–309e).

At any rate, it is clear that human beings cannot be conceived *merely* as a tame herd which could be ruled indifferently for the benefit of the ruler or for their own benefit. They must be *continuously* tamed, but are not found tame already like sheep; it is only the conception of statesmanship as pure nurture, as "shepherding," that needs to assume a fully tame human herd. To say that the statesman rules over tame beings is thus, strictly speaking, only true of the divine ruler in the age of Cronos in the myth, because human beings are then mere sheep, tame and docile, and yet cannot but be ruled by the god for their own good.[86] Thus in the latter part of the dialogue the tame/wild distinction appears to be silently replaced by the distinction between the parts of virtue (the distinction between the courageous and the moderate, 306a8ff.). The wild clearly can be represented as the sharp/courageous (and wildness, like courage, is a purely "Zeussian" characteristic, present only in the age of Zeus, as we shall see), whereas the tame can be represented as the moderate/gentle, even though the Stranger takes special pains not to call the courageous "wild" or the moderate "tame." The full implications of this congruence between the tame/wild and the courageous/moderate distinction will become clearer later; but it must be emphasized that in his (later) recognition of the dual nature of virtue, the Stranger

---

85 Howland (1998, 250), also makes the point that there is a distinction between those animals that are domesticable by means of *logoi* (i.e., human beings) and those animals that are tamable by force, a distinction that is invisible in the Stranger's use of tame fish or geese as examples of "tamable" animals.

86 Cf. Nightingale (1996, 85).

essentially acknowledges that human beings are both tame and wild, and must be both if they are to survive. To be sure, the tame nature is ultimately more fundamental (for human beings are willing to be tamed, they are not by nature recalcitrant), but "wildness" must never be entirely eradicated, since it is at the root of human courage. Yet the reasons for the ambiguous tameness of the human herd will only become clear with the myth, which attributes the wildness of (some) animals, including human beings, to the conditions of scarcity and the lack of divine government obtaining in the present age.

Statesmanship and animality

The remainder of the division up to 267a simply explores the nature of man on the assumption that statesmanship is a form of *nurture* of a fully tame being. From this point of view, some (but not all) of the characteristics that distinguish human beings from other animals are simply "brute facts," that is, purely physical *differentia* that merely distinguish the statesman as the ruler of humans from any (hypothetical) rulers of cranes or other animals. Thus, for example, the fact that the Stranger distinguishes (264d1–9) between tame herds by dividing such herds into those who make their dwelling primarily in water (like fish) and those who make their dwelling primarily in land (like the cranes and the geese), and indicates that "it is obvious to everyone" (264d10–e2) that statesmanship is concerned with the latter, does not actually illuminate the nature of statesmanship (except, perhaps, insofar as it indicates that statesmen do not use ponds to produce human beings). The fact "is obvious to everyone" because we already know that statesmen care for human beings rather than fish.

Similarly, the division of the land-walking animals between those who use feet as their primary means of locomotion (walkers) and those who use wings (fliers; 264e6–11), and the Stranger's strong warning to Young Socrates that even the person most devoid of *phronēsis* (*ton aphronestaton*) will seek the statesman among those concerned with creatures that go "by foot," do not really illuminate anything about the nature of statesmanship: it is simply a brute fact that statesmanship is concerned with human beings, and human beings do not have wings, but the human lack of wings does not imply much, if anything, about the specific nature of the statesman's care. The Stranger has to practically bully Young Socrates into accepting the placement of the statesman over the land-walking (by telling him, essentially, that he would be very dumb indeed not to see it) in order to obscure this inconvenient fact. But given that the Stranger eliminated the criterion of *phronēsis* as a proper criterion for determining the statesman's object of concern, there was really no reason in the nature of the thing not to suppose that cranes and fish have no statesmen (or states-fish or states-cranes) of their own. In Greek, of course, all of these queer personages would be called *politikoi* or *basilees*.[87]

But these two divisions also point to what is missed in the Stranger's rejection of Young Socrates' implicit division of animals into rational and non-rational (the division that was implicit into Young Socrates' methodologically mistaken distinction between humans and non-humans). We find the idea that statesmen are concerned with animals who make their dwelling on land absurd not because the idea is false, but because it seems to miss the point: it is only when human beings have become indistinguishable from living beings without *phronēsis*, in other words, when they themselves have become *aphronestatoi*, that it is possible to think that statesmanship has anything essential to do with "footed" creatures *qua* footed, and hence with the devices that the breeder of birds or fish uses to "tame" and "nurture" his charges. By contrast, Young Socrates' implicit division of the class of living beings into rational and irrational beings had at least illuminated the nature of statesmanship as a form of theoretical-directive knowledge, since such a form of knowledge presupposes the possession of speech,

[87] Indeed, Aristotle, *History of Animals*, 488a10, classed the crane as a political animal. Cf. Campbell (1867, note to 264c).

and indeed some form of intelligence, in its charges, so that they can actually understand and obey the statesman's commands. In fact, it is arguable that all care of living beings without the capacity for *phronēsis* requires a practical (not theoretical) knowledge. In order to get a horse to gallop or an ox to pull actual physical exertion is necessary; a mere command, much less a reasoned argument, will not suffice, since these beings are (for the most part) impervious to reasoned speech. Hence no theoretical-directive form of knowledge, and certainly not the knowledge of the statesman as described thus far, could ever serve to get them to do anything, unless (as in the myth: 272b10) these creatures had the gift of *logos*.[88]

By contrast, the distinctions the Stranger makes immediately following the divisions of animals into land and water dwelling and of the land-dwelling animals into walkers and fliers do tell us something about statesmanship, though in an obscure and ambiguous way that is not fully clarified unless we put these divisions in the context of the myth that follows them. The ambiguities are evident from the beginning, since human beings are characterized by the Stranger's distinctions in two distinct "ways," a "long" one that contrasts human beings with pigs (humans as two-footed swine) and a "short" one that contrasts them with birds (humans as featherless bipeds). Interestingly, the Stranger suggests that this is a general feature of the method of division, since, as he indicates, it was actually possible to characterize the statesman in yet another way, an even shorter way starting at the very "beginning or in the middle" of the division (265b2–6), even though (for pedagogical reasons, as we shall see) they could not have taken that shorter way earlier. In other words, the characterization of statesmanship to which the Stranger arrives appears

[88] Dogs, perhaps, serve as intermediaries between the command of the shepherd and the rounding up of the sheep; but dogs are not ruled entirely by means of *logoi*, as any dog-owner knows.

to be both ambiguous and potentially dependent on contingent pedagogical imperatives, unless we assume that all the alternative ways of reaching the statesman (long and short) are somehow equivalent or at least not incompatible, as the Stranger seems to be suggesting.

In particular, we should note that if the beginning of the search for the statesman was the division of knowledge into theoretical and practical sciences (258b2) and the middle of it (if one assumes that the end is yet to come, at 266e11) was approximately the point at which Young Socrates separated off human beings from the beasts (262a4), then the Stranger is suggesting that there exists an adequate characterization of statesmanship that begins from some modified version of Young Socrates' distinction and is (in some sense) equivalent to (or at least not incompatible with) the characterizations of statesmanship that they actually come up with. As we have seen, a minimal correction by the Stranger at that point (recasting the human being/beast distinction as the "capable of *phronēsis*"/"incapable of *phronēsis*" distinction) could have salvaged Young Socrates' attempted division, and led to a "shorter" division. The Stranger himself indicated at that point that Young Socrates' division was "shorter" and "most beautiful" but that it was not yet "safe" to proceed in that way (262b2–8); Young Socrates had in fact hit upon a true bifurcation of the division into long and short ways, though he was not quite prepared to follow that way, for reasons we have already explored. And, as we shall see, the Stranger's divisions do not deny that human beings are "rational" animals but only deny that such rationality is *per se* important for the determination of the statesman's knowledge.

If such a "shorter" way was already possible earlier, however, then they seem to have already taken the long way: had the choice presented itself at that stage, the short way would have led to human beings as beings capable of *phronēsis*, while the long way would lead, as it in fact does here in both its short and long versions, to human beings as indistinguishable from the beasts (related to swine and to birds). The puzzle, then, is whether the comical divisions that the Stranger now presents (and which he never repudiates, despite correcting other aspects of the division) can be somehow woven together, so to speak, with the never quite rejected idea that human beings have *phronēsis*. Human beings, from the point of view of statesmanship, must be shown to be not only two legged pigs *and* featherless birds, but *also* beings capable of *phronēsis*, or, conversely, statesmanship must somehow take into account all of these aspects of humanity. The short way foreshadowed in Young Socrates' methodological mistake must be woven together with the long way they actually took, and which is now subdivided into a *long* long way and a *short* long way.

The long way

The long way (265b8–d5) has three steps. The first divides the land-dwelling, walking animals into animals bearing horns and animals lacking horns. Human beings are defined here by what they lack, in this case a ready means of defense. The statesman, the Stranger and Young Socrates quickly agree, is to be assigned to the herd without horns. To some degree, this assignment is rather arbitrary, like the previous two steps; horns, or the lack thereof, cannot indicate whether a living being is receptive to the particular kind of theoretical-commanding knowledge of the statesman or not. But the mention of horns does suggest something like the "protective" function of the statesman,[89] a function that is at any rate more clearly indicated, as we have already seen, by the weaving paradigm. Yet the evidence on this point is much too slight to draw any substantive conclusions.

The second step in the division, however, is much more confusing and potentially more interesting (265d5–e5). The Stranger seems to be uncertain about what cut to attempt next, and asks Young Socrates whether he wishes to divide the herd by the "split

89 See Zuckert (2005, 10).

hoof"/"single hoof" distinction or by the *koinogonia* (interbreeding)/ *idiogonia* (non-interbreeding) distinction. Yet he does not let him answer, explaining that horses and asses (both single-hoofed animals), when mating with each other, generate offspring (meaning sterile mules). This suggests that the split hoof/single hoof distinction and the non-interbreeding/interbreeding distinctions are congruent with each other, that is, they both split the herd in the same way: all remaining interbreeding animals are single-hoofed and vice versa, and similarly all remaining non-interbreeding animals are split-hoofed and vice versa.

But do both distinctions yield the same "look" of human being? After all, having single hooves seems to have nothing to do with being able to interbreed: these are "contingently" connected facts, as we might say. Moreover, the first distinction suggests that human beings have hooves, which is quite odd.[90] To be sure, one can interpret *schistos* as referring merely to the fact that human beings, like many other animals, have toes, which would justify the epithet "split-hoofed." But this is a strange way of referring to this fact, in Greek as much as in English.[91] At any rate, the use of this word seems to point to a fairly animalistic conception of human beings.

Having split hooves or not, moreover, does not seem to have any bearing on why the statesman would care for human beings. Both split hooves and single-hooves seem perfectly adequate for the purposes of locomotion, and the single-hoofed animal does not seem to have any advantages or disadvantages with respect to the split-hoofed animal.[92] The statesman's care,

---

[90] The Stranger uses a compound with the word *onux* to signify hooves. *Onux* normally means "claw" and is nowhere else, as far as I can tell, used of human feet or hands; cf. LSJ, *s.v. onux*.

[91] LSJ does not give any instance of *schistos* as referring to human toes, though the word can mean simply "split," said of things as diverse as roads or wings.

[92] *Pace* Zuckert (2005, 10), I do not think that having split hooves shows any kind of human vulnerability. Horses may be faster runners than human beings, but that is not because they have single hooves; deer are fast runners as well, but have split hooves.

it would seem, should not differ at all depending on whether the being he cares for has whole or split hooves, and indeed this seems to be tacitly recognized by the Stranger insofar as the split-hoofed/single-hoofed distinction is silently dropped in favor of the non-interbreeding/interbreeding distinction.

This latter distinction—and the terminology the Stranger uses—recalls the earlier distinction (261d4–e4) between *koinotrophia* (nurture in common) and *idiotrophia* (nurture in private). As we may remember, the art of the statesman was a form of *koinotrophia* at the time (though interpreted as *agelaiotrophia*). *Koinogonia*, however, does not mean here the art of generation in common (e.g., from two people), but the art of generation from two different *genē* or species (e.g., the art of creating hybrid offspring from horses and donkeys). This introduces an ambiguity in the position of human beings, an ambiguity that Young Socrates does not notice. As we saw earlier, it is somewhat unclear in what sense human beings constitute a single *genos*, since each people considers itself to be a sub-*genos* of the *genos* of human beings.

Are human beings, then, *idiogenos*? At the technical level at which Young Socrates, abetted by the Stranger, answers the question, human beings are *idiogenos* since they constitute a single species *vis-à-vis* all other species of animals, with whom they cannot mate. Young Socrates, with his answer, is prefiguring again the rule of the god over the whole *genos* of human beings. At a political level, however, it is not clear that human beings are *idiogenos*. Human beings can mate across *genē*, that is, peoples, and across families (*genē*), which would make them susceptible to *koinogonia*. Such an internal differentiation of *genē* (families, peoples) within a single *genos* (species) of human beings would seem to indicate that while divine statesmen might need the art of *idiogenesis*, human statesmen, who rule not over the entire *genos* of human beings but over one of its sub-*genē*, need the art of *koinogenesis*. This will eventually be confirmed by the introduction of the notion of the statesman as a weaver of the two *genē* of virtue (cf. *genē* 310d3, 310e7, referring to the two kinds of virtue as embodied in two sorts of people) and in particular a weaver of these natures by the judicious use of marriage both within and among *poleis*.

At any rate, the point is that the question of whether or not human beings are *idiogenos* or *koinogenos*, unlike the question of whether or not human beings are split-hoofed or single-hoofed animals, actually matters in determining the kind of knowledge required of the statesman.[93] The two divisions are not equivalent in their power to reveal the statesman and his charges, even if they are empirically (and mathematically) equivalent. They yield two different "looks" of human beings, two different sets of eidetic parts of the *genos* of tame herd animals lacking horns. Mentioning them together points out the limitations of the method of division, since the resulting sets of *genē* are mathematically equivalent, but unequally revealing of the statesman. Only the myth will be able to show how the two distinctions are thus not really congruent from the point of view of the statesman; one applies to the age of Cronos (where no species interbreeds with one another, rendering the second distinction irrelevant), another to the age of Zeus (where human beings constantly "interbreed" in politically significant ways with one another, a tendency that has to be managed by the statesman).

The Stranger's final step in the long way (266a5–b9) takes the form of a laborious joke, ably explained by various commentators.[94] The punch line of the joke is that the nature of human beings (cf. *phusis* 266b2), being like the square root of two (an "irrational" number), is incommensurable with the nature of pigs, which is like the square root of four (a "rational" number). It is only the mathematical procedure of "squaring" these natures—by looking not at the natures of human beings and pigs by themselves, as it were, but at the number of their feet—that makes human beings and pigs commensurable: one kind of animal has two feet, the other four, or twice the number of feet as the first.

---

93 See also Scodel (1987, 65).

94 See, e.g., Campbell (1867, note *ad loc*), and Skemp (1987, note *ad loc*).

Mathematics, in this instance, thus produces a kind of optical illusion: human beings and pigs are made commensurable, and the statesman is given the same rank as the swineherd (266c10–d2), even though human beings and pigs are not, in their nature, commensurable, since human beings are rational beings and pigs are not.[95] The Stranger thus draws the moral of the story (266d7–10): by this method (the quasi-mathematical method of the long way) they have no care for whether some of the *logoi* are "more sacred" than others (*semnoterou* 266d7–8), in an echo of the cranes who made themselves holy by overestimating the significance of their capability for *phronēsis* (263d7). Young Socrates, and human beings more generally, have now been completely humbled: it is not their rationality that would make them an object of the statesman's care if such care is a form of nurture, but merely their animality.

Yet not everything is illusory here. That human beings are kin to pigs is an idea that Glaucon introduced in the *Republic* when he protested that Socrates' "healthy" city was a "city of pigs" (*Republic* 372dff.), a city that, arising out of the spontaneous organization of crafts into a division of labor adequate to the satisfaction of human need, did not require a human statesman. And the *genos* of the pig is said to be "most noble" (*gennaiotatōi*) and most full of ease (*Statesman* 266c4–6), which points to the tension in the human situation evident in the age of Cronos. For human beings to be like the pig they must be placed in a situation which is in some sense nobler—and fuller of ease—than their current situation, as we shall see. But Young Socrates is here invited to laugh at himself. This is a joke, after all; and laughter deflates pride. Yet Young Socrates

95 Some commentators have noted that two-footedness is elsewhere associated with *phronēsis*, something the Stranger does not emphasize. See Dorter (1994, 189), citing *Cratylus* 399c and Aristotle, *Parts of Animals* IV.x.686a27–32. In other words, it is not two-footedness itself that is important, but the nature whose power of locomotion is two-footedness, and thus the divinity of human nature.

does not get the joke. A childish story will be needed to get him to see the point.

The short way

The Stranger gives the short way short shrift by proceeding without Young Socrates' participation (266d12–e11). It is thus physically much shorter than the long way, and it also comprises only two steps, which would make it shorter than the long way in terms of its "elements," since the long way comprises three steps. The division is simple: the class of land-dwelling animals that walk is divided into those animals that use four of their feet to walk and those that use two; these are in turn divided into animals that grow feathers (like chicken, who have wings but do not fly) and those that do not.[96]

The word *pterophuēs*, growing feathers, is very uncommon. Plato uses the word in only two other places in the *corpus*, *Phaedrus* 251c4 (in verbal form) and 255d2 (again in verbal form). In that mythical context, to grow feathers (and thus wings) is to become fully human, to move towards the divine. That the Stranger places human beings among those who are unable to grow feathers thus seems to point to the fact that statesmanship assumes imperfect human beings, that is, human beings that have not grown "feathers" in the language of the *Phaedrus*, and hence have not seen the forms of order. The proper task of the philosopher may be to help human beings grow those feathers; but it is not clear that this is the proper task of the statesman, who may need to take them "as they are." All this, of course, is speculation: but the appearance of this rare word here suggests that Plato was trying to allude to weightier matters than the

[96] Note that the Stranger is not separating winged animals twice, *pace* Campbell (1867, note *ad loc.*), Miller Jr. (1980, 28 and 127n25), Dorter (1994, 181–187), Scodel (1987, 67–68), and Skemp (1987), in the note to his translation of this passage. 264e3–11 separates animals that use their wings for locomotion from those that do not (cf. *xērobatikon* 264d2); 266e6–7 separates animals that use their feet as means of locomotion into those that have feathers and those that do not.

fact that human beings do not grow feathers, which by itself has nothing to do with the knowledge of the statesman.[97]

Shepherds and specialists

At any rate, the Stranger summarizes the results of the division thus far by saying that the statesman turns out to be a kind of shepherd insofar as his task is the "nurture" of human beings. Whether we understand the statesman as a swineherd of two-footed pigs or the breeder of featherless pigeons matters very little in the end, as both characterizations of human beings are essentially identical in identifying the tameness and animality of human beings as their most important characteristics from the point of view of statesmanship.[98] But already the problems with this characterization of statesmanship are evident; for other arts claim to nurture human beings, and thus "dispute" with the statesman (267e4–5). Yet the sheep do not dispute with the shepherd about their own care, since the shepherd combines all the forms of expertise necessary to care for them in his person, whereas the sheep do not have any arts. In relation to the sheep, the shepherd's wisdom is like a god's in relation to man's.

Thus other herders, unlike the statesman, have no rivals who dispute their ability to care for their herds; individual sheep do not have pride in their technical (but partial) knowledge. In particular, the paradigmatic shepherd has all the forms of expertise that, in the case of human beings, are the province of a variety of specialists. A "shepherd" is thus merely the name for the agglomeration of all arts of nurture, unified into a single *epistēmē* (268a6–b7); the shepherd is no "specialist." If the statesman is really like all other shepherds, in other words,

---

97 For an alternative interpretation of this allusion, see Scodel (1987, 67). See also White (2007, 33), and Benardete (1992, 38).

98 Thus in his summary of the division the Stranger ignores the "short way" and simply reports that the statesman is the shepherd of the two-footed, non-interbreeding, hornless, terrestrial animal called man (267c1).

he is much like the—impossible—ideal of the wise man that the sophist imitates (*Sophist* 232e6–233a7).[99]

The reason why other herders do not have rivals, however, is that cows and sheep do not have *phronēsis*, and hence lack all arts. Cows and sheep cannot present themselves as potential rivals to cowherds or shepherds, since all knowledge is on the side of the cowherd/shepherd, while they are (of course) wholly ignorant of the arts. In the political community, on the other hand, knowledge is not only divided among a variety of arts, but is also embodied in a variety of human beings, and not only contingently, as it would be if it were possible for a single person to have all the *technai* (the—impossible—supposition of the sophist), but necessarily.

One could perhaps object at this point that the arts of the cowherd/shepherd can in fact be distributed among different human beings, such as the cow-feeder, the veterinarian (or even the more specialized cow-veterinarian or sheep-veterinarian), the breeding specialist, and the ox-driver. In other words, one might argue that the cowherd/shepherd escapes the fate of the statesman only because the division of labor in late 5th century Greece was insufficiently advanced to allow different human beings to be consistently employed as merely veterinarians, or cow-feeding specialists, or ox-drivers and the like. One could perhaps go further and argue that it is this fact that makes the cowherd/shepherd image unsuitable as a paradigm of the statesman, since by the late 5th century society had become complex enough that the knowledge necessary for managing it could not possibly be embodied in a single person.[100]

There is some truth in this claim, since the complexity of society does prevent the concentration of knowledge, or more precisely its embodiment, in a single person, and the division

99 While the statesman-shepherd is not said to know astronomy and theology (cf. *Sophist* 232c1–2, 232c4–5), he is said to know pretty much everything else: medicine, gymnastics, farming, even music.

100 See Coulobaritsis (1995).

of labor (something which is absent from the Stranger's image of the cowherd/shepherd) is in fact a good indicator of this complexity. But what this interpretation misses is that the skills of the shepherd/cowherd cannot be divided among the sheep or cows, who are *ex hypothesi* unable to do any of the things the cowherd/shepherd does for them. The myth will show that, contrary to the situation holding in the case of the shepherd, the skills of the shepherd of human beings are in fact divided in the age of Zeus among the erstwhile "cattle," that is, human beings, and that it would be only if the difference in knowledge between human beings and their rulers were as large as that between cattle and their herders that the ruler of human beings could be called a "shepherd." In other words, it is only in the age of Cronos that the shepherd of human beings "fits" the paradigm of the shepherd.

Moreover, the fact that the knowledge of the cowherd/shepherd is abstractly "divisible" does not imply that it is therefore merely the side-by-side possession of distinct *technai* that can be simply separated and given to different people, as if tending to a herd were simply the random application of the different *technai* of the shepherd. The *technai* of the shepherd, on the contrary, must somehow be integrated in the task of caring for the sheep, and it is this integrative knowledge (at which the Stranger hints through his choice of examples, which include music and the telling of stories) that must remain for the statesman after he has been "purified" of his associations with the shepherd of human beings and thus with tyranny.[101] The shepherd of human beings remains the model of the statesman, in other words, only insofar as his knowledge allows him to integrate all other necessary *technai* in the task of caring for his herd, but no further.[102]

---

[101] Associations explored by Miller Jr. (1980, 35–48).

[102] It is only to this extent, but no further, that the statesman can be said to be a herder even after the paradigm of the herder has been rejected, as Miller Jr. (1980, 41–52), and Rowe (1995a, 14), argue. By contrast, Delcomminette's (2000) claims for the "herding" interpretation of statesmanship even after

The Stranger even hints at the shape such integrative care takes by further developing the image of the shepherd. Shepherds, according to the statesman, use music and play (as much as the nature of the shepherd's charges, *thremmata*, will take) to enchant and make them tame (*praunein* 268b4). This is the only suggestion in the dialogue that the statesman's task is to tame the human herd, a possibility we had already pointed to when we discussed the tame/wild distinction. But the cowherd/shepherd does not only "tame" the herd; he also "encourages" or "exhorts" it (*paramutheisthai*, 268b4). If we may foreshadow the Stranger's later political theory (306a1ff.), "encouragement," if properly done, induces courage; "taming" or "domestication" does more or less the opposite (though whether it induces moderation is something we cannot explore at this point). Since these activities are in tension with one another, to say that the cowherd/shepherd both encourages and tames his herd seems to indicate that he measures the amount of courage and the amount of moderation required for the herd to function properly, that is, he "weaves" courage and moderation in due measure in the herd, just like the statesman will weave the courage and moderation of his charges (*thremma* 289b2) by means, partly, of play (cf. 308d4, 309a8ff.). The paradigmatic shepherd thus points to the necessarily integrative character of the statesman's knowledge and to his weaving of courage and moderation.

Furthermore, the shepherd is said to be a practitioner of *maieutikē* ("midwifery") and a *numpheutēs* ("arranger of marriages"), two words with strong Socratic overtones.[103] Someone with the true art of matchmaking, that is, someone who prac-

---

the myth go too far: real herders monopolize the knowledge of care in a way that the true statesman does not, and the Stranger's (diminished) use of the terminology of "herds" even after the myth does not show that the Stranger simply continues to believe that the statesman is a shepherd of man, since such use is simply reserved for contexts that show that the statesman's knowledge must be applied to all individuals equally, as I noted earlier.

[103] Cf. Benardete (1984b, 95).

ticed it justly, and who was placed in a supervisory position, like a cowherd/shepherd, would be able to arrange marriages, just like the statesman is said to do at the end of the dialogue (310a7ff.). The paradigmatic shepherd thus partially foreshadows the Stranger's later description of the statesman's task as one having to do with marriages for the sake of properly mixing the souls of human beings (310a7ff.), though he does not appear to be also a midwife of souls, unlike the elder Socrates.

Two changes in the original division that the Stranger makes right after the myth are intended to pave the way for this characterization of statesmanship as an integrative form of care, but they do not immediately accomplish this goal. The first change consists in the substitution of the more generic term "care" (*epimeleia*, which they had already used informally without much precision, as we saw above) for the specific but misleading term "nurture" (275d4–276b6) in the account of statesmanship. Nurture is a form of care, but care is not exhausted in nurture. Once this substitution is made, the original *diaeresis* encompasses the god, the divine shepherd and the statesman, insofar as all of them can care for the human herd (276a6–7); the term care "cloaks" (*perikaluptein* 275e8) the statesman and all other shepherds. The second change (really an addition to the original division) consists in the separation of the care of human beings by the god from the care of human beings by human beings (276c4–d7).

Both changes enable the Stranger to articulate more clearly that the knowledge of the statesman is a form of knowledge that directs and depends on other forms of knowledge, though it hardly ensures this result. Indeed, as the Stranger notes later (279a1–4), the locus of controversy now shifts from nurture (and the arts that also claimed to nurture human beings) to care (where other arts also claim to care for human beings). But whereas the model of undifferentiated nurture set up the god as the statesman's rival (as we shall see in more detail in the next chapter), the model of care by other human beings merely presents the statesman with other human rivals, none of whom can claim to monopolize the care of man (unlike the god, who *can* monopolize the nurture of man in the age of Cronos). The theoretical problem then consists in articulating exactly how the statesman has the "biggest part" of the care of human beings among those contributing to such care (cf. 281c7–d3, 289c4–8), or rather, to use the terminology of the latter part of the *Statesman,* in providing its "measure" (see chapter 4 for more on this idea), not in the (hopeless) task of specifying how the statesman can monopolize the nurture of human beings (something only a god could do). Moreover, as we shall see later, the substitution of care for nurture also gives the Stranger an opportunity to move beyond the idea that the statesman is primarily concerned with the physical "feeding" of human beings. The care of human beings that political knowledge enables, though helping to preserve them physically, moves beyond such physical preservation by helping to educate human beings as far as possible into virtue.

It should be stressed that these changes and additions to the original division do not substantially alter its apparently most puzzling result. Indeed, the Stranger explicitly notes that after substituting "care" for "nurture," the division should proceed as before, ending with the definition of human beings as two-legged pigs. The myth's deepening of our understanding of the role of human rationality in politics (a topic we shall explore in the next chapter) does not substantially affect the main idea of the division: that human beings can be ruled politically not because they are rational, but because they can be tamed. What distinguishes the statesman from the shepherd is not the fact that his charges possess *phronēsis* (though this turns out to matter as well, as we shall see) but that he is a being of the same kind as his charges.

But if these changes to the division do not alter the identification of human beings with two-legged pigs, this does not imply, *pace* Delcomminette (2000), that the Stranger thinks that the statesman is a "herder" of men. The Stranger had already pointed out, even before the myth, that the shepherd was a poor paradigm (cf. 277b4) or image of statesmanship, since the shepherd is defined by his monopoly *vis-à-vis* his charges of the arts of nurture, unlike the statesman (267c–268d). And the corrections and additions to the initial division do not simply "tweak" a basically correct characterization of the statesman as shepherd; rather, the changes and additions help Young Socrates see that the initial identification of the statesman with a shepherd produced an incomplete account of statesmanship (277a5). It is only if we fail to see that the account of statesmanship they have produced is incomplete that we can think that the formal structure of statesmanship is identical to the formal structure of herding. Conversely, it is only once the Stranger has made it clear that the account of statesmanship they have produced thus far is incomplete (even with the various corrections that the Stranger makes to it) that he can start looking for a new paradigm of statesmanship, eventually finding one in weaving. Weaving, unlike herding, provides an adequate image of the complex relationship between statesmanship and the other arts that contribute to the care of human beings while building on the initial (and partial) characterization of statesmanship as the theoretical-directive-autonomous care of tame featherless bipeds. Thus, despite the Stranger's very occasional use of the terminology of herds in the latter part of the dialogue (see above), the Stranger's remarks at 277a–c mark a final rejection of the paradigm of herding for understanding the formal structure of statesmanship.

Willingness vs. unwillingness

A deeper understanding of the inadequacy of the "herding" paradigm for understanding statesmanship will only be possible once we have examined the myth in the next chapter. Before we turn to the myth, however, it is worth noting that the Stranger draws attention to the importance of "tameness" for statesmanship with his last addition to the original division, namely, the separation of statesmanship from tyranny on the grounds that the rule of the tyrant is not voluntarily accepted, but the rule of the statesman is (276d–e).

The potential for confusion between statesman and tyrant is not altogether puzzling: as we saw, the Stranger did identify the statesman with the slave-master (cf. 259b7ff.), and eventually with a shepherd, that is, someone whose power over his charges is absolute, even if he is the same kind of being as they. Yet the Stranger will later claim that the only relevant distinction between the statesman and the tyrant concerns the possession of knowledge, not the willingness or unwillingness of the subjects (291e1–292d1, 300a4–7), implicitly suggesting that the statesman can use violence just as much as a tyrant can, though he never explicitly takes back the original distinction between rule over willing subjects and coercive rule.[104] At any rate, there is a puzzle in the apparent contradiction between the emphasis on consent in the earlier distinction between statesman and tyrant and the apparent radical rejection of consent in the later distinction between statesman and tyrant.[105]

The solution to the puzzle lies in the different roles that these distinctions play in their respective context. In the later passage what is at stake is the *justification* of the statesman's rule. What justifies such rule is not consent but knowledge; after all, people might consent to the rule of somebody without

---

[104] As Rowe (1995b, note to 276e1–2), perceptively notes, the Stranger distinguishes tyrant from king by a different criterion from the one he claims distinguishes them here, but he *does* distinguish them. What seems to be abandoned, in other words, is the "willing/unwilling subjects" criterion, not the distinction between statesman and tyrant.

[105] See Annas and Waterfield (1995, xvi), who consider, without fully endorsing, a solution to this puzzle that is similar to the one I argue for here. See also Skemp (1987, 16–17), who argues, with only slight plausibility, that this "contradiction" shows that the dialogue could hardly have been finished before 360 BCE, the date of Plato's second trip to Syracuse; yet Skemp's argument seems to imply, curiously, that the second part of the dialogue was written before the first.

knowledge (a sophist), which would not thereby make it right for such a person to rule, and occasionally the statesman would need to do things which the people in their ignorance might not accept, which would not thereby make them wrong. But the statesman's knowledge is such that the subjects should ideally consent to his knowledge, and if they do not, it is unclear how the statesman could ever rule. To put the point in a different way, the first distinction between statesman and tyrant grounds their difference in what David Estlund has called "normative consent," that is, an obligation to consent to authority,[106] while pointing to the empirical need for actual consent in most imaginable circumstances in which a statesman could rule. And the need for consent is itself a result of the impossibility of statesmanship over "wild" human beings; statesmanship needs a certain amount of tameness, or at least the potential for becoming tame that could eventually ensure the consent of the subjects to the rule of the genuine statesman.

We can see the importance of consent for the statesman's position in the city by considering the way in which the Stranger introduces the problematic distinction between the rule over willing and the rule over unwilling subjects. The Stranger says (276e1–3) that by not paying attention to the criterion of force and willingness they erred "more naively" (*euēthestera*) than necessary (*tou deontos*, terminology that anticipates the section on measure) in putting together into the same class the king and the tyrant. This is an odd way to describe their mistake, for it suggests that there is a properly naive way of erring in the separation of king and tyrant, a proper measure of *euētheia* concerning their difference.[107] The properly naive way of separating king and tyrant, it would seem, focuses on the difference between willingness and unwillingness; but it is precisely this distinction as a

[106] See Estlund (2008, ch. 7).

[107] Cf. Weiss (1995, 220). Note the presence of terms associated with due measure in this passage, terms that will become important soon enough.

criterion for the separation of king and tyrant that will be rejected by the Stranger in favor of the distinction between the true knowledge of the statesman and the ignorance of the tyrant (cf. 300a4–7). The Stranger thus appears to imply later, through his silence on the difference between these two distinctions, that the properly naive distinction between the willingness and unwillingness of the subjects to be ruled is in essence equivalent to the distinction between the knowledgeable rule of the statesman and the ignorant rule of the tyrant, much as the distinction between split-hoofed and the single-hoofed animals was equivalent to the distinction between the interbreeding and the non-interbreeding animals (265d5–e5; see discussion above).

The implication is not entirely implausible: after all, the rule of the ignorant tyrant is rather likely to employ violence and to be resented. Tyranny just *is* violent rule over unwilling subjects. But the converse proposition—that true statesmanship is rule over willing subjects—does not appear to be true, as the Stranger's own arguments later suggest (297e11–298b7): the knowledgeable ruler is *also* rather likely to be resented, especially if he proposes measures that might cause pain to other citizens. Yet the point of these later arguments is that the citizens are *wrong* to resent the statesman, even when the statesman, like the true doctor, proposes measures that will cause short-term pain. Hence the naive distinction between rule over willing and rule over unwilling subjects captures the normative force of the distinction between knowledgeable and ignorant rule: the citizens should not resent the rule of a knowledgeable statesman; they should be tame in his presence, even if in actual fact they are not always tame. To put the point in modern terminology, what the Stranger is suggesting in the latter passage is that the justification for the statesman's rule is not to be found in the consent of his subjects (whether or not they consent is immaterial to whether or not he should rule over them), but nevertheless a properly open-minded citizenry would in fact consent to the true statesman's rule.

At the same time, the Stranger suggests that they have not even been *properly naive*; they have been too willing to credit the claims of would-be shepherds of human beings without even reflecting on the difference between king and tyrant in the most everyday of terms.[108] The extreme naiveté of Young Socrates—a naiveté greater than that of his untutored fellow-citizens, apparently—is responsible for this mistake; and this extreme naiveté, like that of the philosopher of the digression of the *Theaetetus*,[109] is ultimately caused by a misunderstanding of the dependence of statesmanship on the tameness, or at least the tamability, of human beings and a too great confidence in the power of human *phronēsis* to deal with their potential "wildness." Young Socrates is not suspicious enough of claims to knowledge of the total care of human beings, as he was not suspicious enough of the Stranger's studied ambiguity and strange distinctions. He is too willing to believe in stories about benevolent shepherds of men, despite, or perhaps because, of his fundamentally theoretical bent, and he is thus susceptible to acquiescing to tyranny under the guise of knowledgeable rule. In modern statistical terminology, he is very likely to make type-II errors. By contrast, a cynic—a person with too little *euētheia*—would be too *unwilling* to credit claims to knowledge, and hence would too quickly *reject* the true statesman on the grounds that he must be a tyrant.[110] In modern terminology, the cynic is very likely to make type-I errors.

---

[108] See Miller Jr. (1980, 54–55).

[109] As Hemmenway (1994, 255) notes, in the *Theaetetus* the elder Socrates portrays a philosopher who thinks of statesmanship as a simple form of herding, distinguished from shepherding only by the fact that human beings are more "troublesome" (i.e., less obedient, or less tame and less willing) than sheep and other herd-animals.

[110] See Lane (1998, 154–163, who argues in a similar vein that the "squeamishness" (*duschereia*) of the citizens prevents them from recognizing the statesman.

It is only when a people has the right degree of *euētheia*, good habits,[111] that the statesman would have any chance of being accepted while diminishing the risk that an impostor—an ignorant tyrant—would seize power; good habits means an openness to the rule of the true statesman that is equivalent to genuine "tameness." The naive separation of king from tyrant by the criterion of willingness and unwillingness, though not altogether correct (since there is no guarantee that a knowledgeable ruler will be willingly obeyed, and at any rate his "right" to rule does not depend on the consent of the people), is thus *properly* suspicious of claims to knowledge of the care of the human community and yet open-minded enough to be willing to receive such rule. There is a due measure of "good habits" that makes the city fertile soil for the activity of the statesman, but that Young Socrates has not yet displayed.

It should be noted, finally, that the naive distinction between the rule over willing and the rule over unwilling subjects, like the distinction between rule with and without law, never entirely ceases to be operative in the dialogue. In particular, it retains its importance in distinguishing among what the Stranger calls the "imitative" regimes, and in particular in deciding the worth of a common life in each of these, even though it is of no use in distinguishing the best regime from the imitations, as the Stranger says more or less explicitly later on (cf. 302e4–8). Young Socrates' extreme naiveté concerning tyrant and king thus prevents him from even choosing well in which sort of regime he would best live, and perhaps renders him vulnerable to participation in nefarious plots to overthrow well-established governments, as Plato confesses

[111] Cf. *Laws* 679b7–e3, where the *euētheia*, the naiveté, of the primitive inhabitants of the world is explicitly connected to their being more courageous, moderate, and just, though also more likely to believe "any sort of story about gods as well as human beings."

himself to have felt vulnerable as a young man (*Seventh Letter* 324b8–325a5).[112]

It should be clear from the foregoing discussion that we do not need to accept the "external" hypothesis of formal incoherence (due to a failure to revise the dialogue sufficiently, for example) to explain the discrepancy between the view of statesmanship as a form of rule that is willingly accepted found at 276d–e, and the view of statesmanship as a form of rule that is not grounded on the willingness of the subjects to accept it that we find later in the dialogue. But neither do we need to postulate a difference between an "ideal" statesman whose rule is willingly accepted and a non-ideal statesman whose rule is not, *pace* Delcomminette (2000). The separation between statesman and tyrant on the basis of consent is simply a *naive* (and hence in a sense erroneous) way of understanding the *real* distinction between statesman and tyrant, which is grounded on the possession of knowledge. Yet the naive distinction between statesman and tyrant does point to an important truth: citizens *should* consent to the rule of knowledge, even if sometimes they are not tame enough—they lack good habits, *euētheia*—to do so, or even if sometimes they are so naive (so tame) that they succumb to the first pretender to knowledge that comes their way. The precise degree of human "tameness" (rather than "rationality") that the statesman requires, and which he can help produce, thus appears again as the central problem of statesmanship both "practically" (as the problem of securing obedience to knowledgeable rule, and *only* to such rule) and "theoretically" (as the problem of determining what features of human being make statesmanship both possible

[112] Cf. also Taylor (1961, 232). Taylor notes that Plato there says that it would be "impious" to use force to impose the statesman's will, not that it would be unjust, in accordance with the argument of 296b1ff. But impiety is precisely Young Socrates' deeper fault in refusing to recognize the authority of anything higher than human *phronēsis*, which the Stranger must point out by emphasizing the faultiness of human *phronēsis* and the perfection of divine rule.

and necessary). As we shall see in the next chapter, however, human "tameness" (or its lack) interacts in a complicated way with human "rationality." A fuller examination of the myth is necessary before we can understand exactly what features of human being make statesmanship possible and necessary; and to this task we now turn.

3. Cosmos

THE ATTEMPT TO DESCRIBE statesmanship as a form of nurture led to all sorts of strange consequences: statesmanship appeared as a form of sheep- or swine-herding, and human beings appeared to be either two-legged pigs or featherless chickens. Moreover, the description of the statesman as a sort of shepherd failed to account for the fact that shepherds monopolize the arts of nurture *vis-à-vis* the sheep, whereas statesmen do not.

The Stranger, however, instead of straightforwardly correcting the division (as he eventually does), turns to a rich and puzzling myth that places statesmanship in a "cosmological" context. As we shall see below, this myth imaginatively depicts *both* the condition of the world that would make the conception of statesmanship to which they arrived in the division strictly true (the age of Cronos, which is the literal opposite of ours), *and* the actual condition of the world that constrains any alternative conception of statesmanship (the age of Zeus). In particular, the myth describes the features of the human condition today that make (human rather than divine) statesmanship *necessary*, and at the same time determine its limits. These include material scarcity and the fragmentation of human reason into a multitude of disparate arts, none of which can care for human beings all by itself and yet all of which are needed for human survival. From this point of view, the myth shows how the human possession of reason (*phronēsis*), which had been de-emphasized in the initial division, is in fact relevant for the knowledge of the statesman, both as a source of disorder (insofar as human reason is today divided among many uncoordinated arts) and of order (insofar as human reason is needed for humans to survive in the age of Zeus). The myth thus suggests that even though human beings may not be understood as fundamentally rational animals from the point of view of statesmanship, their rationality both constrains and enables their political care by human statesmanship insofar as it interacts with their "tameness."

At the same time, the Stranger places both conceptions of statesmanship (divine and human) in a *single* cosmological context that clarifies their relationship to one another and to human or divine reason as forms of *care* (*epimeleia*). This cosmological context clarifies the general meaning of "care" and describes the different forms that it can take: of the god for the cosmos, of the gods for human beings, of the universe for itself, of other living beings for themselves, and of human beings for themselves. It identifies both the unity of these forms of care (as ways in which living beings preserve eidetic order in a bodily medium which has a tendency to disorder) and their specific *differentia* (which arise from the prevailing forms of generation and change). But in articulating this general conception of care, the myth also suggests the ways in which the statesman in caring for the *polis* in a sense imitates the care of the god for the whole cosmos. Thus, though the myth is presented as a playful or childish story suitable for Young Socrates' level of experience (268d8, 268e4–6), its importance for understanding the Stranger's conception of statesmanship is decisive. By indicating which aspects of the god's care of the cosmos can be paradigmatic for human statesmanship, the myth shows what makes statesmanship *possible*.

I suggest in this chapter that there are four important parallels between the care of the god for the cosmos and the care of the statesman for the *polis*. First, the statesman's "weaving" of the natures of human beings in the age of Zeus (306aff.) finds its original in the god's "twisting" of the cosmos in the age of Cronos. Second, just as the rule of the god over the cosmos is unsustainable in perpetuity due to the nature of the body, so the perpetual rule of the statesman over the *polis* is unsustainable for the city, and in particular just as the god, as we shall see, has to let go of the cosmos at the appropriate moment so as not to destroy it, so the statesman has to let go of the *polis* when it has achieved its best ordered condition. Third, just as the god takes control of the cosmos again only when the cosmos is in direst straits, so the statesman returns to the *polis* only under conditions of grave disorder. Finally, just as the universe is supposed to "hold on" to its instruction from the god for as long as possible in the absence of the statesman, so the city must "hold on" to its laws for as long as possible.

Taken together, these parallels between the god in the myth and the statesman in the city imply that the statesman's care is a form of emergency care, not a form of continuous care: the statesman, in the end, turns out to be the founding or refounding legislator, not the day-to-day ruler. To be sure, this claim does not depend merely on evidence from the myth: if the argument is correct, it should be supported by evidence from the latter part of the dialogue. But the myth does tell us where to look, so to speak, for that evidence, and how to interpret certain difficult passages in that part of the dialogue. The interpretation proposed here thus strives to achieve a kind of "reflective equilibrium" with the rest of the dialogue both by prospectively using the care of the god for the cosmos to illuminate the care of the statesman for the city and by retrospectively using the later discussion of statesmanship to illuminate the care of the god for the whole.

It may perhaps be objected that the interpretation proposed here reads too much into the myth, especially given the simple purpose for which it is used by the Stranger, namely distinguishing between the divine and the human statesman (274e6–275a6). The Stranger, after all, never explicitly alerts us to the parallels between the statesman and the god that I emphasize here. But as the Stranger himself points out, the myth is too large for its immediate aim (277a6–b8); he only proposes to use a large *part* of it (268d9) to correct the initial account of statesmanship. The Stranger thus suggests, anticipating the discussion of the due measure (283b1–287a7), that the proper way of measuring the myth is not against its use in correcting the initial account of statesmanship (for which purpose it is too large) but against other, not fully explicit purposes. My argument can be understood then as a way of making sense of the myth that ensures that its place within the dialogue is "just right."

I should stress at the outset that my argument does not rest on taking the myth "literally." It does not matter for any philosophically significant purpose whether the Stranger, or Plato, actually "believes" the literal truth of the myth, though as a matter of fact its presentation as a playful story militates against this possibility.[113] If there is any truth to the myth, it is presented in images rather than accurate propositions, and more specifically in "inaccurate" images (in the sense described in chapter 4, pp. 201–205), since the myth depicts the largest of all beings. The truth of the myth, if any, in other words, is the insight into the structure of the cosmos that shapes the narrative and its conceptual framework; but by presenting the myth *as* a story, Plato explicitly signals the inadequacy of such insight. I *am* claiming, however, that the myth serves as an aid to understanding the nature of statesmanship insofar as it presents us with several images of other possible forms of care and forces us to think of their parallels with statesmanship. It thus serves to clarify what is elsewhere in the dialogue the subject of analysis and argument, though there are reasons, both pedagogical (internal to the drama of the dialogue and dependent on Young Socrates' character and preparation) and philosophical (independent of Young Socrates' character and preparation) why the Stranger chooses to proceed by means

[113] *Pace* Brisson (1995, 349). See also Hemmenway (1994, 253–254).

of myth rather than argument. At any rate, we should beware of making too much of the opposition between *muthos* and *logos*, for the Stranger does not do so, and fills his *muthos* with a great deal of argument.[114]

An alternative view

The idea that the statesman somehow imitates the god's care of the cosmos has been occasionally mooted by commentators, though there is little agreement regarding which aspects of the god's care for the cosmos are paradigmatic for the statesman.[115] In recent years, however, a new interpretation of the myth has emerged that claims that the myth describes three ages rather than the traditional two: one where the god controls the movement of the cosmos (the age of Cronos), another one where he is absent (an age where the growth of things is reversed, in some interpretations), and a third where he controls the movement of the cosmos again but in a more indirect manner. This nontraditional interpretation, if correct, has large implications for the political theory of the dialogue that are in conflict with the implications I draw, and hence must be carefully engaged. At any rate, it should be acknowledged that the traditional interpretation is not without some problems, and that its proponents have not always properly articulated the implications of a two-age interpretation of the myth.

The three-age interpretation of the myth has been primarily put forward and defended by Christopher Rowe, Luc Brisson, and, more recently, Gabriela Roxanna Carone.[116] Though they

---

[114] See Horn (2001, 144).

[115] Arends (1999, 109n22), for example, agrees with my view that the myth shows that the statesman acts only when the city is about to be destroyed, though he believes the philosopher and the statesman are identical; Cropsey (1995, 119) argues, by contrast, that the statesman imitates the "shepherds" of men in the age of Cronos, rather than the god who turns the cosmos. Carone (2005) and Delcomminette (2000) both also suggest that the statesman imitates the god, though their differing interpretations of the myth result in different accounts of the political implications of this fact.

[116] See Brisson (1995), Carone (2005), Rowe (1995b), and Rowe (2001b).

do not agree among themselves on the details of the postulated three ages, all of these scholars agree that the traditional interpretation is flawed and should be discarded, and they draw on similar evidence to make their case. Though it has not gained much support so far,[117] has few precedents,[118] and has been vigorously resisted,[119] proponents of this new view of the myth make some arguments worth engaging in some detail.

The main sticking point for the "non-traditionalists"[120] is the (apparent) implication of the traditional interpretation of the myth that we are now living in an era where we lack guidance by the god, a point that seems to be in conflict with various Platonic statements (in the *Timaeus* or the *Laws*, for example) regarding the role of the god in the cosmos. Thus, for example, Carone claims that "it would be quite puzzling (though not impossible) if Plato were trying to make a political point at the expense of either totally diluting a cosmological picture that he had emphasized in other dialogues, or sending a

---

117 Zuckert 2005 toys with it, but does not defend it in her later work.

118 Rowe and Brisson can only cite a 1935 book by Arthur Lovejoy and George Boas, *Primitivism and Related Ideas in Antiquity* (Lovejoy and Boas [1935]), which, in the course of a discussion of various ancient myths, devotes three pages to the myth of the *Statesman* (156–159), and suggest that it appears to describe three ages of the world, though they are not absolutely certain of this. One could perhaps also cite as a precedent (though no proponent of the "revised" interpretation has done so, to my knowledge) George Grote's work (1875, 480–481), since Grote seems to think that the myth unproblematically describes an age of Cronos, a "reversed" age, and an age of Zeus, much as in Brisson's (and Carone's) interpretation. Yet Grote also avers that "[t]here is much in this copious mythe which I cannot clearly understand or put together" (481), and warns that "[w]e cannot fairly demand either harmonious consistency or profound meaning in the different features of an ingenious fiction"; he is not interested in determining specifically whether the age of Zeus goes in reverse relative to that of Cronos, and his view of the myth ultimately does not affect his view of the politics of the dialogue, since Grote thinks that the only contrast that matters is that between the age of Zeus and the age of Cronos, and believes that the age of Zeus is without divine guidance in political terms.

119 See Erler (1995); Ferrari (1995, 394n17); Lane (1998, 103–105); Horn (2001); McCabe (1997); and Nightingale (1996, especially 85).

120 Except for Zuckert (2005).

message that is opposite to it by now denying that we are living under god";[121] and Rowe and Brisson make similar statements. Moreover, the non-traditionalists also claim (to a greater or lesser extent) that the picture of a decaying cosmos implied by the traditional interpretation of the myth conflicts with the political teaching of the dialogue. For example, Carone says that "if Plato means to inscribe human and political occurrences within a larger cosmic picture, it would seem to be rather discouraging or indeed contradictory to be told, on the one hand (as many scholars recognize), that the perfect ruler of the third definition is a prospective ideal whose advent one must remain open to, when, on the other, the standard reading of the myth suggests that things will necessarily go worse in the cycle in which we live."[122]

Non-traditionalists thus might be said to aim to understand the myth in light of what they take to be the true Platonic view about the role of the god in the cosmos, despite the fact that the "traditional" interpretation appears to make good *prima facie* sense of the myth and its political implications. Indeed, until Rowe and Brisson's work, two centuries of modern Plato scholarship had been almost entirely blind to the possibility of an alternative interpretation of the myth.[123] To be sure, earlier scholarship was often quite unconcerned about the specific details of the myth.[124] But the demand for a certain amount of Platonic consistency is not unreasonable; if it is indeed the case

[121] Carone (2005, 126–127).

[122] Carone (2005, 127).

[123] To be sure, there was some occasional discomfort and even confusion about which periods imply what. See, for example, Barker's puzzlement (in 1918) about what he claims are the two "incompatible" images presented in the myth—one of "everything as reversed" in the godless period and one of a "*gradual* departure from the ideal" (Barker [1918, 278n1]). Barker does not suggest that there are three ages in the myth, but he (like Rowe) is resistant to the idea that the "reversed period" is presided over by the god, and hence cannot make much sense of a period of "gradual decay" that is also quite obviously bereft of divine guidance.

[124] An attitude found as late as Guthrie (1978, 183).

that the traditional interpretation of the myth of the *Statesman* implies a radically different view of the role of the god in the cosmos than is found in other dialogues, that would certainly count as evidence *against* the traditional interpretation.

I take it, however, that the fear of inconsistency driving the non-traditional interpretation of the myth is misplaced, both substantively and methodologically. The "teaching" of the myth, such as it is, is a perfectly Platonic one, if we do not come to the table with preconceived notions of what Platonism is about, or about what the Stranger is saying when he suggests that the god in the age of Zeus no longer supervises the cosmos. Indeed, if we understand the myth mostly as a model for the statesman's action in the city (as I do below), the idea that the god "lets go" of the cosmos in our age appears primarily as a political metaphor rather than as a metaphysical hypothesis, unlike the myth of the *Timaeus*.[125] Whereas the myth of the *Timaeus* attempts to explain the order of the cosmos, the myth of the *Statesman* attempts to explain the current disorder of politics, which is clearly not under divine direction, whatever might be said of the cosmos *in toto*; and to the extent that the disorder of politics is assumed to be related to the disorder of the cosmos (in particular, the hostility of nature, as we shall see below), the myth of the *Statesman* necessarily posits a greater degree of divine disengagement and cosmic decay than the *Timaeus*.

Hence Carone's worry about "how can one look forward to the best kind of politics when the universe itself is on the path to decay?" (127) is beside the point: macrocosmic decay finds its microcosmic analogue in the decay of the city's order, and the savior of the macrocosm finds its microcosmic analogue in the statesman. As we shall see below in greater detail, just

[125] See also Delcomminette's (2000) interpretation of the myth, which makes this point at much greater length. For Delcomminette, we might say that while we are politically in the age of Zeus, the stars are not, or the philosophers. His interpretation has antecedents reaching as far back as Proclus.

as the god intervenes as the cosmos is about to fall into the "sea of dissimilarity" (273d6–e1) and sets the cosmos in order again, so the statesman intervenes to save the city and set it in order again; and just as the god lets go of the cosmos so that it can take care of itself, but the cosmos without the god is incapable of holding on to its order forever, so the statesman, having let go of the city (perhaps because he dies), cannot ensure the preservation of the city's order forever, and can only count on the efforts of the city to hold on to its laws for its endurance: the order of the city inevitably decays, just like the order of all corporeal beings does. The cosmic background of the increasing disorder of corporeal being makes it possible to understand why the statesman is needed and why his work cannot endure forever; yet by itself the idea that corporeal being tends to disorder is a commonplace of Platonic metaphysics, even in the *Timaeus*.

Moreover, the return of the god and the arrival of the statesman are both similarly uncertain, indeed "mythical" events: we cannot foresee that they will actually take place, as they are outside the natural order of things. As I argue at more length in chapter 6, the statesman is a kind of freak of nature (a "miracle"): his nature, being unbiased (neither too "quick" nor too "slow," but able to integrate the moderate and the courageous dispositions that are normally found separate among people) is not easily found; and since no cities are actually ruled by true statesmen, his knowledge is also not likely to arise through education. The statesman is, at best, somebody like the Athenian Stranger in the *Laws*, a rare nature who is allowed to grow undisturbed in the unlikely soil of Athens, not somebody we have any right to expect (cf. *Laws* 642c6–d2). Thus Carone's view that one cannot "make sense of the possibility of human and political progress when the universe does not provide proper support" (127) is exactly right, but in a way that she did not intend, for we indeed cannot make sense of such a possibility. The dialogue shows that the universe will not cooperate with the order of the city; political progress is not an assured possibility but at best akin to an act of grace, and a fragile one at that, since the city's order will not survive forever after the statesman departs (or dies). Indeed, the divine gifts do not include statesmanship (274c5–d2; see the discussion below, pp. 172–176; statesmanship is a purely human responsibility, though it must be informed by the traces of divine order in the whole. This may be a bleak doctrine; it is perhaps an even less optimistic doctrine than the one propounded by Socrates in the *Republic*, but it is in no way unplatonic or especially inconsistent with anything that Plato says elsewhere.

Carone (but not Rowe or Brisson) also worries that the two-age interpretation of the myth "promises the abolition of politics in a future [cosmic cycle]." But this worry is similarly misplaced. Such a "promised" abolition is mythical; it is not a promise in historical time. The cosmos may be decaying, but not at an extremely fast rate;[126] the decay of order takes "myriads of revolutions" (270a8). Indeed, as Guthrie once noted,[127] the myth is framed in terms of the mythical "long year" and its *tropai*, its "solstices." From this point of view, the reversal of the cosmos from the age of Cronos to the age of Zeus represents the summer solstice, when the days grow shorter and the good weather goes away, to be replaced by stormy times (cf. *cheimastheis* 273d5); this is the time where the "cloak" of politics, the woolen *himation* that the statesman's weaving will create for the city, is necessary. By contrast, the mythical rescue of the cosmos by the god represents its winter solstice, the nadir of the cosmos, the shortest day, deep in the dead of winter, but indeed the turning point towards the good weather of the age of Cronos. The pattern, if this view is right, is necessarily a cyclical one, but we are in the "fall" of the world, not in its spring, and since it is a mythical pattern we cannot really

[126] *Pace* Carone (2005), who cites 273c5–6 in support of the opposite view. Yet the passage she cites does not show that the "remembrance of god's teaching is extremely brief," but merely describes the broad pattern of decay over the long cosmic cycle.

[127] Guthrie (1978, 194).

expect, except as a matter of faith, any kind of change in the near future. As I show in more detail below, pp. 161–162, this means that we are "in between" a state of full dissimilarity and a state of similarity, a state of complete order and a state of complete disorder; going, indeed, towards greater disorder but not quite there. Carone's interpretation (and other "asymmetrical" interpretations of the myth, like Rowe's and Brisson's) of the myth make such patterns impossible to see.

These considerations do not, to be sure, touch the more specific criticisms of the traditional interpretation that the non-traditionalists make; but it will be better to deal with the more specific complaints they present against the traditional interpretation as I present my own interpretation. To that task we now turn.

Sources of the myth

The Stranger weaves his myth from three distinct sources, earlier myths that provide the raw materials for the Stranger's myth. These are (in the order in which he introduces them) the story of how the quarrel between Atreus and Thyestes was resolved in favor of Atreus (268e8–269a6); the story of the golden age or the age of Cronos (269a7–8); and the story of the earthborn human beings (269b2–4). All of these can be loosely understood as "origin" myths of political order, though they all work somewhat differently: the story of Atreus and Thyestes' quarrel explains how the branch of the house of Pelops headed by Atreus became dominant; the story of the golden age describes a standard from which the present time has fallen away; and the story of the earthborn is both a story about the origin of human beings in general and a way of legitimating the possession of land on the part of some ethnic group, such as the Athenians (cf. *Menexenus* 237b–c).[128] All of these stories combine a "before" and an "after," suggesting a division of time

[128] See Zuckert (2005, 11).

into two periods, the latter of which is continuous with our own age, not a division into three periods.

Proponents of the three-age interpretation, however, have sometimes argued that the story of Thyestes and Atreus actually implies that the reversal of the motion of the cosmos the Stranger will soon describe was merely a short interlude in which the god reversed the movement of the sun but then quickly returned it to its original motion.[129] Yet there is no reason for thinking that the Stranger wants to stress an exact parallelism between the duration of the reversal interval between the story of Thyestes and Atreus and the story he will soon tell.[130] Moreover, even if we accept that the story of Atreus and Thyestes implies that the period of cosmic reversal is short,[131] it is important to stress that the story implies that this period would be precisely the period of divine *intervention*, not the period of divine nonintervention, as Rowe would have it: human depravity and decay leads to a short period of divine intervention, afterwards returning to the usual state of divine nonintervention.[132] Indeed, the myth is silent about the duration of the period of divine rule, but explicitly indicates that the period when the universe is on its own lasts for a very long time (270a8).

Carone raises a different objection to the traditional interpretation of the implications of the story of Atreus and Thyestes, namely, that when Plato integrates the ancient legends in the myth he explicitly says that the god, indeed Zeus, *changes* the motion of the sun towards their current course, rather than letting it go, which is what we would expect if the current period

---

129 Rowe (1995b, note to 270b7–8).

130 See Mattéi (1996, 76n2), and Benardete (1984b, 96).

131 And this is not entirely clear from the sources, which merely speak of the sun recoiling in horror from Thyestes' cannibalistic banquet: cf. Euripides *Orestes* 988f., Campbell (1867, note to 268e12), and Vidal-Naquet (1978, 136).

132 See also Mattéi (1996, 77), who also notes the parallel between Thyestes' eating of his own children and the literal "reintegration" of men into the Earth in the age of Cronos.

were one without the god's guidance (citing 269a1–5).[133] Aside from the fact that this objection works only if we understand the story of Atreus and Thyestes as involving two, rather than three periods, *pace* Rowe, it should be noted that the Stranger uses a rather anodyne word that does not preclude the idea of the god letting go of the sun: he "changed" (*metebalen*) the course of the sun, which is precisely what the god does in letting go of the sun. Even if *metebalen* were taken in a stronger sense as "turned," the Stranger is still saying this *before* he has explicated the mechanism by which the god takes control and lets go of the cosmos, which implies that he need not accept every detail of the ancient stories at this point. And if the story of Thyestes and Atreus implies that the god intervenes for a limited time, afterwards returning the sun to its usual course (as it seems more likely) then Carone's objection fails, since the god's changing of the course of the sun would not refer to the *latest* reversal in the motion of the cosmos but to the reversal *before it*, that is, the reversal that inaugurated the previous age of divine control.

At any rate, Carone is correct to say that the Stranger incorporates rather than rejects the "popular legends" that he uses to construct the myth; but he does not incorporate them uncritically or without transforming them substantially. The attempt to find an exact parallel to the myth in the story of Thyestes and Atreus ultimately runs the risk of misunderstanding the way in which the Stranger uses these legendary stories in the construction of his own myth. The main point he makes is that all of these stories arose from a common "experience" of the reversal of the motion of the universe. This experience was then interpreted in different ways over time, "forgotten" to a greater or lesser extent, and embodied in three apparently unrelated stories, which can nevertheless be unified again by understanding them all as dimly remembered and more or less inaccurate accounts of that original experience (269b5–c2, cf.

[133] Carone (2005, 129–130).

also 271a6–b4). This is precisely what we would expect if the universe had gradually "forgotten" its divine order (273b3–4); forgetting is a reflection of the fact that the universe is no longer perfectly ordered. More importantly, this situation implies that people today can no longer remember the source of their current condition except with the help of philosophical reflection. Hence we need not accept that the Stranger is committed to the view that the current era is one that came about through the active turning of the cosmos by the god; he is only relaying the view that the legend says that "Zeus" turned the cosmos to its present direction of motion, but he never explicitly commits himself to the view that Zeus continues to turn the cosmos, or that the actual turning in question represents anything more than a mythical way of saying that the god let go of the cosmos. The legends do not have authority in themselves, but only when purified through philosophical interpretation.

The Stranger thus implicitly claims to "re-collect" the stories, that is, to collect them together as parts of a single whole, better than the people of his age. Yet he can hardly be said to be "remembering" anything in the normal sense of the word, since the myth is very clearly of his own invention. His capacity for invention/remembrance is not a form of simple "memory," but something similar (though not necessarily identical) to what Socrates in other Platonic dialogues calls "recollection," and which we can understand here more broadly as a kind of insight into the "original" order of the whole. So the Stranger "recollects" the stories (collects them together into a single story) by providing speculative *arguments* for why a reversal of the motion of the universe, with its consequent division between the "before" and "after," is a necessary feature of the world, that is, part of its "order," and linking the main features of each of the stories to those arguments. This is also the kind of recollection that, as we shall see, the universe has of the god's instruction to it (273b2): it is an ability to dimly understand the order of the whole, however blurred this order might become in time. The Stranger "remembers" better only because he has better insight into that order than the people of his age, not because of any special features of the story of Atreus and Thyestes.

The Stranger treats the old stories as containing traces of the true order of the whole, that is, as "reminders" of it; but this is not to say that the story that he fashions from them is something that should therefore be believed literally. On the contrary, the new story is just as much an image of the order of the whole as the old ones, though one that is based on theoretical insight rather than mere hearsay. Its claim to superiority over the old stories is that, as an image, it is a more faithful and more complete approximation to that order; it puts the pieces together better and preserves their relationships more accurately.[134]

The myth that the Stranger now weaves from these three stories divides into four parts. The first part (269c4–270b2) presents the general "mechanism" of the myth, namely, the alternating motion of the universe, as well as the basic reasons behind it: how the god first directs the motion of the cosmos, but has to then release it, and finally must eternally repeat the cycle by taking control of it and letting it go again. The second part (270b3–272b2), accordingly, discusses what happens when the god takes control of the universe, first with respect to animal life in general (270b10–271c1), then with respect to human beings in particular (271c1–272b2). The third part (272b2–272d4) is transitional, and raises the question (without answering it) of whether it is better to live in the age when the god controls the movement of the whole or in the age when he does not. The fourth part, finally (272d6–274d8), discusses the time during which the god does not direct the motion of the cosmos but lets it move under its own power. This last section is divided

[134] On the myth as a visible approximation of an eidetic reality, see Mattéi (1996, 13–16). Mattéi notes appositely that this interpretation of Plato's myths is at least as old as Plotinus, citing *Enneads* III.5.9, 24–29, a particularly concise and elegant statement of the idea.

into a section on what happens to the universe as whole while under its own power (272d6–273e5); a section on what happens to animal life in general at that time (273e5–274b4); and a section on what happens to human beings in particular at that time (274b4–d8).

The motion of the universe: 269c–270b

According to the Stranger, the basic "experience" (*pathos*) of the reversal of the motion of the heavens that gives rise to the old stories results from the fact that, though the god sometimes helps the universe move (in circles, *sunkuklei*, 269c5), he lets go of the whole whenever its revolutions "reach the measure of their fitting time" (269c6–7), which results in an abrupt change of direction in the motion of the whole. Moreover, the Stranger notes that the process repeats itself (cf. 270b); at some times the god controls the movement of the universe, and at other times it does not.

The Stranger stresses that the universe is capable of moving on its own (*automaton* 269c7) in a relatively orderly fashion, since it is an animal, that is, an ensouled being (cf. 261b7–d6) with a share in *phronēsis*. That the universe is a living being with *phronēsis* should be understood as an image of the fact that the movement of the visible whole around us is ordered, that is, that we experience the world as a *kosmos* (cf. *ouranon kai kosmon*, 269d7) that moves in an ordered fashion (in particular, according to the Stranger, it rotates), and that this movement does not evidently come from anywhere outside the universe itself (the *pan*, "all things," 269c4). Like the movement of an animal, the movement of the cosmos on its own (in its current period, as we shall see) is self-initiated and at the same time (partially) ordered. Possession of *phronēsis* is thus understood as a kind of capacity for self-rule, yet as we shall see this capacity for self-rule is insufficient in the long run without connection to the divine. It is also worth noting that by mentioning *phronēsis* here the Stranger introduces the question of the relationship of *phronēsis* to rulership which had been elided in the first genealogy of the statesman; the god "rules over" an animal with *phronēsis*, not an animal without *phronēsis*.

The Stranger also notes that the universe's *phronēsis*, which it uses whenever the god cannot help it move to order its own motion, was a grant from the god "who harmonized its parts" (*tou sunarmosantos* 269d1). As we shall see in more detail below, this must be the same god who turns the universe in the earlier period. Moreover, it is precisely *by* turning the whole that the god harmonizes its parts and grants it a share in *phronēsis* which it can use to move in a relatively orderly way whenever the god cannot help it move. We should also note that this "grant" of *phronēsis* is the cosmic equivalent of the gift of the arts to human beings when the gods no longer rule them (cf. 274c5ff.). Just as the god endows the cosmos as a whole with reason (that is, a capacity for seeing and acting in accordance with divine order) so that it will be able to survive on its own for a time, so he will endow human beings with reason in the form of arts so that they will be able to survive on their own.

At the same time, precisely because the universe is an *embodied* being, the Stranger argues that it cannot *always* move in the same direction as the god (269d5–e1); the universe is not pure soul. The reason, according to the Stranger, is that things which have body cannot remain always the same. There must thus be a change in the direction of the universe's motion. The Stranger briefly considers two other alternatives, rejecting them in turn: a god could turn the universe first in one direction, then in another; but this is not *themis*, not in accordance with the divine nature (269e5–7); or two gods could turn the universe in turn, one in one direction, one in another, as if the gods' *phronēseis* were opposed (270a1–2), but this is also not in accord with the nature of divinity. Hence, the Stranger concludes, the universe must sometimes rotate with the help of the god, but sometimes the god must release it at the appropriate moment (270a2–9; cf. *kata kairon* 270a6), at which point the universe, which has been given an additional lease on life by the god during the time in which it is under its control,[135] goes on to rotate on its own for "many myriads of revolutions," like a well-balanced spindle, until the god has to take care of it again.

Note that the model the Stranger has in mind for the motion of the universe is not that of a single wheel that might slow down and stop when released, but of a Greek spindle being turned by a spinner (the god) which, when no longer helped along to move by the spinner, would stop more or less abruptly and turn in the other direction due to the tension built up in its fibers, balancing on its one foot (see figure 4).[136] The *phronēsis* of the world is strong enough to rotate it in the divine direction with the help of the god, but it is not strong enough to overcome the resistance of its "fibers" to that movement when the world is on its own, even as it "wants" to turn in the same direction as the god; it is therefore not "opposed" to it (270a1–2). The image of a spindle also brings to mind the transformation of disordered and tangled yarn into useful thread as the god "orders" the cosmos, and its slow return to tangled mess as the god lets go of the spindle, anticipating the later description of the universe moving on its own as slowly forgetting its instruction from the god (273b3–4).[137]

---

135 270a4–5: τὸ ζῆν πάλιν ἐπικτώμενον καὶ λαμβάνοντα ἀθανασίαν ἐπισκευαστὴν παρὰ τοῦ δημιουργοῦ; the universe acquires life again by being put in order, and hence its immortality is as it were renewed.

136 Taylor's (1961, 214) uncharacteristically unkind remarks miss the point here; see Schuhl (1968, 83–92) for the correct model. Language suggesting spindles and spinning is found at 270a9 (the universe is the most well-balanced being on a single foot, like a spindle), 273e2–3 (the god saves the cosmos from sinking into the sea of dissimilarity by "twisting" or "spinning" it (*strepsas*), and 273e6–7 (the world is "wound up" by the god, "spun").

137 *Pace* Delcomminette (2000, 179), the model of the spindle does not imply that both cycles are "symmetrical" or make it impossible to see why the god eventually has to intervene again: clearly the "twisting" of the universe under the god's direction is an *ordering* event, and its "unraveling" on its own is a *disordering* event. Delcomminette is on firmer ground, however, when he argues (180–188) that the great reversal must be ultimately interpreted as a reversal in the movement of the soul of the world, not just its physical

Phronēsis, in its worldly and divine incarnations, thus emerges in this image and its associated argument as a principle of order, capable of imposing a regular movement on the world even when it is on its own, but incapable, without divine assistance, of maintaining the divinely-appointed direction of the motion of the cosmos. The bodily component in the mixture that is the world is responsible for the loss of order, as the Stranger repeats at 273b4ff.; but it is an ineradicable part of the mixture, and so the god has to let go of the cosmos.

Figure 4: Woman spinning woollen thread. Pottery jug, Attic, around 490 BCE, found in Calabria © The Trustees of the British Museum

---

movement: the model of the "spindle" is ultimately a mere metaphor for the opposition between the "ordering" of souls under the god and their "disordering" without the god, not a physical hypothesis, as we shall see below in more detail.

It should be stressed that the experience of reversal suffered by the visible whole described by the Stranger does not come at arbitrary times. There is a time for the reversal of motion, for the "unraveling" of the world, a time when it is fitting for the nature of the visible whole to be released, as we might expect from the image of the spindle: "twisting" ceases when the yarn runs out. The Stranger foreshadows his later discussion of the double measure (283d4ff.) by using words like *to prosēkon chronon* (cf. 269c6–7), the time that belongs/is appropriate for the world to turn back, and the *kairos* (270a6), the opportune time for letting go of the cosmos. Moreover, he also foreshadows the task of the statesman, who also must know the *kairos* (cf. 305d4), the right moment for doing anything, and of the process of education, which is analogized to the "twisting" part of the process of making woolen thread (cf. 309a8–b7). This signals the first parallel between the god and the statesman: as the god is the spinner of the cosmos, so the statesman is the weaver of the city; and as the god lets go of the cosmos after he has put it in order, so the statesman lets go of the city when he has put it in order.

If we take the "twisting" imagery seriously, then, we should expect that the god must let go of the cosmos when the cosmos has reached its maximum state of order, that is, when it has become most of all a *kosmos* (cf. 273b6–7, 273e3). But what exactly is this moment? What is the measure of the time for the god to let go of the cosmos? As we shall see, the measure in question turns out to be the measure of the most appropriate ratio of soul to body in the universe so that the universe can rotate on its own for as long as possible, that is, so that it can remember the god's instruction (273b2ff.), and thus preserve its eidetic order for as long as possible in the face of the disordering pressure of the body. The god "measures" the right time for letting go of the cosmos by looking at the ratio of soul to body, that is, of the ordering principle to the disordering principle, and determining what is the highest ratio of order to disorder that the universe can bear due to the fact that it is necessarily mixed with body. The "fitting" time for release would then be the time at which further ordering by the god would not be compatible with the bodily nature of the cosmos, as we shall see in the next section.[138]

The god at the helm: 270b–272b

The model the Stranger uses for how the god determines the right time for letting go of the world is never explicitly stated, and the interpretation below must necessarily introduce more clarity into the text than is actually found there. Yet it is nevertheless useful to provide a speculative reconstruction of the mechanism the Stranger seems to have in mind.

In broad terms (I will fill in the details later), the basic model seems to be the following. First, the Stranger seems to assume that there is a fixed quantity of souls in the world—a quantity of souls that is never destroyed or increased. (Call this the principle of the conservation of soul.) During the "normal" direction of motion of the world souls become associated with distinct bodies, acquiring experience but forgetting their divine instruction or order: they become, as it were, "degraded" or "disordered." (Call this the principle of the progressive degradation of soul when mixed with body.) The influence of body "turns" them, as it were, away from the truth: their "movements"

---

[138] Note that any asymmetrical interpretation of the myth (i.e., any interpretation that postulates three different ages, like Carone's, Rowe's, or Brisson's) must make nonsense of the Stranger's claim that the god only lets go of the cosmos at the fitting time. Why would the god let go of the world when it is clearly unprepared to make a go of it by itself, only to have to intervene again soon afterwards, as if its original letting-go had occurred at an inappropriate time, to let it move again mostly on its own? My own interpretation, by contrast, explains why the god lets go of the world at the moment it does as well as why the world cannot go on indefinitely: the god lets go of the cosmos when it does because otherwise it would lose its nature as an animal, i.e., a combination of soul and body: it would become pure soul. And the god takes control of the cosmos when the cosmos is again about to lose its nature and become pure disordered body.

(desires, etc.) are the contrary of what they should be.[139] When the god takes control of the world, however, he reverses the direction of motion, causing souls to run through life in their previous bodies backwards: starting as old people, they end up as babies. The souls progressively "dissociate" themselves from each of these bodies, which become invisible (non-bodies) once the soul has completed their reverse journey in each of them. This process of dissociation of souls from bodies (and the concomitant "elimination" of body during this period) can thus be understood as a kind of purification or ordering process that minimizes the influence of body in the universe. But this purification process cannot go on forever; otherwise the souls (including the soul of the universe) would separate themselves from their first bodies, breaking their necessary connection with body in general, which would destroy the universe. So the god has to let go of the cosmos at the point of maximum purification, that is, when the souls have gone in reverse through each of their bodies but one. This is the "right time" for letting go of the cosmos.

The reversal of the motion of the cosmos is thus a kind of renewal; by dissociating souls from bodies as much as possible, the god gives the world a new lease on life (270a4–5), "turning" the souls, as it were, towards the truth. Hence the time when the god rules, as we noted earlier, is equivalent to the spring and summer of the world, while the time when he is away is equivalent to its fall and winter, when the cloak of the statesman is necessary for human beings. But let us look at the details of the text.

Effects on animals

When the god takes control of the cosmos (something the Stranger has not said at this point in his narration, but is

[139] See Delcomminette (2000, 180–193) for a more complete version of this view, which connects the changes in the movement of the cosmos to the soul's relationship to the ideas.

confirmed at 271d2–3), and thus reverses the movement of the cosmos, the Stranger says that the most wonder-inducing thing that happens (the thing most likely to induce philosophical reflection, we might say, following *Theaetetus* 155d) is that all the "cyclical" forms of motion in the universe (*tropai*, cf. 271c5; the word also means "solstices") are reversed.

Among those cyclical motions is the cycle of growth and age, which we might call the "life-cycle." Thus, with the reversal of motion, all animals (including, presumably, the universe itself; cf. 269d1) stop aging, and then they grow in reverse (*ephueto* 270e1; they become "naturally" younger). They cease to look older, becoming younger and softer, moving through the life-cycle in reverse towards the nature (*phusin* 270e7) of a new-born child "in both body and soul." Like the universe as a whole (270a4–5), they are thus "renewed." Once a person completes a reverse life-cycle, their bodies become "invisible" (*adēlon*; cf. 271a1), sublimating, as it were, into the non-bodily realm. Moreover, as we learn later, at this point the soul falls to the earth as a seed (272e1–2), "giving back" that particular *genesis*, presumably that particular body with which it was once associated during a forward life-cycle, and "sprouts" again into another body to move backwards through another life-cycle. The Stranger adds that the bodies of those who die violently during the shock of the reversal quickly vanish too, becoming invisible in a few days. The description of this reversal of the life-cycle of human beings (and presumably animals) is enough to tickle Young Socrates' curiosity (271a3–4): if things were as the Stranger describes, how would animals reproduce?

This presents an opportunity for the Stranger to tie in the third source of the myth, the story of the earth-born, into his invented story as the second element of the whole, postponing the centerpiece of the myth, namely, the account of the rule of Cronos (the second source of the myth), to third place but its physical center. The Stranger says that it is clear that "in the nature of the age" (*en tēi tote phusei* 271a6) there was no generation from each other, but from the earth, a form of generation that he describes, significantly, using "twisting" terminology that echoes the "spindle" image of the god's care for the whole discussed earlier: it is a "turning up" or "revolving again" (*anastrephomenon* 271a8) from the earth. Nature thus produces full-grown human beings who emerge from the earth and return to it by becoming younger and younger until they disappear, in a kind of circular motion that repeats itself a number of times in this age. In fact, the Stranger speaks of the cycle of generation in this period as rotating along with the world in a circular motion in the opposite direction as the "normal" direction of the cycle of generation in our age (271b8), and strongly implies that normal reproduction is associated with the current motion of the cosmos, under which earth-generation would not be possible.

The process the Stranger describes presumably continues until all the bodies of human beings (and probably all animals) have vanished, and have thus been "cleared away," so to speak, and the souls have "given back" all the "comings into being" (and thus all the bodies) they were once associated with (272e1–2). The process should thus stop—and the god should release the world—when there are no more bodies left over in the ground from the previous age, that is, when all the bodies that had died in the previous age have resuscitated, lived their lives in reverse, and vanished, except for those who must not vanish if the cycle is to recommence (cf. 271a6–b4, 272d7–e1). In other words, the process stops when all the souls have gone through the reverse generation with each of the bodies with which they were formerly associated *except* one. Otherwise, if those who are alive at the end of this process regressed to the nature of children and then vanished, no more bodies would be left on the ground to continue the process of reverse generation, and the connection between body and soul in the universe would be broken.

Going through the life cycle "backwards" disconnects, so to speak, the soul from the particular body or bodies it was once associated with; it separates the mixture of body and soul by dissolving the body into the invisible (non-body) world, if we may use a chemical metaphor. Hence the process may be seen as a way of making the souls of the world as free as possible of any admixture of body, and thus increasing the total amount of order in the world and leaving the minimal possible quantity of visible animal bodies, living or dead, at the beginning of the present age. These are the bodies which will then multiply and fill the earth through reproduction once the god releases the cosmos again. The forward life-cycle, in other words, proliferates bodies through reproduction, while the reverse life-cycle, which has no reproduction, decreases the amount of "visible" body in the universe. The importance of this bizarre story about reverse generation is emphasized by the Stranger in a passage where he comically scolds their contemporaries for not believing the old *logoi* (271b1–4), something that, of course, every right-thinking person would be inclined to do if these *logoi* concerned human beings aging backwards. The point of this comical reprimand is precisely to emphasize the importance of the process of backwards generation and purification that the Stranger has just described for any understanding of the myth: it is because this is a process in which soul is separated from body as much as possible (and hence in which the cosmos is ordered as much as possible, since the body is the source of disorder in it) that the cosmos can be "renewed" and let go at the right time.

Proponents of the three-age interpretation of the myth have resisted the implication of the traditional interpretation, namely, that we grow "backwards" when the universe is under the control of the god, and argued instead that the growing backwards of human beings and other living things must be a feature of the universe moving under its own power. They see growing backwards as a symptom of disorder, not order, as something contrary to nature. Carone, for example, argues (131–132) that "the close connection between macro- and microcosm" implies that when the Stranger says that the souls "fall into the earth as seeds" this means that they must have followed "the normal process of growth and death, like a plant . . . which suggests that both the era of Cronos and that of Zeus follow the same direction of microcosmic events (from youth to old age) and so therefore should the macrocosm" (131). She further claims that the idea of humans "born with gray hair" suggests a "state of degradation" incompatible with the rule of Cronos.[140]

But it is precisely because the souls of human beings live their lives "in reverse" as it were that they can fall to the ground as seeds, dissociated from their previous bodily experience (which is thus "unlived"); what vanishes or disappears is the body, not the soul of each individual. The seed of each individual is not a bodily thing but each individual soul, and hence it is already invisible; it does not itself disappear as it falls to the ground. But growing "backwards" is certainly compatible with the bodies disappearing; at any rate, when human beings grow "forwards" they do not (unlike plants) "go to seed." They merely die, leaving their bodies behind; but the point of the idea of growing backwards is precisely to explain how the god purifies the cosmos of its association with body, while preserving the souls as seeds. Moreover, if this interpretation is correct, I cannot see how being born with gray hair implies some kind of state of degradation that is not already implied in the depiction of the age of Cronos as a potentially "swinish" age, where human beings might decide to act like the pigs of the initial account of statesmanship. At any rate, the point of the "rejuvenation" of men in the age of Cronos is precisely to cleanse them from the muck of ages of association with the body, which is not incompatible with saying that men begin the age of Cronos in a degraded state.

More generally, we should note that all views that postulate three cycles, two of which include generation from the earth (as in Brisson's and Carone's work), get tangled up in irresolvable

140 A judgment that echoes that of Brisson (1995) and Rowe (1995b, note to 271d7–9), referencing Hesiod, *Works and Days* 178ff., where Hesiod describes a time when babies born gray-haired signal the ultimate degradation of the human race. Note, however, that these gray-haired babies in Hesiod do not become younger, but simply grow old quickly and die; nor do they emerge from the earth, but are born in the normal way.

difficulties about the "synchronization" of the modes of generation with the motion of the cosmos. As we have noted, the Stranger emphasizes that it is "in the nature of the age" (of Cronos) (271a6) that there was no generation from each other, but from the earth. Moreover, his use of "twisting" terminology to describe the form of generation in this age (it is a "turning up" or "revolving again" from the earth, *anastrephomenon* 271a8) alludes to the "spindle" model of the god's care for the universe, where the universe first "tightens" under the care of the god (who spins the spindle to create an ordered thread) and then "unravels" when not under his care. Three-age proponents thus either have to deny that the cycle of generation and the rotation of the universe are coordinated,[141] in flat contradiction with this passage and the usual Greek practice of associating the movement of the heavens with the cycle of generation; or they have to argue that, contrary to all indications, we have three cycles of generation in the myth, two of which share the same direction but a different mode: one in which animals come up from the earth "newborn," one in which they come up from the earth "old," and one in which they reproduce normally. But this contradicts the clear implication of the myth that the entire cycle of generation, and not merely its direction, is associated with the movement of the universe: earthborn in one direction, reproductive in another. It also raises the question of why in the age of Cronos human beings would grow from the earth as newborns (in most earthborn myths human beings emerge fully grown), something the Stranger never says, whereas his only discussion of earth-birth explicitly argues that animals and human beings rise from the earth fully grown. What would be about motion in the age of Cronos or about the nature of the age that demanded earth-birth then but not in the current age, if both ages are supposed to be moving in the same direction? No satisfactory answer has been given by the proponents of the three-period interpretation of the myth.

---

[141] See, e.g., Brisson (1995, 351).

Effects on human beings

Prompted by Young Socrates (271c3–7), the Stranger identifies the age of Cronos—the mythical golden age of abundance—with the period in which generation moved in reverse (271c8–d4): the time when everything came up automatically (*automata*) for human beings, the time of Cronos, when there was no material scarcity, was "least of all" the one that moved with the established movement (*phoras* 271d2, echoing 269e3) of today. Indeed, the stranger explicitly emphasizes that all the cyclical motions of the cosmos at that time (all the *tropai*, including the life-cycle) moved in the opposite direction from the one in which they do now. The Stranger will now explore what we might call the "political" consequences of such a reversal of the life-cycle for human beings.

These consequences include universal abundance. If trees came up from the ground already laden with fruit, grasses full of grain, and so on, there would be no need to wait for them to grow or cultivate them: their emergence in full maturity (and eventual disappearance into nothingness, to be replaced quickly with new plants) would dispense with the need for agriculture, and hence with the need to work for one's daily bread. In fact, by doing away with the need for sexual generation and by providing sustenance automatically to all animals, the reversal of the cycle of generation would make every species and every individual in them independent of each other, which is precisely the situation the Stranger goes on to describe.

As I briefly indicated earlier, the use of the word *tropē* in connection with the description of the age of Cronos adds another image to the structure of the myth, the image of the mythical "great year" with its solstices (*tropai*).[142] The great turn that takes place when the god takes control of the cosmos is equivalent to the winter solstice, presaging the abundance of spring and summer, namely the age of Cronos with its bounty

[142] See Guthrie (1978, 194), for more on this point; Guthrie cites *Timaeus* 39a–d as an example of this usage.

and mild weather and (quite literal!) renewal. We might then say that the point at which the god lets go of the cosmos represents the summer solstice, presaging the hard times of fall and winter, where our present life happens and which require the woolen "cloak" of the statesman; and the point at which the god eventually rescues the universe would represent the winter solstice again, the darkest day of winter, when the universe is buffeted by storms (*cheimastheis* 273d5–e4; note that *cheimōn* also means winter).

During the great summer of the age of Cronos, the god used to rule over the entire rotation (*kuklēseōs*) of the whole, caring for it, just as in turn[143] every part of the ordered whole

---

[143] Following Robinson's (1995) emendation (ὡς δ' αὖ) for the ὡς νῦν of the manuscripts. Carone (2005) has ingeniously argued (130–131) that the manuscript reading provides evidence for her view that the god still takes care of the universe, just as he did in the age of Cronos, and further points to 272b2–3, where the Stranger appears to endorse the view that the "present era" (τὸν νυνί) is "in the presence of Zeus," despite the fact that he distances himself from that view by saying that the present era is only "said to be" under Zeus. Her view depends on an implicit equivalence between the idea that the current age is "under god" and the idea that Zeus directly turns the cosmos. But, as Brisson himself (whom Carone mostly follows) has noted (1995, 357–358), when the god moves away he simply "retires" to his observation post, from which he looks ahead for the coming dangers; we are always "under" the god, whether or not he is actually turning the cosmos. If the idea that the cosmos is currently επὶ Διός (272b2) does not imply that the god is actually turning the cosmos (as Carone's interpretation would require), then her attempt to preserve the manuscript reading ὡς νῦν at 271d4 collapses, since it would make the following κατὰ τόπους incomprehensible: how would it be possible for the god to rule today in the same way as during the age of Cronos but only in some places and not in others? But even if we accept that the manuscript reading of 271d4 should stay, we might understand the Stranger to be referring to places where the god still rules, e.g., the mythical islands of the blessed, and which escape in some way the movement of the cosmos, since the following sentences go on to reconstruct the conditions of a blessed existence. Or we could adopt Delcomminette's (2000) more "metaphysical" interpretation (209–214) of the significance of the ὡς νῦν, according to which the two cycles represent opposed tendencies within the world, and that some aspects of the world remain in the age of Cronos (e.g., the skies, philosophers) whereas others (political life, in particular) are in the age of Zeus; this interpretation, though

(the *kosmos*, cf. 271d5) was under the care of a ruling (subordinate) god (271d4–272b2). Animals represent a set of such parts. They are eidetic parts of the whole or *genē* (the objects of *diaeresis* or division), each species of animal a part of the ordered whole, each *genos* itself apparently divided into herds (*agelas* 271d7),[144] and each herd supervised by a divine shepherd (271d7; note that the word for law, *nomos*, comes from the same root **nem* as the word for shepherd, *nomeus*). Each of these herds, the Stranger emphasizes, was self-sufficient (*autarkēs* 271d7) with respect to everything which it grazed on (*enemen* 271d8, also from the root **nem*). He expands on this curious mention of grazing—for, surely, the animal kinds include carnivorous species—by saying that the self-sufficiency of the herds (and, more generally, of the *genē*) had as a result that no species was wild (*agrion* 271e1), which (in turn) meant that no animals were carnivorous. He also adds, seemingly unnecessarily for most animals except human beings, that the self-sufficiency of each herd meant there was no war or *stasis* at all within any species.

A number of things about this passage deserve some commentary before we move further. The Stranger says that the god "takes care" of the whole rotation of the whole. He practices *epimeleia*, the more general term for care that was earlier confused with herding and that will later be rehabilitated (275c9–e9). It is only the subordinate *daimons* or gods (both terms are used) who are likened to shepherds and said to "nurture" a herd (cf. *trophimoi* 272b8). The general task of

---

it is not my preferred one, is at least consistent with the rest of the myth and has the right political implications concerning the task of the statesman as savior of the world. Indeed, Delcomminette rightly sees that the myth implies that the task of the statesman must be to bring the city into the age of Cronos from its current disordered state, whatever its implications for whether or not the god directs other aspects of the motion of the universe.

144 Though we might claim, as Benardete (1984b, 99), suggests, that each animal species forms a single herd under the supervision of a single shepherd-daimon.

the god (who is left nameless) thus includes the management of the shepherd-gods; but the god is no shepherd himself. He cares for the whole rather than the parts (something emphasized in the opposition of *holē*, whole, to *merē*, parts at 271d), whereas the shepherd-gods care only for their assigned parts. His knowledge is integrative (like the statesman's), and he is not a specialist in the nurture of any single species (just as the statesman is not a specialist in any given form of nurture).

This care for the whole appears to consist in part in the separation of soul from body, that is, in its "purification"; it is thus a care for the soul as well as for the body, or rather for the *eidos* of a species in preventing the disorder of the body from overwhelming the order embedded and preserved in the soul. It also consists in the proper ordering of the parts of the cosmos, that is, in the making of the whole into a *kosmos* (cf. 273b6–7, 273e3), an ordered whole, and the keeping of each part in its own place, unmixed with each other (each *genos* is self-sufficient; cf. *autarkēs* 271d7), as if the god had performed a complete *diaeresis* or division of being (cf. *katakosmēseōs* 271e3, emphasizing the distributive [*kata-*] aspect of this ordering of the whole). The god thus emerges as a possible object of imitation for the statesman, unlike the shepherd-daimons. The statesman's art, like the god's, turns out to be the art of ordering the parts of the city into a proper whole, and it also, like the god's (but less so), rests on the ability to distinguish these parts and keep them from interfering with each other. The difference in this latter respect has to do with the fact that the statesman has to deal with sexual reproduction and the necessary mixing of *genē*, bodily and non-bodily.

By contrast, the subordinate *daimons* deal not with the unity of soul and body throughout the whole, but with the body of each species they shepherd. In particular, they "graze" their herds, that is, feed them; given the condition of the world at this time, they hardly have to do anything else. A god (Cronos; cf. 272b2) is specifically assigned to human beings (271e5–7) to care for their bodies.[145] But only the god who cares for the whole cares for the unity of soul and body (in human beings as in the universe as a whole) by means of the reversal of the cycle of generation, as we have seen.

Evaluating the age of Cronos: 272b–272d

The Stranger concludes his presentation of the time when the world is under the control of the god by telling Young Socrates that such was the life under Cronos, but that the life that the *logos* says is under Zeus,[146] the one now, he can perceive for himself, since he is present in it (272b1–3). These are the two possible lives: there are no other alternatives to consider. But Young Socrates has not yet considered them in their full significance, and the Stranger has to prompt him: would he be able and willing to decide which one is the happiest (272b3–4)? Young Socrates is unable and unwilling, and for good reason: after all, the expectation that the "golden age" would be unproblematically happiest has been confounded by the association of that age with the reversal of the cycle of generation.[147]

The Stranger thus offers to show him in what way to judge between them, but not to actually answer the question. The judgment, he indicates, turns on the presence or absence of philosophy in the age of Cronos, something the gods apparently cannot force human beings to practice, even after satisfying

---

145 Cronos is not the name of the god that orders the whole (that god always remains nameless) but simply the name of the shepherd-god that rules over that eidetic part of the whole comprised by human beings.

146 The Stranger refuses to commit himself to the view that life now is under Zeus: the god does not "control" the universe in the current period, though he oversees the motion of the cosmos and, as we shall see, has taught the universe what it needs to know to move on its own. Note also that earlier (270a1–2) he had explicitly argued that the cosmos could not be turned by two different gods, so either Zeus and Cronos must represent the same god (contrary to the Stranger's implication), or the cosmos is not being turned by Zeus.

147 Young Socrates is more cautious in this respect than some modern scholars, who simply assume that the "golden age" just has to be happier than this age of "Zeus." See for an example of this incautiousness Horn (2001, 159).

all their necessary desires and granting them the power of conversing with animals; it all depends on whether human beings have a desire for knowledge and argument.[148] Though there is some reason to think that philosophy would be highly unlikely in the conditions of the age of Cronos,[149] the Stranger neither denies nor unequivocally asserts that human beings are capable of philosophy in that age, and there is indeed no reason to categorically doubt this possibility. We will only note that if the god cannot ensure that human beings will be happy in the age of Cronos, then *a fortiori* a statesman could not do so either. Happiness depends on philosophy, not on statesmanship. Moreover, the practice of philosophy in the myth appears precisely as a possibility for *all* human beings, not as the wisdom of a few; and though philosophy is necessary for happiness or the good life,[150] and hence, in a sense, is more important than statesmanship, it is also *easier* to acquire than statesmanship, since it depends merely on a desire for knowledge and does not necessarily need to deal with the intractable problems created by scarcity and disorder in the age of Zeus.

Regardless of whether or not human beings can engage in philosophy in the age of Cronos, when they are directly "nurtured" by their own *daimōn*, it is worth stressing that the picture of the age of Cronos that the Stranger presents retrospectively illuminates many of the puzzling features of the first division or genealogy of the statesman.[151] In particular, the depiction

---

[148] See Brisson (1995, 358); Rowe (1995b, note to 272c5–6).

[149] There is a great deal of controversy on this point. Many commentators believe that philosophy is impossible in the age of Cronos due to the lack of memory: see Brisson (1995, 358); Griswold Jr. (1989, 151); Rosen (1979, 78); and Scodel (1987, 81n9). For contrary views, see Carone (2005, 143) and Rowe (1995b, note to 272c5–6); both of them argue that human beings have the possibility of philosophy even in the age of Cronos, though both of them also argue that in the age of Cronos there is no reverse generation, contrary to the interpretation proposed here (and to the traditional view).

[150] A point rightly stressed by Arends (1993).

[151] See Benardete (1963), Griswold Jr. (1989), and Scodel (1987, especially 85–86).

of the age of Cronos illuminates the emphasis of the original division on external marks to distinguish human beings from other animals and its denigration of human reason.

As we saw earlier, in the first division of the statesman human beings were characterized in terms of purely physical characteristics: they have two feet (unlike pigs), which they use as their normal means of locomotion (unlike most birds); do not have horns (unlike most cattle) or wings (unlike flightless birds), have split "hooves" (unlike horses and asses) and live on dry land (unlike fish). In our everyday understanding, none of these distinctions seem important for understanding the kind of knowledge that the statesman has, for the simple reason that whatever vulnerabilities they may imply are remedied by all the other *technai*, as the Stranger suggests later (274b4ff.), not by statesmanship: lack of speed in locomotion by the arts concerned with "vehicles" (288aff.), lack of protective physical features by the arts of armor and arms-making (288b1ff.); even lack of wings and the inability to survive underwater by in modern times the arts of aviation and submarine-making, in ancient times by the arts of Daedalus and the ship-makers. In the age of Zeus, in other words, human beings are not the vulnerable animals these characteristics may imply simply because, as animals with *phronēsis*—the capacity for reason—they are able to develop all the arts necessary to supply the deficiency, arts that are different from statesmanship. Whatever vulnerabilities statesmanship protects against must arise out of this very use of *phronēsis* and *technē*, but these vulnerabilities are not the purely physical defects of human beings.[152]

Since, however, in the age of Cronos the arts are unnecessary, as the shepherd gods supply the entire nurture of human beings (making "protection" unnecessary), the distinction between animals with *phronēsis* and animals without *phronēsis* collapses. If a god takes care of the entire "nurture" of animals, then the only criteria that matter for picking out human

[152] See, for more on this, pp. 167–173 below.

beings from among the other animals are purely physical ones: that they are land-walking animals, without wings or horns, with split "hooves," and so on. Moreover, since individuals in a species are no longer related to each other by relations of descent and generation, only external marks can group together members of a single species: the ability to breed or not with others is irrelevant.[153] The Stranger, in other words, was right to reject Young Socrates' division between animals with and without *phronēsis* at 262a3ff., after the care of the statesman for human beings had been deemed to be a form of nurture (261e1ff.), since, once the task of the statesman comprises their entire nurture, then human beings might as well be beings without *phronēsis*.[154] They would then be, after all, no better than cattle, ignorant of all the arts, in the hands of a shepherd who knows all of them (cf. also 268a6–b7).

However, there are three specific distinctions the Stranger makes in the first division in order to characterize the kind of animal over which the statesman exercises his knowledge that seem to lose their point in the age of Cronos. These are the distinction between interbreeding and non-interbreeding animals, the distinction between tame and wild animals, and the distinction between herd and non-herd animals.[155] These distinctions lose meaning because in the age of Cronos all animals are non-interbreeding, tame, and form herds due to the action of the god, which makes species and individuals independent of each other. Hence they cannot be differentiae of the kind of animal over which statesmanship (or shepherding) is exercised in that age.

---

[153] As Cole (1991, 199) notes.

[154] Cf. Benardete (1984b, 114): "The deficiency in Young Socrates' answer [at 262a3–4] did not lie in its brevity but in the assumption that man as a rational animal was relevant to political science if the model of ruling was the divine shepherd."

[155] Benardete (1984, 99) also makes this point, though only with respect to the last two distinctions, that between tame and wild and that between herd and non-herd animals.

The fact that the myth draws our attention to these specific distinctions in turn "problematizes" them in the age of "Zeus," that is, in our age. As I indicated in the previous chapter, in our age it is not clear that human beings are non-interbreeding in a politically significant sense, since the term *genos* means not only species but also "people" and even "family," and human beings clearly interbreed across peoples and families in politically significant ways, even if they normally choose not to (cf. 262d3–5 and 310c4ff.). Furthermore, it is not clear that human beings are fully tame in our age, given their propensity to war and *stasis* (cf. *Sophist* 222b7–c8). And finally, it is also not clear that human beings can be properly ruled perfectly merely by means of collective care, that is, as a herd (cf. *Statesman* 295a10–b3 and context), given the dissimilarity of their characters and circumstances.

The myth suggests, in other words, that only the reversal of the cycle of generation (life in reverse!) could ensure that human beings would be perfectly non-interbreeding, tame, and herd-like. In the age of Zeus, by contrast, the human species interbreeds in politically complicated ways that the statesman must control, as it emerges at the end of the dialogue (cf. 310d3–6, where *genē* mean the character traits that must interbreed); its tameness is never assured, due to the conditions prevailing in the age, but must rather be achieved by statesmanship; and though the species is taken care of collectively, in cities, the dissimilarity of characters and circumstances prevailing in our age makes it impossible for a human statesman to perfectly care for each member of the herd while caring for the whole (cf. 294b2–3). The myth therefore prepares us for the discussion of the statesman as the weaver of souls (who interbreeds different *genē* of human beings), as well as pointing to the difficulty that the *polis* will have in accepting a true statesman, both because human beings are not perfectly tame, that is, not perfectly obedient, and because they are also not perfectly homogeneous, which means that the rule of law is an imperfect expedient. In all three cases what the god achieves by means of separation—making each species and individual independent of each other—has to be achieved by the statesman by other means, primarily proper combination: of *genē*, arts, and law.

Two other claims (not precisely distinctions) made in the first division are also interestingly illustrated in the age of Cronos, and problematized by contrast in the age of Zeus. These are the claims that the knowledge of the statesman is the same as that of the slave master, the king, and the household manager (259a1–c4) and the claim that the statesman rules by means of commands. The first claim is either literally true or meaningless in the age of Cronos, since there are neither families nor political regimes at that time, while it is clearly disputable in our own age.[156] The second claim is also problematic in a similar way in the age of Cronos, as there can hardly be any gap between the god's knowledge and the performance of any action in the world, unlike in the case of the statesman of the age of Zeus. A command implies the possibility of disobedience, something that the god does not face; he does not need to cajole, persuade, or threaten anybody. *Vis-à-vis* the god, no human being is free to disobey.[157] Conversely, we might say that human beings are perfectly tame in that era, whereas they are not perfectly tame in our era.

The same point is illustrated in the relationship between the god at the helm of the whole and the subordinate shepherd-gods or shepherd-daimons. This relation is not, strictly speaking, a hierarchical one, where the god at the helm of the whole issues the commands and the shepherd-daimons act like heralds, transmitting them to their charges. In fact, the Stranger takes great care not to suggest that the shepherd-daimons are anything less than fully commanding rulers, since they must "fit" the result of the division, which had characterized the shepherd of human beings as an autonomous ruler. Thus,

[156] Moreover, the shepherd-daimon erases the distinction between household manager and slave master, as Griswold Jr. (1989, 151) notes.
[157] See Nightingale (1996, 85).

he calls them the "co-rulers" (*sunarchontes* 272e7) of the god, and refers to them interchangeably as *daimones* and *theoi* (cf. 271d7, 272e5, 272e7), just as the god at the helm of the whole is occasionally called a *daimōn*, even if he is also said to be the greatest of them (272e7). The greatest god does not have to tell them to do anything; once he lets go of the whole, for example, they let go of the parts of the whole assigned to them, "already knowing" (272e8) what had happened, unlike workers employed in building a house, who have to be told what to do, not knowing the purposes or plans of the architect. The tasks of both of these gods can thus be seen as two aspects of a single form of divine care, as the interchangeability of the appellations *theos* and *daimōn* suggest.[158]

By contrast, in the age of Zeus the question of the effectiveness of commands (and thus the relationship of statesmanship to the *technē* of rhetoric, cf. 304a1–2) becomes a pressing issue, since the knowledge of the statesman requires the cooperation of other arts to be effective in the world, as we have seen. In particular, the forms of knowledge represented by the *technai*, which supply the lack of divine shepherding, are no longer automatically in accord with the knowledge of the statesman or ruler of the whole; and a relationship which in the age of Cronos is devoid of dispute now becomes the subject of contention. The *technai* dispute the claim of the statesman to rule, even after statesmanship has been separated from the art of nurture, as the sequel to the myth shows. They may agree that statesmanship has the "largest" part of the care of the *polis*, as the great god is the "greatest" *daimōn* (cf. 281b7–d3, 287a7ff.); but they claim a share in this care too. This is the ultimate reason why the myth does not manage to produce a complete and clear picture of the statesman, since there is no

---

[158] See Miller Jr. (1980, 128n5): "the key distinction is not that between god and demi-god, theos and daimon, but, rather, that between the god as such and the shepherd form he assumes in the age of Cronos. This is the difference between the god seen theo-logically, as in 269b–270b, and the god seen mythically, as in 270b–274e."

divine analogue in the relationship between the greatest god and the other *daimones* to the contentious relationship between the statesman and all the other artisans. The statesman, after the myth, is merely the greatest "caregiver" among them, like the god among the *daimones*, but this, as the Stranger will implicitly point out (281c7–d2), is insufficient for the full determination of statesmanship. Let us now turn our attention to the age of "Zeus" in order to flesh out these claims.

The universe under its own power: 272d–274d

The final section of the myth is in a way the most confusing, since the Stranger describes both the moment in which the god lets go of the cosmos and the moment in which he takes control of it again before returning to a description of the period during which the god is not in control of the motion of cosmos. Though the Stranger signals at 273e4–5 that the narrative is to be read discontinuously—in other words, that one must understand the section from 272d to 273e as a description of the effects of the release of the cosmos by the god on the cosmos as a whole until the god decides to take control of the universe again, and the section from 273e to the end as a description of the effects of the very same release on animals and human beings—the transition is obscure, which has enabled some commentators to claim that the Stranger must be describing at the very end of the myth (from 273e onwards) a third period of control by the god.[159] As we shall see, however, the Stranger follows the same pattern as in the first part of the myth: he first describes the effects of the original experience at the root of all the three stories that are the sources of the myth (the great reversal of motion) on the universe itself; then specifies the effects of that reversal on animals in general; and finally draws the "political" implications of the reversal for human beings more specifically. Thus, while in the first part of the myth he explains the effects of the reversal of this motion in one direction for the universe,

---

[159] See especially Carone (2005, 129–130).

animals, and human beings, he now explains these effects when the reversal happens towards the present direction.

These effects are, broadly speaking, as follows. First of all, the universe, after a brief adjustment period, tries to hang on to its divinely imposed order, caring for itself; but over time the bodily element in its constitution disorders it, to the point that the god must step in again to rescue it and repeat the process. Second, each animal species must also attempt to preserve itself, imitating the universe, since animals are no longer under the care of distinct gods. But in doing so each animal species must come into conflict with the others, which generates disorder, and must reproduce itself sexually, which also generates certain kinds of disorder. Finally, human beings must also attempt to preserve themselves through the use of their god-given *phronēsis*, just like the cosmos, but their *phronēsis* is split into the different arts and crafts, which generates further disorder and necessitates the cyclical intervention of statesmen. Let us examine each of these effects in more detail.

Effects on the cosmos as a whole

The Stranger first proceeds to describe (272d6–e3) the moment in which the god releases the universe, which we have already discussed in some detail (see above, pp. 134–145). This is the time when the earth *genos* is exhausted, that is, when the maximum number of bodies, deposited there in the previous age of Zeus by the normal pattern of generation, have come up from the earth and vanished, and thus there are no longer any left there. It is also the time, as we saw earlier, when each soul has given back all of its generations, that is, when it has lived backwards in all the bodies with which it was previously associated in the previous age when the universe was moving under its own power, and thus the time when it has fallen into the earth as seed (for each successive backwards reincarnation) for the appointed number of times (272e1–3). It is at this time that the helmsman of the whole lets go of the handle of the rudder and retires to his observation post (*periōpēn*).

The god thus ceases to guide the whole, but remains present as an observer, at the prow of the ship looking ahead for the dangers to come rather than at the stern guiding its course.[160] Similarly, the subordinate gods let go of the parts of the whole which they used to supervise, ceasing to care (*epimeleias* 273a1) for them. Someone else is at the stern, hand to the tiller, namely, the "fated and inborn desire" (*epithumia*) of the universe itself and its parts. This appears to be the desire of the cosmos for its former state, that is, its previous order (*kosmos*) under the god.

After an initial disruption caused by the change in direction as the god lets go of the cosmos (273a1–3), the "phronetic" element in its constitution reasserts itself, and the cosmos now goes on arranging/ordering its own course (*katakosmoumenos* 273a7, echoing what the god himself did earlier, *katakosmēseōs* 271e3, that is, making itself into a *kosmos*), since it has power and care (*epimeleian* 273a7) over itself and its parts, like the gods used to have over it and its parts (cf. 273a1). This ability to arrange its own course, to make itself into a *kosmos*, an ordered whole, depends, the Stranger now says (273b1–3), on the cosmos' ability to remember the god's instruction, that is, the order granted to it by the god, which it desires.

The cosmos' ability to remember the god's instructions (and hence to hang on to its order) is affected by the passage of time (273b3–4). At first, the cosmos is close to the god, and thus remembers those instructions clearly, or rather, fulfills them clearly (*apetelei* 273b3). In this state the world is full of good things, and its order is well preserved. At the end of the cycle, however, the god's instruction is only remembered or fulfilled in a blurred sort of way, though it never, the Stranger

[160] See Brisson (1995, 357), and Skemp (1987, 97). The god never completely abandons the whole, contrary to what is sometimes too glibly asserted. Like the captain of a ship, he must sometimes be at the prow and sometimes at the stern.

implies, ceases to be fulfilled in some way. In this state, by contrast, the world is full of evils.

The reason for this forgetfulness or inability to hang on to its god-given order (273b4–7) is that the *sōmatoeides*, the bodily *eidos* (a wonderful oxymoron of Platonic metaphysics) in the mixture that is the cosmos—that is, a mixture of the bodily *eidos* and the soul, as a living being—does not allow it. The *sōmatoeides* is the ordered form (the *eidos*) of body, *sōma*, which is the original nature or condition (273b5, b8) of the whole before the god orders it; but the body, as the principle of disorder in the universe, ultimately reasserts itself, giving birth to all the things that are harsh and unjust in the universe.

Remembrance is always of things that have an *eidos*, a form, never of chaos. For the cosmos to remember the god's instructions thus means for it to preserve the *eidē* that make indeterminate body into ordered body, into the *sōmatoeides*. But the nature of body is entropic, to use a modern term: it tends to lose structure, not to gain it, to cease to have looks (*eidē*), and thus to look "blurred," eventually sinking into the sea of dissimilarity (273d6): the place, in other words, of what is unlimited (*apeiron* 273d6), to which reason or form does not belong, in which likeness, which makes bodily things categorizable into *eidē* (by giving them distinct looks), has ceased to subdue the chaotic nature of body. Only soul (or life, as modern science would perhaps say) struggles, though ultimately (in the very long run) in a futile way, against the creeping disorder, preserving the structure of parts of the whole while that which is without soul simply runs its course and decays into disorder, slowly or quickly.[161] Care, we begin to understand, is a process by which soul makes body achieve and preserve form (*eidos*),

[161] It should be noted, if only in passing, that in some ways this is a picture not entirely dissimilar to that depicted by some modern cosmologies: losing organization or complexity (eidetic structure), expanding ad infinitum, the universe eventually dissolves into the chaos of random motion and atomic decay.

or, perhaps better, the process by which soul orders body so that it resembles as much as possible its proper *eidos* (e.g., the *eidos* of its proper animal "species").

The Stranger suggests that such is the final stage of the universe in which we live, the "end of the universe" (*telos hapantōn* 273e4–5), and the end of the story in chronological terms; no other periods are described after this.[162] It is at this point that the god, who cares for the whole, having put it into order (*kosmēsas* 273d4, having made it into a cosmos), and who does not want to see it sink into the boundless sea of dissimilarity, again resumes his position at the tiller, restarting the whole cycle all over again. At the end of the world the god saves the disintegrating whole and redeems it by making it immortal once again, that is, by renovating its order and thus preparing it for a further journey on its own (cf. 273e5–6). To be sure, this is not the end of the world in the sense that it is merely the start of another cycle; but it is the end of this world, the world that we know, and which we perceive (cf. 272b3). As the Stranger puts it, what he has described is "this end" of all things (*touto . . . telos* 273e4–5), namely one end of all things in an endless cycle in which things are again renewed by the action of the god and once again meet their end.

What the Stranger's story means, in other words, is that the present world is "in between." It has not, and will not for a long (mythically long: "myriads of revolutions" 270a8) time reach the "end of all things" that the Stranger has just described; but it is not, either, close to the moment when

[162] Rowe (1995b, note to 273e3–5) sees that the Stranger must refer to the end of the world, though he takes it, incorrectly, to mean that what the Stranger has described as "ending" is not the age of Zeus but some other age, i.e., that "the end of all things" means "the end of the [previous] cycle." But for the Stranger to speak of the "end of the world" makes much more sense if he means the end of this age, the one we live in, which indeed represents all things to us. At the same time, the Stranger is also noting the chronological boundary of the story he is currently telling; so, in this sense, Skemp's translation of *touto . . . telos hapantōn eirētai* as "this is the tale full told," also seems to capture part of the Stranger's meaning.

the god lets go of it, and in fact it is also separated from that moment by a mythically long time. Present human life is thus located in between an original condition of order and similarity, full of goods, and a final, not yet reached (nor strictly speaking "reachable" in historical time) condition of disorder and dissimilarity, full of evils.[163] This is a condition of only partial dissimilarity and disorder, and thus partial intelligibility and order, where bodies can, for the most part, be categorized according to *eidē*, but where they are not identical to these *eidē*. The flux of *genesis*, in other words, is not entirely without patterns and regularities; the universe hangs on to its order with decreasing effectiveness, but with some effectiveness nonetheless.

Effects on animals

The Stranger resumes the story by skipping over the intervening age of Cronos; if the god rescues the cosmos, he must then get it ready for release again. Having "twisted it" or "wound it up" again (*strephthentos . . . au* 273e6–7), so that it is now ready to unwind, that is, to move in the direction of the present cycle of generation, the god releases it and the process recommences.[164] The "age" of all creatures stops again,

[163] Cf. *Theaetetus* 176a5–8, where Socrates tells Theodorus that there must always be something contrary to the good in human life: the world is full of evils and goods, not one or the other.

[164] *Pace* Carone (2005, 130), *strephthentos* at 273e7 does not imply that the god takes control of the motion of the cosmos in the present period. Because she is antecedently committed to her three-period view, she does not see that the Stranger is merely summarizing what happens in the age of Cronos, namely the "twisting" of the world's disordered yarn again into thread, or the recurrence of the age of Cronos. The Stranger is thus saying that once the cosmos has been put in order or "wound up" after almost falling into complete disorder (turning into yarn again, we might say) it is let go again for another cycle, but while earlier he described what happened to the entire cosmos during that cycle (273a1–273e5; note *metastrephomenos*, which one might translate "unwinding" at 273a1, contrasting with *strephthentos* at 273e7), he will now discuss what happens to the animals and human beings in it. The persistent impression that the Stranger must be describing three

and "new" contrary things are given back to them, to wit: they start to age, to die, and their bodies (rather than their souls; cf. 272e1–2) fall to the earth in the end, that is, they start new lives and hence acquire new experiences. In doing so, the Stranger emphasizes that all things imitate and follow (*apomimoumena kai sunakolountha* 274a1) what happens to the whole.

This means, first of all, that just as the whole gets old—that is, experiences the life cycle as a form of aging, going inexorably towards its death—living beings do so too. The Stranger goes on to emphasize the concomitant aspects of the process of aging (274a1–3): conception, generation, and nurture, the three main aspects of the life cycle. The "imitation" represented by these three things began to "accompany" at this time (*suneipeto*) all the parts of the whole "by necessity." It is not, however, entirely clear what this means, since the cosmos is neither conceived nor generated nor nurtured, and hence living beings would seem to be unable to imitate it by conceiving, generating, and nurturing themselves.

The Stranger clarifies this somewhat in the next sentence (274a3–b1). Just as the cosmos is now *autokrator*, that is, responsible on its own for its self-care (which, as we have seen, consists in the preservation of its god-given eidetic order) so now each part of the whole is also responsible for its

rather than two cycles is due to the Stranger's way of telling the tale: first the age of Cronos is described in detail, then the letting go of the cosmos is described in detail along with the effects on the whole, then the Stranger notes that the cosmos is saved and put back in order (the god comes back), and then he returns to discuss what happens to animals and people during that time when the universe is forgetting its instruction from the god, especially what happens to people ("the point of the tale," 274b1). At no point does the Stranger ever suggest that there is some third period that is important for understanding the point of the myth. We need not speak here about all the other problems involved in postulating a third cycle for the economy of the myth and its political point: why would the god decide to return but not rule human beings directly through the various subordinate divine presences present in the age of Cronos? Did the god decide that he had made a mistake during the age of Cronos, and has now "learned" the correct way of ruling human beings?

own care "as far as possible," which consists principally in its own (ultimately futile) attempt to preserve itself as a distinct *eidos*, or, more precisely, to preserve its constitutive unity of body and form. Care in both cases (the universe and each living being) is what we might call *eidos*-preserving behavior. This is why the parts of the cosmos can be said to imitate the cosmos, even though the cosmos does not reproduce or nurture itself, since conception, generation and nurture are precisely those processes in the life-cycle of living beings that ensure the minimal continuity of the species (the *eidos*) in both space and time.

The god's injunction to each part of the universe to take care of itself by itself, that is, to be *autokrator*, like the cosmos, is qualified: they are to do so as far as possible. Their ability to tend to themselves on their own is limited in two basic ways: first, each individual animal must preserve itself by feeding on other living beings which are not necessarily at its immediate disposal; and second, (most) species depend for their preservation over time on sexual reproduction, that is, on the contingent cooperation of pairs of its members. By contrast, in the age of Cronos nourishment was always at the disposal of all animals, which meant that each animal was independent of every other animal in this respect; and no sexual reproduction existed, which meant that each species preserved itself over time automatically, independently of the actions of its members and without "mixing" among them.

These two sorts of dependence of each living being on other living beings for its own care imply that nurture and reproduction in the age of Zeus can only imperfectly preserve the unity of *eidos* and body that constitutes each species, since their normal operation disturbs the balance of the *eidē* in the universe. This is so because (one presumes) as the numbers of each species fluctuate wildly, and some die off, in the "struggle for existence," and because offspring vary, unpredictably, from their parents, each species comes to "look" different, and thus eventually comes to embody—with the passage of time—a different *eidos*, or rather, falls away from its original *eidos*. What was a static equilibrium among all species in the age of Cronos is now dynamic due to the operation of nurture; what was perfectly regular in the self-perpetuation of the unity of *eidos* and body in a species by means of earth-birth (which, we might imagine, was a kind of "cloning") is now unpredictable, slowly effacing the *eidos* of the species.[165]

More precisely, the regular operation of the processes of nurture and reproduction slowly destroys the unity of *eidos* and body that constitutes each species and the whole, a unity that the god put together in the age of Cronos. This leads eventually to the condition of "dissimilarity" that the Stranger noted was characteristic of the end of the world: each individual body becomes unlike all others, losing its connection to the *eidē*. Generation and its associated processes (conception and nurture) are both preservative and destructive of eidetic order in the cosmos, and thus (presumably) also in the city, since they are both the way in which each living being reproduces the bodily manifestation of its *eidos* and the way in which they efface it from the world, that is, the way in which they sever the connection between *eidos* and body. This is something that the statesman will have to take into account, as indeed he is shown to do at the very end of the dialogue (310a7ff.): he must take care to preserve the delicate balance between the *eidos* of courage and that of moderation, both of which can be effaced (by becoming overly exaggerated or distorted, as it were) from the city through the normal process of reproduction (see chapter 6). The myth thus brings out the essential features of the cosmos (or rather, of life) that limit the potential of statesmanship to order the city.

---

[165] Modern evolutionary biology would, of course, argue that some *eidē* vanish but new ones emerge. Yet in the myth the process accords with the general decay of the whole into dissimilarity.

Effects on human beings

Let us now turn to the final and most important sections of the myth. The Stranger once again says that we are now at the point towards which and for the sake of which the entire *logos* has rushed (274b1–2). What follows is a description not of what happens in general to living beings in the cosmos with the turn and the coming of the age of Zeus, but of what happens to human beings in particular, and indeed the "political" implications of this turn.

The Stranger declines to go into details as to what in particular happens to any other species (274b2–4), as this would take too long. Yet what happens to human beings has something to do with what happens to other species generally (274b5–d2). While human beings were deprived (they are left alone, as the Stranger says: *aperēmōthentes* 274b6) of the care of the *daimōn* who possessed and grazed them in the age of Cronos, a care which tended to their every bodily need, the other beasts, and in particular those whose nature was harsh to begin with but was suppressed under the rule of the gods, became wild (274b8). Human beings, at the time, were weak and unguarded, and thus an easy prey for the beasts; in particular, they were without contrivances or machines (*amēchanoi*) and without the *technai* (274c1), and thus did not know yet how to provide for (*porizesthai* 274c3) or to protect themselves, since need (*chreian* 274c4) had never before compelled them to do so; their nurture was "automatic" before. They were thus in great *aporia* (cf. 274c5), like the cosmos at the end of time (273d5), without resource or way out, a *poros*, that is, something that would allow them to provide for themselves/make their way in the world.

The Stranger now says that it is from this situation that we get the old legends (*ta palai lechthenta* 274c5–6) concerning the gifts that were given by the gods, gifts that were accompanied, he adds, seemingly irrelevantly, by a necessary teaching (*didachēs*) and education (*paideuseōs*; 274c7). The gifts are the *technai* and a few *mēchanai*, contrivances, "machines" or ready-made technologies (274c7–d2) such as fire or seeds. These are not granted to human beings "ready to use," so to speak, but require much of that "necessary teaching and education" that the Stranger suggested accompanied them in order to become truly useful. The Stranger does not say, however, that the gods simply gave these gifts to human beings; that would be a too blatant contradiction with what he has just said, namely, that human beings had just been left alone by the gods, or rather, that they have just been bereft of their care (274b5). What the gods (or rather, the god) seem to grant human beings is *phronēsis*, just as the god gave the universe *phronēsis* (269d1). But since *phronēsis* is always granted in the form of arts or skills ("cognitive capital," we might say) that cannot all be embodied in the same person, the ancient legends speak of different gods granting us different arts.[166]

The *technai* allow human beings to exercise care over themselves (cf. 274d6), and in particular over their nurture; they therefore cannot be said to constitute a direct form of care on the part of the gods, even if the Stranger were to endorse the

---

[166] The idea that the arts of care cannot all be embodied in the same person is only implicit in the dialogue (see the discussion above of the problems with the shepherd analogy), not explicitly stated at this point in the myth (though it *was* stated at *Sophist* 232e6–233a7) . It is worth noting that in the myth told by Protagoras in the *Protagoras* (a similar story about how human beings acquired the arts, though with some significant differences, as I note below), Prometheus distributes each art (except statesmanship, to which he had no access) to different human beings because one person's knowledge "suffices to take care of many others" (322c–d). It is only the knowledge of statesmanship (glossed in Protagoras' myth as "justice and a sense of shame") that is distributed to all, since one person's knowledge of justice or virtue does *not* suffice for many others; all must have it. Ironically, though the Stranger's arguments contradict Protagoras on this point (statesmanship is certainly not granted to all, or even to anyone!) it would seem that the Eleatic stranger agrees with Protagoras that the knowledge of the statesman does not suffice to *fully* take care of many others. Ideally, *everyone* would have the knowledge of statesmanship, and law would not be needed (see 295b and discussion in chapter 5).

truth of the reports. The *technai* make the shepherding care of the god unnecessary; they distribute some of the knowledge which before was the province of the gods (cf. the multiple *technai* of the shepherd, 268a6–b7) to human beings. Insofar as each of the arts are developments of human reason (a divine gift by the god to the cosmos, and by extension to human beings) that substitute for one or more of the tasks that the gods used to perform for us, then it is divine. However, the Stranger associates the discovery of the arts not immediately with the gods but with necessity (274c4); without the arts, human beings would have been destroyed by predation. Without the whip of necessity, in other words, human *phronēsis*, the gift of the gods, would have remained unused, and would not have developed into the several arts.

The *technai* thus are and are not the gifts of the gods: they are in the sense that their discovery is only possible by means of the *phronēsis* which derives ultimately from the divine, and in fact is nothing other than the divine in us (the result of the providential ordering of the whole by the god), and to that extent the stories preserve a truth; but they are not in the sense that no Olympian gods ever came down from heaven to grant them to us, and to that extent these stories, like the stories from which the myth itself is woven, distort matters. Only the situation of human need forces human beings to exercise that gift, and thus to discover (some of) the *technai*. Without such need it is unclear whether human beings do exercise *phronēsis*, as the picture of life in the age of Cronos, and the Stranger's doubt as to the happiness of human beings in that age, sufficiently showed.

At any rate, and more importantly for our purposes at this point, need makes human beings exercise this gift in specific ways: the *technai* that are discovered are those that make life "livable," as Young Socrates will unwittingly imply later on (299e8–10), that is, comfortable enough for the human *eidos* to be embodied and preserved into the indefinite future and to free human beings for other things. In other words, need does not make human beings exercise *phronēsis* so as to find all the *technai*, but only some particular ones, as we can gather from the Stranger's choice of examples.[167]

The first *mēchanē* (let us think for the moment of *mēchanai* as ur-*technai*, originators of *technai*) the Stranger mentions is fire, proverbially stolen from heaven by Prometheus ("foresight"). Fire, and the *technai* that depend on the use of fire, are all related to the care and preservation of the species (the human *eidos* in its bodily manifestation). The fire-arts warm human beings during the inclement winters of the age of Zeus (contrast with the age of Cronos, 272a5–7), keep away the wild beasts, and provide energy for cooking and the making of metal implements, an art that is associated with Hephaistos, god of the forge, who is named next. Fire indeed promises to preserve the *eidos* of human beings in its bodily manifestation into the future, as befits an art said to come from "foresight." Fire, furthermore, is associated in Plato with the primeval illumination of the understanding (cf. *Philebus* 16c5–7), that is, with the very origin of all the *technai*.[168] It illuminates the night of the world, just as *phronēsis*—the "fire" given by the gods to human beings—illuminates the place of increasing dissimilarity that is the bodily world, and thus staves off the vanishing of the *eidos* from the age.

The mention of Hephaistos and his "fellow-artisan" Athena immediately after the mention of Prometheus signals a clear allusion to the story of Prometheus and its consequences for human beings as told in Hesiod, for it is only in that story that Athena appears as the "co-artisan" of Hephaistos, helping

---

[167] Cf. Miller Jr. (1980, 52).

[168] As the passage in the *Philebus* makes clear, Prometheus brings fire as well as the method that Socrates recommends to Protarchos, and that is further described in 18b7ff., for the discovery of eidetic structure in the unlimited and multiplicity in what is a unity; the method is furthermore characteristic of all the *technai*, according to Socrates. Fire is characterized by Socrates as that which illuminates the most (16c7), just as the method he is about to recommend illuminates the world more than anything else.

him build Pandora. According to Hesiod, who tells two versions of these "old tales" (see *Theogony* 536ff., *Works and Days* 42ff.), Zeus wanted to punish human beings for the trick that Prometheus had played upon him once. This trick is described in the *Theogony* as follows: there was once a "test," which consisted in the division of an ox between gods and human beings. For reasons that are not clear, Prometheus—human foresight—got to perform the division, daring "to match his wits against the almighty Zeus" (Dorothea Wender's translation). But instead of dividing the ox honestly, Prometheus attempted to trick Zeus by presenting him with the worthless bones wrapped in fat, and giving the valuable "marbled inner parts," wrapped in the worthless stomach, to human beings. Symbolically, Hesiod seems to be suggesting that human foresight "got ahead of itself" and failed to honor the gods properly by keeping from Zeus what was Zeus' due.

In the *Works and Days* the narrator does not describe the particular trick that Prometheus played on Zeus, but prefaces the entire narrative by saying that the gods "desire to keep the stuff of life (*bion*; cf. *bion* at *Statesman* 274d3) hidden from us"; otherwise human beings would have a careless existence, without labor, much as in the age of Cronos in the myth of the *Statesman*. Prometheus, or human foresight, therefore, wanted to alleviate the cares of human beings, indeed, to abolish labor, and at first succeeded in part by stealing fire, which Zeus had hidden as punishment to human beings for the trick that they (that is, their foresight) had tried to play on him.

But Zeus then came up with a different idea. He ordered Hephaistos and Athena (Hephaistos' fellow artisan in this enterprise) to make a lovely woman, Pandora. In the *Works and Days*, which contains the more detailed version of what follows, Pandora brings a gift—a beautiful box—to Epimetheus ("hindsight"). Epimetheus thoughtlessly (that is, without foresight) opens the box, which contains all the evils that beset human beings in this life, and which fly away, instead of being safely contained. Only "hope" is left in the box. In the shorter version of the story told in the *Theogony*, Pandora is given to human beings in general, who are seduced by her erotic charms; from her comes the "race of womankind" who, the narrator says in very bitter tones, bring harm to human beings and are no help to them in poverty. Pandora, the product of Hephaistos and his fellow artisan Athena, is thus associated both with the evils of the human condition and with the erotic necessity of human life.

In the myth, the Stranger associates Hephaistos and his fellow artisan with the *technai*. Implicitly, therefore, he is suggesting that the *technai* are, colloquially, a "Pandora's Box." They are seductive, indeed truly beautiful, but dangerous. The gifts of Hephaistos and Athena are in no way unambiguously good. When used without foresight, they unleash a myriad of evils on the world, though the hope always remains that they can be used for good. In particular, Hephaistos presides over the arts of making metal implements, which allow human beings to wage savage war on one another, while Athena, the armed goddess, who is said to have sprung from the head of Zeus in full armor and who counsels Zeus "in both good and evil plans" (Hesiod, *Theogony* 886–900; the quotation is from line 900), stands for the arts of generalship, judgment, and rhetoric (cf. *Statesman* 303d4–305d1), which counsel the statesman but can themselves be used for both good and evil purposes. Neither the arts of war nor those of peace, however, are identical with statesmanship, as the Stranger will show later (303d4ff.).[169]

The arts that Hephaistos and Athena provide to human beings thus allow them to become "wild" rather than "tame." To be sure, this wildness protects them against the natural wildness of many other animals (274b7–c1) in the age of Zeus: with metal weapons no animal is a match for a human being, and in fact many of them become his prey. But this presents

[169] Contrast this with the myth told by Protagoras in the *Protagoras*, where Protagoras claims that the art of war is a part of the art of statesmanship (322b).

a problem, since human wildness can and is normally turned against members of their own species. Neither Athena nor Hephaistos provide human beings with a *technē* for taming themselves in their relations with their fellows; neither, in other words, stands for the art of ruling. Athena, it is true, in standing for the noblest "political" arts, makes the *polis* in some sense possible, but it is a diseased *polis*, a *polis* without statesmanship, like Athens (the city of the two Athenas).

In fact, the Stranger conspicuously fails to mention Zeus, the god who stands for the art of statesmanship itself, among the gods that grant human beings gifts of *technai*.[170] The implication seems to be that human beings are not compelled by need to discover the *technē* of statesmanship. This point should be stressed, for it is the source of much misunderstanding of the lessons of the myth: statesmanship is not among the *technai* said to be discovered by necessity; it is rather associated with "hope," what was left in Pandora's box. But how can this be so?

As I remarked earlier, the situation of need is what compels human beings to use the gift of the god (*phronēsis*) to find a solution to the problem of their own preservation, that is, of the preservation of the human *eidos* in its bodily manifestation in the age of Zeus. But the *technē* or *epistēmē* of statesmanship seems to be unnecessary for this task, as the Stranger implies later with some amazement (302a3–6): the *polis* is strong by nature, not (or not simply) by *technē*. The *polis* is a self-organizing being, that is, one that usually preserves its *eidos* without the operation of a supervisory *technē*, merely

[170] Contrast, again, with the myth of the *Protagoras*, where Protagoras explicitly notes (322c) that Zeus granted human beings the equivalent of the art of statesmanship (a sense of justice and shame and the art of war, which is a part of the art of statesmanship). The myth of the *Statesman* is thoroughly anti-Protagorean in its political implications. See also Narcy (1995, 230), Schäfer (2001, 127–128), Howland (1998, 265), and Miller Jr. (1980, 52) for different views about why the Stranger fails to indicate that Zeus grants the art of statesmanship to human beings.

on the strength of its laws, which are decidedly second best in comparison with the knowledge of the statesman.

This is reflected too in the general scarcity of statesmanship. While farmers, smiths, rhetoricians, generals, weavers, and judges of varying but undoubtedly real knowledge can be readily found in all times and places, true statesmen are exceedingly rare (cf. 292e4–293a4, where the Stranger and Young Socrates agree on this point); indeed, our normal "political" experience tells us that this is so. We are apt to bestow the title of "true statesman" only on few, very select individuals, whom we think of as saviors, if not so much of the whole human race, at least of our particular polity: Solon, Lycurgus, Washington, Lincoln, Churchill, FDR. Only extremely acute need, in other words, caused more often by human beings rather than by nature, seems to be able to compel human beings to discover the *technē* of statesmanship; otherwise, the human *eidos* seems to muddle along, if in a decaying fashion.

Yet the *polis* without statesmanship is always at risk. The arts that ensure the self-preservation of men in the face of the wildness of nature in the age of Zeus do not give anyone full insight into the divine order of the whole; they depend on partial insights that can be exploited for specific tasks (building fortifications, killing animals, forging weapons), but not for organizing the whole of human life (deciding when fighting is appropriate is not the province of the general, for example, as we learn later). Moreover, the possession of such arts makes human beings proud (a point that the Stranger does not emphasize, to be sure), inciting them to conflict. We might say that the gifts of the gods, like the evils in Pandora's box, save human beings from the wildness of nature at the expense of destroying their original tameness.

Statesmanship is necessary if this condition of technically-mediated conflict is not to eventually destroy the city. Thus, though statesmanship is a protective art just as many of the *technai* are, and as the rest of the dialogue clearly implies, its protection is required not against the hostility of nature (for that, the arts under the aegis of Prometheus, Hephaistos, Athena, and Demeter suffice) but against the ravages of the *technai* themselves, the evils (or dubious benefits) of Pandora's box.[171]

We can now see the deeper parallels between the statesman and the god. The god, after all, "saves" the cosmos only at the time of its direst need; only then does the god return to the tiller again. Similarly, the myth suggests, the statesman can only emerge at the time of direst need; at any other time he would not be accepted.[172] He will appear like a god among human beings (303b4) not just due to his superior knowledge, but insofar as he can only be awaited, not produced on demand. The idea of the statesman is the hope of salvation, like the mythical hope that the god will save the universe again from falling into dissimilarity.

Furthermore, just as the god's taking control of the cosmos to save it involves a certain amount of death and destruction, so does the arrival of the statesman in the city (cf. 308e4–309a7); people must be killed, others made into slaves. The providential return of the statesman is not without some (necessary perhaps) disruption. And as the god leaves the cosmos to its own devices

---

[171] This identification of kingship as regulator of the *technai*, determining what are their real benefits and harms and thus deciding if they are worth learning, is also found in the short myth about writing that Socrates tells Phaedrus in the *Phaedrus* (274c5–275b2; see especially 274e7–9). See also *Laws* 678a–679d and context, where the Athenian attributes human conflict to the discovery of the *technai* unregulated by law or statesmanship. Thus, contrary to Griswold Jr. (1989, 152), and Rosen (1995, 68ff.), statesmanship is not simply, in Griswold Jr.'s words, "the art of defending the citizens from a fundamentally hostile nature"; in fact, the myth suggests that if political science is necessary to human beings, it is not necessary for protecting them against a fundamentally hostile nature but to protect them from the unbridled consequences of the uses of the arts. This is never stated explicitly by the Stranger, but it is implicit in much of the argument of the rest of the dialogue; at any rate, the unnamed *technē* that decides whether music and all the other *cheirotechnai* are to be learned is surely no other than statesmanship itself (cf. 304b1–c6).

[172] See chapters 5 and 6. Cf. also Arends (1999, 109n22).

after ordering it properly, the statesman leaves the city to its own devices after ordering it properly, as we shall see (311a1–2; see also chapter 6), that is, after giving it laws or creating the imperfect order to which the city must always hold, despite its increasing inappropriateness to conditions dissimilar to those for which it was created (cf. 294a10ff., 295c7ff.), like the universe holds on, with increasing difficulty, to the instruction of its creator before nearly sinking into the sea of dissimilarity.

Moreover, just as the god regulates the universe in part by regulating its mode of "generation," the statesman does a similar thing in the city, as we have already indicated. He regulates marriages in order to counteract the destructive tendencies of natural generation by "reversing," through proper education, the natural tendency of human beings to seek partners similar in character to themselves, just as the god reverses the normal cycle of generation, suppressing sexuality and entirely eliminating the destructive tendencies of generation.

Finally, the fact that it is only in the age "which the *logos* says is under Zeus" (272b2) that statesmanship is supposed to emerge points to the fundamental absence of statesmanship in our age. "Zeus" in the Stranger's story stands for the absent god (for our age is devoid of gods, cf. *aperēmōthentes* 274b6) and at the same time for the highest god (since "Zeus" in Plato usually denotes the highest god). The god who stands for statesmanship, unlike Athena and Hephaistos, is the god conspicuous for its absence in the story about the gifts of the gods. Similarly, statesmen are always conspicuous for their absence, hoped for in our need but more often than not absent, like the "Zeus" of the age. One might say that "Zeus" stands for the need to cope with the absence of the statesman.

The Stranger concludes the myth (274d4–e3) by repeating that human beings are no longer under the care (*epimeleias*) of the gods, and thus that they started to take care of themselves by means of all these *technai* and *mēchanai*; in particular, it became necessary for them to take charge of their own care (*epimeleian*), just as the entire cosmos does. Human beings jointly imitate and follow the cosmos all the time, now in this way (the way just described), then (in the age of Cronos) in that other way (namely, by growing younger and letting themselves be taken care of by the gods). Statesmanship must also be, therefore, a form of imitation of the kind of care the god provides for the cosmos in the age of Cronos, but the Stranger has not yet fully described it as an art; right now it appears to be, like the god who directs the whole among the shepherd-daimons, only the biggest of the arts, imitating the activity of the highest god as the other arts jointly imitate the divine shepherd of human beings. In order to determine its exact place among the arts, we will require a new paradigm, that of weaving, which indicates, as we have seen, how the statesman organizes the great hierarchy of arts that gives rise to the city in such a way so as to mitigate the conflicts that the possession of arts would otherwise give rise to.

4. Knowledge

THROUGHOUT THE *STATESMAN,* the Stranger assumes that statesmanship is a form of knowledge which can also be understood as an art (*technē*). As we have seen, this knowledge is characterized as theoretical, directive, and autonomous early in the division, and as a productive art later. Moreover, in the myth the Stranger suggests that the knowledge of the statesman has something to do with the intuition of the traces of divine order in the cosmos, and in the section on the rule of law the Stranger will further argue that those who do not have such knowledge are somehow capable of imitating it, sometimes well and sometimes badly. Yet it is not entirely clear what the Stranger means by saying that the statesman has a form of knowledge or an art, or how such knowledge can be used to regulate the disorder of human affairs. In any case the Stranger nowhere explicitly clarifies what he means by knowledge.

To be sure, the Stranger does give us some important clues about his views, but these clues are scattered throughout the *Sophist* (in the discussion of images and of true opinion) and the *Statesman* (especially in the discussion of paradigms and measure). In this chapter we shall take a detour from the main thread of the argument in order to see how these disparate discussions suggest that the Stranger understands the knowledge of the statesman as a capacity to "read" the eidetic order of the cosmos, not just a knowledge of some eidetic structure or another, and in particular to "read" the forms of order—the noble, the just, and the good—in such a way that these forms of order can serve as concrete standards for particular actions. Moreover, the Stranger's implicit view of knowledge also has as a consequence that "opinion" or "judgment" is nothing but the imitation of knowledge (though true and false opinion represent two different kinds of imitation), and that knowledge of eidetic structure can secure the truth of some of these judgments.

Technē and epistēmē

Statesmanship in the *Statesman* is characterized as both a *technē* (e.g., 287d4, 296c5, 300e7, 311c1–2) and an *epistēmē* (e.g., 258b3–5); and the Stranger does not appear to make a distinction between these terms in the *Sophist* either. He nowhere proposes a division of *epistēmē* into technical and non-technical forms, and the modern terminological distinction between "art" (*technē*) and "science" (*epistēmē*)—the one imprecise and not governed by rules, the other precise and governed by rules—is alien to the dialogues of the trilogy (*Theaetetus*, *Sophist*, *Statesman*) and indeed to Plato.[173] Moreover, it is generally accepted that Plato, unlike Aristotle, does not use "technical" terminology, and often uses more than one word to mean the same thing. Commentators have therefore tended to assume, with some justification, that the terms *epistēmē* and *technē* are used interchangeably in the dialogue.[174]

Yet the view that Plato does not use technical terminology does not imply that Plato is careless about his word choices.

---

[173] Though it is perhaps prefigured in the discussion of more and less precise forms of knowledge at *Philebus* 55c4ff. My reading of this section suggests that there the term *epistēmē* is especially reserved for the "precise" part of a form of knowledge, leaving *technē* for the non-mathematical, imprecise aspects of it; cf. *epistēmēs* at 55d6 with *technas* at 55e7. Even here, however, the term *technē* is sometimes used to refer to the "precise" part of knowledge (cf. 56c8).

[174] See, for example, Annas and Waterfield (1995, 3n5); Gill (1995, 294); Griswold Jr. (1989, 162n6); Lane (1998, 23); Nussbaum (1986, 443–444n10), with extensive citations to earlier work; Rowe (1995b, note to 258d5); Skemp (1987, 23n2 and 121n1).

Indeed, if we examine the matter closely we shall see that the terms *technē* and *epistēmē* are not entirely interchangeable in either the *Sophist* or the *Statesman*. Two patterns of usage are visible. First, the term *epistēmē* is especially reserved in the *Statesman* for those forms of knowledge that have something to do with the good, the just, and the noble, that is, those forms of knowledge that can justly lay claim to the title of "wisdom" (*sophia*), and is never used of the art of the sophist.[175] Second, the term *technē* never denotes a mere grasp of "facts" or "propositions," but always implies a *capacity* to "read" many eidetic structures and to use such structures as concrete standards for measurement or action. Let us consider the evidence in greater detail.

The word *epistēmē* occurs only 11 times in the *Sophist*, in contrast to 47 times in the *Statesman*. (The word *technē* occurs 49 times in the *Sophist* and 73 in the *Statesman*). *Epistēmē* never applies to the sophist, as we can easily see: 233c10 (the sophists seem to have *epistēmē* about everything, but do not; also 233c1, they seem to hold themselves *epistēmonos* in respect of that which they refute/dispute, but are not), 235a3 (the Stranger asks whether the sophist has the *epistēmai* he seems to have or is an imitator; note that the sophist's imitative art is not an *epistēmē* but a *technē*), 249c7 (not about the sophist; in the argument against the friends of the forms, which makes all *epistēmē* vanish), 253b10 (in the argument about the science of the free), 253c4 (Theaetetus' agreement that they are in presence of an *epistēmē*), 253c8 (the *epistēmē* of the free, that is, that of the philosopher), 253d3 (the *dialektikē epistēmē*), 257c8 (the nature of the other is broken up into small change like *epistēmē*), 257d2 (*epistēmē* is one, but the part that becomes applied to something holds some peculiar

[175] A few scholars have noticed this last point, though they have not made much of it: so Sayre (1969, 149, 175–179) who claims that this shows that the knowledge of the philosopher is not merely a *technē*, and Lane (1998, 23), who also notices this but thinks its significance is merely to "cast a faintly pejorative shadow back on the status of sophistry."

name of its own; hence there are many *technai* and *epistēmai*; note that this is not a hendiadys), 265c10 (as part of a question to Theaetetus, the god creates things with *logos* and *epistēmē*), 267e2 (distinguishes between imitation with mere opinion and "inquiring" imitation, the latter of which has *epistēmē*; see also *Statesman* 301b2). Furthermore, the word *epistēmōn* occurs only 2 times in the *Sophist*, and in both cases the sophist is explicitly declared not to be *epistēmōn*: at 232a1 (whenever one seems to be *epistēmōn* in many things but is called by the name of a single *technē* this appearance is to be doubted), 233c1 (the sophist seems to be *epistēmonos* in respect of that which he controverts, but is not). By contrast, the word is used 10 times in the *Statesman*, often of the statesman himself (cf. 293c7, for instance). In general, then, Plato appears to take care to reserve the word *epistēmē* and related words for the statesman, even as he also calls the knowledge of the statesman a *technē*.

A further piece of evidence for the view that there is a distinction between *epistēmē* and *technē* is the fact that the only arts (other than statesmanship) that are dignified with the appellation *epistēmē* in the *Statesman* are generalship, true rhetoric, and judicial knowledge, the true servants of statesmanship (cf. 304c10, 305a9, 305c11). Apart from these arts, the appellation *epistēmē* is reserved for "generic" forms of knowledge, such as *gnōstikē*, which denote broad categories of knowledge rather than specific skills. Thus, *pezonomikē* (265c6), *gnōstikē* (267a8), and *koinotrophikē* (267d13) are all referred to as *epistēmai*. The Stranger, by contrast, never calls any of the arts that constitute weaving, or even any of the arts of the city, an *epistēmē*, with the exception of (genuine) generalship, rhetoric, and judicial knowledge, though individual arts may partake of a part of *epistēmē* (cf. 290c5).

Only statesmanship and generalship are called both *epistēmē* and *technē* (cf. 305a5). This seems to indicate that these forms of knowledge transcend merely technical knowledge (though they are also forms of technical knowledge), in particular through their entanglement with the knowledge embodied in the "moral" virtues. It is possible to be a good weaver and be a terrible person; it is impossible to be a good general and lack courage. Similarly, it is impossible to be a good rhetorician, in the sense discussed by the Stranger, and be a sophist (cf. 303e10–304a2); or a good judge and take bribes or be intimidated (cf. 305b4–c2). The statesman's activity is itself said to be that of a wise and good man (296e3) and to be accomplished with both *technē* and *nous*, not *technē* alone (297a7–b1).

Moreover, the term *epistēmē* is also connected in the dialogues of the trilogy with the idea of *sophia*, wisdom, in ways in which the term *technē* is not connected. For example, at the very beginning of the *Theaetetus* Socrates identifies *epistēmē* and *sophia* (145e6 and context), while *technē* is nowhere identified with *sophia*. Moreover, while Plato might sometimes write that a person who has a specific *technē* is someone who is *sophos* concerning that subject (cf. *Statesman* 290b2), he never, to my knowledge, implies the converse: the *technitēs* is never the simply wise man. The underlying idea seems to be that wisdom—*sophia*—as well as knowledge—*epistēmē*—can be "of the whole," so to speak, whereas *technē* must always have some restricted field of application, and hence cannot be identified with wisdom *tout court*.

In this respect, the Stranger's use of the term *epistēmē* to designate statesmanship from the very beginning thus suggests a tight connection between wisdom and the art of the statesman. This is reflected in the usage of the words *sophos* and *sophia* as applied to the sophist and the statesman. The word *sophos* occurs 44 times in the trilogy (32 times in the *Theaetetus*, 7 times in the *Sophist* and 5 times in the *Statesman*). To be precise, *sophos* occurs at *Sophist* 230a7 (on the people who think themselves *sophos* not being such, and their imperviousness to admonition), 233b2 (the sophists are in some way able to give the young the impression of being *sophōtatoi*, wisest of all in all matters), 233c6 (the sophists seem to be *sophoi* to their pupils), 234c7 (the art of the sophist makes him appear wisest, *sophōtaton*), 268b10 (is the sophist wise or merely "sophistic," in the last division?), 268b11 (Theaetetus emphatically replies that he cannot be wise), 268c1 (the sophist is an imitator of the wise), *Statesman* 284e11 (critique of the *kompsoi* who think they are saying something *sophos* when they say there is a science of the measure of everything), 290b2 (on the heraldic race and those who become *peri grammata sophoi* in serving others; apparently the same as the *pandeinoi* or the "all-around-clever" at 290b3; there is some irony here), 296e3 (the wise—*sophos*—and good man manages [*diokēsei*] the city in the interest of the ruled; this is the criterion of the true regime), 299c6 (one must not be wiser, *sophōteron*, than the laws, under penalty). The sophist, unsurprisingly, is never described as truly *sophos*, but only as seemingly so. But the statesman is strongly implied to be *sophos* in the last definition of the *Sophist*, where the parallel sophist/imitator of the wise and statesman/wise is nearly inescapable (cf. 268b7–c4), and actually called *sophos* at *Statesman* 296e3, where he is said to manage the *polis* in the interest (the *sumphora*) of the ruled (language reminiscent of the discussion of justice in the *Republic*, by the way; cf. *Republic* 343b1ff., especially 343c4 and elsewhere). Plato thus implies that the statesman's *technē* is either itself a form of wisdom or enables him to be wise, that is, it is a form of real knowledge (*epistēmē*), while the sophist's *technē* remains a "purely technical" capacity, so to speak.

The connection of the statesman's *epistēmē*/*technē* to wisdom is further enhanced by the terminological ambiguity of the phrase *basilikē technē*, which would at first glance seem to offer irrefutable evidence regarding the interchangeability of *epistēmē* and *technē* in the *Statesman*. Like the English "kingly art," the Greek *basilikē technē* is ambiguous between the sense "art of the king" and the sense "art which is like a king to the other arts."[176] In the first sense, the *technē* of the king is a *technē* among many others: a *technē*, one might say, that has rivals for the title of wisdom, just as the king as shepherd of human beings encounters rivals for the title of nurturer of human beings, or a *technē* that cannot pretend to represent the whole of *epistēmē* (cf. *Statesman* 267d7–268c4, *Sophist* 257c10–d2). In the second sense, the kingly *technē* orders and rules all the other *technai* and *epistēmai*, as indeed it turns out to be the case (cf. *Statesman* 304a6–305e6): it is integrative, like wisdom, rather than narrow and focused, like a regular *technē*.

Similarly, the phrase *politikē technē*, also used by the Stranger to describe the statesman's knowledge, denotes both one *technē* among the arts that care for human beings and the *technē* that preeminently cares for human beings, insofar as it cares for the whole in which such care takes place, namely the *polis*. It cares not for a part of the *polis*, as all the other arts do, but for the whole of it (*Statesman* 305e2–6). The *technē* of the statesman—*politikē*—thus in some sense includes all the other arts in the *polis*, which suggests that it looks like wisdom, just as the art of the sophist looked like wisdom in its apparent gathering together of all the human forms of knowledge (*Sophist* 233a–c). The difference is that the statesman does not know or pretend to know everything that the other arts know, unlike the sophist. Rather, his knowledge includes the other arts insofar as he integrates them into the common task of caring for the *polis* (cf. *Statesman* 279e5–280a6); and, to that extent, it is no regular *technē*.

Nevertheless, we need to note the limitation that the name *politikē* (unlike the name *basilikē*) imposes on this *technē*/*epistēmē* as a claimant to the title of wisdom; for *politikē* is

[176] A contrasting ambiguity haunts the phrase *mimetikē technē* (the "mimetic art"), which describes the sophist. This is at the same time the *technē* that uses *mimēsis* (the *technē* of imitation) and the practice that camouflages as knowledge (the *technē* that imitates *technē*, is merely a *mimēsis* of *technē*, i.e., is not really a form of knowledge in the final analysis).

concerned with a merely partial whole (namely the *polis*), not with the whole as such, with the *kosmos*. The art that appears to be concerned with the whole as such is called *dialektikē* (or philosophy, cf. *Sophist* 253c9). Unlike *politikē*, the art of the statesman, *dialektikē*, the art of the philosopher, is never called a *technē*, which perhaps suggests that it is more worthy of the title of wisdom than statesmanship, even as *dialektikē*, unlike *politikē*, seems not to use or be the art of measure that determines whether specific actions are just or unjust, courageous or moderate, in the city. In other words, while *politikē* seems concerned with a narrower whole than *dialektikē*, *politikē* also appears to be concerned with particulars in a way that *dialektikē* is not. Indeed, the term *technē* appears to indicate a form of knowledge that can make judgments about particular actions and objects, unlike the term *epistēmē*.

But *technē* is also contrasted in other Platonic dialogues to the mere "empirical" ability to guess correctly about such particulars. For example, in the course of a discussion about the nature of rhetoric in the *Gorgias*, Socrates makes the claim that rhetoric is not a *technē* but a skill rooted in mere "experience" (*empeiria*, sometimes translated "knack," *Gorgias* 462c). The distinction is further elaborated at 463a and 465a, where Socrates distinguishes between the ability to "guess" correctly about something (in the case of rhetoric, whatever produces pleasure in some particular crowd) that someone with experience of past events has, and the ability to give an appropriate account or *logos* of why something ought to be done or not done in any particular case that someone with *technē* has. In Socrates' view (see also 501a), skills rooted in mere experience (in contrast to *technai*) lack a reliable account of both the proper *end* of the activity (so sophistry and rhetoric lack a proper account of what is beneficial, and hence aim at pleasure instead, unlike genuine political science) and of the proper *means* to accomplish that end (so sophistry and rhetoric cannot explain *why* certain devices produce certain effects under particular conditions, but merely rely on the fact that they *have* had such effects in the past or have been at least correlated with them). Someone who lacks a reliable account of both the ends and the means of some activity cannot be said to understand either *what* he is doing or *why* whatever he is doing "works." Hence such a person cannot have an *art* in the proper sense of the term.

As others have noted, the fact that arts are distinguished from experiential skills on two dimensions (the account of the *end* and the account of the *means*) leaves open some space for ambiguity in the determination of which capacities are genuine arts and which capacities are merely experiential skills.[177] One could certainly imagine skills that lack an appropriate account of (and hence fail to understand) the *means* to accomplish some effect, but nevertheless aim at the correct end; medicine, which aims at health, may be one such skill. (Doctors more often than not—and certainly more so in Plato's time—lack a good account of the causes of disease and the reasons for why a particular treatment works in particular cases, though they do have a reasonably good understanding of the end of medicine, namely health; see also the discussion in chapter 5, pp. 263–265). And by the same token, one could imagine a skill that has an appropriate account of the means to accomplish some effect but lacks a good account of the end; imagine a "scientific" rhetoric in the Aristotelian mold that nevertheless aims at pleasure rather than what is beneficial (cf. also *Protagoras* 354b–c, where Socrates entertains the possibility of pleasure as the good).[178]

---

177 See Irwin (1979, 135).

178 Moreover, the idea that arts possess an *account* (of either ends or means) is ambiguous: does the genuine craftsman need to be able to *explain* in each and every case (and in changing circumstances) why what he is doing *works*, or does he simply need to *know* why it works in some nonverbal way—know the causal relations that can be exploited to produce a certain effect? Socrates typically seems to assume the former (as in the *Meno*), though the Stranger does not. We shall nevertheless ignore this problem for the moment; suffice it to note that it reemerges in the relationship of statesmanship to the law, since the genuine account of *why* the law works

The tight link that Socrates emphasizes between the lack of an account of the proper end and the lack of an account of the proper means in the case of rhetoric seems to have something to do, as Dodds notes,[179] with the fact that rhetoric aims at the pleasant rather than the good. The pleasant, as a person's "apparent" good, is intrinsically tied to that particular person rather than to persons in general: only a particular individual can judge ("feel or perceive") what is pleasant to him or her at any given point in time, whereas he or she is not always the best judge of what their own *good* is, even if we understand their good as some maximum of pleasure over an entire life (something which requires calculation, not merely some incorrigible "perception" of pleasure at a particular point in time). But because persons are different, we can never tell what will make any particular person feel pleasure; we can only be guided by experience in our selection of the proper means to provide him or her with pleasure, though of course we may be able to establish statistical regularities that help in this process, like, e.g., most people like sweets. In other words, to say that an activity aims at the pleasant is to say that there can be no general account of the means that accomplish its end. But the converse is not true: even if an activity aims at the correct end (e.g., the good rather than the pleasant) it may not have a proper account of the means to accomplish the end. Experience may be the best we can do even in cases where we have the correct account of the end, or even if we somehow aim at the correct end even though we lack a correct account of it.

The point is important since the distinction between *technē* and *empeiria* will reappear in the *Statesman*'s discussion of the rule of law, as we shall see below in more detail (chapter 5). The Stranger claims (300b) that law (or at least certain kinds of law) is not based on *technē* but on mere *experience*, yet law is not

or fails to work is always far more complex than the law itself, and cannot necessarily be communicated to those who are under its rule.

[179] Dodds (1959, 229, note to 465a2–5).

necessarily formulated with a view to what is pleasant. In fact, law is formulated with a view to the preservation of the city (a proper end), but only on the basis of experience of those things that have in the past served to preserve it; and the "skill" of the city in framing this law lacks an account of *why* these things served to preserve the city in the past, or *why* other things might be necessary under changed circumstances. This reevaluation of "empirical" but nontechnical skills is evident already in the *Theaetetus*, where Socrates had acknowledged that skills like cookery *could* have significant predictive power (178d9–10) even with respect to pleasure, and implicitly accepted that a good prediction of what would be *good* for a city need not be rooted in genuine knowledge of either means or ends. From this point of view, the argument on the rule of law that the Stranger will develop in the *Statesman* represents a more serious attempt to grapple with the distinction between *technē* and *empeiria* than Socrates' argument in the *Gorgias*, and it issues in a more positive evaluation of *empeiria* than Socrates provides.

At any rate, in the *Gorgias* Socrates never fully articulates the connection between, say, the knowledge of what is beneficial of political science, and the knowledge of what *actually* makes people better or worse in particular circumstances. In fact, during the course of the discussion he conspicuously fails to make Callicles a better person; on the contrary, he seems to make him *worse* rather than better, contrary to his boast that he alone among all the Athenians is the true statesman, that is, the person who aims to make citizens better rather than worse (521d–e).[180] The *Gorgias* thus indirectly raises the question of whether it is enough to have the right account of the end; the *technē* of statesmanship appears to be more difficult than Socrates believes.

We have thus far seen that the distinction between *technē* and *epistēmē* has something to do both with the relative value of the two (only forms of knowledge that deal with the highest

[180] A point perspicaciously noted by Arieti and Barrus (2007, 1–2).

forms of order, properly speaking, are referred to as *epistēmai*) and the ability that a *technē* gives its possessor to make correct judgments about particulars, an ability that seems to be rooted in some "account" or some "understanding" of cause or form. I want to suggest the dialogues of the trilogy focus precisely on what connects *technē* to *epistēmē*: how can the possession of an *epistēmē* also provide a person with a *technē*? In fact, the key "epistemological" issue in the *Statesman* is precisely how the statesman can link a knowledge of the highest forms of order (an *epistēmē*) to both the production of particular effects in the world of becoming and the responsiveness to particular circumstances that requires reliably making correct judgments (a *technē*). How is the statesman's knowledge of the good, the just, and the noble (which was identified with the knowledge of the statesman or philosopher-king *simpliciter* in the *Republic*) connected to the actual production of the city's order in varying and unpredictable circumstances? How is the knowledge of justice itself, for example, connected to the judgment that *this* or *that* action is actually just, and ought to be done? And how is the justice of the statesman connected to the city's ability to survive in a changing political context? These questions all concern the relationship between knowledge of the forms of order and correct judgment about particular actions or people, and they were never fully resolved elsewhere in the Platonic *corpus* by Socrates.

That this is an important issue for the *Statesman* is already evident in the *Theaetetus*. The dialogue begins the trilogy with a discussion of the question of knowledge: what is *epistēmē*? Yet while it is clear that in the *Theaetetus* the term *epistēmē* includes the *technai*, as Theaetetus' first (and inappropriate) response to Socrates' question concerning knowledge, as well as Socrates' response to that response, shows (*Theaetetus* 146c7–147c6; see also 197a5ff.), it is striking that the discussion of knowledge throughout that dialogue is conducted in splendid isolation from the *technai*: Socrates always asks what *epistēmē* is, never what *technē* is. But the question of *technē* is never too far from the surface of the discussion: for example, the Protagorean thesis that knowledge is perception flounders in part on its inability to account for any expertise, including Protagoras' own (see, e.g., 177c2–179b9),[181] and the "aviary" image describes the *technē* of arithmetic (198a5) as a kind of "hunt" for the birds that represent "pieces of knowledge," yet proves unable to give a good account of this hunting. More generally, in its concern with judgment (opinion) and what relationship, if any, such correct judgment, has to knowledge, the dialogue again points to the *technai*, which work by somehow enabling their possessors to make *correct* judgments and yet are *more* than correct judgment. As Socrates and Theaetetus struggle with the possibility of "true and false opinion" (with or without an account), they thus implicitly raise the question of what "opinion" or "judgment," especially of particulars (e.g., judging correctly whether Theaetetus is standing or sitting) has to do with any sort of expertise.

The *Theaetetus* is of course a rich and complex dialogue that has supported more than one interpretation, and I cannot here do even the most minimal justice to its arguments without digressing too far from the main themes of this study. To some, the dialogue shows Plato's increasing awareness of the problems with his "middle period" two-world epistemology and ontology, which sharply distinguished between opinion and knowledge and becoming and being, especially insofar as this epistemology denied the possibility of what we might call "empirical" knowledge.[182] And in fact the dialogue's focus on judgments *about* particulars (e.g., "Theaetetus knows Socrates"), and its extended treatment of the thesis of knowledge as perception, suggests a newfound preoccupation with the possibility of making knowledge-claims about things other than forms. For others, however, the *Theaetetus* simply points the

[181] See Burnyeat (1990, 39–42) and Sedley (2004, 86–88).

[182] See Burnyeat (1990, 127) for some discussion and references. Burnyeat himself seems to have inclined to that view.

way to the very epistemology and ontology of the *Republic*.[183] For example, in a recent book,[184] David Sedley has argued convincingly that the dialogue shows Socrates as the "midwife" of Platonism, showing how Socrates helped Plato "give birth" to the two-world epistemology and ontology of the *Republic*. On this view, the dialogue leads Socrates and Theaetetus to the brink of the "classical" Platonic metaphysics, but does not take us across the threshold, even as it indicates how *Plato* did give birth to genuine offspring rather than "wind-eggs." In support of this view, we can point (for example) to the way in which the dialogue disposes of the thesis that knowledge is perception in part by redescribing the domain of perception as a realm of Heraclitean change where stable knowledge is impossible, and the dialogue's clear reassertion of the classic Platonic separation between true opinion and knowledge. On both views, moreover, the *Sophist* solves the problems that the *Theaetetus* raises, though there is little agreement regarding *how* it does so.[185]

I do not pretend to intervene in this debate so much as to bypass it. For my purposes, all that matters is that the *Theaetetus* reopens the question of the relationship between true opinion or correct judgment and knowledge properly speaking that is at the heart of the Platonic problematic of *technē*; and that the *Sophist* and the *Statesman* articulate this connection in a way that preserves the possibility of the standard "two world" epistemology and ontology of the *Republic*, as we shall see. Already in the *Meno* (98a1–2) Socrates had guessed that *epistēmē* somehow makes true opinion or correct judgment "stable," tying it down "by means of calculation [*logismos*]" to the grounds of the judgment itself, and suggests that this is what "recollection" means, but he does not give a

[183] See, for example, Cornford (1935). This interpretation has of course much older antecedents: most of the Ancient Platonists read the *Theaetetus* in precisely that way, as Sedley (2004) notes.
[184] Sedley (2004).
[185] See, e.g., Kahn (2007).

full account of how such "tying down" of true judgment with a *logos* is possible, and does not claim that he *knows* that this is what knowledge is. In the *Theaetetus*, however, Socrates examined several senses in which knowledge may be said to be correct judgment plus an account and rejected them all (201d–210b), as each of the rejected "accounts" of knowledge as true judgment plus an account seems unable to "tie down" true opinion to anything beyond itself. The specific reasons Socrates gives for rejecting these "accounts" of knowledge have been the subject of considerable scholarly controversy;[186] yet it is worth emphasizing that Socrates assumes throughout that knowledge must involve an *ability* to produce correct judgments in different circumstances and about a variety of related objects, as when he discusses the example of writing the first syllable of Theodorus and Theaetetus' names (207e7–208b6). Merely being able to correctly enumerate the letters in the first syllable of Theaetetus' name cannot count as knowledge of grammar if this ability does not *also* enable one to correctly enumerate the letters in the first syllable of Theodorus' name, and merely being able to indicate the distinguishing mark of some object (the third account of "account" Socrates considers, 208cff.) cannot indicate knowledge unless this ability *also* enables its possessor to indicate the distinguishing mark of a variety of related objects. Knowledge, in other words, must be conceptualized as a *technē* if a definition of it as "correct judgment [or true opinion] plus an account" is to be made to work.

The *Sophist* and the *Statesman* tackle different parts of the challenge of the *Theatetus*. In the *Sophist* the Stranger develops a conception of opinion or judgment as a specific kind of image that either preserves or fails to preserve the structural relationships among the *formal* parts of something, which he uses to illustrate how false opinion is possible as a kind of distortion. In the *Statesman*, by contrast, he implicitly develops a conception of *technē* as a capacity that, using two forms of

[186] See Burnyeat (1990, 128ff.) for an exhaustive account.

measurement, enables its possessor to reliably *produce* such images on the basis of insight into formal structure. The art of measure (or rather, the component of all art that consists in measurement in its two varieties, as we shall see) enables the craftsman (including the statesman) to produce what is needful in particular times and contexts, *including* correct judgments or true opinions about particulars, by relating the atemporal perfection of form to the particulars of time and place. We might then say, roughly, that the *Sophist* is fundamentally a dialogue about the nature of opinion (including false opinion), while the *Statesman* is fundamentally a dialogue about the nature of art; and that in these dialogues the Stranger comes to understand *technē* as *epistēmē* plus measurement, and the products of all *technē* (including correct judgments) as images of formal structure.

Before we can appreciate the Stranger's account of knowledge, however, it will be necessary to take a brief detour into the "standard" account of *epistēmē* that Plato puts in the mouth of Socrates in the *Republic*, especially as this account is in many ways related to the problem of *political* knowledge that is our central concern in this study. We shall then be in a position to understand more clearly in which respects the Stranger remains within a broadly "Socratic" orbit, and whether any departures from the "Socratic" (or Platonic, for that matter) position as expressed in these dialogues represent a theoretical advance by the Eleatic. As I shall try to show, the Eleatic never rejects the basic epistemology and ontology of the *Republic*, but merely articulates the connection between its two realms differently.

Knowledge and opinion in the *Republic*

In the *Republic* Socrates produces a far more sophisticated account of knowledge, and in particular *political* knowledge, than anything we find in the *Gorgias*. The literature on Plato's theory of knowledge in the *Republic* is vast (indeed, almost coextensive with the literature on the *Republic* itself), and for our purposes it is not worth discussing in detail the many controversies that Plato's great images of the sun, the line, and the cave have generated. I limit myself to what I take to be the best account of knowledge that makes sense of what Plato is trying to say while remaining relatively plausible as an account of knowledge, and pointing to its application to the problem of political knowledge.[187] My presentation is thus necessarily incomplete; there is much I do not discuss, since this is not a study of the *Republic*, and I gloss over many points in ways that may appear cavalier to the specialist. My purpose is simply to articulate the basic Platonic/Socratic framework for understanding knowledge in the *Republic* in such a way that a productive comparison with the Platonic/Eleatic framework of the *Statesman* is possible.

The basic framework seems to be as follows. Knowledge is a capacity to grasp "what is" (476e7–9), where "what is" is contrasted to things that both "are and are not," that is, are something in some respects but are not that thing in other respects (479a–d). These things are grasped by a different capacity, "judgment" or "opinion" (478d). More generally, "what is" can be glossed as *invariant* or *atemporal structure* or *form* (cf. 500b–c),[188] whereas what is between being and non-being manifests such form or structure in manifold associations and relationships to different degrees, which makes it appear sometimes as something, sometimes as something else. Socrates thus speaks, for example, of the invariant structure of beauty *itself* as what *is* (beauty can never *not* be itself), and hence as knowable, whereas the many beautiful things, which manifest (or "imitate") the structure of beauty in some respects but not in others, thereby appearing beautiful at some times and in some relations but not others, are in between being ("being something," namely beautiful) and non-being ("not being

[187] I have learned much about these passages from Reeve (1988); Denyer (2007); Sedley (2007); and (especially) Miller (2007), on which I draw extensively. I do not note below my disagreements with these authors.

[188] The invariance of the forms cannot be fully understood as "eternity in time"; it is rather a kind of independence of time or atemporality.

beautiful"), and hence are not properly speaking knowable. To *know* is thus always to grasp fully some invariant structure, or some structure that does not appear different when seen in the light of different relationships, whereas to *judge* (or have an opinion, a *doxa*, a "seems to me" condition) is always to grasp something that could be otherwise, either because it can change (what is big can become small) or because it may appear differently in different relationships (e.g., what is big with respect to something may appear small with respect to something else and vice versa). Hence while knowledge of something is guaranteed to be correct by the invariance of its object (the invariant structure is always what it is and not something else), a judgment or opinion that X is Y can be either true or false, and more importantly for our purposes it can *change* its truth value either because its object changes (e.g., X becomes Z), or because the object appears to judgment only in *some* relationships and not in others (X is Y in context A, but not-Y in context B).

Note that in identifying knowledge and judgment as distinct capacities concerned with different kinds of objects, Socrates implicitly opens a gap between the ability to *know* some invariant structure (e.g., the laws of physics) and the ability to *judge correctly* some fact (e.g., the position and momentum of some specific object), a gap that he never fully closes in the dialogue. Moreover, this relatively simple picture is complicated by the analogies of the sun, the line, and the cave, all of which introduce further difficulties for our understanding of the relationship between knowledge of invariant form and the particular judgments about specific things. Let us look at these analogies in some detail.

In the line image (509d1–511e5), Socrates divides all of being into a sensible realm and an intelligible realm, and distinguishes within each realm between images or representations of things, and the things that are the originals of these images. In the visible realm we thus find representations of visible things (like stories about just men and just actions), and the sensible things themselves (like just men and just actions), whereas in the intelligible realm we find first what we shall call "models" of forms (like mathematical entities, but also such things as theories of justice or things like the aviary model of knowledge in the *Theaetetus*, which would otherwise find no place within Socrates' ontology) and the forms or structures of reality themselves (like the form of justice itself). Socrates illustrates the relationship between these entities (510c1–511a8) by talking about the practice of geometers: the geometer uses visible figures (e.g., triangles in the sand) that represent intelligible entities (triangles) to derive intelligible conclusions (geometrical theorems), but in the process assumes that certain intelligible hypotheses (e.g., the parallels axiom) faithfully represent a real invariant structure or form; to grasp the reality of the hypothesized principle one has to travel *using* these intelligible hypotheses (theories or models, we might say) to what is properly "unhypothetical" (511b6), that is, not merely posited for the sake of argument but actually grasped as the intelligible structure underlying the theorems, something that seems to require the geometer to grasp the principle of perfection or the good insofar as he needs to understand the sense in which, for example, the intelligible triangle is a *perfect* triangle.[189]

But for our purposes it seems to me that the point Socrates is trying to make is better grasped by thinking about a non-mathematical example. If we start from "actions or persons that are (believed to be) just" (which are in the sensible realm), we can use these as stepping stones in a ladder of abstraction to create intelligible *models* of justice (definitions of justice, for example), and in turn use these intelligible models to arrive, via dialectical argument, at the underlying form of justice itself, which we can only fully grasp when we understand why our model of justice properly identifies perfect justice, that is, when we grasp the form of justice in the light of the good or

[189] I follow here Miller's (2007) superb discussion.

perfection itself. This is close enough to the procedure Socrates actually uses in the *Republic* to arrive at the form of justice, or at least as near to it as possible, though a demonstration of this claim would require a full interpretation of the *Republic*: initial models of justice are first tested against our intuitions of what specific actions or people are just (consider, for example, Socrates' refutations of various definitions of justice in *Republic* I), and then discarded or refined dialectically by means of more purely theoretical ("intelligible") considerations. One is tempted to liken what Socrates does to Rawls's discussion of "reflective equilibrium," which also starts with our considered judgments of what things are just and unjust, develops an initial model of justice, and moves on to dialectically test it both against these judgments and against alternative models until we arrive at a model that, having survived these tests, we feel confident enough represents a good approximation to the real structure of justice.

Socrates indicates that in respect of truth, the relationship between what is knowable and what can only be judged is like the relationship between originals and their images (510a9–10). Though his meaning is not altogether clear, he seems to be pointing to the fact that an image always falsifies its original in some respect. Moreover, a single original may have multiple images, similar in some respect to the original, but all of them somewhat different: the image can be false in many ways. This is true in both the visible and the intelligible realm: just as there may be many tellings of the story of Socrates, all of which falsify the real actions and character of Socrates in some respect, so there may be many definitions (intelligible models) of justice, most or all of them potentially wrong in some respect given the real structure (form) of justice, though most of them capturing *some* aspect of the underlying form of justice. And it is also true across the line that divides both realms: actions or individuals may only imperfectly manifest some intelligible model of justice. The image is ontologically dependent on the original in such a way that it is never *simply* like the original.

Since representations are images of sensible things, sensible things are images of intelligible models, intelligible models are images of real structures or forms, and all of these things are "illuminated" to different degrees by the first principle of things (the good or the principle of perfection, represented by the sun), the line analogy suggests an ascending hierarchy of truth, which Socrates articulates by pointing to four distinct "conditions of illumination" in the human soul, each one progressively "clearer" than the previous one with respect to some particular structure or form. Consider again the example of justice: at the lowest level of clarity and truth (*eikasia*), one *imagines* stories about just people and just actions; at the next level (*pistis*), one can *believe* that particular people or actions are just; a further level of clarity (*dianoia*) is achieved when one can *think* abstractly that justice is such and such; and the highest level of clarity and truth (*noēsis*) with respect to justice is attained finally when we *understand* that justice is genuinely such and such, that is, when we truly grasp the structure of justice, and do not merely image it through theoretical constructions.

Note that one can imagine relatively accurate stories of just people and actions (e.g., the stories that would be admitted to *kallipolis* after Socrates' censorship) as well as relatively inaccurate stories (e.g. the Homeric stories before Socrates' censorship); and similarly one can believe correctly or incorrectly that some people are just or unjust, and think correctly or incorrectly that justice is such and such (has some structure or another). But at the highest level of illumination there can be no error: one cannot understand incorrectly that justice is such and such, since in genuinely understanding one fully grasps the original—the form or structure of justice—rather than the model or image. This implies that knowledge properly speaking is only possible as understanding: even at the level of models (which includes mathematics) there is at best correct judgment (opinion), not knowledge, even though Socrates suggests that the level of thought is between opinion and understanding (511d4).

Yet the line image is static: even Socrates' geometrical example at 510c1–511a8 tells us very little about how we might move, for example, from imagination to belief to thought to understanding without losing our way (by, for example, relying too much on incorrect representations of just actions or persons to develop models of justice). In particular, the connections between the *understanding* of form or invariant structure and the production or grasp of *correct* images of such form in thought, belief, and imagination remain obscure. For further (yet still insufficient) clarification, we need to turn to the even more complex image (or better yet, model) of the cave (514aff.).

In order to understand the basic thrust of the cave image, it is worth keeping in mind two points. First, the cave sets the line in motion: it depicts how, starting from representations, someone might achieve enlightenment, that is, grasp the real invariant structures (forms) of reality, and indeed the structure of all structures (the good, the general principle of order of all things), and then return to the cave. But second, and most importantly, the cave image is specifically concerned to describe the achievement of *political* knowledge and its contribution to the order of the city. Yet for all its brilliance the image remains obscure; it leaves Glaucon (and perhaps us, too) dazzled and at the level of *eikasia*.

The cave appears to contain two kinds of people: the prisoners, who only observe the shadows on the wall, and the people who carry the statues (the originals) that cast the shadows. The people carrying the statues can be likened to the producers of "culture," including presumably the poets, whose stories about just and unjust people and actions (and many other things besides) determine the extent of the views of virtue of the prisoners. Most people in the city thus must remain at the level of *eikasia*, their views fully determined by the "media." Yet they may acquire an experiential skill that enables them to identify the shadows and predict their order (516d), that is, allows them to identify what conventional stories say about justice or injustice, virtue and vice, and to live their lives by the standards implicit in these stories, imitating such people and such actions. Those who can best identify the shadows and their usual relations are thus rewarded with prizes and other honors. But what about the carriers of the statues whose shadows are cast on the wall? Socrates does not say this, but it seems natural to suppose that they are skilled at identifying the *statues* they carry, and not just the shadows, in the dim light of the fire in the cave; as cultural producers they set the tone for the entire society. Yet if the fire in the cave is sufficiently dim, or the statues they carry reflect poorly the originals *outside* the cave, then their experiential skills at identifying the statues they carry will also be deficient. These people are thus at the level of belief, having views (accurate or not) about just people and just actions, and more generally about virtuous or non-virtuous people and actions.

Socrates says that if a prisoner were compelled to turn around towards the light, he would be at first dazzled: his experiential skill with the shadows does not allow him to identify the originals of the shadows (515d). We might imagine, for example, that the prisoner would be at a loss to identify just people or just actions as such. As he moves up the cave, he thus loses the experiential skill to function according to the particular standards of his society, unable to properly identify the shadows or their sensible originals, much less to gain honor by living his life according to these conventional standards. This is a painful experience; Socrates thus stresses that the prisoner has to be dragged all the way out of the cave, away from the familiar certainties of his culture.

Once the prisoner arrives outside the cave, moreover, he is not immediately able to see most *real* things. He sees at first only shadows and images in water (516a6–7)—including images of men, which, according to the image of the line, would represent the originals of the statues of men whose shadows are cast on the walls of the cave. In other words, the now liberated prisoner at first only recognizes distorted and dim images of the real structures of reality: we might say that he now has "theories" about justice and virtue and all such other things, but he cannot tell for sure how close they are to the true structures of reality. It is only after a long time that he is able to look at the originals of such things directly, and only at the very end of the process he is finally able to look at the sun, the good itself, and understand that the good is responsible both for the truth and beauty of everything.

The image of the sun had been introduced earlier (507a1–509c2) as a representation of the good. These passages are among the most contentious and difficult in Plato's entire *corpus*, and I cannot pretend to offer a definitive interpretation. I follow Miller in thinking that the good is perhaps best thought of as the principle of *perfection* or *order* itself.[190] To the extent that it is possible to say what Socrates has in mind on the basis of a sensible image (the level of *eikasia* or at best *pistis*!), we can perhaps think of the good (at the level of *dianoia*, mere theory: we ought not to claim understanding!) as determining the ways in which the invariant structures of things—including the invariant structures of justice, beauty, and so on—are forms of *order*, that is, impose normative standards on the sensible realm. Such order is ultimately expressed in proper proportion or *summetria*, the (sometimes mathematically determinable?) relationship of the various parts of a thing to one another, so that justice, for example, appears as a certain relationship between the parts of the soul. But such proper proportion is seen only *in light of the good*, that is, in light of a consideration of the principle of order itself. Hence the good could be characterized, in Aristoxenus' famous report of Plato's lecture on the good, as "the one,"[191] that is, the principle that reveals the manifold structures of being as all equally forms of order or perfection, and hence as the originals of which sensible beings are merely images that *lack* such perfection; and it could also be characterized as responsible not only for

[190] See Miller (2007, 327).

[191] Aristoxenus *Harmonics* 122.13–14.

whatever epistemic access we might have to such structures but for their very being as *proper* proportions (cf. 509b6–8).

Socrates had earlier indicated that when the soul fixes its gaze on something that is "illuminated by truth and what is" (508d4–9), "it understands, knows, and apparently possesses understanding, but when it focuses on what is mixed with obscurity, on what comes to be and passes away, it opines and is dimmed, changes its opinions this way and that, and seems bereft of understanding." But remember that in the cave image only the things *outside* the cave are fully illuminated by the sun; the things *inside* the cave are mostly illuminated by a fire halfway up the steep path. Only opinion or judgment is possible in the cave. And indeed, as the philosopher is compelled or decides to come down from the cave, his insight into the invariant structures that are ultimately the originals of the shadows and the statues inside the cave cannot help him "dispute about the shadows of justice or the statues of which they are the shadows and to dispute about the way these things are understood by people who have never seen justice itself" (517d8–9). The knowledge of the man who has achieved enlightenment is (at least at first) useless for living according to the standards of the city, and even for identifying genuinely just actions or people. Again the problem of the connection between knowledge of form and the correct judgment about just actions and people raises its head; and Socrates will not ultimately be able to articulate this connection fully. The most Socrates can say is that a soul that has been turned "towards the light" eventually adjusts to the darkness of the cave and is able to see "vastly better" *both* the statues and the shadows (520c3–6), and hence both the actual just people and actions and their images in stories, myths, and the like.

Knowledge and opinion in the *Sophist*

How, then, does the Eleatic Stranger articulate the connection between knowledge and correct judgment, between the understanding of form and the judgment that *this* action is just and ought to be done? The short answer to this question is "through the concept of measurement." But before we can understand what this means, it is necessary to first take a brief detour through the arguments on imitation in the *Sophist*. The conception of imitation developed there will eventually be used to explain what it is that the statesman does and why the law cannot do what he does, and it will help us understand how the statesman's "measure" functions.

According to the Stranger, there are two kinds of images or appearances: *phantasmata* and *eikones* (235b8ff.).[192] *Phantasmata* are images that look like something but are not actually congruent—do not share the exact same proportions, or the same common "measure," *summetria*—with what they look like (236b4–7). They are "distorted" images: statues where the head is actually bigger in relation to the torso than in the original, for example. But such images distort the proportions of the original only in order to save the phenomena, so to speak: without the distortion, the images would look different from what they represent from the point of view from which they are usually seen. The Stranger thus implies that *phantasmata* can "correct" for the fact that the point of view from which we look at big and beautiful things is not optimal; thus big statues of gods need to distort the regular proportions of the human figure if they are to seem beautiful to people viewing them from below (235e5–236a1), even though they can also of course be used to obscure the actual relationships obtaining among the parts of the original (making an ugly thing appear beautiful, for example, or for that matter, as we shall see, the weaker argument appear stronger). The point to note is simply that such images may be pedagogically useful even if false in

[192] Many scholars have found the distinction problematic, even otiose: see, for example, Cornford (1935, 198); Philip (1961, 459); and more recently Ambuel (2007, 67–81). As we shall see, I do not think the distinction is otiose; the problems that scholars have had with it are partly a result of attempting to assimilate the doctrine of images that the Stranger develops to the Socratic doctrine of images, which is indeed quite different.

the sense of not preserving the correct measure of the relationships among the parts of the original, since they can preserve, through distortion, other important qualities of the original. Incidentally, this implies that we should not be too quick to think that a philosopher could not make use of such images, contrary to what is sometimes asserted.[193]

By contrast, *eikones* are images that, in preserving the exact proportions of the original, can appear distorted to those who are not properly situated to appreciate them, though they are not thereby identical with the thing they image: they merely preserve the proportions of the original without correcting for the point of view from which the image is to be seen. So, for example, an *eikōn* of a big and beautiful man might look distorted (the head might look too small, for example) when viewed from below. At the same time, an *eikōn* of a thing remains an image, rather than a duplicate of the thing: the common measure holding its parts together (e.g., the relationship of the size of the head to the size of the torso, or of a thing to its quality in the case of verbal images) duplicates the relationship between the different parts of the original, but does not replicate every element in it (so the head of the statue is made of stone, not of flesh; and the statement uses words, rather than simply duplicating the reality it addresses). The *eikōn* is "the same" as the original only with respect to the proportions among the parts of the original, not their material; it is not the perfect duplicate of the original that Socrates suggests in the *Cratylus* would not be an image at all but simply another original (*Cratylus* 432c).

The distinction between *phantasmata* and *eikones* thus implies that an image is something that is related to an original insofar as the image preserves, or seems to preserve from some point of view, a measurable relationship between the various

[193] See Nightingale (2002) for a similar view, as well as Blondell (2002, 365ff.). I have also benefited tremendously from the stimulating, though at times opaque, discussion of this passage in Benardete (1984a, 105–112).

parts of the original thing without duplicating exactly the thing itself. So statements about things can be understood as images of these things (cf. *Sophist* 260c), even though words are obviously not identical to the parts of the things they represent in combining with one another. What matters for the accuracy of an image (that is, for whether we consider the image to be an *eikōn* or not) is not the identity of the parts or aspects of the image and the parts or aspects of the original, but the relationship among the parts: the image is accurate if the parts of the image preserve the proportions of the original, and inaccurate otherwise. But this means that an accurate image (e.g., a verbal representation of some state of affairs) may not "look" at all like the thing it (accurately) represents, whereas an image that superficially duplicates aspects of the original (e.g., colors) while changing the original proportions so as to make the original appear more "pleasing" from some point of view may appear to the inexperienced like a more accurate representation of the original.

This distinction can help us clarify the account of false statements (and false opinion) that the Eleatic Stranger develops later in the dialogue. In the Eleatic's account, a true statement turns out to be a kind of likeness in speech, preserving the relationships (the combinations) between the parts of speech that would obtain among the parts of reality, whereas a false statement would not preserve such relationships and yet may (from some point of view) "appear" as though it did preserve them, that is, a false statement would be a *phantasma*. More specifically, words that come together in propositions when the forms to which they refer do not in actual fact come together thus distort real relationships (261dff.): they produce images that have different parts and proportions, as it were, than the original. If this interpretation is correct, the Stranger's view is in this respect quite similar to that of the early Wittgenstein: words may refer to things (may be arbitrary tokens or labels for things), but would not themselves be images of them, whereas sentences would be images ("pictures" in the terminology of the early Wittgenstein) of things insofar as the relationships between the words in the sentence are the same logical relationships as the relationships among the forms in which a thing participates.[194] To be sure, this "solution" to the problem of false statement is not put in terms of *phantasmata* and *eikones* (though these and related words do appear throughout these passages; see 260c8–9, 264a6); the Stranger speaks of mixtures, not of proportions, and he does not refer back, except implicitly, to the original discussion of images. Yet the best understanding of what he is saying implies that what is preserved in speech-images is precisely the intelligible connections between forms, the "proportions" of a fact: it is possible to speak true and false sentences precisely because the parts of the image do not need to be the same things as the original, they only need to preserve the relationships of "mixture" obtaining among those original parts.[195]

Imitating knowledge

If an "image" of something is an arrangement of elements that refer to the parts of the original in particular proportions—sometimes preserving, sometimes not preserving, these proportions—then the idea of imitating a certain situation or state of affairs makes sense: we imitate it truly when we preserve the relationships among its parts in the image (and hence produce "true opinions"), and falsely when we do not (even though perspectival distortions may make accurate images appear inaccurate and vice versa). But what would it mean to imitate an art, not just a thing like a landscape or a human

[194] See Wittgenstein (1992 [1919]).

[195] See, for a similar view, Dorter (1994, 172). Ambuel's (2007) argument that the Stranger fails to give an appropriate account of false statement because he fails to give an appropriate account of images would thus be incorrect: on the contrary, the Stranger proposes an alternative to the Socratic treatment of images and originals, one which does not depend on the problematic notion of degrees of being but nevertheless manages to make sense of the idea of an image as different from, yet related to, an original.

form? In order to see what it might mean to imitate a form of knowledge, it will be useful to proceed as the Stranger does in the *Sophist*, namely, by looking at a small example first before we look at larger cases. The example of "angling," used by the Stranger to show Theaetetus the way to proceed at the beginning of the *Sophist* (218e2–221c3), should serve our purposes.

Angling is described by the Stranger by means of an ordered list of the elements or eidetic parts (cf. *Statesman* 262a9–263b11) that together constitute the *eidos*, the characteristic look of angling as a particular power to do something (cf. *Sophist* 219a6). Each of these parts represents a "dimension" of angling, being itself divisible into further parts, some of which do not belong to angling. Of the proper eidetic parts of angling, some refer to characteristic actions (such as upward motions), others to the characteristic circumstances of angling (such as daytime), others to characteristic instruments (such as rods), others to the characteristic beings captured by the angler (fish), and yet others to the immediate purposes pursued by angling as such (the capture of fish). But the most important of these elements is the only one that cannot be directly observed, namely *technē*. *Technē* gives the measure of all the other eidetic parts of the *eidos* of angling (rods, motions, immediate purposes, circumstances, etc.) and arranges them into a whole that is reliably able to do the work of angling, that is, catch fish. *Technē* is, to put the point in slightly different terms, what provides the different parts of angling with their *summetria*, their proportions relative to one another. Insofar as the Stranger knows what angling is, however, the division should capture (as an image) the characteristic relationships between all the different parts of angling: it should be an *eikōn* of angling.

Such a list of elements of angling can itself serve as a model that can be imitated, if one so wishes. To imitate an angler means, primarily, to look like an angler (or to create a painting or a discursive account of an angler) without actually being one. Thus, one could imitate an angler by sitting at a riverbank, attempting to catch fish using upward motions with a rod during the daytime hours. From a distance, it is possible that such a performance might confuse somebody into thinking that the person imitating the angler is actually an angler, though one's purposes in doing so need not be deceptive: one may be trying to learn to fish, for example. But so long as one does not have the *technē* that gives measure to all the external marks of angling, that joins them together in their proper proportion (their *summetria*), one cannot be said to be an angler; and this *technē* is not fully captured discursively in the divisions of the angler but merely mentioned.

Note that, in imitating the knowledge of the angler without the possession of the *technē*, the image—the look or *eidos*—produced is necessarily distorted *vis-à-vis* the original, for it does not normally preserve the proper measure among all the eidetic parts of the original. If the imitation did preserve the proper measure of all the parts, this would constitute a mark of knowledge: for only somebody with the *technē* of angling could reliably produce an image of angling that preserved the measure of all its proper parts. Somebody with knowledge of angling could still produce a distorted image of angling for some particular purpose, but no one without knowledge of angling could produce a non-distorted image of it except accidentally (cf. *Statesman* 300d4–e2).

These considerations straightforwardly generalize to the "imitation" of more complex forms of knowledge, like statesmanship. In order to produce an *eikōn* of statesmanship, one would have to reproduce the relationships between the elements of statesmanship in a dynamic context, not just in this or that situation. The performer in his performance of statesmanship, in this case, would be indistinguishable from the statesman, and the *eikōn* would indeed be indistinguishable from the original (cf. *Statesman* 300e1–2, *Cratylus* 432b1–432c6).[196] It is

[196] See Blondell (2002, 26–27) for further discussion. This is the same principle behind the Turing test of artificial intelligence: if a machine could perfectly imitate a human being in intelligent conversation (i.e., produce an *eikōn* of intelligent conversation), then the machine should be considered intelligent. At the same time, the attempt to create an intelligent machine

in this sense that accurate images of statesmanship can only be created by a statesman, and that only the statesman can accurately mimic another statesman, just as only an angler could ultimately produce accurate images of angling (even the division of angling is a "phantasm" of angling, though a useful one for pedagogical purposes). Indeed, as we shall see below (see chapter 5), even the law cannot accurately imitate statesmanship. The law is always a distorted image of statesmanship.[197]

Note that, if my interpretation of the Stranger's distinction between accurate and inaccurate images and of their connection with knowledge and opinion is correct, it is easy to see that knowledge must be understood always in terms of the preservation of what the Stranger will call "due measure" in the *Statesman*, even if the Stranger does not make this connection explicit. If knowledge is concerned with the accurate reproduction of the *summetria*, the common measure, of a set of elements (e.g., forms) in words, then knowledge can also be understood as the preservation of the *metron*, the measure, of these relationships. Moreover, if knowledge preserves such relationships, then one can arrive at an approximation of knowledge by studying paradigms or examples, that is, images that preserve some of the relationships among eidetic parts across the target of study and the paradigm, as weaving does (imperfectly!) for statesmanship. Indeed, the discussion of paradigm turns out to be essential for understanding how *technē* links knowledge of form and correct judgment, so we shall turn to

---

might involve creating a machine that would "imitate" what intelligent beings do. See Turing (1950); note that Turing called his thought experiment "the imitation game."

[197] The Stranger makes a number of further distinctions in the art of creating distorted images on the way to locating the sophist that suggest that there is more than one way in which distorted images may be produced, not all of which are equally bad. In particular, the Stranger will distinguish between "knowledgeable" and "non-knowledgeable" distorted imitation (*Sophist* 267b7–8), as well as between "ironic" or "dissembling" and "naive" distorted imitation (267e11–268a4). Distorted images are not all equally bad, as we shall also see when we come to the discussion of the rule of law.

it first before discussing the section on due measure and its connection with the knowledge of the statesman.

Knowledge and paradigms: 277d–279a

As Jacob Klein has noted,[198] the Stranger's methods up to and including the myth and the immediate corrections after the myth can be characterized as forms of *apodeixis* (cf. 277a2): the Stranger has attempted to derive the character of statesmanship directly from (*apo-*) larger or more general beings, without resorting to small examples, in contrast with their procedure in the *Sophist*, which started with the paradigm of the angler. The problem with such methods is that large beings (like the statesman, cf. 277b4) are difficult to grasp directly, because their internal structure is very complex. Using another large being (e.g., the god) to illuminate the structure of the first (the statesman) merely compounds the problem. This is not to say that the results of their investigation thus far are worthless; as we have seen, the account of the statesman they have produced is incomplete, not wrong. They have, after all, managed to roughly characterize statesmanship. But, as the Stranger will argue, for complex beings it is best to start from images that have less internal structure than the object that one wants to know. Such images can then be placed, as it were, side by side (*para-*) with their original in order to bring the latter's structure to light; they are *paradeigmata*, "models."[199]

It is important to note that the "size" of a model has nothing to do with its worth. So, for example, the shepherd of men at first appeared to be as humble as the swineherd Eumaeus (cf. 266c11–d2). The shepherd, in other words, appeared to be small, smaller even than the king should be. One can imagine the Stranger starting from this humble figure as a paradigm

[198] Klein (1977, 165–166).

[199] "Models" in this sense seem to me to be a kind of *phantasma*, chosen to correct for the low point of view from which we always start, as we shall see. But a full elucidation of this problem would lead us too far from our main argument.

of the king, just as he started from the angler to get at the sophist and will begin from the weaver to get at the statesman; but the humbleness of the shepherd was deceptive. The statesman as shepherd humbled human beings as the cattle of the shepherd, but exalted the shepherd himself with divine knowledge, granting him all the arts (which the sheep, by definition, lacked) rather than a supervisory knowledge that is one among all the other forms of knowledge. A "small" model may be likely to be a humble art, but the converse is not true; a large paradigm may also give the appearance of being a humble art, as the shepherd did. But how can appropriate models help us understand "large" and complex beings like the statesman?

The Stranger begins by saying that each of us apparently knows/has seen "everything" as if in a dream vision, and yet we ignore all things once again when we try to know them as if awake. "Everything" here seems to mean the eidetic structure of the whole, the universe of eidetic "words," the meaning of being. This dreamlike awareness of eidetic structure is such that when we try to examine it under the cool gaze of reason, what we seemed to know appears indistinct and unknowable; being recedes into indeterminate formlessness, into the "unlimited." What seemed vivid in a dream can often no longer be described or named when awake. The wakeful knowledge of being thus involves being able to perceive the eidetic elements in the indeterminate-seeming manifold of a given whole.

There are echoes here of the idea of "recollection" in the *Meno*, though the Stranger does not introduce any specific theory of how we have this sort of *a priori* awareness of eidetic structure. The dim—dream-like—awareness of this eidetic structure can also be fruitfully compared to what Heidegger referred to as the "hermeneutical circle of the understanding."[200] The "hermeneutical circle" refers to the circular structure of

---

[200] Heidegger (1962). See also Arends (1999, 101–102), and Arends (2001), who refers in both cases to Gadamer's more extended treatment of the issue in *Truth and Method* (Gadamer 2003 [1960]).

all understanding: we understand particular things in light of the whole to which they belong; hence we must have some pre-understanding of the whole to which a thing belongs in order to understand them; and this, in turn means that we must have some pre-understanding of all of being, or rather, of being as such, in order to understand anything at all. Being in Plato, however, is always (at least partially) eidetic structure or form; thus our understanding of anything is always informed by a dim and dreamlike pre-understanding of eidetic structure.

We can speak of this pre-understanding of eidetic structure as "mythical." Like dream-visions, myths like the one the Stranger had just finished telling Young Socrates offer synthetic glimpses of the eidetic structure of the whole; yet such insight as the myth offers has to be made useful by other means, that is, the eidetic elements depicted in it have to be picked out and shown to correspond to the eidetic elements in the being under examination (e.g., the statesman). Examples of this abound in the Platonic dialogues. For example, the knowledge of grammar involves recognizing the eidetic elements—letters, in their individuality and in their kinds—in the indeterminate manifold of voice, as Socrates explains in the *Philebus* (18b6ff.). The use of paradigms helps bring this mythical or dream-knowledge into focus; it is a way of awakening us to the eidetic structure of a larger whole by focusing our attention on the eidetic structure of a well-known smaller whole that contains much the same eidetic elements or exemplifies the same (or similar, but with lesser complexity) relationships among eidetic elements (cf. 278e9–11). The experience of learning is another "large" being, we soon discover; for it requires a *paradeigma* itself. The Stranger puts the point in somewhat paradoxical language: they now need a *paradeigma* in order to show what *paradeigma* means, that is, what the use of *paradeigmata* accomplishes for our knowledge.

The Stranger concedes that to speak of knowledge in terms of dreams and visions is a very strange way of speaking; and indeed it seems to him out of place (*atopōs* 277d6) to have brought up the way in which we experience the acquisition of knowledge at just this point in the dialogue. Why bring up a discussion of knowledge now? They are at an impasse: the Stranger has indicated that the genealogy of the statesman they have produced thus far is "incomplete" (277a5) and that they have rushed without paying attention to the right time (*para kairon*) for saying things (277a6), going sometimes too fast, and sometimes too slowly, and thus failing to attend to the proper proportions of the statesman, like bad sculptors. They have created a distorted image of the statesman. One suspects that part of the problem is that they did not discuss knowledge before rushing to define the knowledge of the *Statesman*, in contravention of standard Socratic practice, and must now do so at the wrong place in the dialogue, so to speak; but their lack of measure also exhibits, in a theoretical context, the very problem that the statesman must confront, namely, how to determine the *kairos* of action, and so what one must do in particular circumstances and with respect to particular individuals. The Stranger has proved to be deficient in the art of the statesman; he will now use that failure to teach Young Socrates about due measure. The dialogue's disorder in its first part will now yield to the Stranger's ordering dialectic; thus the dialogue's action mirrors the mythical pattern, and the statesman's action.

It is also worth noting that in having the Stranger speak of "dreams," Plato also recalls the "dream" of Socrates in the *Theaetetus* (201d8ff.), namely, the "theory" of knowledge that Socrates dimly elaborated at the end of that dialogue in attempting (unsuccessfully) to make sense of Theaetetus' proposal that knowledge is correct judgment with an account. For now the Stranger will articulate something that sounds very much like a version of that theory, complete with a discussion of the same example of letters and syllables that Socrates had used then.

What, then, is the paradigmatic experience of knowledge? How does knowledge happen to us? He starts by saying: "we know" (*ismen* 277e3). A paradigm is only useful when we start from the known, and yet it is necessary when we do not know.

The known is small (277e6–7): there must be an immediate knowledge or awareness of the eidetic elements of some things, else there could not be knowledge of anything, as the Stranger emphasizes later (278d8–e2). Here the Eleatic indirectly rejects the basic assumption of the "dream theory" of the *Theaetetus*, namely, that in generating an account we start from unknown, even unknowable, elements (*Theaetetus* 202d10–e1). What Young Socrates knows, according to the Stranger, is a small thing: children. Young Socrates, in other words, knows something of himself; for, as we might remember, when it comes to the bigger things, Young Socrates is still a child (*Statesman* 268e5–6), and has at any rate not long left that age.

These children are becoming experienced (*empeiroi* 277e3) with the various elements of the words they are to spell, that is, with the letters in isolation. Again, this is something within Young Socrates' range of experience: he knows that he himself is not yet fully experienced with letters, though he is becoming such, as Theaetetus had the previous day acknowledged with some vehemence (*Theaetetus* 207e5–6). They are familiar, or, as the Stranger puts it, they perceive (are passively aware of) each of these elements distinctly in small combinations; they fail to perceive distinctly the same elements in larger combinations, however. The use of words for "perception" in this passage recalls the arguments of the *Theaetetus* to the effect that perception is not knowledge; but the mention of experience suggests a role for experience as a precursor of knowledge, again in keeping with the dialogue's revalorization of experience in the production of law (see chapter 5). Familiarity with the elements of things does not imply knowledge of such elements in the full sense of the word; such knowledge comes, as we shall see, with the recognition of arbitrary combinations of these elements. But this recognition appears to be built up from a foundation in experience.

Children can identify these elements (*stoicheiōn* 277e6, recalling *Theaetetus* 201e2ff.) when they appear in simple and short syllables or combinations. The Stranger does not say anything about the nature of these elements; but it is important to stress that he does *not* say that they are unknowable or that we cannot say anything about them, contrary to Socrates' problematic assumption in the *Theaetetus*. No metaphysical assumptions are made about them, but it is reasonable to think that these elements can be formal or eidetic elements, given the Stranger's own practice in building up the divisions of various beings, and that they are themselves knowable in *some* sense.[201]

Children are able to "say the truth" about such short syllables: they have true opinion, but not knowledge. What they lack is practice and experience with letters, and what they are to achieve is proficiency in recognizing these elements in all possible combinations, not just in the simple ones. It is such proficiency in identifying these elements in all sorts of combinations, not the mere familiarity with particular elements in particular combinations, that truly counts as knowledge. So long as they do not have this practice, the children make mistakes; and these mistakes are much like those described by Socrates in the *Theaetetus* (207a9ff., especially 207d8–208a8) in trying to elucidate the second meaning of *logos* as a "list of elements." Socrates described there how a student might be able to correctly spell "Theaetetus" but be unable to spell "Theodorus" (thinking it starts with T instead of Θ). The mistake is pardonable: Θ (the letter with which both Theodorus and Theaetetus start) sounds very much like T at the beginning of a

---

[201] In the *Theaetetus* Socrates had characterized the elements in such a way that they appeared to be purely material, perceivable but not knowable (see Sedley [2004, 153–163]). Yet individual letters, as the discussion in the *Philebus* shows (18b6ff.), are themselves *eidē* that "pick out" form out of the unlimited manifold of voice; and the Eleatic does not explicitly exclude that elements could be *formal* (and hence knowable) components of things. To be aware of letters "in simple combinations" should thus not be identified with an awareness of pure individuals (in the sense in which "elements" appear to be used by Socrates in *Theaetetus* in 201d8ff., or even in the Wittgensteinian sense of the *Tractatus*), but with an awareness of *types* of things, even if imperfect. See also the following discussion, three paragraphs down.

word. Yet if someone is able to spell correctly the first syllable of Theaetetus' name but not the first syllable of Theodorus' name, even though both start with the same two letters, he cannot yet be said to know "letters" properly (he does not have the know-how of spelling). He does not yet have the ability to identify the elements of the whole with which he is concerned (namely, the Greek language) whenever and wherever they occur, and in particular is unable to say when the elements of some particular syllable are the same and when they are different to those of some other syllable (cf. *Statesman* 278b6–c1). Knowledge could thus not be merely the ability to identify and list the elements of some particular complex being (e.g., a word), even if such a list were correct (this is merely true opinion); one must be able to recognize these same elements when they turn up in arbitrary combinations.

The Stranger now describes the "easiest" and "most beautiful" way to leverage the correctly judged combination of elements to produce a correct judgment of the not yet correctly judged combination, that is, to "apply" the empirical familiarity with the elements in the smaller syllables to the attempt to correctly judge the composition of the larger or more complex syllables or combinations.[202] The procedure is as follows: first, the child must be shown the combinations in which he has the correct opinion about the elements; then these combinations must be set next to the combinations not yet known, so that

[202] The use of paradigm is in this case set in a pedagogical context, where the Stranger already knows which paradigms will be most useful for Young Socrates, as Arends (2001) rightly stresses against the view of Lane (1998); but there seems to be no reason to think that paradigms cannot also be on occasion used to generate new knowledge, as Lane wants to argue, *pace* Arends, even if they are not so used here. Mathematicians, for example, often generate new knowledge by focusing on less complicated versions of a given problem or abstract object; see for example Polya (1971) or Ruelle (2007). Indeed, Arends seems to concede the point when he writes that the dialectician must "analyse all 'simple' 'perceivable' things," since "the entrance to the 'greatest things' may only be found by means of the right paradigm" (133).

the elements in both combinations can be shown (presumably, but not necessarily, by the teacher) to be the same or different (278a8–b5). As a result, the student now correctly judges the composition of *both* syllables, not just the first one (278c5–6).

Note that what is the same in both combinations or syllables must be *eidē*, looks or aspects. The element of "carding" in weaving and part of the element of "education" in statesmanship are the same in that they both participate in the same *eidē*, that is, insofar as both are arts of separation; but carding is not education, just as the Θ of Theaetetus is not physically the same as the Θ of Theodorus but merely a different instance of the *eidos* of Θ. Moreover, the success of the comparison procedure depends not only on finding "words" that contain the same eidetic elements (such as, e.g., Socrates and Theaetetus, both of which contain the element α), but that contain the same elements in the same order or eidetic relationship (such as Theaetetus and Theodorus, both of which contain the syllable "Θε"). It is the earlier (correct) perception of elements in easier combinations that is leveraged for learning the more difficult combinations or syllables, not the bare perception of letters. True opinion of a complex whole like statesmanship, we should emphasize, is true opinion of structure, not just of isolated elements.[203]

Note also what this implies for the proper size of a paradigm: a paradigm of something should be small enough so that all its elements are distinctly perceived by the learner, but large enough to contain the eidetic structure of the larger whole. There is a tension here, for the paradigm in some sense cannot have a structure as complex as that of the thing it is a paradigm of, since it is a "smaller word." Indeed, the paradigm of weaving fails to contain the fullness of the structure of statesmanship: statesmanship coordinates and gives

---

[203] Cf. Rowe (1995b, note to 278e10–11): "[t]he claim seems to be that—if a model of a suitable sort is available—they do in fact know what statesmanship is, insofar as they understand the same configuration in the other simpler ('smaller') case." I would say that they do not *know* but are able to judge correctly what statesmanship is.

meaning to a larger set of arts and activities, as we have seen. The Stranger leverages the discussion of weaving into a way to gain insight into the (more complex) structure of statesmanship and its formal elements, but statesmanship itself is never fully modeled by weaving. Weaving is thus a distorted image of statesmanship, not an *eikōn* of it; and so is every model used for educative purposes.

The Stranger stresses that the result of any single side to side comparison of two "syllables" (the paradigm and that of which it is a paradigm) is true opinion (not *epistēmē*) about the eidetic structure of the more complex one: the student now comes to judge correctly of the composition of the more complex syllable (278c3–6). In the terminology of the *Republic* (discussed previously), after using a paradigm one acquires true opinion (judges correctly) about the *model* of the initially unknown syllable, e.g., one acquires true opinion about the proper model of statesmanship (recognizes the correct model of statesmanship) from the side-to-side comparison with the correctly specified model of weaving, but one does not yet have a full grasp ("understanding") of the formal elements underlying the model. The implied point seems to be that knowledge (*epistēmē* or *technē*) is manifested not in the correct judgment about the formal structure (the model) of this or that particular complex being—just as knowledge of letters is not manifested simply in the fact that the pupil learns to spell a few more complex words after a short period of practice—but in the skill, that comes with much practice, of distinctly grasping these formal components of reality (the *eidē*) in all their possible combinations, which would thus allow one in turn to *have* true opinion about all complex beings within some domain. At the highest level, this is simply dialectics (cf. 285d7), the art of the philosopher, whose domain is the whole of reality, but the same should be true of all arts, whose domain is more restricted.

More generally, knowledge (*epistēmē* or *technē*) now appears as the know-how (skill or art) that leverages a grasp of formal elements to judge correctly arbitrary combinations of such elements, yet we *acquire* a secure grasp of these formal elements by leveraging our correct judgments of particular combinations of them. By learning to judge correctly the multiplicity of combinations of formal elements (and hence their similarity/difference, their "contrast" with all other formal elements) we eventually come to *know* each of these formal elements, and in *knowing* these formal elements (and hence being able to recognize them whenever and wherever they appear) we can correctly *judge* their combinations.[204] Knowledge is thus normally acquired *via* true opinion (278a5 suggests there may be other, harder and less beautiful ways of acquiring knowledge), and yet it makes true opinion secure.

Knowledge and measure: 283b–287b

We are now in a better position to understand how statesmanship can leverage a grasp of formal structure to decide *which* actions are just at particular times and places, but we still need one more element: the concept of measure, which the Stranger introduces after the discussion of weaving.[205] To "measure" anything, in the Stranger's presentation, is to find a measure for it, that is, a standard that allows us to place the thing in relation to the ideas of "excess and deficiency," or more and less; and this can be done in two ways.

---

[204] The basic idea is in the spirit of the *Sophist*'s solution to the problem of false judgment. Just as false judgment is possible because "not being" is simply "otherness," and hence we can come to judge of something that it is other than what it is, knowledge of form becomes possible when we learn to recognize how each formal element of reality is both the same (in some combinations) and other (in other combinations) than all the other elements.

[205] This section has given rise to a vast and not always very useful literature. See, for a critical account of some of the more bizarre interpretations of the section on measure, Lafrance (1995). A very careful reading of this section, from which I nevertheless sometimes differ, is found in Sayre (2005). Delcomminette (2000) is also essential for understanding the connections between measure and the forms. Other useful discussions of this section are found in Harvey (2009), Hoffmann (1993), and Tordesillas (1995). An earlier version of what follows has been published before in Márquez (2006).

We can measure "excess and deficiency" in one way by relating the "greater" exclusively to the "smaller" and vice versa (283d11–e1). This means that given two objects A and B of some kind (such as two pieces of woolen cloth, for example) we can find some respect (such as length, breadth, or area, all "numerable" dimensions; cf. 284e4–5) such that we can say that A is either greater or smaller than (or equal to) B. B is here the measure of A in that A appears great (or small) in relation to B, and vice versa: hence A and B are measured against each other only (283e11), regardless of whether the greatness (or smallness) of either is sufficient for anything else. That there is an art to this sort of measurement is evident in this example since it is not always immediately clear, given two pieces of woolen cloth of similar dimensions, which one has the bigger surface area. A certain know-how is here necessary to ascertain excess and deficiency, a know-how that may involve (but does not always require) the use of a common measure in the narrow sense (such as the square meter) and the performance of arithmetical calculations that render the two pieces of cloth measurable in the respect of interest (in this case, area).[206] At any rate,

[206] Cf. Rosen (1995, 120). Oddly, Sayre (2005, 9) argues that the first sort of measurement cannot be of specific quantities (as when we say that Socrates is a foot shorter than Theaetetus), and goes as far as to suggest that these arts of measurements are not really arts at all, but mere guesswork (22). Sayre's argument relies on a peculiar interpretation of *arithmos* as measure, but seems to be internally contradictory, since it would demand that the art of measurement according to more and less not be an art at all (contrary to the explicit statements of the Stranger), whereas the art of measuring with actual numbers (by correctly judging, for instance, that Socrates is a foot shorter than Theaetetus) must always be an art of measuring according to the mean, even though such "mean" measurement cannot be found in the example. Sayre relies on a specific reading of the *Philebus* for this interpretation, but the passages he cites do not support the conclusion that the kind of measurement the Stranger is speaking of here can never be numerically precise, only that it sometimes may not be. To use one of Sayre's examples, two armies can indeed be compared to each other "roughly"—without counting the exact number of soldiers—but they can also be compared "precisely" without for that reason involving the measurement according to the mean. See also Harvey (2009).

the specific procedure which we might use to accomplish this measurement may vary, but the point is clear: such measurement can only tell us that A is bigger (or smaller) than B (by so much), a fact that is disclosed in the act of measurement, but never that A is "too small" or "too big" for some X.

But there is another way in which we may measure something: A may be too small (or too big) for some purpose, regardless of whether A is smaller or greater than B in a relative sense. Too much is always too much for something. Thus it may be that a piece of cloth A is larger than B in a relative sense, but still too small for the purpose of creating a cloak that fully covers a particular person's body. A in that case falls short (or is bigger) than the quantity or number C (or range of quantities C) of A's material in some respect (length, breadth, or area, for example) that makes X actual (here a warm cloak). Here A is not measured against any arbitrary thing B, but against that quantity C of something (which may not in fact exist) that is actually needed to *produce* X. Note, incidentally, how this sort of measurement is essential to the production and judgment of *images*. To say that an image is accurate or inaccurate is always to make a determination of whether its parts are "too large" or "too small" relative to the corresponding parts of the original, which serves as the measure of the image. Moreover, in making this sort of determination we can also *bring into being* an accurate (or intentionally inaccurate, for that matter) image of this original.

This quantity or number C can thus be called the necessary quantity or number for the generation of X, and hence this sort of measurement can be said to be "according to the necessary being of the generation [of something]" (283d8–9). Furthermore, this quantity C (of length, breadth, or area, in this case) is such that we can say that it is "in the middle": more or less than C means that X fails to be produced or is produced incompletely. C can thus be called the "mean," *to metrion* (283e11), and this sort of measurement can thus be said to be in respect of C or the mean, *pros to metrion*.

Later, in his formal division of the art of measurement (284e2–8)—an art which would seem to be implicit in all arts, as we shall see below—the Stranger extends his conception of this second sort of measure beyond the mean. He thus speaks not only of *to metrion*, the mean, but also of *to prepon*, the fitting; *ton kairon*, the opportune; *to deon*, the necessary; and finally of "everything that is settled away from the extremes into the middle." These characterizations of the measure in question are all related, but they nevertheless refer to different things. The mean points to the dimension of quantity (the quantity C of something necessary for producing or acquiring X), the fitting and the necessary to the idea of things that belong together (the thing C without which X cannot be produced or acquired perfectly or even at all), and the opportune to the dimension of time (the time T at which some specific action must be done so as to produce or acquire X). The final description, everything that is settled away from the extremes and towards the center (a description that is the very center of the dialogue, incidentally) describes a general characteristic of all these measures, namely, that they provide the standard against which we can speak of the "center" and the "extremes."

Note that these are not necessarily measures of "quality" as opposed to "quantity." The weaver (to take the example that motivates the digression on measure) does not measure the amount of wool he has against any random amount of woolen cloth, but against that amount of wool that would be required to create a *himation* that actually protects a man from the harshness of the weather; and such an amount can often be quantitatively determined. In order to create a good cloak for somebody, the weaver must know how much wool he needs, that is, how much wool is neither too much nor too little if the cloak is to fulfill its function in a particular case; and in actually carrying out this sort of measurement, he must determine whether any particular piece of wool is bigger or smaller than the "standard," that is, he must carry out a measurement of the first kind as well. Similarly, in order to create a good picture of a person, the painter must measure the parts of the original relative to each other. The second kind of measurement may thus (but need not) include the first kind.

Note also that this sort of measure does not determine or help us know the purpose or activity X which gives it meaning. Such purpose must be already posited in order for this sort of measurement to take place, but this sort of measure is nevertheless involved in all purposive activity as it allows us to calibrate means to ends, and hence in all moral activity, as the Stranger makes clear (283e6). Insofar as the good is an end, therefore, being a good or a bad person involves a measurement of one's activity against that ("ideal") activity that brings about good things. It is thus correct to understand this sort of measure as involved in purposive activity, but incorrect to understand it as a definition of the good except insofar as it determines what actions or things bring about states of affairs that can be said to be good for a given activity, or, in shorthand, insofar as it helps bring about the good in concrete instances. The mean is not itself the good, but that particular thing C that is required to bring about a concrete good thing in concrete circumstances, and that particular thing itself varies from context to context: it *connects* the determinate good of some practice to the particulars of the sensible world. So one cannot imitate a form of knowledge by always providing exactly C in order to do X, for C will vary depending on circumstances; it is the task of the art of measurement to determine C in light of the forms of order (the "originals") that regulate the production of X. More generally stated, the measure of the mean "mediates" between the general knowledge of the purpose of some activity (e.g., weaving, which intends to produce cloaks that protect from the cold) and the concrete situation (e.g., the fact that this person requires a cloak)—as the argument of the dialogue demands of the statesman (cf. 294a4–b6, 295b1–5). It is only by means of measurement that any know-how finds purchase in the flux of bodily reality as a way of connecting form and concrete judgment, and can thus exist as a know-how properly speaking, as the Stranger goes on to explain.

The Stranger says that the arts and their works, including statesmanship and weaving depend on the existence of this sort of measurement, which he characterizes as something hard but not impossible to achieve (284a5–b2). Their inquiry itself would be fruitless should this sort of measurement not exist (284b4–5), and so they must assume the "existence of a measure in relation to the generation of the mean." The passage is obscure.[207] If we take the "mean" to be the due measure that is instantiated in some particular activity for some concrete purpose (e.g., the size of the cloth that is necessary for creating a cloak that is large enough to cover a specific person well), then the Stranger seems to be suggesting that there must exist a measure of measures, that is, a measure that determines whether any given mean is actually too much or too little for some ultimate purpose (e.g., the good of human life). In a compressed way, the Stranger would be alluding to the good itself as the measure against which all other measures are either too much or too little, and indeed to the thesis of the *Republic* that knowledge is ultimately possible *only* in light of the good. On this view, arts are only possible if the knowledge they embody is connected to some insight into the good, insofar as the good provides a determinate measure of what needs to be done in the particular circumstances to produce the proper end of the activity (e.g., health, justice, etc.). For example, it is only in light of the good that the doctor can understand (the form of) *health* as a certain proportion among the parts of the body, and hence act to preserve such proportion; without the good as a superordinate measure, there can be no standard by which the doctor can measure his activity, and hence no art of medicine properly speaking.[208]

---

[207] See Sayre (2005, 6, 19), and Hoffmann (1993) for some useful discussion.
[208] On this view, the idea of measurement does *not* represent a real change from the *Republic*, but rather a fuller articulation of what it means for knowledge to be possible only in light of the good.

But the Stranger could also mean that whenever somebody with an art engages in measurement—e.g., when the weaver measures the amount of yarn he or she needs to weave a cloak, or how much tension the warp and the woof must have, or the appropriate "straightness" of the web, such measurement is not made against some ideal standard accessible independently of the practice of weaving; on the contrary, the practice of weaving must itself bring into being this standard concretely (in, e.g., the selection of the amount of yarn or the tension of warp and woof or the straightness of the web). More formally, if we take the mean to be that quantity C of G that makes X possible, then to measure A or B against C is to measure them against that quantity of G that must be generated or brought into being if X is also to be brought into being. A or B are measured not against C "abstractly" but against the coming into being of C, which would ensure the desired effect X. But C is not ascertainable outside the practice or art: to know C is to know how to bring it about, as we can see when we reflect on an art like weaving.

On either of these interpretations, however, art or *technē* always requires a link between the abstract understanding of how much is too much or too little for bringing about some state of affairs and the concrete application of such understanding to concrete cases. All successful application in some sense "brings into being" the mean for a particular context, not being content with simply observing it. Conversely, without the possibility of bringing into being the quantity of something that is "just right" for bringing about X, no one could ever have an art related to the practice of bringing into being X (cf. 284b7–c4). Thus, if it is impossible for the weaver to bring about the requisite straightness of the web or the appropriate tension of warp and woof, then weaving as an art becomes impossible. The *testimonia* of the *technai* themselves, however, is at this point and for their purposes sufficient to guarantee that such a form of measurement exists (284d2–d9) since the dependence of *technai* and this sort of measurement is mutual: if one exists, the other does, and vice versa, and they can see that the arts exist, so some such measure must also exist. We should note, however, that this assumption only holds for the arts as a whole, not necessarily for any particular art. Their assumption does not compel the existence of a measure for the art of statesmanship, unless we take the first interpretation strictly and make the measure of statesmanship the good itself.

Why is this sort of measurement connected to the *technai*? If the *technai* are the forms of human know-how, as we have indicated already, to have a *technē* is to know how to reliably produce or acquire some X in some restricted field of human endeavor, and this implies being able to determine what quantity or number or kind of a certain thing A reliably produces or acquires X under any given circumstances. Thus the doctor must know the proper dosage of a drug to cure a disease for a given person of a certain size and age, and similarly the shoemaker must know how much leather he needs to use to create shoes that are comfortable and durable for a given person of a certain size and age, among other things. Should this sort of measurement not exist, all the *technai* would be no more than experienced guesswork. On the first interpretation of the measure of the generation of the mean, moreover, we could argue that even highly reliable guesswork would produce effects that are too much or too little in relation to what is good for us.

Consider the example of "cookery," which Socrates suggests in the *Gorgias* is nothing more than guesswork (cf. *Gorgias* 463a6ff., and the discussion above). The cook cannot know in advance given a person of some size or age, how much sugar will be necessary to give that person pleasure. Experience can make cooks learn to please particular people, and even large classes of people, but they cannot reliably produce pleasure by their art. But even if they could, they would not necessarily know what food is actually good for people, since pleasure and the goodness of food are not directly related: we can experience pleasure by eating food that is not healthy for us. To say that this sort of measurement does not exist in any given area, in other words, is thus to say that there is no reliable way of determining what quantity or number of C of G produces or acquires the explicit goal of the practice in any given situation, and thus whether or not quantity or number A of G, which is at hand, is in fact too much or too little for producing or acquiring the explicit goal of the practice; or else to say that even if C could be reliably determined for *that* goal, it could not be determined for our ultimate purposes, that is, our good. We could not tell, for example, why health and not pleasure is the appropriate end of the activity, or what combination of these ends is appropriate for us.

A presupposition of the existence of this form of measurement (and conversely, of the arts) is the regularity of nature in its causal relations. The *technai* are only possible if nature is reliably regular in its productive aspect, and hence if it is possible to measure, given some situation, how much of G will be necessary to bring about X. But to the extent that the picture of the cosmos the Stranger presented in the myth is true, the world only imperfectly holds on to its order; and this would seem to imply that in its productive aspect, nature is also only imperfectly regular. The imperfect regularity of nature is only implicitly acknowledged by the Stranger when he says (284a8–b1) that the *technai* preserve the mean only with difficulty, though they do preserve it, that is, that the determination of the more and the less than the mean is not something impossible (as it would be if nature were completely irregular) but only difficult (as it is given the "intermediate" condition of the universe). The existence of the *technai* is thus not a complete proof of the regularity of nature in general and of the existence of this sort of measurement in particular; for that, a consideration of "the precise itself" (and thus of the limits of measurement and art) would be required, and such a demonstration would be longer, according to the Stranger

(284c7–d2), than even the demonstration of non-being in the *Sophist*.[209]

The difficulty of the sort of measurement the Stranger has described, shown in the drama of the dialogue by the errors that they commit throughout their discussion, makes it clear that all *technē* is a fragile achievement, statesmanship perhaps more so than any other art. If Young Socrates can see this, he will indeed have understood something about statesmanship and about art in general, and will be less willing to believe that his own art of mathematics, which seems more precise than all other arts, gives him any sort of immunity from this human predicament.

The Stranger described the necessary art of measurement for the production or acquisition of things, but he has not yet said anything about whether or not such things are worth pursuing. He has not said, in other words, in relation to the production or acquisition of *which* state of affairs the art of measurement should be employed. In particular, from what he has said it would be possible to apply the art of measurement to the Stranger's speeches and find out that they have been too long for the production of pleasure or the presentation of the account of the weaver. The "means" have been discussed; now

[209] As Lane (1998, 129–130) notes, the Stranger applies a form of "meta-measurement" here, contrasting the sufficient with the precise itself, and thus the *technai* as they really are (ultimately devoid of full precision) with philosophy. For a contrary view, see Tordesillas (1995), who believes that all of these measures must be independent of chance and the disorder of the cosmos. But that is precisely what the myth shows cannot be the case entirely. Howland (1998, 271) seems to go too far in the other direction when he claims that the mean is restricted to *technē* rather than *epistēmē*, and can never be known scientifically but only by way of familiarity. I do not think this is necessarily the case, since I think knowledge of the mean is bound up with knowledge of the productive regularity of nature in some field of human endeavor, though it is not necessarily a matter of knowing rules. It is true that the mean in any given circumstance is not known "scientifically, after the manner of unchanging beings," but it is also not known by mere experience: there must be insight into the regularity of nature.

the ends against which the measurement is to be carried out must be discussed, if briefly (285c4ff.).

In order to present the ends against which measurement is to be carried out, the Stranger asks Young Socrates (285c8–d3) whether those learning about letters are supposed to consider a problem about the letters of a specific word more in order to learn the letters of that specific word or in order to become more expert about letters in general, and thus to be able to spell all sorts of words. Note the Stranger's use of the comparative *mallon*, more (285d1); even if understanding a specific word is not the whole point of learning to spell, it is *part* of the point, however small. Young Socrates of course answers that learners tackle such problems for the sake of learning about letters generally; learning about one thing is not yet knowledge, as we saw earlier, but merely a part of a practice that leads eventually, and after much effort, to *technē* or *epistēmē*, that is, to know-how rather than to mere true opinion.

Tackling a particular spelling problem thus makes sense mostly in the context of a practice in spelling that will allow one eventually to read and thus to learn about other things, not just about words. The Stranger thus poses the question more generally. Is the search for the statesman more—note again the comparative *mallon* (285d6)—for its own sake or more for the sake of becoming more expert about the eidetic structure of all things, that is, becoming "more dialectical about all things" (285d5–7)? Clearly, Young Socrates answers, it is for the sake of learning about the eidetic structure of all things. Hence, *a fortiori*, the Stranger points out, learning about weaving is not for its own sake (285d9–10).

This does not mean, however, that learning about the statesman is valueless. The argument of the Stranger clearly implies a hierarchy of things to be learned, at the bottom of which are those things that are perceptible or have perceptible likenesses, and at the top of which stand the things of which there are no such likenesses, and thus require to be shown by means of *logoi* alone (what I have called models: recall the discussion of knowledge in the *Republic*, above). The former are "smaller," the latter "bigger," not only in mere size but also in honor (285d10–286b1).[210] The Stranger does not tell Young Socrates to what category the statesman belongs. It is not entirely clear whether the statesman has a clear perceptible likeness (as the facts that he can be shown in part by means of the weaver, and that the statesman has a body, suggest) or not (as the facts that a long argument is necessary to bring him to light, and cannot be simply pointed out, unlike the weaver, and that statesmanship is a bodiless thing, suggest); but it seems plausible to consider the statesman one of the greatest beings. After all, though it has perceptible likenesses, they are not sufficiently clear to bring him to light (cf. *enargōs* 286a2), as the drama of the dialogue has amply demonstrated.[211]

Whatever the case, it is clear that the Stranger believes that the discussion of the statesman, though important in its own right, is subordinated to the task of becoming expert in understanding those things that have no bodies. (And it may be that Young Socrates is simply more interested in becoming an expert in dialectics than in statesmanship.) Abstract knowledge about statesmanship must always constitute a lower form of knowledge than this other expertise, though it is unclear whether this implies that the expertise of the statesman is also a lower form of expertise, especially since it is likely to involve knowledge of such bodiless beings as justice and the good. It is reasonable to suppose that becoming more "dialectical" about all things—that is, knowing more about the eidetic structure of all things—is a necessary step in becoming a statesman; and hence that it is not possible to determine anything about

[210] This passage has generated an extensive literature, starting from Owen (1973). The concerns of this literature, however, are not relevant to our concerns at this point.

[211] Contrary to what Klein (1977, 176–177), seems to imply by suggesting that weaving is the sensible resemblance of statesmanship. But the Stranger speaks of *sufficiently clear* perceptible resemblances, and weaving can hardly be said to be a sufficiently clear resemblance of the statesman.

the relative wisdom of statesman and philosopher from this passage.[212] Dialectics would then be preparation for statesmanship, and philosophy would be, as I have stressed throughout, on the way to statesmanship but not necessarily identical with it. At the same time, however, it is worth stressing that the Stranger does not explicitly say anything about the relative value of statesmanship and philosophy.

I have not said much thus far about the context of the discussion of measure and paradigms, discussing their substantive content without commenting on their place in the overall structure of the dialogue. The discussion of paradigms came about due to the failure of the shepherd as a paradigm of the statesman. Indeed, the problem was less that they had chosen an inadequate paradigm than that they had not chosen a paradigm at all (contrary to the Stranger's methodological strictures in *Sophist* 218d): the implicit model of their division was discovered only after they had already been led astray.[213] After the discussion of paradigm, the Stranger introduces the paradigm of weaving, which, as we saw in chapter 1, serves as a model for the entire task of discovering the statesman. But the utility of the discussion of weaving is not immediately apparent,[214] and so the Stranger introduces the notion of due measure, presumably in order to show that their discussion has not been a waste of time. But he does not, in actual fact, then justify the length of the section on weaving;[215] he merely suggests that whatever they are doing, they are doing for the sake of becoming more dialectical.

---

212 See, for a more extensive defense of this view, Arends (1999, 102). Arends rightly notes the connection between "dialectics" and "intertwining," connecting the latter with the activity of the statesman.

213 See Benardete (1992, 43).

214 As it is clear not only from the Stranger's own words, but also from the reactions of modern commentators: see, e.g., Annas and Waterfield (1995, 47n45).

215 See Benardete (1992, 25).

The Stranger is clearly inviting us to see for ourselves how the discussion of weaving actually helps us understand the structure of the conversation; we cannot make progress in understanding statesmanship unless we figure out by ourselves how the two parts of the division of statesmanship fit together in much the same way that the two parts of the division of weaving fit together, as we saw in chapter 1. Being able to see this for ourselves involves an increase in one's dialectical abilities; it shows that one has grasped the formal structures common to both weaving and statesmanship, and hence that one has become more "dialectical." Hence the Stranger rightly declines to engage in a detailed justification of the length of the discussion of weaving; doing this work for us would not help us become more dialectical.

Moreover, without the discussion of measure we would have little understanding of how the knowledge of the statesman could regulate the disorder of human affairs by means of the intuition of order that the myth suggested. Indeed, the apparent disorder of the dialogue also indicates something about the difficulties of statesmanship: the regulation of the disorder of human affairs may itself appear as a form of disorder, a lack of structure. In this sense, the *discussion* of statesmanship through the dialogue is a more accurate image of statesmanship than even the *division* of statesmanship, though for reasons discussed earlier, no *static* image is ever a fully accurate picture of an art.

5. Law

AS WE SAW IN CHAPTER 1, the Stranger resumes the discussion of statesmanship after the section on measure by separating the statesman from all the other arts that contribute to the care (or indeed the production, broadly understood) of human beings. But the Stranger soon runs into difficulties; some of the "rivals" of the statesman for the care of human beings turn out to be harder than expected to separate from the statesman. Some false rulers take refuge in the majesty of the law, and so the rule of law must be shown to be inferior to the rule of knowledge. The rulers without knowledge or law, by contrast, are easily dismissed once the law has been shown to be inferior to knowledge.

These sections of the dialogue constitute the heart of the political theory of the *Statesman*. Yet the Stranger's arguments about the nature and limits of the rule of law are complex and poorly understood.[216] The best way to approach them is to notice that the Stranger explores the relationship between the knowledge of the statesman and the law from two distinct and opposed perspectives, that of the genuine statesman and that of the city. From the point of view of the genuine statesman,

[216] Much controversy surrounds the interpretation of the relevant passages, with some scholars suggesting essentially that the whole argument is incoherent. For a sense of the variety of positions that have been taken on this question see Klosko (2006), Neiman (2007), Rowe (1995b, 2001a, 2005), Samaras (2002), Teisserenc (2005); I address some of the specific arguments made by these authors in the notes below.

the law is the instrument that he is forced to use in view of the fact that he cannot be everywhere he is needed, and which he is free to disregard when he is present. From the point of view of the city, however, the law is the instrument that it uses to protect itself from what it sees as potentially malicious uses of office and of the knowledge associated with rule by codifying the city's experience to date of the things that have helped preserve it.

The Stranger's argumentative strategy in this section thus consists in showing that from either perspective (that of the city and that of the statesman) the rule of law is inferior to the rule of knowledge, but that nevertheless the rule of law would be better than any alternative form of rule not involving genuinely knowledgeable individuals even if the laws in question had been created by the city without the help of knowledgeable individuals and made unchangeable and unrevisable. His argument does not, however, suggest that this is the best possible "implementation" of the rule of law, or speculate about potential improvements to it. His main concern is to show Young Socrates that, if we take a suitably adequate view of what law is, then at its best (when made by a genuine statesman) the rule of law would still be worse than the rule of a knowledgeable statesman, and at its worst (when created by a city without much participation by knowledgeable individuals and made unrevisable) it would still be better than the alternative of the rule by ignorant individuals in their own interest. Hence in the end the difference between the laws that a genuine statesman would create and the laws that a city would make for itself turns out not to be especially important: all law is at best a kind of "true opinion," and hence inferior to knowledge, though superior to ignorance.[217]

[217] There turn out to be minor differences between the laws that a genuine statesman would create, and the laws that a city would make for itself, but both kinds of laws remain mere images of the knowledge of the statesman.

The Stranger's argument about the relative value of law has some important implications. In particular, it shows that the perspectives on law of the statesman and the city are in practical conflict: because the city cannot distinguish with any degree of certainty between genuine and virtuous statesmen and malicious or ignorant imitators, it insists on law the most when someone claims to have such knowledge; but it is precisely when someone actually has this knowledge (that is, when someone is truly a statesman) that the law is least useful. In the Stranger's view, the city in its second sailing thus maneuvers between the Scylla of accepting the claims of false statesmen (and hence rejecting law when the rule of law is better than the rule of false statesmen) and the Charybdis of rejecting the claims of true statesmen (and hence accepting law when the rule of the genuine statesman is better) if it wants to endure for as long as possible in the best possible state. Given the scarcity of genuine political knowledge and the abundance of malicious imitations, it is generally (but not necessarily always) better to err on the side of law; but if the city always erred on the side of law it could never be open to the transformative knowledge and action of a genuine statesman, and hence would be trapped in what we might call, using modern terminology, a suboptimal equilibrium. This practical dilemma is not insoluble, to be sure, but it is beyond the scope of the Eleatic Stranger's argument. It is only in the *Laws* that we can see the full extent of Plato's efforts to overcome it through institutional innovations like the Nocturnal Council, as we shall see.

The argument of this chapter thus has some important implications for how we understand the politico-philosophic project of the *Statesman*. First, contrary to some widespread views,[218] my argument implies that Plato does not believe in the *Statesman* that the best form of the rule of law is one in which

[218] See Klosko (2008), for example, whose views I argue against at more length in Márquez (2011), as well as Neiman (2007).

the laws are unchangeable and unrevisable, and it certainly does not imply that Plato was committed to a defense of the rule of law that rules out the possibility of their gradual change informed by experience and Socratic-style inquiry (though not necessarily knowledge) into the virtues. On the contrary, as we shall see, the Eleatic Stranger's argument implies that any philosophically informed "implementation" of the rule of law should have *space* for inquiry within the bounds of the law, and in particular makes conceptual *space* for the kinds of "institutions of inquiry" represented by the Nocturnal Council in the *Laws* and the Academy in Athens as necessary complements to the rule of law.

Second, and relatedly, the argument implies that the best ruler of the city in the absence of the true statesman turns out to be the man who knows that he does not know (and in particular the man who knows that he does not have the science of the statesman). This is the Socratic philosopher, whose knowledge is of his own ignorance, and who is therefore not tempted to claim that he knows better than the laws, though he wishes to know and hence engages in inquiry into the nature of virtue and justice. The argument thus implicitly vindicates something like the Socratic philosopher as king, that is, as the best ruler of the city in the likely absence of the statesman.

I stress that I do not claim that the Eleatic Stranger explicitly argues either for an institution like the Nocturnal Council of the *Laws* or for the desirability of "philosopher-kings" as the second-best alternative to the rule of genuine statesmen. The purpose of his argument is simply to show Young Socrates that the rule of law is inferior to the rule of knowledge from any perspective, though superior to the rule of ignorance, not to construct a theory of the varieties of the rule of law and of the ways in which systematic inquiry can complement it without necessarily undermining its authority, or to solve the practical dilemmas faced by a city that is considering whether to stick to the rule of law or to heed the claims of would-be statesmen. He does not mention philosopher-rulers at all, and in general seems to consider both the law-abiding and the non-law-abiding rulers sophists, since the rule of law as it is commonly understood (though not necessarily as a philosopher would understand it) prevents the kind of inquiry into the good, the noble, and the just that is essential to philosophical activity. But I do argue that, suitably understood, the presuppositions of the Stranger's defense of the rule of law suggest that there is a space between the rule of unchangeable, unrevisable laws and the rule of the statesman, and that the logical way in which this space is filled is through institutions of inquiry that enable the rulers of the city to engage both in Socratic inquiry about virtue and in "comparative" political inquiry about the laws and their performance while nevertheless safeguarding the law's authority, that is, institutions like the Nocturnal Council in the *Laws*, or indeed the Academy in Athens.

In what follows, I develop these arguments in greater detail. The first section examines the statesman's view of the law. I show how the Stranger establishes the scarcity of political knowledge, how the need for law directly results from and is intensified by such scarcity, and how law is nevertheless seen by the genuine statesman as an inferior expedient. The second section examines the people's view of the law. I show that the Stranger thinks that from this point of view the law is properly conceived as a form of protection against those who claim to have knowledge, how this protection works by codifying those practices that have in the past helped the city, how such codification leads to inferior institutions than the rule of the genuine statesman yet even at its worst leads to superior results than the rule of the ignorant. The final section explores and dismisses some potential problems with the Stranger's arguments, and argues that these arguments are consistent with the view of the rule of law that the Athenian Stranger develops in the *Laws*.

The scarcity of statesmanship and the need for law: 291d–296a

The Stranger's examination of the perspective of the genuine statesman on the laws has two major parts. In the first part, the Stranger argues that political knowledge cannot be a common attribute of individuals or political regimes, that is, he establishes its scarcity. In the second part, he uses this fact to argue that the statesman must therefore make use of laws, since the single statesman could not take into account all the particular details of individual situations as they arose. Concurrently, however, he argues that law is nevertheless an inadequate substitute for the statesman's knowledge, an image of the statesman's genuine wisdom, though an image that, as we shall see, stands to his expertise as true opinion stands to knowledge.

Political regimes and the scarcity of political knowledge

The Stranger begins the argument for the scarcity of political knowledge by introducing the notion of a *politeia*, a political regime (291d7). The *politeia* is the form of political rule (291d1), the ultimate order of the *polis*. To ask what is the *politeia* of a particular *polis* means to ask who rules, for what end, and how.

The Stranger first surveys what he takes to be the common answers to this question: what are the political regimes? In common opinion, cities differ with respect to their regime along four dimensions. First (291d1–9), they differ in the number of their rulers. This yields three basic sorts of *politeia*, namely, monarchy, oligarchy, and democracy. Later on the Stranger will further characterize this dimension as that of the strength of the ruler(s) to impose his (their) order (cf. 303a2–b2); the greater the number of rulers, the greater the dispersal of power and hence the greater the difficulty for the ruler(s) to impose his (their) order.

Second (291e1–3), in common opinion, the *politeiai* differ in a) the way in which the rule of the one, few or many is experienced by the ruled, that is, whether they submit "willingly" or "unwillingly" to it; b) the poverty and wealth of the rulers, and hence their material interests; and c) the way in which the rulers actually rule, that is, whether by means of general rules or arbitrarily, with or without law. These three dimensions further differentiate the three basic sorts of *politeia*, in effect doubling their number. First, there is monarchy and tyranny, a distinction that emerges primarily—but not exclusively—out of the experience of the people of the rule of one, that is, whether they bear this rule willingly or unwillingly, or whether they think it is according to law or not. Second, there is aristocracy and oligarchy, both of which seem to be the rule of the rich (cf. 301a6–8), presumably in their material interests, though such rule is carried out differently by the rulers: in an aristocracy according to law and (hence) willingly accepted, in an oligarchy not according to law and (hence) not willingly accepted. Finally there is just democracy, which is the rule of the poor (291e10–292a3), presumably in their interest, though the Stranger admits that democracy can vary according to whether the rich accept the rule of the poor willingly or unwillingly, and according to whether this rule is according to law or not.

The Stranger does not spend a lot of time straightening out the ambiguities and contradictions of the common opinions about *politeiai*; at any rate he will collapse all of these distinctions later into the distinction between rule by law and lawless rule (302e7–8) as the only distinction that describes anything of significance. Only law turns out to be an image of knowledge; force or consent and material interest are not such images. To be sure, the distinction between rule willingly and unwillingly accepted in a sense "maps" onto the distinction between lawful and lawless rule, as Young Socrates' reaction to the idea of lawless rule suggests (293e7–9); but in any case it is only the distinction between lawful and lawless rule that retains any direct connection to knowledge.

The Stranger uses this quick and dirty discussion to note that if statesmanship were indeed a form of knowledge as they have described it (292b3–c4) their task would reduce to determining whether or not any of the dimensions of a regime they have identified is a sign that knowledge is actually present in the city. Does the fact that a city is ruled by one or a few people, or lawlessly or by law, or in a way that elicits consent, imply that it is ruled by people with knowledge?

The first of the dimensions they examine is the number of rulers. Is a majority of the citizens capable of having the knowledge of the statesman (292e1–2)? The question is ambiguous. The Stranger could be asking whether the knowledge of rule is the kind of knowledge that can be possessed by many people in a city (as many people in a city possess the knowledge of farming to some degree), or whether the decisions of the majority—obtained through deliberation and majority voting procedures—reflect political knowledge even if the individuals composing the majority do not themselves have this knowledge.

The Stranger ignores the latter possibility, namely, that though no individual member of the city may individually have the relevant form of knowledge, the ignorant all together may display some wisdom due to the diversity of their perspectives and the aggregation of their small bits of knowledge.[219] His concern is to establish the absolute scarcity of the embodied knowledge of statesmanship, and only then to consider how such scarcity may be remedied by whatever flawed expedients may be at hand.

---

[219] Aristotle argues in the *Politics* 1281a39ff., that the many as a whole may have better judgment than the few, mostly due to the diversity and complementarity of their perspectives; for some discussion, see Waldron (1995). This is of course a staple of modern arguments for democracy; for an accessible, nontechnical presentation, see Surowiecki (2004). See also, for a more scholarly presentation of these arguments in the context of non-political judgments, Page (2007); and on the specific application of these ideas to democracy, ancient and modern, see Dahl (1989), Estlund (2008), and Ober (2008). Note that Plato himself seems to have been open late in life to some form of this argument, as the comments of the Athenian Stranger on the ability of the many to make good judgments regarding character at *Laws* 950b–c suggest, though there the Athenian does not suggest that this is a consequence of the aggregation of their judgments, only a fact about the average level of these judgments.

Young Socrates agrees with the Stranger that no such knowledge is to be found in the majority of people. But the Stranger does not leave it at that; he asks further whether in a *polis* of one thousand people there could be found one hundred or fifty even that had this knowledge sufficiently (292e4–5), that is, whether five or ten percent of the citizenry might have this knowledge. Now, we might think that if the wise were between five or ten percent of an assembly that deliberates about questions of war and peace, presumably the wise would have some influence (cf. 298d5–7), and hence their voices would not be simply overwhelmed by the ignorance of their fellow citizens. Furthermore, in a situation where most decisions present choices between boldness and moderation (cf. 307e1ff.), the votes of most citizens would presumably cancel each other out (about half of them voting for the policy that encourages boldness, another half voting for the policy that encourages moderation), leaving even a small block of five to ten percent of the votes of the wise with disproportionate influence in determining a correct policy. So the Stranger has to argue that the wise are exceedingly scarce, not just relatively scarce, if his argument is to be at least plausible.

Young Socrates replies to the Stranger's question about the possibility that five to ten percent of the population have the requisite political knowledge with an uncharacteristic outburst, giving his longest speech in the dialogue (292e6–293a1): if this were the case, he says, the *technē* of statesmanship would be the easiest in the world to have of all the *technai*. For, he adds, we know that it would be hard to find a hundred or even fifty checkers players (*petteutai* 292e7) in a thousand people good enough to play against the best in other Greek cities.[220] The

[220] It is worth noting that the *petteutēs*, the checkers player (the exact nature of the game of *petteia* is unknown, but it is thought to be similar to the modern game of checkers) is an image of the god in the *Laws* (cf. 903d6), where it also seems to be used as an image of the statesman or legislator himself (*Laws* 739a1ff., though the reference there is not unambiguously to the legislator).

conclusion he draws is that *a fortiori* it would be much harder to find a hundred kings among a thousand human beings, a phrase whose startling ring he softens by reminding his listeners that they had earlier agreed (cf. 259b3–5 and context) that the "king" is the person who has the kingly *epistēmē*, whether or not he rules in fact.

It should be noted that Young Socrates cannot be saying that the members of the multitude cannot have any art at all. In fact, one may think that he forgets much too easily that the majority of the people already have arts (indeed, the city is in a sense nothing but the gathering of the artisans of human care), and that in a city of a thousand human beings one could well find more than a hundred farmers and other artisans. His answer is cast in a comparative form. It is not the case that one cannot find fifty or a hundred mediocre checkers players, but that one cannot find fifty or a hundred checkers players good enough to compete against, and best, the best in Greece, just as among a thousand people one would be hard-pressed to find a hundred farmers or shoemakers or the like good enough to rival the best in Greece. One could, however, easily find a fair number of mediocre farmers or shoemakers, who despite their mediocrity nevertheless do possess the arts of farming or shoemaking, in whatever small degree. Indeed, such mediocre farmers or shoemakers may be considered excellent in comparison with earlier farmers or shoemakers, assuming that farming or shoemaking admit of progress.[221]

Nevertheless, though one may find a variety of artisans in the city (even large numbers of them in some cases), the very fact that the people already have arts constitutes an obstacle to their having an additional art, especially one as difficult as statesmanship is claimed to be. This is part of the point of Young Socrates' comparison of statesmanship to checkers-playing. If

[221] As the Stranger indeed appears to assume, cf. 299b2–e5; something like this is assumed in Protagoras' argument for the wide distribution of political expertise (justice) in the *Protagoras*.

something as frivolous and inconsequential as the game of checkers requires absolute dedication in order for a person to master it, then statesmanship, which is infinitely more difficult, could hardly be learned on weekends and lazy evenings. One can learn to play checkers or chess in one's spare time, and even become a mediocre player, but, barring exceptional gifts, only a professional, who devotes all his time to learning the *technē* of checkers or chess, can really become a competitive player in world tournaments. This of course means that the majority of the population of the city, the artisans already separated off from the statesman, can hardly be expected to become excellent at a difficult art that they have no time to learn since they are busy practicing their own arts. The division of labor and knowledge, we might say, is the iron cage of democracy, at least on the assumption that statesmanship is indeed a difficult art.

Young Socrates' comments, however, seem to imply that statesmanship can be possessed to some degree among the people, just as a large number of people can become mediocre *petteutai*; what cannot be possessed is the highest degree of statesmanship. And yet the Stranger implies, by his framing of the question, that what matters is the highest degree of statesmanship, that only that degree is sufficient (cf. *hikanōs* 292e5) for the needs of the *polis*. This points to a fundamental difference between statesmanship and many of the other arts in the city. The city can do very well, for example, with a hundred mediocre farmers in every thousand human beings; perfect excellence in the arts is not required for their usefulness. Why, then, do Young Socrates and the Stranger insist that the statesman must not merely have the art of statesmanship but be excellent at it? Why does the Stranger want to suggest that it is the enormous relative scarcity of statesmanship that counts?

Though the Stranger does not directly address this question, the main reason for his insistence on the supreme excellence of the statesman seems to have something to do with his (and Young Socrates') conception of the context of politics.

The *polis* exists in a context where conflict is pervasive (the "age of Zeus"), such that a failure by the city to make correct judgments about the proper responses to conflict may result in its eventual destruction (cf. 307e). The constant threat of annihilation in war would demand a high degree of excellence in political action by the rulers of a city. Young Socrates' choice of image, the competitive *petteutēs* who is in constant battle with his counterparts all across Greece, suggests something of the sort: the "game" of politics appears to be too high-stakes to tolerate mediocre statesmanship.[222]

This unarticulated assumption about the fierce competitiveness of the context of politics merely expresses what Plato might have considered to be the obvious truth about all politics: the Greek *polis* existed in an extremely competitive "ecology" of cities engaged in constant conflict with one another, and where "state death" was a likely consequence of policy failure.[223] In such a competitive ecology, only the highest level of political knowledge, capable of providing the *polis* with the best possible long-term institutions, would seem to make the city capable of weathering the many challenges it is likely to encounter.

On the other hand, we will soon learn that cities without any form of statesmanship survive, sometimes for long periods of time (cf. 302a5–6). The institutions of some cities seem to embody the kinds of experience that enable them to survive in the competitive Greek context, even though they may not have been expressly designed by knowledgeable legislators. Their superior performance against varied challenges over time shows that there is something good about them. As we

[222] This suggestion fits the interpretation of the dialogue proposed by Arends (1993), though Arends himself does not analyze this passage: the statesman's primary responsibility is foreign policy in a hostile world.

[223] See Ober (2008, especially ch. 3). The phrases "competitive ecology" and "state death" are from Ober. Though it is not possible to calculate a meaningful hazard rate from the evidence we possess, Ober provides good evidence that the Greek *poleis* were subject to a higher risk of being completely destroyed through interstate competition than modern states.

shall see, the cities that survive in this context do so precisely because they hit upon a close enough equivalent of statesmanship, an imperfect but relatively effective way of making the city resilient and resistant to the evils brought about by the prevalence of conflict in the age of Zeus.

The argument thus far can be recast as follows: statesmanship is not merely scarce in absolute terms (given that it is a difficult form of knowledge to learn and that most people already have arts that keep them from learning statesmanship) but the demanding competitive context in which it must be practiced implies that it is exceedingly scarce in relative terms as well. Hence the correct regime could not be one in which the majority of the people simply ruled, since in such regimes the influence of the statesman would be minimal, and the majority of the people could not supply the defect of his knowledge sufficiently given the large competitive pressures faced by the city. The Stranger concludes that the right regime (the one where the true statesman rules) would thus be one where only one or a few people rule, since only one or a few people would have the sought-after knowledge.

The question remains, however, as to whether any of the remaining distinctions (e.g., the distinction between rule with or without law, or rule accepted willingly or unwillingly, or rule by the rich or by the poor) among political regimes indicate that the city is ruled by people with the sought-after knowledge. The Stranger will now deny this. Even among the regimes where only one or a few people rule, there is no guarantee that such people will have knowledge if they rule according to law or with the consent of the people, or if they rule in the interests of one or another group.

The argument depends on one of Plato's favorite analogies, namely the analogy between the doctor and the statesman. He says (293a6–c3) that the statesman shall be considered a statesman (*nomisteon* 293a8, punning on *nomos*, law: the statesman is to be "legally" considered a statesman) so long as he rules according to *technē*, whether or not this rule fits within the distinctions they had previously assumed to be important, by analogy with doctors, whom we do not consider (*nenomikamen* 293b1; note again the pun on *nomos*) to be doctors any less just because we are willing or unwilling to be treated by them, or whether or not they cause us pain or act according to written rules or are themselves rich or poor, so long as they take care of us knowledgeably, acting for the good of our bodies, that is, healing us.

We should be careful here about what the Stranger is claiming. We do not think that somebody is not a doctor because one or more of his patients refuse to be treated by him, but because we think he does not have knowledge of medicine; as the Stranger suggests, it is conceptually true of doctors that the willingness or unwillingness of patients to be treated by them has no bearing on their possession of the knowledge of medicine. To be sure, the fact that one or more of a doctor's patients refuse to be treated by him might be counted as evidence that he does not have the requisite knowledge of medicine that would make him into a doctor, even though he claims to have it. There are quacks who claim to have the knowledge of medicine but do not have it, and it is not always unreasonable to be unwilling to be treated by someone who claims to be a doctor but whom we believe is not actually one.[224] Yet this sort of evidence is not decisive; some people refuse to be treated simply because they fear the pain that the doctor may cause them, even if they think—correctly—that the doctor has knowledge of medicine (they may misjudge their own good, or suffer from weakness of the will), or because they have the false opinion that the person who is to treat them does not really have knowledge of medicine, or similar things. Similarly, the fact that a doctor does not treat his patients according to

[224] As Benardete (1984b, 128–129) notes however, it is easier for us to tell the quacks from the real doctors than it is for the city to tell the sophist from the true statesman, though we should add that it has never been very easy to tell the real doctors from the quacks.

generally established rules, or even that he is poor rather than rich, is at best to be treated as empirical (and hence, to some extent, unreliable) evidence that he does not really possess the art of medicine, but not as the grounds of his being or not being a doctor, since a real doctor (one with knowledge of medicine) could ignore such rules, or be rich or poor indifferently. Thus, the immediate point at issue is not whether the doctor is entitled to use violence to cure us (he may or may not), but the *definition* of the doctor in terms of knowledge.[225]

Nevertheless, the Stranger will now use Young Socrates' agreement with this conceptual point to push the analogy further and apparently justify the use of violence by someone who has knowledge. Just as a doctor remains a doctor regardless of whether or not they rule over us willingly or unwillingly or with law or without law or whether they are themselves rich or poor, so does a genuine statesman remain a statesman whether or not they do any of those things (293c5–d2); whether or not a statesman uses force or consent is independent of his possession of the knowledge that makes him a statesman, though perhaps prudent or imprudent in particular circumstances. After Young Socrates readily agrees, the Stranger illustrates the point more concretely (293d4–e6), detailing the specific things a true statesman might be justified in doing for the sake of the good of the *polis*, such as killing people, sending out colonies,[226] bringing in new citizens, and so on. Only the concrete imagery of the statesman's actions, done without recourse to the law, manages to shake Young Socrates; it is only at this point that he admits to being troubled about the fact that the true statesman may act without law (293e7–9). Yet it is worth

[225] *Pace* Annas and Waterfield (1995, xvii and 59n56).

[226] "Like a swarm of bees," 293d5; this is later echoed in the Stranger's remark that statesmen are not born superior in body and soul, unlike a queen bee (301d8–e1). This suggests that the Stranger recognizes perfectly well that such uncontrolled action by a true statesman is highly unlikely, if not impossible, for it would imply that human beings are like bees, i.e., that they recognize the true ruler when they see it.

emphasizing that the Stranger is even here not arguing that *any* use of violence by a true statesman would be justified or prudent; it may turn out that violence is hardly ever useful to the statesman, as the earlier "naive" separation of the statesman from the tyrant portended (276e1–2). The Stranger's main point remains conceptual: the willingness or unwillingness to cooperate of subjects are not themselves characteristics of the statesman, who remains a statesman even if his subjects, not trusting his knowledge, refuse to cooperate with him.

Yet, as Young Socrates' discomfort indicates, the Stranger's conceptual point (which is irreproachable) easily shades into a practical justification for whatever the person claiming knowledge of statesmanship says it is necessary to do, whether or not it is actually necessary to do any of these things. Moreover, the analogy between the doctor and the statesman obscures the fact that the violence of the doctor falls on parts of a single person, whereas the hypothetical violence of the statesman falls on distinct persons; one may fairly accuse the Stranger of not taking seriously "the distinction between persons," like any modern utilitarian.[227] So in the *polis*, unlike in a single patient, the "parts" (the citizens) might disagree that what is in the interest of the whole of the "patient" (the city) is also in their own interest; and they might disagree that what preserves the city as a whole also makes it better rather than worse, two disagreements that do not arise in medicine.[228] This disjunction between what the statesman thinks is best and what individual citizens think is best surfaces in the Stranger's remark that the statesman uses both knowledge (*epistēmē*) and justice when treating the city (293d8–9), even though nothing he has said

---

[227] Rawls (1999, 24).

[228] See Stern (1997, 268). The conflict between the good of the parts and the good of the whole is more clearly seen in the analogy of the statesman to the gymnastics trainer at 294d4ff.; from the perspective of the law such conflict is inevitable, though the Stranger implies (by comparing the *phronēsis*-governed city to a single body) that this is not so in principle, *contra* Stern (269). See also Benardete (1984b, 132).

before would lead us to think that the knowledge of the statesman fails to include the knowledge of justice. Nevertheless, what from the theoretical point of view—that of the statesman himself as well as the philosopher—is merely a redundant addition, looks, from the point of view of those lacking this knowledge (such as Young Socrates), dangerously separate.

It is also worth noting that it is only with the help of concrete imagery that Young Socrates sees that the good of the city and the good of the parts of the city can at least in appearance diverge. As usual, the "abstract" or general perspective (the purely conceptual point that stresses that consent or violence are not constitutive of the knowledge of the statesman), is not sufficient for Young Socrates to "connect the dots," so to speak. This parallels his inability to understand the first account of weaving until the Stranger used concrete images (cf. 280b6ff., and context), and even his inability to understand the implications of the first account of the statesman until the Stranger used a myth. Most commentators seem to suggest that Young Socrates' reaction is simply a reflection of his being so to speak a good Athenian.[229] But it should be emphasized that he expresses his discomfort only after the Stranger has resorted to very concrete imagery of killing and radically changing the body of citizens. The abstract idea of rule without law does not faze him. All this seems to indicate that Young Socrates has difficulty "connecting" the general to the concrete, that is, he does not have a *technē*.[230] We might say that Young Socrates is utterly lacking in the rudiments of statesmanship—he remains utterly "naive," as we noted previously (chapter 2, pp. 111–117)—which must be able to connect the general to the particular in each and every case, and to determine not only that violence may be abstractly justified but whether actual conditions justify its use. Until concrete instances of particular actions are presented to him he does

[229] Cf. Cooper (1997, 101n38), Gill (1995, 292–293).

[230] Stern (1997, 268), argues for the same point on slightly different grounds.

not see the problem in connecting the general knowledge of the statesman (which, presumably, includes knowledge of justice) to the particular circumstances of diverse human beings.[231] It is thus no wonder that the Stranger now proceeds to criticize the general perspective of law, which also fails to notice its lack of applicability to particular cases.

At any rate, the Stranger says (293e10–294a4) that he was just going to ask Young Socrates whether he truly accepted all that he had said or whether he experienced a certain repugnance (*duscheraineis* 294a2) at what they had just said.[232] Since Young Socrates feels some repugnance, the Stranger will now defend the position that the statesman should rule without law, though he cannot fully dispense with it. He will then explain why a certain kind of good law (cf. *eunomous* 293e4) is nevertheless necessary for a regime to be a "more beautiful" (*epi ta kalliō* 293e5) imitation of the true regime, that is, the regime of the statesman not bound by law.

The inadequacy of law

The Stranger makes clear that he is not suggesting that lawmaking has nothing to do with statesmanship: in some way, he says (294a6–8), *nomothetikē*, the art of legislation, belongs to *basilikē*. But, he claims, the best situation is not for the laws to rule but for a kingly man with *phronēsis*. The reason for this, in brief (294a10–b6), is that *nomos* is unable to comprehend what is best (*ariston*) and what is most just (*dikaiotaton*) together, and hence to command what is best (*beltiston*), whereas the man with *phronēsis* can.

Note that what appeared as a disjunction between knowledge and justice in the eyes of the citizens (293d8–9) reemerges

[231] This is not to say that a statesman could never do the things the Stranger says he might do without acting in contravention of the principles of justice and his own knowledge.

[232] The importance of the notion of "repugnance" in the reactions of the citizens to the statesman's potential actions is well emphasized by Lane (1998, 162–163).

here as a disjunction between the best—in the sense of the *ariston*—and the most just from the point of view of general simple rules (laws). This disjunction is such that their common product, so to speak, (which should be the best in the sense of *beltiston*) cannot be commanded by the law, that is, cannot be encompassed in a simple command. Any rule or command that could do this would be too complicated to be useful, though not necessarily impossible in principle, and any rule simple enough to be useful would inevitably compromise the just at the expense of the best (*ariston*) for some, or vice versa, thereby failing to attain the best (the *beltiston*). The reason for this is simply that, as the Stranger goes on to note, human beings are too various, and their circumstances too diverse, for a simple rule to command the best (the *beltiston*) for everyone at the same time.

This "dissimilarity" of human beings and circumstances appears to be ultimately rooted in the nature of the cosmos, as we have already noted (cf. chapter 3, section 1): the dissimilarity (*anomoiotētes* 294b2) of human beings and their actions, is derivative of the general tendency towards dissimilarity of the cosmos (cf. 273d6).[233] More specifically, the fact that human affairs never keep still, does not allow any *technē* whatsoever (not just political science) to make visible or bring to light "a simple instruction concerning all matters and for all time in anything whatsoever," as the Stranger says. *Technē* must constantly rediscover what is best for any particular set of human characters, actions, and circumstances, and hence mediate between the eternal forms of order and the changing circumstances of human life.

It should be emphasized that this does not mean that *technē* is merely knowledge of particulars. The Stranger is not saying that we simply cannot know anything about human affairs in general terms, as he would be if we took "law" to mean simply any general understanding of things. In fact,

[233] A point also perceptively noted by Lane (1998, 150).

there may be rules—even simple rules—that specify what is best for a particular sort of human being, or for a particular set of circumstances, or even in reference to a set of actions. In ethical life such rules may even be extant as proverbs that express a preference for one or another action in most circumstances.[234] But there are no simple rules that are able to articulate what is best in every circumstance and for every human being; all simple rules admit of exceptions. The Stranger, in other words, articulates a basically consequentialist standard of evaluation for political decisions.[235] The right decision is that decision which is best overall, all things considered, but the grounds of such a decision are too complex to articulate in a simple rule: there are simply too many potential different circumstances and individual human beings to consider, and hence too many potential (and potentially conflicting) simple rules, all of which would apply to some range of circumstances and character profiles.

The judgment of *technē* is the "compact" version of that enormous set of simple rules, and thus cannot itself be expressed as a simple rule.[236] To have a *technē* means to be able to generate the rule for person of character ***n*** in circumstance ***c*** who does ***p*** without looking it up in a table; but this can only be done if there is some ultimate regularity—though not necessarily a simple or even clearly expressible one—underlying the rules, such as the form of justice. In other words, the "compact" understanding of the world by *technē* is ultimately a general

---

[234] Cf. Benardete (1984b, 131). Benardete cites the proverbs "he who hesitates is lost" and "look before you leap" as examples that embody the tension between moderation and courage. He concludes correctly that the law, like the proverbs in question, is thus unable to inculcate "true virtue."

[235] See Parfit (1984) for a thorough examination of consequentialism. Note that consequentialism is not equivalent to utilitarianism, which is only one version of consequentialism, and one which Plato would not accept.

[236] The term "compact" comes from modern computer science, in particular the field of artificial intelligence; much of what the Stranger says about *technē* and rules is in fact a live issue for this field. For an interesting introduction, see Baum (2004).

understanding of nature in the regularity of its productive or generative aspect, as we saw in our discussion of the section on measure (chapter 4, pp. 226–227). That this regularity of nature cannot be expressed in simple rules is a testimony to the difficulty of discerning underlying similarities in a universe that has a tendency towards dissimilarity. But the fact that *technē* can generate simple rules for a variety of occasions, and indeed that law sometimes works decently well, is only possible because the universe is not entirely devoid of similarity in this age: it is, as we noted earlier, "in between."

Another way of articulating these points is to see that law is to the art of the statesman as opinion is to knowledge.[237] Any given person may hold true opinions about all sorts of things. I may, for example, have the true opinion that murder is wrong, or at least that some particular killing is wrong. But this does not mean that I have knowledge of justice: that I correctly guessed that murder is wrong, or that this or that killing is wrong, does not mean that I will be correct in guessing the right or wrong action in some other set of circumstances, or even the right or wrong rule for the actual circumstances in question. (Consider: is insider trading wrong?) To have knowledge, as we saw in chapter 4, means being able to produce in principle true judgments in a particular field given the particulars in question (e.g., being able to accurately say whether some particular action is right or wrong, given the particular conditions in which the action takes place) because of some grasp of the underlying form of order or relevant invariant laws (rather than, say, some mysterious "sixth sense" for justice). Thus the knowledge of statesmanship, based as it is on the correct understanding of justice and the good, would be able to articulate the best response for the

[237] The distinction between knowledge, opinion, and ignorance, common in the *Republic*, does not play a large explicit role in the *Statesman*, though it does appear in the *Sophist* and the *Theaetetus*, as we have seen in chapter 4, and appears to structure the discussion of the place of law in relation to both the knowledge of the genuine statesman and the ignorance of his sophistic imitators.

city in the widest possible range of circumstances and for the widest possible range of character profiles, whereas law cannot compactly encode the genuine knowledge of justice without ceasing to be expressible as a set of simple rules, and hence can at best remain true for some narrow range of circumstances and character profiles, even when it has been created by a genuine statesman. It is "true opinion" rather than "knowledge": it says (perhaps rightly, given some set of circumstances and character profiles) "this is just" or "this is unjust" or "this is best for the city" without possessing the resources to change itself when this is no longer just or unjust.

The need for law and the scarcity of statesmanship

Yet the Stranger thinks that there are reasons why it is nevertheless necessary for the statesman to legislate, even though the law has been shown to be inferior to knowledge. The reason boils down to scarcity: it is because the knowledge of the statesman is not always available when and where it is needed that he must use law. From this point of view, law is the inferior expedient that the statesman must use because he cannot be present "at everyone's side" (295b1–2) to command what is appropriate at every moment, or, more precisely, because the necessary knowledge of the statesman is not evenly distributed, so it is not always available when it is needed.[238]

---

[238] It is worth stressing that the Stranger's point is not the "paternalistic" one that we need someone at our side to direct our actions at every point, but that we need knowledge in order for our lives to turn out in the best possible way, whether this knowledge is our own or another's. So, for example, for us to be as healthy as possible we would need to have the knowledge of medicine "at our side," whether our own or that of a doctor, and similarly for us to have as good a life as possible in common with others we would need to have the knowledge of the statesman "at our side," whether our own or that of another. Yet this knowledge is not widely or evenly distributed (in contrast to the knowledge of medicine, which seems to be more widely available); hence the need for law. Contrary to Castoriadis (1999, 160), the Stranger does not assume or imply that we are all "sick," merely that we do not normally have the knowledge necessary for us to be always as healthy as possible.

This is the basic point of the two analogies the Stranger uses, the analogies between the statesman and the gymnastics trainer and between the statesman and the doctor who goes away on a trip: the law is unable to respond to the particular circumstances of individual people (it treats people in groups, rather than individually: 294d–295b), and it is unable to quickly adapt to changes in circumstances (it remains the same even as conditions change: 295b–296a), yet the genuine statesman must nevertheless use law, since there are just too few statesmen to attend individually to the needs of every citizen and to remain in every city for ever. Law is thus a partial remedy for the scarcity of statesmanship insofar as it embodies a kind of "snapshot" of the practices that the statesman would use at a particular time and given some particular group of people, but which are only guaranteed to work at that particular point in time and for that particular group, not in general. In this sense, law is a static picture (an "imitation" or "image") of the dynamic knowledge of the statesman.

But these analogies also reward deeper examination. The analogy of the statesman to the gymnastics trainer injects again a competitive context into the discussion, much like the analogy of the statesman to the draughts player did earlier; and the analogy of the doctor to the statesman suggests that statesmanship is not a form of knowledge that can be reproduced within the city. Let us therefore examine these analogies in more detail.

Just as the trainer prepares individual athletes to participate in athletic competitions, so the statesman's task seems to be to prepare individuals to compete in a "political race" (the competitive context of international politics, perhaps), where the community is constantly threatened. Yet just as the relative scarcity of trainers *vis-à-vis* athletes does not thereby make it impossible for athletes as a group to be more or less properly trained, the potentially bad effects of the scarcity of statesmanship are also mitigated by the possibility that general rules will produce acceptable performance by the city as a whole. Even if the talents of gifted individuals are not fully developed or the special needs of others addressed, the group as a whole may still place high enough in a competition, even if it does not collectively win a victory; similarly, the city may not gain world-historical fame or produce outstanding exemplars of individual virtue, but it may still be preserved for a long time. Implicit in the trainer analogy is the idea that, though law is not as good as individualized knowledge, it is good enough for most situations; the statesman, like the trainer, can recognize substantial similarities among people that make general commands possible.[239] The trainer is thus justified in dealing with human beings "in herds" (*hathroois* 294d5, *agelais* 294e10), that is, without special regard to the variations among human beings.[240]

The idea that statesmanship, like gymnastics training, depends on a competitive context also suggests that the function of the statesman with respect to the city is primarily preparatory rather than fully directive. Just as a trainer is an enabler, that is, someone who prepares others to do certain things that the trainer himself does not do (and which need not be done in the trainer's presence), so the statesman seems to be someone who prepares the city for a competition in which he himself need not participate. He prepares the city as a whole to run the race of politics on its own (cf. 311a1–2), but does not run the race himself, just as the trainer does not run the race for the athletes he trains. And just as the trainer cannot ensure the athlete's victory, so the statesman cannot ensure the city's victory by means of the law he creates.

---

[239] See Teisserenc (2005, 370).

[240] The reintroduction of the herd terminology, which otherwise drops out after the myth, as I noted earlier (see chapter 2, pp. 78–79), is noted by Stern (1997, 269–270). Like Stern, I am inclined to think that its reappearance here points to the scarcity of the knowledge of the statesman, in fact to the great gulf between his knowledge and that of those he rulers, a gulf nearly as large as that between the shepherd-god and his human herd. Nevertheless, it should also be noted that the terminology of herds drops out again from the rest of the dialogue.

The model of statesmanship implicit in the trainer analogy thus seems to depict the statesman's task as a constitutional one: the statesman sets up those basic institutions that prepare the people to act appropriately in the competitive environment in which the city is placed, even when he is not himself present in it. But this constitutional role necessarily opens a certain scope for the autonomous activity of the citizens in the best regime, even if such scope is not large. The Stranger of course does not argue that the citizens would be self-legislating—the statesman will legislate for them, after all—but he does imply that the statesman could not even do everything political for them, just as a trainer cannot run the race for which he has prepared the athlete. Indeed, as we shall see (chapter 6, pp. 329–336), the statesman can at best prepare the citizens to make relatively good political decisions in some range of circumstances, and hence he must prepare them to be relatively autonomous under the law, even if he cannot give them knowledge.[241]

The doctor analogy (295b2ff.) works similarly to the trainer analogy, and has some of the same implications, but whereas the trainer analogy focuses on the "spatial" scarcity of statesmanship, the doctor analogy focuses on its "temporal" scarcity. Here laws are conceived as instructions that a statesman or a doctor might leave behind if he were to absent himself from the city for some extended period of time, reminders of the things those they care for need to do in his absence (295c). Yet why must the statesman leave behind instructions? When a doctor goes away for an extended period of time, supposing he practices in a city and not in some extremely isolated area, his patients can usually count on another doctor; he need not leave any instructions but can instead refer them to another practitioner of the art. The knowledge of medicine is rarely entirely absent from the city, even if particular doctors are.

---

[241] This point is noted by Howland (1998, 274), though a bit more strongly than I would.

The complete absence of such knowledge is unlikely because the city can normally ensure its reproduction. It "reproduces" itself in institutions (such as universities or apprenticeships) that allow people without the knowledge in question to "imitate" the practitioners and learn the principles of the art, becoming in turn doctors and trainers. The Stranger, however, seems to assume that this is not possible in the case of the statesman: the city cannot simply train another statesman to take the place of the departing one. His absence is much more thoroughgoing than the absence of a given doctor or trainer. The apparent impossibility or difficulty of institutionalizing the reproduction of statesmanship is the more distant reason why law is necessary: it is a stopgap measure necessary while the city waits for another statesman.

From the perspective of the statesman, then, law is designed to hold the city together until he (or, more precisely, his knowledge) can return, and hence something that he feels free to set aside whenever he is actually in the city. Yet it is worth noting that despite its "stopgap" character, the law does not necessarily make things worse. Indeed, the Stranger stresses (295c7–296a3) that the patient who follows a prescribed regime may get unexpectedly better "thanks to Zeus" (the god who represents statesmanship, incidentally), and so similarly the condition of the city may actually improve even when the statesman is absent. Just as with the trainer analogy, the doctor analogy implicitly suggests that the inadequacies of law are not insurmountable.

Note that the Stranger, in the case of the doctor, stresses the unlikelihood of his early return, an unlikelihood that is only compatible with an extreme scarcity of knowledge of medicine. In this case law, with its implicit guarantee of permanence, is required; and the point is emphasized by the Stranger's characterization of the simple notes left by the doctor as *tarchaia . . . nomotēthēnta* (295d3), the ancient laws, a strange turn of phrase if the notes in question were merely reminders of a doctor's prescription meant to tide the patient over for a short time. Law is not merely a short-term expedient; its force derives from the near-certainty that the statesman who framed it will never return. The statesman thus appears again in the guise of a founder figure rather than day-to-day governor, as the doctor who comes infrequently and changes the constitution of the city to ensure its long-term health.[242]

By the same token, though it may be laughable from the point of view of knowledge for the doctor and the statesman to be bound by the laws they or somebody like them instituted earlier, the sacralization of these laws by time hints at the empirical difficulty of changing them on his return. Changing the laws, from the point of view of the citizens, is never a laughing matter, despite the Stranger's assertion that in truth it would be so;[243] and perhaps it is more difficult if, for whatever reason, the patient seems to be doing better, as the Stranger suggests (why change the instructions that seem to be helping, then?). The Stranger hints here at the practical conflict between the perspective of the city (which is well advised to hang on to its laws at nearly all costs) and the perspective of the statesman, who finds it "laughable" to keep the laws of the city if he knows they must be changed.

Law as an image of wisdom: 296a–303c

The law has emerged thus far as the inadequate, but necessary, instrument of the statesman given the scarcity of his knowledge. Properly crafted law (that is, law crafted with knowledge) provides a reasonable substitute for the statesman's absence, but it must fall silent when he is present. Now, however, the Stranger will examine law from the point of view of the many rather than the statesman (296a5–6). He does this by discussing several examples that reflect the crafting of the law by a people.

---

[242] See also Stern (1997, 270).

[243] As Benardete (1984b, 134) notes, "[o]nly in truth is [changing the laws] laughable."

In these scenarios, the people are especially concerned not with their own arbitrary preferences or desires but with their own inability to determine who will or will not harm them; their concern is primarily protective. They do not deny, as we shall see, that political knowledge or statesmanship is possible, and they do not in principle deny that they themselves do not have this knowledge, but because they are mistaken about its nature, they fear that the people who do have such knowledge may want to harm them. They thus primarily want to be persuaded (296a8–11) that any changes to the law are actually for their own good, on the assumption (unstated by the Stranger) that they would then be able to judge whether the change will harm them or not.[244]

Young Socrates thinks this is a perfectly reasonable idea: are they not right? The Stranger does not say straightaway that the claim of the many is wrong (296b1); indeed, as we shall see, his argument implicitly gives support to the views of the Athenian Stranger in the *Laws*, who ultimately agrees with the people's concerns on this point. Yet instead of agreeing that the people's concerns are reasonable, the Stranger presents Young Socrates with a series of analogies designed to show him that the fact that some law is voluntarily accepted cannot count as evidence that it is based on knowledge, and the fact that some measure must be violently enforced cannot show that it is not.

The justification of force

The first analogy draws again on a parallel between medicine and statesmanship. The Stranger presents Young Socrates with the case of a true doctor (that is, a doctor who truly has the *technē* of medicine) who forces a patient to do something

[244] Note that the many, in the Stranger's presentation, cannot conceive of anything better than the rule of law; what is better than the current law is always another law, something that can be legislated, not a deviation from the law. But the statesman's knowledge resists being legislated; all legislation is a falling off from it, even if a necessary one. See Benardete (1984b, 134).

against the established written directions (perhaps the very same directions he had given him beforehand) for his or her own good. The violence that such a doctor uses, the Stranger argues, can be classed with anything except, *ex hypothesi*, with those things that make one ill and those things done without knowledge, whereas every mistake in medical science can be classed with those things that make one ill.[245] If violence makes us healthy in some circumstance, then it must not be excluded from the art of medicine; we do not base our judgments about whether or not someone is a true doctor on whether he persuades or forces us to follow a specific treatment, but on whether he can cure us (or at least on whether he does not make us sicker).

It should be emphasized that the Stranger is not saying that doctors are justified in using violence, only that *if* some prescription violently enforced could restore us to health, we could not thereby claim that such prescription was not part of the art of medicine. To be sure, violence is hardly ever the best way of treating a patient, even though it may succeed in making him better on occasion. Such force, furthermore, can only be an unavoidable necessity when the doctor feels duty-bound to help an ignorant patient or is himself forced to do so by somebody else, as when a parent tells a doctor to heal an unwilling child. In fact, the Athenian Stranger will argue (cf. *Laws* 719e7–720e6, 857b9–e5) that the law should contain both an element of persuasion and an element of force, but the element of persuasion appeals to our better part and is therefore superior to the ineliminable necessity of force.

The same is true of the violence a statesman may employ against the laws for the good of the *polis* (296c5–297b3), though here the Stranger's argument needs to be a bit more delicate.

[245] This implies, incidentally, that the doctor *qua* doctor never makes a mistake, a claim that the elder Socrates had shown to have some paradoxical consequences in *Republic* I when Thrasymachus put it forward (cf. *Republic* 340cff.).

The analogy suggests that the kind of force the statesman uses to do things that are more just or better or nobler than those enjoined by the laws cannot itself be called unjust or worse or ignoble, or at least that the people who are subjected to it cannot say that they have suffered shameful or unjust or just plain bad things. Yet surely the fact that the statesman is forced to use violence already argues for a certain failure in his task. The people who suffer the violence of the statesman may think they have suffered bad things at his hands, even if in fact they have not, and thus he may appear to them as a tyrant, rather than as a statesman (cf. 276e1–14). If a person's limb could feel wronged at the doctor's use of amputation to save the patient, it probably would do so, even if the patient did not; similarly, since the violence of the statesman affects people unequally, not everyone would be convinced of its necessity. Thus, while the statesman's violence may not be called "unjust" or "bad" or "ignoble," it may perhaps be called by other names, some no less damaging to the statesman's prospects for long-term success: impious, for example. It is worth remembering that in the *Seventh Letter* Plato (or the author of the letter) disavows violence as impious, though not necessarily unjust; and impiety may be a formidable practical barrier in its own right.[246]

Furthermore, while we can relatively easily say whether or not a doctor has cured us (or at least not made us sicker) by

---

[246] *Seventh Letter* 331a–d; Taylor (1961, 232). It is unclear what this implies for our views of Plato the man; it is nevertheless clear that if the violence of the statesman is seen as impious, then it is not likely to be of much use. To be sure, some people (see Klosko 1986, 187) date the *Statesman* to before Dion's expedition, arguing that Plato only changed his position on the use of violence after the failure of that expedition, which illustrated quite clearly the dangers of using force to achieve fundamental political transformation. I think it is unlikely that such an obvious thought would only have occurred to Plato then, and find attempts to date the *Statesman* so precisely unconvincing. But whatever the case, it is clear that the moment of founding or re-founding a political regime has the potential to be a violent one, and such violence, even if counterproductive, is not necessarily "unjust" in any obvious sense; see Voegelin (1987 [1956], 160), Davis (1967, 325), and more generally Arendt (1963).

amputating a limb, that is, it is relatively easy to distinguish good doctors from bad doctors,[247] it is not nearly as easy to say whether or not a statesman has "cured" the city by exerting violence on some of its parts (or indeed, by doing anything at all). The many look to persuasion as a "proxy" for good statesmanship in a way that they would not for in medicine in part because they are less able to identify optimal outcomes in the case of politics. They may be able to say what a bad outcome is (e.g., civil war, external conquest) but not necessarily what an "optimal" outcome would be, especially if statesmanship, in contrast with medicine, deals with a more comprehensive good, which is harder than health for most people to judge.

It is nevertheless important to note that with this argument the Eleatic Stranger is certainly not recommending violence; ideally, the rule of the statesman is always willingly accepted, just as they had said earlier (cf. 276e1–14, as well as the discussion above, chapter 2). What he is saying is only that the use of violence cannot be evidence that someone *lacks* the art of the statesman, though it is also not evidence that someone *has* the art of the statesman.[248] He is simply reiterating, from a different angle, the conceptual point he had made earlier concerning the relationship between violence and knowledge (293a–c; see discussion above), not suggesting that violence will be the right course of action for a statesman in any particular set of circumstances.

It is also worth noting that despite Plato's fondness for the analogy between doctor and statesman, medicine is actually a rather poor example of a *technē* in the strict sense of the term. Both ancient and modern medicine are hugely dependent on guesswork (though modern medicine has made some progress

---

[247] There are some qualifications here. The best doctors may be those who take on the hardest cases, and therefore fail more often, and information about success rates is not always easily available. See Gawande (2004).

[248] There is no "reversal" in Plato's position, *pace* Annas and Waterfield (1995, 62n58).

on this score),[249] and precise accounts of the causes of particular diseases tend to be in short supply: the doctor who succeeds in treating a patient is nearly as likely to be ignorant of the deeper reason for his success as the patient, and before the germ theory of disease was perhaps in a worse condition of ignorance than the patient, given that the patient might have at least acknowledged his or her ignorance, while the doctor would have espoused a false theory of the causes of disease. Ancient medicine at any rate was just as likely to kill as to heal, and modern medicine, despite enormous progress in some cases, is only a bit better in the aggregate.[250] It is hard to imagine that such poor knowledge could ever justify any degree of violence, and it is difficult to believe that Plato thought the medicine of his age constituted a genuine science rather than (at best) a form of systematic inquiry. As Plato was well aware, political science also fails this test; and hence it is hard to imagine that Plato thought that whatever poor knowledge of politics he and his contemporaries actually *had* justified any degree of violence.

All in all, one sometimes wonders (speculatively) whether Plato's use of the doctor analogy (and, to a lesser extent, of the ship-captain analogy, which suffers from some of the same problems, though for slightly different reasons: navigation depended enormously on the cooperation of nature, over which the ship captain has very little control, as the Athenian Stranger acknowledges in the *Laws*) is not intended to point

[249] Doctors normally do not know why the drugs they use work and cannot account for why they fail in some cases, for example, even though they may "know" that the use of some drugs is associated with the improvement of some conditions; but such purely "statistical" knowledge at best constitutes "experience" from Plato's point of view, and it is only a bit better than the folk-experience that associates particular remedies with specific maladies, sometimes quite successfully.

[250] Most improvements in modern life expectancy and disease control are due more to sanitation and "public health" than to medicine, though of course modern medicine is an improvement over ancient medicine in its treatment of *some* wounds and *some* diseases, and in its knowledge of the causes of disease more generally.

to the enormous distance between a genuine statesman and the "state of the art" of the knowledge of statesmanship of the age. Just as the best doctor in Plato's time (and today, to a lesser extent) was at best a kind of lover of the knowledge of medicine—someone who is interested in learning about health and the body, but who actually knows very little about either—so, we might think, the actual "statesman" in Plato's time would be at best a lover of the art of statesmanship, someone who is interested in learning about how to rule a city but actually knows very little more than the untutored others whom he wants to rule; in other words, a kind of philosopher, but by no means a genuine statesman in the strict sense. So the Stranger's insistence on the genuineness of the doctor in the analogy is perhaps significant as an acknowledgment that the argument he is presenting would make the genuine statesman an impossible ideal; in the actual world we live in, the statesman is always at best a sort of philosopher, that is, a lover of wisdom, not an expert.

At any rate, the conclusion of the argument appears to delegitimize violence in the real world. The Stranger says that violence does not become just or unjust by being committed by the poor or the rich, or by being accompanied by persuasion, or by being done according to written rules; only the combination of both wisdom (cf. *sophos* 296e3) and goodness can justify political violence, and only this combination is the genuine definition of the correct management of the *polis* and of the interest of the ruled (296d7–e3). The requirement that the statesman must be *sophos* (a word not used lightly by the Stranger in non-ironic contexts) suggests that even a philosopher would have a hard time justifying violence, since he is himself not *sophos*, but is at best a lover of wisdom.

Note again that the Stranger feels the need to emphasize that the true and genuine ruler has both wisdom and goodness, something that he will reiterate a bit later, when he says that the true ruler rules with both *technē* and *nous* and distributes to the citizens that which is most just (297a7–b1). Yet nothing he has said so far suggests that knowledge is different from goodness; in fact, the previous argument clearly indicates that ignorance about the just, the good, and the noble leads to injustice and badness, while knowledge leads to justice and goodness (296c5–7). The fact that he still needs to use this formula indicates how hard it is to convince the people (including Young Socrates, a receptive audience) that virtue and knowledge are one. To say that the statesman acts with knowledge does not appear to be sufficient to convince the people that his rule is better than the rule of law, unless they are convinced that he also acts with goodness. We shall see later how this fear shapes the law and why it may be justified to some degree (297e11ff.).

The Stranger uses one last analogy to argue that the law, as understood by the people, is inferior to the unfettered rule of the true statesman, this time to the ship-captain (296e4ff.): to bind the ship captain to inflexible rules and procedures is to limit his ability to react quickly and properly in case of danger, and thus to thwart the point of having a ship captain at all. The analogy works only if we think that politics is like a voyage through stormy seas (cf. 273d5, where the whole world is compared to a storm-tossed ship), where every decision is a matter of life and death, and there is no room for discussion.[251] But we have seen that there are grounds to doubt this view of political life, since the *polis*, as the Stranger will confirm, seems perfectly capable of enduring for long periods of time without the benefit of statesmanship. In at least some contexts (perhaps contexts that are quite common) political life is not a matter of life and death. When disorder becomes an existential threat law is indeed seen as a constraint; but this experience can be exploited by sophists as well as by true statesmen. Statesmanship not bound by law can only seem acceptable to the many, in other words, in emergency situations, and indeed

[251] See Rosen (1995, 167).

it is in the decision to go to war or not that the Stranger thinks statesmanship is most sorely needed (cf. 305eff.).[252]

Law as the codification of experience

The Stranger now reiterates his contention that the *politeia* ruled by knowledge is to be found among those ruled by one or a few, but that the other *politeiai* are merely imitations of it, some more beautiful, some less (297b7–c4; cf. 293e4–6). This statement now needs the explanation that was postponed by Young Socrates' unease with the possibility that the statesman rules without law; as he says now, he did not really understand what the Stranger meant then.

The basic idea is that the imperfect *politeiai* imitate the genuine regime "beautifully" when they use the "writings" of the best regime (the regime ruled by the statesman), or, in other words, when they use those writings that a true statesman would have left for them upon going away had he been present earlier (297d6–8), the reminders they are to use for the duration of his (possibly permanent) absence, and punish those who violate them with the greatest severity. A city that ignored its own laws, by contrast, would imitate the statesman badly (300d–e).

But this is hardly enough to support the rule of law in most cities, for it seems to require that all laws be created by a genuine statesman. Yet not all laws are created by a Solon or a Lycurgus; the argument in fact seems to disqualify most law from having real authority. "Normal" law could be neither first nor second best, but perhaps third best, if that, since it does not have its origins in the instructions of a true statesman but at best in experience or trial and error (300b); yet the Stranger insists (cf. 297e5–6) that the rule of law in general—not just of those laws given to the *polis* in the past by a true statesman that is no longer present, but even laws created by a city apparently in the absence of a statesman—is in fact second best. Moreover,

[252] See also Arends (1993).

the Stranger appears to endorse the even more extreme position that the city must never change its laws, whatever their origin (299b–300a, 301a), which would seem to be too strong a conclusion to draw if the city's laws have not been drafted by a genuine statesman.

How are we to understand the Stranger's apparent endorsement of all law in the absence of the statesman, and in particular his view that the rule of law, whatever the origins of such law, is the "second best" imitation of the knowledge of the statesman? Two broad solutions have been proposed. The more "traditional" position, defended with vigor in recent times by Samaras (2002), is that the laws that a city creates in the (relative) absence of knowledge imitate the truth precisely insofar as they embody a certain kind of "experience," which is understood as a kind of trace of knowledge. Their content approximates the content of the laws that a genuine statesman would create for the city, though it would not be identical with it. On this view, Plato truly endorses the rule of unchanging experience-based law as a "second best" rather than merely a kind of necessary evil: such laws have real positive value due to the fact that they embody the experience of the city. As Rowe (2001a, 66–67) has pointed out, however, if Plato is endorsing the rule of experience-based laws, he would also seem to be endorsing, absurdly, as a principal component of the rule of such laws a prohibition on Socratic inquiry into the matters regulated by the laws (cf. 299b–e), even though these laws are not produced by knowledgeable individuals.

It is therefore best to distinguish, the argument goes, between the laws that a genuine statesman would create with his knowledge,[253] and the laws that a city would create based on experience.[254] Only the former are referred as "imitations of truth" in 300c and given real positive value, according to

[253] And which, in Rowe's view, would not prevent inquiry: see Rowe (2001, 74).
[254] See also Klosko (2006, 212).

Rowe,[255] whereas the latter could be said to imitate the truth only insofar as they have the "second-order feature," as Lane says (1998, 159), of not being changed in the absence of expert knowledge. Such laws would not necessarily be similar in content to the former, and would not necessarily have real positive value, since they would be produced by individuals without knowledge, advised at best by clever rhetoricians. They are really "third best": better than the lawless rule of ignorant individuals, but not obviously much better. The problem with this argument, as Klosko among others has pointed out, is that the context of 300c suggests that the Stranger is speaking about the laws that a city would create based on experience, not about the laws that genuine statesmen would create.

As we shall see, Rowe is correct to argue that the *Statesman* cannot endorse a strong prohibition on Socratic inquiry as an essential and important part of the rule of law, yet he errs in his assessment of the role experience plays in giving value to law, which leads him too quickly to the view that laws can only be changed by those with full-blown knowledge and that only laws created by such people have real positive value. Indeed, contrary to Rowe's view (and in accord with Samaras's view), the argument of the *Statesman* suggests that all (proper) laws (whether written by genuine statesmen or not) "imitate the truth" through their content, both insofar as they are written "as far as possible by those who know" and insofar as they embody a certain kind of experience, though of course the balance between experience and knowledge varies for any particular law, and it can still be argued that the laws created by a genuine statesman imitate the statesman's knowledge "more beautifully." More importantly, in arguing for this position the Stranger presents a view of the connection between experience and knowledge that does not, despite appearances, commit him to saying that laws could only ever be changed by genuine statesmen and indeed seems to leave open the possibility of

[255] See also Teisserenc (2005, 378).

an institution like the Nocturnal Council that could properly revise the laws of a city without necessarily possessing full political knowledge.

The argument again proceeds by analogy to the ship captain and the doctor, but it is a more extended analogy, indeed a whole story about how law might come to be. The story imagines a people that, concerned with protecting itself against the misuse of power and expertise by doctors or ship captains, creates laws that end up choking the development of the arts of navigation and medicine. It is important to stress that in this story the people do not deny that there is expert knowledge of medicine or ship-navigation, and by implication of statesmanship. Indeed they may even recognize the experts among them, though they mistake their intentions. Moreover, they are solely concerned with their own protection, rather than with their own aggrandizement or with some other dubious or factional purpose. Plato was of course very much aware that some law is simply a way to further the private interests of some over others; this is simply the argument of Thrasymachus in the *Republic*, and it is reiterated in the *Laws*, where the Athenian Stranger notes that most cities are really factional despotisms (713a). The point of this argument is thus not to defend or condemn all law without qualification, but to redefine proper law as that law that is formulated with the intention of protecting the city from harmful or ignorant rulers, and to show that even such law is inferior to the rule of the statesman, though better than the alternatives.

The key premise of the argument is that the people are unable to distinguish between a genuine expert who wants to help them and a malicious person who does not.[256] So the Stranger tells Young Socrates to imagine (298a1ff.) a situation in which we (the people) thought that we were suffering the most terrible things at the hands of the noble (*gennaion* 297e11) ship

[256] As Neiman (2007) rightly sees, though I do not share the conclusions he draws from this fact.

captain and "the doctor worth many doctors" (297e11–12). The people may think this, for example, because they suffer pain at their hands—the doctor might cut or burn them, for example, all the while telling us it is for their own health. Similarly, a people may think that its leaders are making it suffer terrible things while telling them such things are for their own good, and thus come to resent them, as the Athenians resented Pericles' policy in the initial stages of the Peloponnesian war (Thucydides, *History of the Peloponnesian War* 2.59), even if that policy was the right one in the circumstances.

The people do not think that they are suffering at their hands, however, because they believe that ship captains and doctors are incompetent, and thus capable of inflicting evil through ignorance; on the contrary, it is their very competence that makes them dangerous in their eyes (the eyes of "everybody").[257] The point should be stressed: the Stranger's argument assumes that we think some people are genuine doctors or captains, not that nobody has such knowledge, and we think that precisely *because* the doctor and the ship captain have knowledge of medicine and navigation they are able to benefit or harm whoever they wish. We think of art, in other words, as the ability to "err willingly."[258]

Since the doctor and the ship-captain can harm us (they can "err willingly"), we can also imagine that they will do so if we attribute to them corrupt motives (298a5–b7). We can, for example, imagine that they charge large amounts of money,

---

[257] Note that the Stranger uses the first person plural, emphasizing it with the adjective *pantes*, "all of us." He does not exclude anybody from his argument.

[258] The idea of *technē* as the ability to err willingly (rather than unwillingly) is expressed in many of the so-called "Socratic" dialogues (see, e.g., *Hippias Minor* 366e–367a and passim, *Republic* I.333e3–334b6), and is deeply rooted in Greek thought. See, for some discussion, Penner (2005, 59n24). Penner cites Aristotle *Metaphysics* 1078b26–27 and *Nicomachean Ethics* 1129a11–17, 1140b20–25 as well as various Platonic texts, and argues convincingly that in Plato it is only the expertise of justice (in this case statesmanship) that escapes this possibility: it is true only for that expertise that no one errs willingly.

little of which (in the case of doctors) goes to treatment, while most of it goes to themselves and their dependents; that they can be easily bribed by our relatives or enemies to do us in; and that all the while they can justify (or so we think) what they are doing on the grounds of medical or navigational necessity, even if we cannot see it, taking advantage of our ignorance. Thus we—everybody—see a disjunction between the technical competence of the doctor or the ship captain and his "moral" competence. And indeed, technical knowledge, insofar as it is not knowledge of the just and the good, is in a certain sense amoral. The Stranger thus characterizes the error of the doctor as that which makes one ill, not as that which is unjust (296b9–c3); it is at least theoretically possible for a doctor to unjustly either heal or make ill other people. That this is possible, indeed even likely, stems from the fact that the doctor *qua* doctor does not have the knowledge of the just and the unjust, the good and the bad, and the noble and the shameful, and thus may decide to misuse his art ("err willingly") in pursuit of some mistaken view of his own good. This is why the Stranger feels the need to speak in the story not of a run-of-the-mill captain but of a noble ship captain and a doctor "worth many others" (297e11–13), adjectives that, though they may refer to the excellence of the specific competence of the captain and the doctor, suggest rather their moral superiority to other ship captains and doctors, since otherwise the suspicions of the people would turn out to be well founded.

The Stranger's parallel between doctors and statesmen thus indicates that the people believe that statesmanship, like medicine, is a purely technical capacity that can be disconnected from the virtue of its possessor. But this is not true: genuine statesmanship, insofar as it is fundamentally connected with the knowledge of the good, the just, and the noble, cannot be used to "err willingly," that is, do what is unjust, or wrong, or ignoble (cf. 296c9–d5), in the same way as the doctor's knowledge can be used to poison others. Such willing error is possible only on the assumption that the artisan mistakes the just and the unjust, the good and the bad, and the noble and the shameful, in order to gain some imagined advantage from the misuse of his art, something which the statesman *ex hypothesi* does not do. Thus, while there are doctors who use their expertise justly, doctors who do not do so, and imitators of doctors, there are only genuine statesmen and people without the expertise of the statesman, that is, imitators of the statesman. Yet the uniqueness of statesmanship in this respect gives rise to a persistent illusion that in fact the statesman's knowledge is like all the other amoral forms of knowledge, as the Stranger occasionally acknowledges by speaking of a "good" as well as wise statesman (296e3), even though both the goodness and the wisdom of the statesman must be intimately connected, if they are not altogether identical. As a conceptual matter, in other words, the statesman cannot do what is unjust; but as a matter of empirical fact this is not always so clear. Indeed, all experience is against it; and, as we shall see, experience is all that the people can base their judgments on.

The people, then, are unable to reliably distinguish genuine statesmen (who could not harm them) from others (who may). Thus, insofar as they remain primarily concerned with their own protection, they forego the possibility of an "optimal" outcome (the unconstrained rule of a true statesman) for the sake of a "safer" one. The problem is that they do not, however, believe that they are truly making a tradeoff; on the contrary, they believe that they can have the benefits of the statesman's knowledge without the risk of misidentifying it (incidentally a very large risk, given the scarcity of genuine political knowledge). They think this is possible because they appear to believe that the relevant knowledge of the statesman can be codified in the law in such a way that it cannot be misused. But this is, again, a mistake, and one that is less forgivable: as the Stranger just argued (291d–296a), the real knowledge of the statesman cannot be codified in law.[259] But though they are mistaken about this, this does not mean that the process through which they go about attempting to codify this knowledge has no value. Let us now examine this process in detail.

The Stranger imagines the people setting up an elaborate system of law, with appropriate enforcement and monitoring mechanisms, restricting the things that the practitioners of the arts under suspicion can or cannot do, and in general confining their actions to the letter of the law. This system is presented in four steps, the first three of which have parallels in Athenian legal practice. At each step the people introduce increasing degrees of constraint on the activities of the arts; as the Stranger says, their resolution is to prevent medicine and the art of the ship-captain from being exercised by people who are *autokratores* (cf. 298c1), self-rulers.

The word *autokrator* had been used in the myth (274a5) to describe the way in which the universe and its parts were supposed to exercise their care over themselves by themselves, that is, in a self-directed fashion. The removal of *autokrateia*, self-rule, from the arts thus implies their subjection to somebody or something else. This is not, by itself, incorrect; after all, insofar as the arts do not know the just and the unjust, and insofar as their effects impinge on the achievement of the just and the unjust in the city, then they should find themselves under the authority of the statesman (cf. 304a6ff.), which is another way of saying that only the statesman could be *autokrator*, since only his knowledge is fully self-commanding, and only his knowledge could include the good, the just, and the noble. And we have seen (chapter 1) that the arts that constitute the city are arranged in a continuum of self-directedness where only the art of the statesman is truly self-commanding. But the people

[259] Thus, *pace* Gill (1995, 297–300), the error of the political community described here is not that the people think that there is no scientific knowledge of politics, but that they think such an art could be codified in law so as to avoid its misuse.

in the story place all the arts under the authority of law, not of statesmanship, which, on the Stranger's view, is a mistake at least for the case of the art of the statesman.

The first step in the story of this process of eliminating the self-rule of the arts—in particular the arts of medicine and navigation—is taken by the assembly, and results in what we normally call law. In its fear of those who claim to have knowledge (and indeed, in the Stranger's analogy, actually have this knowledge), the people thus decide to write down explicitly those of its practices that they have seen have served in the past to heal the sick or reach port safely (300b1–2), and to distill the knowledge of the doctor and the captain into simple rules, specifying the sorts of tools they may use, the way these may be used, and the typical actions that are to be taken in typical circumstances. As a result, the people codify into law the practices with which it is familiar and rejects those with which it is not familiar, considering them dangerous innovations. For example, the city might regulate the practice of naval warfare by requiring the use of long ships (298d4), an obsolete practice which nevertheless was useful in the past, and in general would codify the knowledge of the navigator by specifying that navigators use the instruments and techniques with which the people have long been familiar, and no new ones.[260]

Such associations are certainly possible for ordinary people, since they can tell what it is to be cured of a disease and what it is to prevail in war without having knowledge of medicine or strategy; but they do not, properly speaking, count as knowledge, because there is no guarantee that the association between a practice and a particular outcome will continue to hold in the future absent a correct account of the causal relationship between the practice and its outcome, that is, absent genuine knowledge of the overarching practice, which is precisely what the assembly lacks. Conditions might change,

[260] Note the emphasis on military technology. See also Skemp (1987, 205n1), and Campbell (1867, note *ad loc*).

and associations might be spurious: fighting with long ships, which might have been an effective way of fighting at sea in the past, may no longer work against new forms of trireme warfare, and drugs that appeared to work in the past might have been spuriously associated with the improved condition of the patient. Correlation, as the saying goes, does not imply causation. So the Stranger still considers law, all things considered, a "mistake" (cf. 300b4–5), insofar as spurious correlations, or correlations that no longer hold given changed circumstances, might lead to mistakes about the proper way to, e.g., treat sickness or fight naval battles.

The laws of the city, at least when they have been framed by the city with the intention to protect itself from abuses of power, are thus similarly the misguided attempt to codify the knowledge of the statesman, and they similarly succeed at best in writing down those practices that have served in the past to preserve the city, not at embodying the reasons for why these practices worked to preserve it. Such law at its best embodies the experience of the people, the fruits of its trial and error (300b1–2). But experience is not knowledge: the people do not have the wherewithal to distinguish which of these past practices will be useful in the future and which will be harmful. They mistake correlation for causation, so to speak. Only the knowledge of the statesman, that is, a full account or understanding of the kinds of things that help preserve the city's unity and virtue, could determine in every situation which past practices are useful for its preservation, or even whether (and which) new practices are needed.

We learn later in the dialogue that the statesman is centrally concerned with the dangers of external and internal war, both of which can be understood as the disease of cities (cf. *nosos* 307d7 and context), and both of which are remedied by the statesman using his own "drug" (*pharmakon* 310a3). We might thus surmise that correct "political" legislation by the city involves the codification of those practices of the city that have been associated in the past with internal peace and victory in war. To the extent that the laws of the city are simply the codification of these practices, we can then understand them as "imitations" of the practices that knowledgeable individuals would use to protect the city (300c5–7). Such laws are likely to be the constitutions of cities that have lasted for a long time, despite the absence of genuine statesmen ruling over them (302a5–6): they are likely to have hit upon, through long experience, practices that preserve the city from the twin dangers of internal and external conflict. Law that codifies these practices is based on opinion rather than knowledge (cf. 301b2), since it is created without a full understanding of the causes of conflict or of the true good of the city, but such opinion is likely to be close to the true opinion, at least for a given range of circumstances.

Thus, though correlation is not causation, it is good enough if the conditions under which the city has survived up to now do not change very much in the future. This is noted by the Stranger with some amazement (302a1–2): it is a fact deserving of wonder (and thus of philosophical reflection, we should note: cf. *Theaetetus* 155d) that some cities are not easily destroyed, even though (it is implied) their laws have not been created by knowledgeable statesmen.[261] The embeddedness of experience in the law, despite its inferiority to knowledge, enables it to achieve adequate enough results (measured by the endurance of the city), because experience produces an image of the truth (that is, of the actual practices that would protect the city).

---

[261] It is worth noting, however, that the fact that some cities endure is not perfect information regarding the goodness of their laws. As the Athenian Stranger notes in the *Laws*, "many routs and pursuits have occurred, and will occur again, without a clear cause. So we should always set down victory or defeat in battle not as a clear but as a controversial criterion for whether practices are noble or not. The fact is, bigger cities defeat smaller ones in battle" (638a–b, Pangle translation). Resilience to external conflict is no guarantee of good institutions, though it provides some evidence of them; note that in the context of the passage the Athenian is criticizing Spartan institutions, which he considers better than average but by no means good.

Though the Stranger does not emphasize this point, it is worth noting that one way in which the law prevents internal conflict is through its presentation of itself as a full account of the good, the just, and the noble (cf. 299c5–8). Insofar as the law is "sovereign" in this sense, it keeps all practitioners of the arts from misusing them for their own partial vision of the good, just as the law of the statesman would do. It thus keeps the arts within their own competence, weaving together the forms of care represented by all the arts of the city for the sake of its vision of the good of the *polis*. This vision may be substantially wrong, but according to the Stranger's argument any account of the good set in law is substantially wrong, including the statesman's own, since it cannot account for itself and hence cannot adapt to changing circumstances. Law simply cannot be a complete and correct account of the good and the just, regardless of whether or not it is created by the statesman, though it can be a correct opinion of the good and the just valid for some range of circumstances. Yet insofar as the law of the city keeps the artisans from overstepping their own competence (and thinking they know about the good and the just when they do not), it does substantially the same thing as the law that a true statesman would give to the city. The laws then essentially say that every person should do his or her own job within the bounds of the city's "knowledge" (that is, opinion) of the good, the just and the noble.[262] The only difference between the laws of the city and the laws of the statesman in this respect is that the laws of the statesman may be correct for a longer period of time, or be more correct for the specific circumstances in which they were created; but from the point of view of true knowledge, they are both insufficient, insubstantial images. They, too, in the absence of the true statesman, become "idols" of the good, the just, and the noble; yet without such idols not even the makeshift web of care formed by the artisans in the city in the absence of the

[262] Cf. *Republic* 433a–434d.

statesman would hold, and human beings would perish in the attempt of every possessor of knowledge to misuse it for his or her own mistaken purposes.

Moreover, the Stranger stresses that in a process of law-making such as he has described, that is, one concerned with the protection of the city against the misuse of expertise and rule, the knowledgeable may not be entirely powerless to affect the content of the laws. Thus, the Stranger emphasizes in the story that participation in the assembly that makes the laws is not restricted to those without knowledge of medicine or navigation, but allows (though does not privilege) people with the arts to be codified to make their voices heard and to give advice (298d5–7).[263] So the law may approximate with greater or lesser exactness the kinds of rules that a knowledgeable individual would leave for the city, that is, it may be "truer" opinion. The greater the influence of doctors and ship-captains in crafting laws about medicine and navigation, the greater the closeness of the laws of the people to the laws a great doctor or a ship captain would have constructed on his own in case he needed to do so, and hence the greater the number of practices closer to the "state of the art" that would be enshrined in writing. By analogy, the real laws of a city, if they were made through a process that included some people with some degree of knowledge, can be said to come "as far as possible" (cf. 300c5–7) from those who know (that is, as far as possible given their limited numbers in the assembly), and hence they can approximate, with greater or lesser exactness, the "true" set of practices that preserved, and is likely to preserve, the city, for some greater or lesser range of circumstances.

Yet though the protective effect of laws is of course amplified if the laws are written "as far as possible" by those who have knowledge (300c5–7), in the end all laws (whether based on

[263] Cf. also 259a1–9, especially *sumbouleuein* at 259a2. Nothing bars the true statesman from offering advice to an assembly and thus helping shape the laws.

experience or created by individuals with knowledge) are mere imitations of the truth (cf. 293e4–5) insofar as they represent purely static "snapshots" of the kinds of (changing) practices that would actually preserve the city's unity and virtue in a changing world. From this point of view, the law that a city creates for itself, embodying its experience of the things that have preserved it from conflict in the past, is functionally identical to the law that a genuine statesman would create for it. Both kinds of law represent accounts of the practices that make the city united and resilient to conflict and which are valid only for some limited range of circumstances; recall that a true statesman understands that law is not valid for all circumstances, even if he made it himself. The law that a genuine statesman might create might be better in degree, but not in kind; it might be a somewhat more beautiful imitation (a less distorted imitation of his knowledge) than the law that a city gives itself, but both remain imitations. They are both like old "snapshots" of the practice of real knowers, distorted ("phantastic") imitations of the knowledge of the artisan rather than live forms of knowledge (cf. 300c5–7; see also chapter 4), although they look to the people to be accurate and complete representations of the knowledge of the statesman.[264] At the margins, it may matter a bit whether these are knowledgeable distorted imitations or not (cf. *Sophist* 267b7–8), since the true statesman presumably has a better idea of which laws may preserve the city over a wider range of circumstances, but they are both insubstantial images compared to the real knowledge of the statesman. Hence the Stranger sees no need to distinguish

[264] Palumbo (1995, 179ff.) argues, to the contrary, that law is an "eikastic" or nondistorted imitation—an exact copy—of the art's practice. But the point of the Stranger's story is that the people select those practices with which they are familiar, that look beautiful and useful to them from their position, rather than create an exact copy of the "state of the art," which would include practices with which they are unfamiliar. Only someone with knowledge could make such an imitation of his own art, as we saw in chapter 4, pp. 205–209, but even then it would not be a fully accurate image of his knowledge over time; all law is ultimately "phantastic," not "eikastic."

between the rule of law in the sense of holding on to the laws that a genuine statesman would create for the city, and the rule of law in the sense of holding on to laws created by the city by codifying its experiences: all of them "imitate the truth," but are not *the* truth.[265]

Law is thus not a form of knowledge, but a form of opinion, which may, in some circumstances, even be true. Its origin (whether created by a genuine statesman or by a city) only affects the range of circumstances for which it is true, not the fact that it is limited in this range. The problem with law is that it remains opinion; even if it was true in the past, it may not remain true in the future, and it has no resources to change so that it remains true in the future. Conversely, insofar as it is *mere* opinion the law acts as a restraint on those who actually do have knowledge.

Yet the story the Stranger has told up to this point does not fully reflect the degree to which genuine statesmanship is restricted by the rule of law in actual cities. All that is implied by the story thus far is that those who are the recognized practitioners of the arts (genuine doctors and ship-captains) must practice them in accordance with certain rules, a proposition that need not strike us as absurd. Indeed, it strikes Young Socrates as merely "strange" (298e4), but not as intolerable. Thus far, the people's understanding of the rule of law is not

[265] The debate between Rowe, Samaras, Teisserenc, and others surrounding the interpretation of 300c5–7, and in particular regarding the question of whether *tauta* at 300c5 (which indicates the laws that are to be called "imitations of the truth") refers "backwards" to the laws created by the assembly without the participation of the true statesman or "forwards" to the laws created by those with knowledge, is misconceived. That law is an imitation of the truth is not primarily a statement of praise but of fact, since all law is a mere imitation of the truth, a mere "picture" rather than the living reality of the thing itself (cf. also Samaras [2002, 175]), and hence the *tauta* at 300c5 can refer indifferently to both sorts of law; recall in this connection that the Stranger argues that sophistry is an imitation of wisdom (*Sophist* 266a–268d), and that he calls all the rulers of the law-abiding cities "sophists" (*Statesman* 303c).

in deadly conflict with the statesman's understanding of it, and one might imagine a form of the rule of law that stops at this point.

But now the Stranger imagines a further way in which the people may restrict the practitioners of the arts of medicine and navigation. Instead of allowing only genuine doctors or ship-captains to practice these arts, or at least those who have had the requisite education (and hence to retain some measure of self-rule), they restrict their practice to people selected, by the more or less random process of election and the certainly random process of the lot, from among everybody (298e5–9). It is at this point that the Stranger's example starts to seem truly comic, for we do not normally think that doctors should be selected at random or by election from among the people, including people who know nothing of medicine, and this is reflected in Young Socrates' response, suggesting that if this were the case the situation would be harder than if there merely existed some regulation or codification of technical activity (298e10).

Once again, the people's misunderstanding of the nature of knowledge affects the kind of institutions they create. Thinking, erroneously, that the knowledge of the arts can be distilled into simple rules, they now believe that such knowledge is available to anyone who can read, and hence (logically) that anybody can practice it. The analogy with statesmanship is clear: not only is the knowledge of the statesman more or less codified (erroneously) in actual cities, but it is practiced by people who have been selected by lot, much as in Athens, rather than by people with the requisite knowledge.

Yet this is not enough, for it does not ensure that knowledge may not be misused. If knowledge is available to everybody in the form of written rules, then it follows that it may be misused by anybody who can read. The Stranger thus imagines that the people create courts and other mechanisms which further restrict the self-rule of the arts of medicine and navigation. Malpractice suits and the like are allowed, a fact that Young

Socrates, who is imagining this, greets with what amounts to a dismissive "serves them well," saying that people who would willingly practice the arts under such conditions would most justly suffer whatever punishments are meted out to them (299a8–b1). He does not appear to be entirely wrong about this: if people willingly submit to practice the arts under these conditions, there is a sense in which it is just that they be punished if they break the rules (cf. *Crito* 49e–53a). This could be the reason why Plato depicts Socrates as consistently refusing to participate in politics narrowly understood: he was not willing to practice statesmanship under these conditions, preferring to converse with the young privately.[266] At the same time, the possibility that the laws may themselves be unjust or the jury improperly swayed does seem to cast doubt on the justice of the entire system. This question is raised most pointedly by the detour the Stranger's argument now takes. For he will now appear to describe the case of Socrates.

The Stranger says that it still seems necessary to the people to set up another law in addition to the laws they have described already, namely the laws codifying the arts and the laws restricting the power of their practitioners. This new law restricts inquiry on the part of the already regulated practitioners of the arts (299b2–d1). While the first law codified the practice of the arts (was in fact nothing other than the codification, or image, of the art that the assembly created) and the second and third established enforcement mechanisms and regulated the power of the practitioners of the arts, the whole system of law thus far had not entirely closed the possibility of improvement in the law by means of inquiry or research. One might imagine the regulated practitioners of the arts introducing proposals in the assembly for the people to judge. If the people accepted them, these proposals would then become part of the established law. But this new law regulates not only the practice of the arts but their very development, prohibiting further change.

---

[266] Cf. Strauss (1989, 227–228).

The law thus presents itself not only as a codification of the knowledge of the ship-captain or doctor, but as a *complete* codification of this knowledge. Those who, contrary to the law, engage in research into the matters that the law images, thinking that such knowledge as is embedded in the law is not complete but can be increased, are called *meteōrologoi* and garrulous sophists (cf. 299b7–8), as the elder Socrates was called by Aristophanes, and are further accused of corrupting the young by persuading them to act contrary to the established nautical or medicinal practice (299b8), just as Socrates was accused of corrupting the young. They are accused, in other words, of persuading the young to think of themselves as *autokratores*, self-rulers, and therefore of violating the very intention of the laws, namely, that no practitioner of any art is to be *autokrator*, self-ruling in it (298c1), but that all must be subject to the law.

Unlike the other laws that the Stranger has described in the story so far, this "new" law does not correspond to a particular Athenian practice.[267] To the extent that there is a parallel here with Athenian practice, the parallel is to the Athenian understanding of the implications of Socratic inquiry into the laws. The argument seems to be that the Athenians wrongly believe that their laws represent a complete account of the good and the just, just as the people in the Stranger's story wrongly believe that the laws they are setting up wrongly believe that their laws represent a complete account of the healthy and the nautical, when they are merely distorted images of the relevant knowledge. And because they wrongly believe this, they think that any attempt to inquire into the laws is an attempt to discredit what they take to be the true conception of the good and the just, that is, to corrupt the citizens and in particular the youth (299c3–d1). Thus the Stranger's analogy seems to suggest that the Athenians' mistaken understanding of the nature of law led to the conviction of Socrates.

[267] See Lane (1998, 154n37).

So understood, the Stranger's argument suggests that the key problem with the law as cities conceive it (not necessarily as a philosopher might conceive of it) is that it fosters a particularly misleading understanding of the nature of the just, the noble, and the good that tends to preempt further inquiry into these matters. Indeed, its authority depends to a great extent on the shared but necessarily incorrect belief that what the law says is a relatively correct or undistorted account of the just and the good. There can be no Socratic humility to the law if it is to be effective: the law never says that it does not know the just and the good.[268] And the more effective the law is at inculcating this conviction of its rightness in the citizens, the harder it is to change, and the more law-abiding the citizens.

Yet though the law thus seems to lead by its own inner logic to the ban on inquiry into itself (and hence, we might say, to Socrates' murder, insofar as Socratic inquiry would necessarily *appear* to undermine the authority of the law),[269] the Stranger implicitly suggests that law is nevertheless able to stop short of it.[270] The Stranger (or rather Plato, in this context) is not absolving the Athenians from the murder of Socrates, but he attributes it, paradoxically, to an excess of

[268] This is so even under a modern understanding of the proper role of law. The law necessarily postulates its own view of the good and the just as correct and sets it down as authoritative (punishing those who overstep its limits), even if this view of the good and the just law is "permissive" enough to allow many others to pursue their own interests according to their lights, i.e., even if the law is indifferent regarding (some) competing accounts of the just and the good.

[269] It is worth stressing that throughout this passage, Plato (and not just the Stranger) seems to assume as a matter of course that Socratic inquiry, properly conducted, *cannot* corrupt the youth; the Athenians are simply depicted as wrong on this count. Nevertheless, the Stranger implicitly grants the point that Socratic inquiry can undermine the *authority* of the law by showing its incompleteness as an account of the good, the just, and the noble, as we shall see.

[270] Thus Lane (1998, 161) notes that later none of the "law-obedient constitutions is said to ban investigation," which suggest that this feature of law is not strictly necessary.

lawfulness: the Athenians were not measured enough in their understanding of the shortcomings of the law, believing that their laws represented a complete account of the good and the just and the noble when it was merely a distorted image of it, and hence wrongly condemning Socratic inquiries that showed it to be incomplete as a form of corruption of the youth.[271] By presenting an account of the nature of law that shows its incompleteness, Plato (through the Stranger) is thus attempting to restore a measured understanding of law to the city, and indirectly arguing for the freedom of inquiry that was denied to Socrates: a correct understanding of law must make *space* for philosophy, because a correct understanding of law recognizes that the account of the good and the just that the law offers is ultimately incomplete, though insofar as such inquiry *also* undermines the authority of the law it will perhaps have to be carefully circumscribed, as we shall see.

This seems to be the point of the Stranger's exchange with Young Socrates at 299e which concludes the story about the origins of the law. After reciting a list of seven arts and kinds of arts he asks Young Socrates to consider what would happen to life if all of them were regulated in the four ways he has described, and in particular if a prohibition of inquiry were to be made effective in each of these arts. Young Socrates, in an unintentional foreshadowing of Socrates' famous speech in the *Apology*, says (299e6–10) that in the situation the Stranger describes it is clear that all the arts would be completely destroyed and that they would not emerge in the future due to the obstacles placed in the way of inquiry by the law; so that life, which was already hard, would become completely

[271] This does not mean, *pace* Rowe (2001a), that all law will lead to the death of Socrates; only that this is an inherent tendency in the law that must be checked by the correct ("philosophical") understanding of its shortcomings as an account of the just and the good. Cf. also Voegelin (1987 [1956], 165): the "culmination of lawfulness" is the "murder of Socrates," but, I would add, not measured lawfulness. There is a mean of lawfulness too.

abiōtos, unlivable.[272] And indeed, without the arts, life would be literally impossible for human beings, since they would be destroyed by the harshness of nature (274b5–c5); but Young Socrates, like the elder Socrates, is pointing to the necessity of inquiry, that is, philosophy, broadly understood, for the arts (including the art of the statesman) to develop. It is not the mere regulation of the arts that destroys them, but the prohibition of even regulated inquiry. It is only when the Stranger suggests that the people would in addition prevent all inquiry into the matters regulated by the laws that Young Socrates declares the situation unbearable (299e6–10). Thus, of the four "components" of the rule of law discussed by the Stranger (codification of past practices, selection of practitioners of the arts by means of lot or election, examination of these practitioners after their time in office, and prevention of inquiry), only the prevention of inquiry is judged to be unambiguously bad, or rather, only the combination of all four components is explicitly condemned by the argument. Similarly, the elder Socrates will stress in his upcoming trial that the unexamined life, the life without "talk about virtue and the other things about which you hear me talking and examining myself and others" (*Apology* 38a), that is, the life without inquiry into the good, the just, and the noble, which are precisely the objects of the art of the statesman, would be unlivable, but that a life under the law that included inquiry would be quite livable.[273]

[272] Cf. *Apology* 38a5–6: ὁ δὲ ἀνεξέταστος βίος οὐ βιωτὸς ἀνθρώπῳ, "the unexamined life is not livable for a human being." For more on the significance of Young Socrates' echo of the elder Socrates, see Miller Jr. (1980, 99–100). Miller argues that Young Socrates, with this response, passes the "test of recognition" that the elder Socrates had set up at the beginning of the dialogue, and thus demonstrates his philosophical nature. For a less sanguine view of Young Socrates' nature, see Stern (1997, 273n44).

[273] Arends (1999, 114n27) rightly sees that Young Socrates' response is in accordance with the myth, but he wrongly denies a link to the *Apology*: what makes possible all arts is "inquiry," i.e., "philosophy." Strauss (1989, 228) notes that "Socrates obeyed without flinching the law which commanded

As I briefly indicated above, foreclosing inquiry into the just, the good, and the noble would not only result in the death of Socrates, but also more generally would close off the possibility that a statesman might emerge in the city; for how else could a genuine statesman acquire the knowledge he needs except through inquiry? In other words, it is not the mere fact of the rule of law but the excess of lawfulness culminating in the prohibition of inquiry that makes the emergence of statesmanship impossible, and hence in the long run guarantees the destruction of the city, just as the universe would eventually be destroyed if the god did not come to rescue it, renovating its instruction. If this possibility is not to be completely foreclosed from within the city itself, the law must thus find a way to accommodate some form of inquiry into the objects of which it claims to be the authoritative account.

One may object that the Stranger says (at 301a) that imitating the true constitution well requires the citizens, once their laws have been laid down, never to do "anything contrary to their written and ancestral customs" (301a3), which suggests that the Stranger is endorsing a more extreme version of conservatism. But this formulation does not prevent inquiry and improvement of the laws in accordance with the laws; it is only if we read 301a, illegitimately, as including the kind of prohibition on inquiry described in 299b, that we get the strong legal conservatism assumed by some commentators. All that the passage says is that the city imitates well the true constitution if it respects the experience embodied in its laws and hence refuses to go beyond it at any given time. In that case, the city's constitution is a good imitation of the true constitution not because it has been designed by a true statesman or because the citizens refuse to change it,[274] but because it embodies an intermediate degree of truth, lying in between the extremes

him to die because of his alleged corruption of the young; yet he would not have obeyed a law formally forbidding him the pursuit of philosophy."

[274] *Pace* Lane (1998, 157–158).

of completely ignorant rule (300d9–e1, always wrong) and completely knowledgeable rule (always true, 300e1–2): it has laws that may be appropriate for some circumstances and characters but not others, embodying opinions (cf. 301b2) which may be true in some cases but not always. Since the citizens do not have reliable means to determine *in general* the circumstances under which these opinions are true and under which they are not, they should not, on their own authority, do anything contrary to them, and they are perhaps well advised not to change them often; but the argument does not imply, and the Stranger nowhere says, that the citizens should never attempt to change these laws in accordance with experience through institutions like the Nocturnal Council.

It is true that the Stranger does not argue for any of this. At best, he implicitly (but not really explicitly) points out the dilemma in which the city is caught, namely, the tradeoff between the need to retain the authority of the law and the need for some degree of inquiry. The point of his argument is simply to show Young Socrates that even if the law were to prohibit inquiry it would still be preferable to the situation in which the ignorant ruled without respect for the law. Given the enormous scarcity of genuine political knowledge, it is less risky for the city to err on the side of refusing to hear the voices of those who claim political knowledge (and hence occasionally rejecting genuine insight) than to depart from its hard-won experience (which at least correlates with the kinds of things that have helped the city survive up to the present time): it would be better for the city to close itself off *entirely* to the possibility of political knowledge than to risk being ruled by the ignorant (300a1–301a4).[275] Indeed, if the consequences of error are dire, genuine knowledge extremely scarce, and circumstances relatively stable, as in the highly competitive

[275] "[B]etter a city ruled by bad laws [including laws created by the people] than one ruled by incompetent governors": Pradeau (2002, 98).

ecology of the Greek world,[276] then the Stranger's argument becomes very powerful: a conservatism of experience is then almost always better than ignorant and lawless innovation. Such extreme conservatism has in fact helped many societies survive for relatively long periods of time in precarious environments, though it has often ultimately led to their demise, just as the Stranger would predict.[277]

This kind of conservatism often seems extreme to modern commentators.[278] Moreover, it seems to encourage the worst kind of political messianism: the city is to hold on to its laws, no matter how bad these may be or how bad the consequences may seem, until such time as it judges that a true statesman is in its midst (a judgment that it may at any rate be unqualified to make), and then it is encouraged to throw caution to the wind and embrace the "reversed" world of the lawless rule of the statesman. The Stranger's (apparent) conservatism appears to stand at an enormous distance from the organic conservatism of experience advocated in modern times by thinkers as diverse as Burke, Oakeshott, and Hayek, and even from the kind of conservatism advocated by the Athenian Stranger in the *Laws* or by Aristotle in the *Politics*.

If it is better for the city to forbid inquiry than to run the risk of being ruled by ignorant men who ignore the city's hard-won experience, it would be even better if the city could find a way to be open at least to philosophical inquiry into the laws and the virtues without undermining its authority, and the Stranger nowhere forecloses this possibility. So long as the prohibition on investigation or inquiry is not an essential

---

[276] See Ober (2008, ch. 2).

[277] See, for example, the account of the survival and eventual demise of the Norse in Greenland in Diamond (2005, ch. 7 and 8, especially 239–240). Norse conservatism was necessary in a harsh environment were the margin for error was small, but it became a liability once circumstances changed (climate, trading relations, and the technology of neighboring Inuit communities).

[278] Cf. Annas and Waterfield (1995, 68n65); Klosko (2008, 470–471).

element of genuine law, as I have argued it is not, then it would not be altogether out of the question for the city to consider legal changes when its accumulated experience dictates, so long as it can be ensured that those proposing the changes do not act with a view to their private profit and that excessive changes do not undermine the authority of the law. The Eleatic Stranger's arguments could thus implicitly accommodate the proposal of the Athenian Stranger for a "Nocturnal Council," an institution for the accumulation of experience suitable for protecting the city against internal and external conflict and for integrating this experience into the legal system of the city.[279] The "messianism" of the argument is merely an effect of the way in which the Stranger sharpens the alternatives, not a necessary result of conceiving of law as the codification of a people's experience.

It is worth examining in some detail the way in which the Athenian Stranger in the *Laws* overcomes the dilemma identified by the Eleatic Stranger in the *Statesman*. As others have noted, the legal system described in the *Laws* is designed to be quite conservative.[280] The Athenian discourages innovation in education as a danger to the state insofar as it leads to the desire to change the laws (797a–d); claims that it is only when the laws are seen never to have changed that they are "reverently upheld" (798a–b); and even praises the Egyptians for the fact that their laws have endured for ten thousand years without change (656d–657a). Moreover, the Athenian repeatedly warns about the dangers of innovation, especially innovation "from abroad" (952e–953a), and his only discussions of procedures

[279] My position thus implies that Plato already believed that radical conservatism was untenable, and did not change his mind when he was writing the *Laws*, *contra* Klosko (2008).

[280] For details, see Klosko (2008); Stalley (1983, 81–82); Vanhoutte (1954). Bobonich (2002, 395–408), and Morrow (1960b), have a more expansive view of the degree to which the laws of Magnesia can be changed, but they still see it as quite conservative. At any rate, that the legal system is designed to have a conservative bias does not imply that it is never to be changed, however, as I show in detail in Márquez (2011).

to change the laws (with some minor exceptions) make such change difficult, requiring the concurrence of the people, the officials, and the oracles (771a–772d). The Athenian is especially concerned with sustaining the authority of the law, and he believes that the best way of achieving this is through the maintenance of shared beliefs in the completeness and sacredness of the laws.

Yet the Athenian clearly shares the Eleatic's view that the best thing is not the rule of law, but the rule of those with knowledge, indeed the rule of reason. For example, in a prelude to the criminal law (874e–875d) he says that "no law or order is stronger than knowledge" (875c6–7, Pangle translation), and that if there arose a person with the appropriate nature and the requisite knowledge, it would be wrong to subordinate such a person to the law. But human nature being what it is, such a person is not likely to arise or to be able to resist the temptation to pursue his own private interest: the knowledge and virtue required are simply too scarce.[281] Hence we need law, which is only second-best with respect to the rule of the truly knowledgeable individual. This short argument, to be sure, is not intended as a full-blown philosophical examination of the rule of law, much less as a justification for a form of the rule of law that prevents inquiry or legal change, but it is safe to assume that the Athenian would agree with most if not all of the more complex argument of the Eleatic Stranger in the *Statesman* regarding the specific value and limits of the rule of law.

Yet though the Athenian designs the legal system of Magnesia to have a "conservative bias," he does not entirely dismiss the possibility that legal change may be necessary in the distant future, when he is not around. He indicates that he does not believe his own lawgiving is necessarily exempt from error (cf. 769a–d, 857c, 859c), which suggests that he

[281] Though not, it should be emphasized, utterly impossible; the Athenian's position is compatible with that of the Eleatic.

understands perfectly well that there may come a time when the laws he lays down will need to be changed (cf. 840e), and though the procedures he devises for changing the laws are necessarily restrictive, they are not impossible to use, and indeed the Athenian says that such change may eventually become necessary (772c7). In order that such change may not threaten the survival of the city, the Athenian thus introduces an institution, the "Nocturnal Council," which is intended to let the city steer a relatively safe course between the Scylla of excessive conservatism and the Charybdis of excessive and unreflective openness to legal innovation, which is the very dilemma implicitly depicted by the Eleatic Stranger in the *Statesman*.

As Morrow rightly noted (1960b, 507), "whatever else the Council may be, it is first of all an institution for the higher education of its members." It is the only institution in Magnesia where Socratic inquiries into the nature of virtue, and in particular those virtues that ensure the city's unity, can be freely pursued, alongside with more empirical inquiries into the comparative performance of the laws of the city and those of other cities. The Athenian does not promise that such inquiries will lead to actual knowledge, but they do amount to the kinds of inquiries that the form of the rule of law espoused by the people in the Eleatic's story (at *Statesman* 299b) would ban. At the very least, the institution is carefully designed to keep the stock of the city's experience as current as possible. Thus one major focus of the institution is to listen to the reports of observers to other lands (951d–952d). Moreover, its members are likely to have privileged access to interesting visitors from foreign countries (953d), and they are the only citizens allowed to interact with atheists (909a), a provision apparently designed not merely to punish the atheist but to keep the members of the council "sharp" and capable of fielding challenges to their own laws and institutions (cf. also 951b).

Yet the Athenian Stranger is very careful to prevent unchecked inquiry into the nature of virtue and laws. This is the reason, for example, for the web of restrictions surrounding the handling of information about other cities by the Nocturnal Council: travelers abroad must report to the Council on their observations of the laws of other cities, but if the Council decides that this knowledge is corrupting, they must not communicate it to anyone, on potential pain of death (951d–952d). Inquiry can undermine respect for the laws, according to the Athenian, and hence the Council must have a very conservative bias in its mandate: it must err on the side of rejecting innovation. In a sense, Plato is suggesting here that the people in the Eleatic Stranger's story (who stand in for the Athenians) were not wholly wrong to be worried about the effects of unchecked Socratic inquiry. The Council represents Plato's ultimate response to this fact, balancing the need for inquiry if eventual changes to the law are to be maximally informed by experience and true opinion (but not necessarily by knowledge) with the need for retaining maximum reverence for the laws.

Both the *Statesman* and the *Laws* stress that laws are not to be changed easily, and that legal change, especially when it is motivated by private interest, is easily harmful to the city. But both dialogues also recognize the need to integrate inquiry into the rule of law if the rule of law is to be anything more than the least bad option for a city. Though the Eleatic Stranger does not propose institutions like the Nocturnal Council, the presuppositions of his arguments about the value and limits of the rule of law directly lead to a solution like that of the Athenian Stranger, or indeed, like that of Plato in real life, namely the Academy.

Imperfect political regimes

Once the case for conservatism is complete, the Stranger can then return to the classification of constitutions (*politeiai*) or forms of political order, though his remarks there are not strictly essential to the search for the statesman. There are three basic sorts of *politeiai*. The first is the *politeia* that the statesman himself rules directly, and that is the kind of *politeia* where there are no laws properly speaking, since in it all laws—pictures of knowledge—are revocable in the presence of living knowledge. In such a regime, the statesman has the correct causal account that ties particular practices to the preservation of the city (or its flourishing, for that matter).

The second is the imitation of the first kind of *politeia* in law, a "picture" of knowledge in action preserved by the laws of the city in the absence of the embodied representative of living knowledge. Though, as we have seen, there are some differences between the kind of picture that a true statesman would create of his own practice and the kind of picture that an assembly would create on the basis of its experience of political knowledge (that is, of its "view" or "opinion" of the practice of those who are recognized as having political knowledge, 301b2), in the final instance they are both pictures of knowledge, rather than the real thing, and hence liable to become quickly obsolete and even harmful without the living presence of the statesman. We might think of these as the regimes based on mere correlations between particular practices and the preservation of the city, rather than on real understanding of the causes of the city's preservation.

The third *politeia* is the one where there is no longer even a picture of knowledge in action, as the laws are disregarded or changed on the basis of personal whim. This *politeia* is an imitation of the characteristic gesture of the true statesman (rule without laws) but it is an empty imitation, since it is no longer even a picture of his knowledge. It is like a snapshot of the wrong thing; the regime is based not on opinion (true or false) of some correlation between the practices of the city and its preservation, but simply on desire and ignorance (301c3). The first kind of imitation is thus preferable, as closer to the truth of the statesman's presence, than the second; as imitations, however, the Stranger will soon suggest that neither of them really is a *politeia* but merely a *stasiōteia*, a factional order for the sake of a part and not the whole (303b8–c5).

The Stranger uses this insight now to reclassify all the *politeiai* (301a6–c9). There is only one true regime, namely kingship, and the other regimes divide according to whether or not they imitate the true one by holding to their own laws or by disregarding them, that is, whether the rulers rule according to opinion (which may more or less approximate true opinion) or according to private desire and ignorance. These distinctions yield seven regimes, namely the true one plus six imitations, but only five names (301b7–8), since the kingship of the true statesman and the kingship of the imitative king share a name, and democracy, whether according to law or not, still has only one name.

The Stranger pauses to explain why only five regimes are normally recognized by people, rather than the six/seven he has described (301c6–e5). The explanation centers on the difficulty human beings have believing that a true statesman can exist, that is, on the difficulty people have in believing in the conjunction of technical competence and moral *epistēmē*, a point we have already encountered in the Stranger's story. They think such competence as a statesman would have would be necessarily misused in harmful ways to them, not understanding that the statesman's competence, being the knowledge of the good, the just, and the noble, cannot be misused. They are thus distrustful of would-be monarchs (*duscheranantōn* 301c9), that is, they find a single monarch of that sort hard to take, just as Young Socrates had found the fact that the true statesman rules without law hard to take (cf. *duscheraineis* 294a2), and do not believe that anybody could ever be able and willing to rule with both virtue and knowledge.

At any rate, the distrust of the people is well-founded given the evidence available to them; as the Stranger says, kings do not emerge among human beings as among bees, immediately identifiable as such for their evident excellence in body and mind (301d8–e2). The king really is like a god among human beings (cf. 303b4–5, where the Stranger makes the comparison explicitly), though a hidden god, a god that returns to impose order in the city but must always recede into invisibility. Though the Stranger does not assert this, we might say that only situations of extreme emergency would allow the king to emerge to impose his order, presenting the people with the alternative of either complete destruction or trust in the statesman, just as it is only the near-death of the universe that makes the god return to reorder the cosmos.

The non-recognition of the true statesman by the people, and thus their necessary reliance on law, is the reason, the Stranger suggests, why cities are full of evils (301e6ff.). This is not surprising, since such complete reliance on law would destroy the products of any other art (302a1–2; cf. 299e6–10). Hence what is deserving of wonder (and thus of philosophical reflection, we should recall: cf. *Theaetetus* 155d) is the fact that cities are not easily destroyed, that in fact they are strong by nature (302a3–4), at least some of them, despite suffering all sorts of evils. Some cities (amazingly!) endure for a long time without being overturned. It is understood that these are the cities that are the good imitations of the true *politeia*, though the Stranger does not say so. By contrast, those cities governed by people who think they have the *epistēmē* of statesmanship but in fact do not have it are constantly being overturned (302a5–b3).

Why are some cities preserved? There are a number of possibilities, though the Stranger does not speak in any detail about them. First, and most obviously, there is the possibility of belief in the divinity of the laws (see, e.g., *Laws* 624aff.): piety then makes rulers believe that they do not know better than the laws. (Yet, as the Athenian Stranger argues in the *Laws*, belief in the sacredness of laws, though important to their preservation, is not enough; a specific constitutional structure, which came to be called a "mixed" constitution, and which the Eleatic does not discuss, is necessary.) Or it may be that in some cities the citizens have a healthy enough fear of being duped by fake statesmen and an awareness that they cannot tell who the true sophists are, and hence prefer to put their trust in laws that are designed to prevent the misuse of knowledge by people without virtue. In this case it is the nature of human beings—their natural distrust of the possibility of a coincidence of virtue and knowledge, the evidence of which is all around them in the possible amorality of all technical knowledge—that leads them (in some cases) to construct cities that, in spite of everything, endure for a long time. Such cities have laws that are the functional equivalents of laws that a true statesman would have established for the duration of his absence, that is, laws that codify correlations between certain practices and the preservation of the city, even as the citizens fail to understand why these practices result in the preservation of the city and thus fail to see when the same practices may no longer work. Whatever the case, the Eleatic Stranger's argument suggests, but does not state, that the cities that endure have within themselves something very much like the Socratic "I know only that I do not know" better than the laws, induced either by piety or by genuine awareness of ignorance, whereas the other cities do not know that they do not know, thus displaying the worst kind of ignorance, and hence are easily destroyed. The Stranger does not continue this fruitful line of thought; the strength of the city by nature is left as something that is *thaumaston*, worthy of wonder and thus of philosophical reflection, but also something for a different time.

Instead, he now turns to something he terms a digression (*parergon* 302b8), yet a digression of the utmost "practical" importance for the life of human beings (302b8–9): which of these imitative *politeiai* is best?

The basic argument is quite simple (301c1–303b7): considering all six imitative forms of government, the two dimensions of power (cf. 303a4–7) and closeness to the true *politeia* determine the degree to which a common life (*to suzēn* 302b6) is tolerable in them. The rule of one is highest in power, that of many lowest; the rule of law is closer to the true *politeia*, that of human beings without knowledge farthest. This leads to a complete ranking of all the regimes: lawful monarchy first (closest to the true *politeia* and highest in power to do good), lawful oligarchy (aristocracy) second, lawful democracy third, unlawful democracy fourth, unlawful oligarchy fifth, and tyranny last (farthest from the true *politeia* and greatest in power to do evil). The best place to have a common life is under a kingship according to law, and the worst is under a tyrant. Conversely, it is better to live under a lawless democracy than under tyranny; democracy is the "middle" or "mean" form (303a2–3), the natural outgrowth, one might say, of the general distrust of the coincidence of *technē* and virtue that gives rise to the law itself.

The position of democracy within the ranking of regimes deserves further thought. As we saw, the Stranger's hypothetical "story" about the origins of the rule of law took democracy, not monarchy or, despite some minor references, oligarchy, as its paradigmatic case.[282] Democracy was paradigmatic because it showed precisely how the fear of the disjunction between *technē* and virtue gives rise to law, and how this fear is assuaged by restrictions on the power and knowledge of all artisans, who in turn form the city. Moreover, most law-abiding regimes are "democratic" not in the sense that the people have any input over the day-to-day activities of rulers, but in the sense that the laws of the law-abiding regimes are always distillations of the common experience of the entire community of those things that preserved it in the past, not just creations of the (*ex hypothesi* ignorant) rulers.

Yet the confusion of names between the two forms of democracy—law-abiding and lawless—is not accidental, but the result of the necessary lack of self-control of democratic politics: the multitude can always be convinced, sometimes with good reason, to change the laws. What the assembly, in its fear, makes, it can also unmake. Democracies are not necessarily conservative regimes. It makes a difference for living whether

[282] Cf. Benardete (1984b, 124).

the laws are or are not respected there, but this difference is not manifested clearly enough for people in general to come up with different names for the two forms of democracy.

Similarly, monarchy, even if law-abiding, always falls under the suspicion that the monarch might one day abuse his power and knowledge; hence lawful monarchy or kingship, shares a name with the true *politeia*, suspicion of which gave rise to law. Though the Stranger does not elaborate on this point, all monarchy already points to the demise of law: in its bad form this is by definition; in its good form by its closeness to the lawless rule of the true statesman, which (we might suspect) the lawful king is always tempted to imitate, despite his lack of knowledge. A lawful king must have veritably Socratic self-control, that is, must know that he does not know how to rule, a difficult thing for a monarch to know.[283]

This double ambiguity (the same name for the true regime and the regime of the lawful monarch as well as the same name for both lawful and lawless democracy) thus points to what we might call the fragility of the law. The Eleatic Stranger has no argument for a regime that preserves the law better than others; his only concern is with simple evaluation. For such an argument, we would have to turn to the Athenian Stranger in the *Laws* and the doctrine of the mixed regime (cf. especially *Laws* 693d–e, on the "two mothers" of regimes, namely monarchy and democracy).[284] This is another way in which the natural "strength" of the *polis* was merely characterized as wonderful (302a3), that is, as worthy of philosophical reflection, though such reflection was not further pursued. Reflection on that strength should lead (and it does not do so here) to a consideration of what forms of law, and under what conditions, make a city and regime "strong" and "stable."

---

[283] Cf. Roochnik (2005, 12–13).

[284] I discuss the doctrine of the mixed regime in the *Laws* in detail in Márquez (2011).

Finally, we must note the shift from common life (*suzēn* 302b6) to merely life in the lawless regimes (303b1–3). The absence of law means, in a certain sense, the absence of community; the regime without law is clearly a factional regime, as the Stranger notes (303c2), though his charge applies to all imitative regimes, whether lawful or not. Hence only a privately good life, rather than true common life, is possible in the lawless regimes. Only the rule of law allows what is strictly speaking a factional regime to form, for a time at least, a genuine community, allowing for true living together, though we should have to say that the instability of the rule of law in such circumstances (when one "faction" rules over another) eventually destroys whatever community emerges in these regimes. We would need the doctrine of the mixed constitution developed by the Athenian Stranger, once again, to see how to move beyond a purely "factional" regime.

The digression on law concludes here with the complete separation of the "false rulers" from the true rulers. It should be noted that at no point in this discussion have these false rulers been denied a certain role in the making of the web of politics. Though ignorant of true political knowledge, the false rulers must have a certain skill in sustaining the illusion of the law's rightness in the absence of the statesman, and hence some ability to see that they do not know better than the law if they are to rule well (perhaps because they think the laws are divinely ordained, or are otherwise "legitimate"). At their best, such rulers are "Socratic" in the sense that they abide by the laws because they know that they do not know, while still leaving open the possibility of inquiry; at their worst they are clearly sophistic insofar as they ignore the law and imitate the knowledgeable ruler without having his knowledge. But all of them must have a kind of imitative art, which makes them, as long as they actually rule, sophists (303c4–5), since all of them ultimately imitate the knowledge of the genuine statesman (either lawfully or lawlessly) without actually having it.

The Stranger's harsh assessment of all existing rulers is not tempered by his implicit concession that the city must get by, somehow, in the absence of genuine knowledge, and that such knowledge will be rare and generally lacking. But he does acknowledge, however indirectly, that if the city needs illusion in the absence of the statesman, then this illusion should be based, as much as possible, on true opinion and experience, and not merely on the private interests of the current ruler.

6. Statesman

WITH THE ARGUMENTS ON THE SUPERIORITY of the statesman's knowledge to the rule of law, the Stranger has essentially separated statesmanship from all the false or sophistic rulers, and indeed from all the arts that make possible the actually existing city in the absence of genuine knowledge. Yet two tasks still remain.

First, the Stranger still needs to separate statesmanship from those arts that are directly responsible for the true or best regime (and not just for actually existing cities). These arts are true rhetoric, generalship, and the art of judging. Like the arts of carding, fulling, or twisting, which were shown to be directly responsible for the woolen cloak in the discussion of weaving, these arts are directly responsible for the true regime; and just as the weaver had to coordinate the activities of the carder, the fuller, and the warp and woof-makers in order to properly complete the cloak, the statesman must coordinate the activities of rhetorician, the general, and the judge so as to successfully weave the genuine web of politics, that is, the true regime. Such coordination involves the determination of the timing of the activities of the rhetorician and the general and the framing of the laws that constrain the activities of the judge so as to preserve the city from both external and internal threats. The need for such coordination, however, implies that in the absence of the statesman the rhetorician, the general, and the judge simply become the false rulers, both lawless and lawful, that have already been separated from the statesman.

Second, even after separating the statesman from true rhetoric, generalship, and the art of judging, the Stranger still needs to fully characterize the positive role the statesman plays *vis-à-vis* the city as a whole, that is, the task that only the knowledge of the statesman, and no other artisan, can perform in the city. The Stranger characterizes the task of the statesman as an educational and legislative one: he provides the citizens with firm opinions that minimize the destructive effects of their systematically biased judgments, especially in foreign policy. Once again the statesman appears to be primarily concerned with the timing of certain actions, since the dispositions of the citizens may be systematically biased either towards recklessness or passivity, both of which threaten to destroy the city in the absence of knowledge.

Yet as we shall see in this chapter, the statesman cannot simply substitute his judgment for that of the citizens. His role turns out to be, paradoxically, to prepare the city for his absence, and his presence in it turns out to be self-limiting, because he cannot ensure the reproduction of his knowledge. The statesman's task, I shall argue, can thus be understood as the creation of institutions that are resilient: they can function, in his absence, to minimize the unavoidable risks to the existence of the city that come from the fundamental division of human characters into so-called "courageous" and "moderate" dispositions.

The rhetorician, the general, and the judge: 303d–305c

The three arts that are yet to be separated from the art of the statesman, namely, those of the general, the judge, and the genuine rhetorician (303e10–304a2),[285] are "kin" to the art of the

[285] The Stranger does not explicitly say that these are the only arts that remain to be separated from the art of the statesman, but after completing the division of statesmanship from these arts he no longer attempts to separate it from any other arts. Late in the dialogue he talks about "educators" (308e5), but he nowhere attempts to separate these from the statesman. A reasonable inference is that the "educators" are simply musicians and gymnastics trainers, already separated from the statesman earlier (287c1–4,

statesman (303e9), that is, they perform tasks that are tightly related to the task of the statesman and require his coordination, as we shall see. Without these arts, the knowledge of the statesman could never become effective in the city; but by the same token, without the guiding knowledge of the statesman these artisans degenerate into false rulers.[286]

These arts also represent the penultimate step in a progression from more to less embodied in the arts of the care of human beings in the city. As we saw (chapter 1, pp. 51–57, 63–67), the Stranger first described the things that the "indirect" causes of the city produced. These were the physical things that human beings need to take care of their own bodies, and they could, in turn, be likened to the physical body of the city: its fortifications and houses, its vessels and vehicles, its tools and decorative artifacts, its foods and medicines, even its evanescent theatrical performances, and ultimately all the human beings that use and consume them. The Stranger then described the people that directly produced the actually existing city and regime, ending with the false rulers. These people emerged out of the growth of desire in the city and were themselves its managers, creating a sort of illusion of order through the legal or alegal imitation of the true statesman's regime. They could be likened to the "disordered" soul of the city. The Stranger will now emphasize the powers (*dunameis*; cf. 304d9, 304e3, 305b2) that make the statesman's true order effective in the city, which can be likened to the agencies of the soul that mediate between reason and desire, and he will end with the ordering principle of the city itself, the technical *epistēmē* of the king, which can be likened to reason or *phronēsis* in the individual. The properly ordered city (the city with the true regime) thus emerges from this

288e9–289a5, who exercise their arts under the close supervision of the statesman; the statesman's educative function—as the creator of the "curriculum"—is not usurped by them. There is, in other words, no separate art of education distinct from the knowledge of the statesman, *pace* Dixsaut (1995, 266), and Cooper (1997, 90).

[286] See Miller Jr. (1980, 104), as well as Rowe (1995b, note to 303d4–6).

progression as an analogue to the perfected or properly ordered human being, though this is something the Stranger chooses not to emphasize in any particular way and the analogy is at any rate imperfect, even if Plato gives us enough hints to make the connection.[287] Such an analogy results not so much from the deliberate intention of the Stranger's presentation (unlike Socrates' analogy of city and soul in the *Republic*) but from the real structural similarity Plato sees between the care of human beings in cities to the care of human beings individually. The important point here is not so much that (or whether) there is such an analogy, but that the arts—the uses of *phronēsis*—in the city become increasingly "theoretical" as the Stranger proceeds with his work of separation. Yet, as we shall see, the gap between the practical knowledge necessary for human care and the theoretical knowledge of the statesman that can alone give proper direction to such care is no more easily bridged in the city than in the human soul.

The Stranger compares the experience of separating these arts from statesmanship to the experience of those who purify gold (303d6–304a4). Gold is at first mingled with dirt and stone, which are more or less easily separated from it, just as they have separated all the other arts of care from the statesman. After this separation is complete, however, there still remain those things that are kin to gold, which are *timia*, valuable, and separable from gold only by "fire" (always a symbol of *phronēsis*, as we have seen; see chapter 3, p. 169). While, in other words, the exercise in separation of all the other arts might have appeared pointless to some (who is going to confuse statesmanship with vessel-making?) the remaining exercise in separation itself demands great *phronēsis*, for the arts that remain are in fact confused with the statesman: the heroic general, the master rhetorician, and the upright judge are all obvious representations of the statesman. The gold-refining metaphor the Stranger employs suggests, furthermore, that

[287] Cf. Benardete (1963, 212–213).

these arts are not always found separated "in nature," as it were; only the light of analysis (the "fire" of *phronēsis*) can ultimately separate them. Yet in another sense it is only when they remain together that the knowledge of the statesman can be made effective as the order of the city.

The Stranger first separates rhetoric from statesmanship by the following argument (304a6ff.). Using the example of playing musical instruments as something that is learned in the city, the Stranger asks whether there is also a form of knowledge that determines whether it and other handicrafts should be learned at all or not (304b4–6), and which is in turn different from it. This form of knowledge is then said to rule over those other forms of knowledge rather than the other way around (304b11–c6): the art that teaches some specific skill is ruled by the art that determines whether something should be learned. The Stranger then claims that the same thing that is true of teaching and learning is true of persuading and being persuaded (304d2). There must thus be an art of persuading a crowd of people through "storytelling" (304d1), namely the art of the rhetorician, and an art that determines whether persuasion is to be employed rather than force or nothing at all (304d4–6), an art that is to be identified with statesmanship (304d8–9).

Though the argument the Stranger uses is superficially clear, it raises the more general and more difficult question of the specific relationship between statesmanship and all the other arts. On one view of the matter, the argument suggests not merely that rhetoric is to be distinguished from statesmanship, but that statesmanship is the art that determines which arts are to be learned in the city, and indeed that statesmanship is in principle concerned with when each of these arts are to be used.[288] It would seem reasonable to suppose that the statesman would know about the benefit or harm any other art would bring to its possessor and to the city, since the statesman's art is closely tied to knowledge of the good, the

[288] See Lane (1998, 145), for an argument along these lines.

just, and the noble, unlike any other art. Indeed, in the myth on the origins of writing in the *Phaedrus*, Socrates attributed this sort of knowledge to the true king (*Phaedrus* 274c5–275b2). Moreover, as we saw in the discussion of the implications of the myth, it is reasonable to conceive of statesmanship in part as the art that prevents the unchecked effects of the use of all the practical arts (see chapter 3, pp. 171–174). The doctor does not know the good *qua* doctor; he only knows what makes one healthy or unhealthy. The statesman would then be someone who is concerned with what all the citizens of the city must learn, including the specific mix of arts that is most conducive to the city's preservation and flourishing, and (in principle at least) with the conditions under which these arts must be used for the good of the city.

But the Stranger does not explicitly identify statesmanship with the art that determines which arts are to be learned in the city. The reason seems to be the following. As we shall learn, the statesman is primarily concerned with the causes of conflict, and especially the causes of those conflicts (both external and internal) that have the potential to destroy the city. Such conflict can arise from the misuse of knowledge, since most artisans do not know the good, the just, and the noble in their capacity as artisans. Yet in general most arts are not the main causes of conflict in the city, since the artisans aim at some kind of good (health, etc.) and are normally subject to the law and hence guided by whatever values are embodied in it. It is only the arts of rhetoric, generalship, and judging, that pose a serious problem. Their misuse, unlike the misuse of medicine, can quickly make the city vulnerable to conflict, since these arts can be used to pervert the values embodied in the city's laws. Moreover, with respect to these arts the statesman could not be content with determining the mix of artisans that will practice rhetoric, generalship, and the art of judging; he must necessarily be concerned with when and under what circumstances these arts are actually used, whereas it would seem impossible for him to be concerned with the timing and circumstances of each use of say, medicine, despite the fact that the doctor, *qua* doctor, does not know the good, the noble, and the just.[289] The statesman is not concerned with supervising whether or not a doctor should use his knowledge to heal this or that particular patient at some particular point in time, unlike the statesman's concern with whether or not the rhetorician should use his art at this or that particular moment; as the Stranger puts it later, he is only concerned with the right time for the use of the "greatest" arts (305d3). If statesmanship is to be a realistic possibility, it must stand in a direct relation to only some, but not all, of the arts in the city, and at best only indirectly regulate all of the other arts in the city.

Moreover, while the absence of supervision by the statesman might lead the artisans into error regarding the good, the noble, or the just in any particular case, it does not lead them to error regarding their own arts: the doctor knows what actions cure the patient whether or not the statesman is present (that is, he knows the healthy). The absence of supervision by the statesman does not affect the ability of the practical arts to do their own (necessary) work; yet the absence of the statesman has much more deleterious effects for the rhetorician, the general, and the judge, since the essence of their task is precisely to "translate" the statesman's knowledge into persuasive speech, action in the battlefield, or specific rulings that solve individual conflicts. To exaggerate a bit, they are nothing without him. Given these facts, the most the statesman could do with respect to the practical arts would be to legislate something like a conception of justice to which all of them should subscribe, that is precisely what the Stranger says the statesman does in creating the "divine bond" (309c). In the case of rhetoric, generalship and the power of judging, by contrast, the statesman must necessarily concern himself with whether these arts are used at any particular moment or according to any particular standards (cf. the emphasis on the *kairos* at 305d4). Since they

[289] As Arends (2001, 141–142) sees, *pace* Lane (1998, 145).

are the arts that "mediate" between the statesman's knowledge and the citizens, without his presence they must necessarily set themselves up as sources of the good, the just, and the noble and cease to be themselves to become imitations of statesmanship. Hence the statesman cannot be content with simply setting the general parameters under which they operate, since the essence of these arts simply is to faithfully actualize the statesman's knowledge in different contexts (the assembly, war, and the private relations and contracts among citizens). They are like the arts of the herald that were discussed and separated from statesmanship earlier (260d11–e9), which merely receive commands, but do not generate such commands on their own; and their proper virtue is always a form of (potentially Socratic) self-restraint, as we shall see.

The rhetorician

The art of persuading crowds by means of myth makes sense only insofar as it mediates between the statesman and the citizens considered as an assembly—that is, a law-making body. Such an art might seem unnecessary, since we have seen that the statesman operates above the law. But, as we also saw earlier (chapter 5, section 1), the statesman needs to use law even when he is present in the city (though he might need to change it often); and he cannot hope to impose laws on the citizens without something like their consent, since force is not part of his art and obedience does not come naturally to the citizens. Moreover, though it would seem that people must be either forced or persuaded to accept the statesman's commands, apparently making the rhetorician and the general two sides of the same coin,[290] the Stranger nowhere mentions the existence of an art of applying "internal" force to enforce the statesman's commands; whatever physical force the statesman's commands require seems to come, in keeping with the general "statelessness" of Greek cities, from the physical force of the

[290] See Miller Jr. (1980, 104).

citizens themselves, who are persuaded to support the law.[291] Persuasion must thus be the primary instrument by means of which the statesman makes his commands—and thus political order—effective in the city; even those commands of the statesman that must be "enforced" against some in the city depend to a large degree on a kind of consent, as the Stranger had earlier obscurely noted (276e; see also the discussion in chapter 2, pp. 111–117). Hence the claim that true rhetoric cogoverns (*sundiakubernai* 304a2) action in the *polis*; for without it, practically no action directed by the statesman can truly take place.

Persuasion, to be sure, comes in two flavors, as the Stranger has indicated (304d1–2): there is persuasion by means of "myth" or storytelling and persuasion by means of "teaching." The first seems to apply in particular to the multitude, though the Stranger's use of some form of "mythology" in his conversation with Young Socrates should warn us against taking this restriction too strictly. Indeed, a mixture of myth and argument is used by the Athenian Stranger in the *Laws* to persuade the citizens of Magnesia to accept his laws. On the other hand, there does not appear to be a persuasion of the multitude through *teaching* properly speaking, even though one-on-one teaching does exist, as the conversation itself proves. Such "teaching" persuasion would also appear to belong to the art of the statesman or the philosopher, who could use it to provide the rhetorician with at least a true opinion (but not knowledge, or else it would be possible to turn the rhetorician into a statesman) about the good, the just, and the noble.[292] The rhetorician, in turn, armed with this true opinion, would then use his own art to persuade the multitude to pass laws that embody this true opinion.

---

[291] There is no art of "police" for the Stranger, and no sense that the internal structure of the community requires this role, contrary to the Weberian understanding of the state.

[292] Cf. Cropsey (1995, 138).

If this reconstruction of the potential relationship between the rhetorician and the statesman is correct, then the former must be willing to be taught the just, the good, and the noble by the statesman. But such willingness is only possible if the rhetorician has a "Socratic" attitude towards his own knowledge, that is, knows that he does not know about the good, the just, and the noble. In the absence of this attitude, however, (an absence that the Platonic dialogues show is extremely common and hard to remedy) the rhetorician will always be strongly tempted to substitute his own judgment about the good, the just, and the noble for that of the statesman, and hence to use his skill at persuading the crowd to pass laws in his own interest, which would make the rhetorician into the representative ruler of a lawless democracy or oligarchy. The proper relationship between statesman and rhetorician is thus exceedingly fragile, and their separation is fraught with difficulty, as the Stranger warned us (303d4ff.), especially since the statesman cannot ensure his own permanence in the city.

The general

Just as the art of the true rhetorician mediates between the statesman and the citizens considered as an assembly of voters, the art of the general mediates between the statesman and the citizens considered as soldiers. He translates the statesman's commands into "force" against other cities, just as the rhetorician translates them into laws freely accepted and convictions fully internalized. And just as in the case of the rhetorician, the proper relationship between statesman and general requires that the latter be willing to be guided (or taught) by the statesman's knowledge of what would constitute an advantageous victory for the city and what would not, which in turn would require a great deal of Socratic self-restrain on the part of the general, that is, a knowledge that he does not know about the good, the just, and the noble in matters concerning the victory of the city.

More specifically, the general does not know which victories would actually lead to the preservation of the city, or which battles are worth fighting for the sake of its the long-term survival, or which victories or techniques of warfare (cf. *Laws* 706b) would be good for the character of the citizens. But just as the absence of this attitude would produce in the rhetorician the temptation to substitute his own judgment for that of the statesman concerning the good, the just, and the noble of which the city must be persuaded, the absence of this attitude in the general would make him easily tempted to substitute his own judgment for that of the statesman in its external affairs. This temptation would be all the greater since, in contrast to the rhetorician and the judge, the general actually "rules" a herd of human beings and, like the king, (and even more so than the true rhetorician), his art is one of understanding and seeing the right moment for doing anything, for holding back as well as for rushing forward. All of this suggests that a (good) general is in a position to believe himself (incorrectly) deserving of kingship and thus to set himself up as a tyrant, as the Stranger intimates by describing the art of the general as a great and terrible one over which the true king must exercise a kind of despotic power (305a4–6), something which would be of course very hard to do in the inevitable absence of the statesman unless the general can be counted on to abide by the law. Thus, just as the rhetorician becomes the representative of lawless democracy or oligarchy as soon as he abandons his Socratic self-restraint, the general similarly becomes the representative of lawless monarchy, that is, tyranny, as soon as he stops recognizing the authority of the statesman.[293]

The judge

The art of judging represents a form of mediation between the statesman and the citizens considered as individuals. It

[293] In fact Plato thinks that some (false) regimes are not very different from armed camps. Cf. Benardete (1984b, 141), and *Laws* 666e1ff.

presupposes the law (305b5), in contrast to the art of the rhetorician (which is used to make law) and that of the general (which operates beyond the borders of the city, that is, beyond the confines of the law). With the help of the law (which the statesman may of course change so long as he is present) the judge mediates between the general insight of the statesman and the specific case at issue, though, like the statesman, the judge can do no more than "declare" the just. His art is as theoretical, in some sense, as the art of the statesman, since it does not contain the ability to enforce his decisions; he might at best count on the respect of the citizens.

Just like the rhetorician and the general, but perhaps more clearly, the judge must have an attitude of Socratic self-restraint towards his own views of the just. Since he does not have the actual knowledge of justice *qua* judge, if he did not accept the law as the truth concerning justice, he would be tempted to substitute his judgment for that of the law unless he understood that he does not know better, becoming a lawless ruler. His art would thus ideally consist of the ability to apply the statesman's general laws to specific situations. Hence though all the mediating arts are in some sense "heraldic," the art of the judge is more heraldic than that of the rhetorician or the general, since it is more exclusively concerned with interpretation and demands fewer additional skills. Nevertheless, though this interpretive skill must clearly be an element of his art, the Stranger emphasizes rather the judge's character strength (cf. *rōmēn* 305c6; 259c7) for resisting temptations (such as fear or gifts or pity or hatred or friendship) that might bias his judgment away from what the law says. The art of interpretation of the judge seems to be thought of as straightforward once these biases are overcome, potentially making every citizen into a judge, since the strength that allows the judge to overcome these biases does not appear to be a form of knowledge, and is presumably the especially successful result of the general education that the statesman will provide to the citizens: the judge is simply a citizen who has an enduring true opinion of the just, the noble, and the good, and is not unduly biased in either the "courageous" direction (making him too likely to succumb to hatred) or in the "moderate" direction (making him too likely to be a pushover).

This strength, however, is also emblematic of the inflexibility of the rule of law: the judges, by disregarding all these factors, might indeed do something that, though perhaps just according to the law, need not correspond to the true knowledge of the just for that particular situation. Indeed, this inflexibility might imperil the ability of the statesman to render justice to the citizens, since the judge substitutes the law (which is at best the true opinion of the just) for the judgment of the statesman (which is the knowledge of the just). Their judgments, in other words, would always need to be supervised by the true statesman if their art is not to degenerate into a form of law-governed rule, that is, a form of "good" sophistry. But since rule by rhetoricians or generals in the absence of the statesman is always a form of lawless rule (oligarchy or democracy for rhetoricians; tyranny for generals), the power of the judge, even when deprived of the guiding knowledge of the statesman, is superior in rank to that of the other two "kindred" arts to the statesman, and hence rightly discussed last, as closer to the statesman, so long as the judge accepts that the law is the truth of justice. The rule of the statesman decays into the rule of judges.

The statesman and the problem of conflict: 305d–311c

The Stranger and Young Socrates are now ready to discuss statesmanship itself. What is the positive knowledge of the statesman, if his knowledge is not identical with the knowledge of any of the other figures they have discussed thus far? What is the role of the statesman in the city? What is his primary responsibility?

The Stranger characterizes the statesman's knowledge in the first instance in terms of his ability to determine the right time (the due measure of such time, that is the *kairos*, cf. 305d4) for action or non-action with regards to the preservation of the whole city. The idea that the statesman's knowledge concerns the timing of action or non-action regarding threats to the city has two aspects, however. The first relates to the control of the timing of the use of rhetoric and generalship and the second relates to the sources of the biases that distort our judgment of the right time for action or inaction.

Rhetoric, as we have seen, is the art that is needed when one needs to speak to an assembly, either to create new laws or to persuade other cities to act in particular ways, whereas generalship is the art that is needed when one needs to engage in war. Rhetoric thus deals primarily, though not exclusively, with the potential for "internal" conflict, whereas generalship is more narrowly oriented towards the potential for "external" conflict. Yet both arts transcend legality, in contrast to the other "noble" art, the art of judging: rhetoric because it can be used to change the laws, and generalship because war is generally conducted beyond the reach of "domestic" law. We might therefore gloss the statesman's knowledge as knowledge of the time and the mode of transcending the law.[294]

From this point of view, the *kairos* that the statesman must know is simply the right time for changing or establishing the fundamental laws of the city (via the use of persuasion), an activity that clearly could not and should not be undertaken every day, as well as the right time for undertaking bold action to change the "external context" of the city (by shaking off the chains of imperial tyranny, for instance). Both of these activities are undertaken by the statesman in exceptional circumstances in order both to preserve the city and to make it better rather

[294] Note that the Stranger excludes the art of judging from among the arts concerned with the "greatest actions" of the city. The reason seems to be that the art of judging cannot transcend the law (at least on a fairly simplistic conception of the interpretive task of the judge which the Stranger seems to accept), and hence that the art of the statesman is only concerned with the art of judging insofar as it frames the laws by which the judge has to judge the cases that come before him.

than worse in the long run (297b2–3), just as the god both preserves the universe and puts it in its best possible condition (see chapter 3). The statesman appears here as a revolutionary figure, who determines whether the conflicts threatening the city's existence demand the framing of new laws or the use of force at a particular and exceptional moment in its history, and intervenes decisively to save it.[295]

There is, however, a second aspect to the statesman's knowledge of the "right time." If the long-term preservation of the community entails making it less vulnerable to internal and external conflict beyond the time in which the statesman can intervene (that is, beyond the time in which he is physically present in it), then the statesman must know the most general causes of such conflict and take action to prevent them as much as possible from becoming operative in his absence. His task is to create a community that is resilient to his absence, not one that is dependent on his physical presence, especially since the Stranger (for reasons we shall explore in greater detail later) does not appear to think that the city can successfully reproduce, on a regular basis, the knowledge of the statesman. Indeed, as Arends has pointed out,[296] some of the Stranger's recommendations—such as the marriage policy designed to establish the "human bond"—only make sense as expedients for the *longue durée*, when the statesman is no longer present in

[295] It is important to note that the Stranger never suggests that the statesman's goal of preserving the city can be usefully distinguished from his goal of making the city better rather than worse, contrary to the views of Arends (1993), Kochin (1999, 70–71), Rosen (1995, vii), and Zuckert (2005), among others. The way to preserve a city is to make it less vulnerable to internal and external conflict, and the way to make it less vulnerable to internal and external conflict requires the framing of institutions that are in an important sense just and make people better rather than worse: one preserves the city by putting it in right order, though, to be sure, in making the city less vulnerable to conflict in the long run the statesman may need to resort to "conflictive" measures (cf. 293b–c), just as the god by reversing the motion of the cosmos necessarily creates a certain amount of destruction.

[296] See Arends (2001, 136).

the city. But, as the Stranger now argues, the most fundamental threats to the city come from the citizens' ignorance of the right time for action or inaction, that is, their ignorance of the time for actions that transcend the rigid prescriptions of the law, especially in the realm of foreign policy. The statesman's role then appears not as using his own judgment of the right time for decisive action or inaction, force or persuasion, in the face of threats, but of establishing institutions that diminish or at least make less harmful the citizens' ignorance of the *kairos* for transcending the laws. In this sense the statesman necessarily has to concern himself with the citizens' *virtue*.

The conflict between the parts of virtue

The problem of the establishment and preservation of the order of the city in the face of internal and external sources of disorder, and indeed of threats to its own physical existence thus forms the background to the discussion of the "conflict" of the parts of virtue (306a8–307d5). The problem, as the Stranger describes it, is that "moderation" and "courage," both of which are thought to be "parts" of virtue, are opposed, indeed appear to hold a "hatred" for each other and to be in a state of war (*stasis*) with one another (306b9–11).[297] Each of these "parts" of virtue is expressed in a disposition to value and praise certain kinds of things: the "courageous" disposition tends to value and thereby praise quickness and sharpness in everything (306c10–d5), whereas the "moderate" disposition tends to value and praise slowness, deliberation, and quietness in everything (307a7–b3). Yet what appears valuable from one point of view in a given situation will often seem dishonorable or not valuable from the other point of view.

---

[297] At this point in the argument it is not yet clear whether the Stranger believes moderation and courage so understood are *truly* parts of virtue, or, as it becomes clearer later, merely character dispositions that are fully virtuous only when manifested in ways that are in accord with the *kairos* for action or inaction in particular circumstances.

The problem for politics is that these dispositions tend to produce different evaluations of the appropriate responses to external threats by the city: courageous dispositions tend to positively evaluate hawkish policies and to find dovish responses cowardly and dishonorable, regardless of the underlying situation, and moderate dispositions tend to evaluate dovish policies positively and to find hawkish responses crazy or hubristic, regardless of the underlying situation (307e1–308a9). But given the condition of the cosmos in the age of Zeus, neither policy is always appropriate, and if people with either disposition become dominant in the city the result is the city's ruin (307e1–308a9), since neither the courageous nor the moderate fully base their evaluations of the right policy on real knowledge applied to the specific situation but instead tend to prefer certain policies merely, or at least mostly, because these policies agree with their particular character dispositions. Moreover, even if neither disposition becomes fully dominant, their conflict still indicates a "sickness" in the city (*nosos*, 307d7), since there is no guarantee that people of either disposition will accurately assess the city's situation whenever they happen to be in charge, and their judgments will be fiercely contested by people with the other disposition, indeed perhaps to the point of civil war (cf. *stasin* 306b11), since people of each disposition tend to find the actions praised by the other disposition contrary to virtue.

The problem the Stranger describes is not that people with the "courageous" or the "moderate" disposition are simply irrational, insisting on a maximalist hawkish or dovish policy every time; if that were true, then the Stranger's prescription for "mixing" these dispositions would seem hopeless, and his insistence that these dispositions are real parts of virtue (e.g., 306a8, 306c1) would seem pointless. What the Stranger is saying is best understood in terms of the kind of uncertainty that every political community faces. What a community ought to do in the face of a potential threat is seldom obvious, and in general there will be a colorable case for both "hawkish" and "dovish" policies. In this situation, the vast majority of people, not having genuine political knowledge of or even good information about the situation (which is, after all, uncertain and only imperfectly known), will tend to evaluate a policy according to the particular disposition they (imperfectly) embody (that is, what in general appears valuable or honorable to them) rather than according to the reality of the situation (which is in any case uncertain). Their judgments will be "biased," but there will be no guarantee that the overall bias of such judgments in the city will tend to its preservation.

Though the Stranger does not say this, we may assume that the judgment of the genuine statesman, by contrast, is not biased; his evaluation of the right policy depends entirely on his knowledge of the just, the good, and the noble as well as on the available facts of the situation (which may not necessarily be perfectly known). The statesman may perhaps err due to the genuine uncertainty inherent in all political life, since he does not necessarily have a superhuman grasp of such particulars, but he does not err because his judgment is colored by a disposition to value quick and violent action over deliberation and diplomacy (or vice versa) that is unrelated to the particular situation at stake. In other words, while most people have at best partial virtue insofar as they tend to value particular sorts of things more or less independently of the reality of the situation and the demands of justice, goodness, and nobility, only the statesman has complete virtue, since his valuation of various things, and in particular of the policies appropriate to a city *vi-à-vis* external threats, is dependent only on knowledge of the good, the just, and the noble, as well as the available facts of the situation. For the Stranger as for Socrates, genuine virtue is knowledge.[298]

[298] The sometimes expressed idea that the Stranger abandons the familiar Socratic teaching of the unity of the virtues (e.g., Barker [1918], Crosson [1963, 37], with some reservations; Irwin [1995, 339–340]; Mishima [1995], Scodel [1987, 163]; Skemp [1987, 223n1], with some reservations) seems to be based on an elementary misunderstanding, since the Stranger never says that genuine virtue is in opposition to itself, only that parts of virtue

But the Stranger does not propose to substitute the unbiased judgment of the statesman for the judgment of the city with its random mixture of dispositions, as we might expect if the Stranger were simply describing a regime over which the true statesman would rule as an absolute monarch. His recommendations assume that the task of the statesman is to prepare the city to make unbiased judgments for as long as possible in his absence, not to rule over it; he conceives of the statesman as legislator and founder, not as a dictator, a point all too often overlooked in discussions of the dialogue and of Plato's political theory more generally. Unlike Machiavelli in *The Prince*, who similarly understands the problem of the state's preservation in terms of the "mismatch" between impetuous or cautious dispositions and the temper of the times (cf. *The Prince*, chapter XXV), the Stranger is not interested in the preservation of the city of a specific ruler; his concern is with how to stably embed an unbiased judgment of the right time in the city as a whole, so that the city can respond to the challenges of the "age of Zeus" more or less successfully in the short as well as the long run.[299]

Moreover, in grounding the vulnerability of the city to both internal *stasis* and external war on character dispositions rather than on economic or other social conditions, the Stranger signals that the problem of the preservation of the city's order is fundamental, tied to the current cosmic era rather than to whatever social conditions may exist in a particular time and place. In other words, the Stranger seems to be suggesting

appear to be in opposition to one another because what each of these parts would demand in a given situation is the opposite of what the other would demand. Such opposition can only be overcome through knowledge, a view which is identical in its essentials to the standard Socratic view. For a more complete exploration of the issues involved in this debate, see Bobonich (1995, 313–314); for a similar conclusion to mine, but on other grounds, see Miller Jr. (1980, 108).

[299] As Arends (2001, 136) rightly notes, the "ES aims at the prevention both in the short and the long run of intellectual stasis concerning decisions about war and peace."

that even if property in the city were distributed correctly and sexual desire were properly regulated (as in the *Republic*), the city would still not be rational enough to confront the challenges that the world would throw at it, for these expedients would be unable to rid the city of biased judgments about the *proper time* for action.[300]

The fundamental or basic nature of the problem of political conflict and its grounding on a "natural" division in the distribution of human dispositions is reinforced by the clear resonances of that division with both the division of the cosmos into two alternating ages and the earlier division of all animals into tame and wild (see chapter 2, pp. 91–94).[301] Thus, for example, though human beings in general were classed with the tame animals, it is clear that some are more or less "tamable" than others (cf. 309e1), indeed that some are excessively fierce and some excessively slavish. This fact complicates the task of the statesman, requiring him to engage in a process of selection of the citizenry whereby the excessively wild or courageous are to be killed and the excessively tame or moderate are to be enslaved (cf. 309a1–6).[302] Yet the division of human beings into moderate and courageous, unlike the division of animals into tame and wild, could not have been fully discussed at that time, since the statesman needs to deal with both of its branches.

Similarly, the division between courageous and moderate dispositions also seems to map onto the Stranger's division of the cosmos into two ages in an illuminating way. If human beings lived in the age of Cronos, it is clear that only slowness or moderation would be required of human beings, since there

---

300 A point that Klosko (1986, 193) misses in his evaluation of the Stranger's argument.

301 The Stranger is always careful to suggest that some people perhaps cannot be characterized as having either of these dispositions, by which he probably means that the naturally philosophical are not biased in this way. See Dixsaut (1995, 261–262, 264). Dixsaut refers incidentally to the fact that dogs, who represent "le naturel philosophe," were left out of the division of human being.

302 Cf. Dixsaut (1995, 270).

is no *kairos* in that age that would demand forceful action, quickness, and energy. We might thus say that, even though the virtues properly speaking are unnecessary in the age of Cronos, "moderation" is the virtue of the "golden age." This is indicated by the identification of moderation with *kosmiotēs*, orderliness (307b2; cf. 307e2), and thus with the ordered cosmos of that age. Moderation, at any rate, is required only when things are already in order, since it preserves that order: in the most general terms, this is the virtue that "restricts" motion so that order is not disturbed. The "slow" accept whatever order is given around them, something that is perhaps fine if human beings are ruled by a god, but not necessarily if they are ruled by human beings. In general they mind their own business (307e3–4), that is, they are "just" in the sense of the *Republic* (433a–434d);[303] yet their justice is insufficient to deal with the possibility that some people are not just in this sense. We might call them "conservatives" if that term were not fatally anachronistic, and we may note that such people are intrinsically law-abiding, regardless of the "content" of law.

Courage becomes necessary, and also problematic, because we live in the age of Zeus. With the release of the cosmos by the god, and its increasing disorder, times arise when quickness, sharpness, energy, and the like, in short, what in other Platonic dialogues is called "thumotic" action, is demanded of human beings. Such action is required when order needs to be restored or forcefully preserved. When the *polis* or the cosmos is not fully ordered, the action of man is required to reimpose a modicum of that order; hence the name of the virtue, *andreia*. The "quick" fail to accept the order or disorder around them: they are "revolutionaries" or "radicals" in the basic sense that they are dissatisfied with the order of things and act to change it. However, they also tend to forget that the order of the whole is not made merely by human willfulness; they forget the

[303] Note moderation is closer to justice than courage: cf. 309a1, 309e1, as well as Bobonich (1995, 324).

divine sources of order (cf. 309a1), and consequently threaten to increase disorder rather than restore order by their misguided, out of *kairos* interventions for the sake of restoring that order. The virtue of courage is thus fundamentally a virtue of this age: the virtue that ensures that wrongdoers are punished, but also the virtue that disrupts the rule of law.[304]

Weaving the virtues, educating the citizens

The cosmic source of the division at the heart of human being implies that conflict is not something that can be transcended by art, or finessed by appropriate economic arrangements, though it may be tempered by these things. The weaving of the web of politics is not merely a contingent policy, appropriate for some cites and not others, but a permanent necessity for all political communities.

But how, exactly, can the statesman weave together these two conflicting dispositions so as to increase the ability of the city to preserve itself and its order? Weaving turns out to be a kind of education, though not an education that results in knowledge properly speaking or occurs one-on-one. Rather, it results in secure true opinion (309c), and it occurs in common. Only a certain kind of individual education, not the kind of collective care that the statesman provides, could possibly lead to knowledge, and in particular to the kind of knowledge of the good, the just, and the noble that the statesman has and which constitutes genuine virtue, though the Stranger nowhere describes this education, and it may not in fact exist. The statesman's education of the city (a "civic" education) thus at best results in something we might call (though the Stranger does not do so) "civic virtue," understood as secure true opinion. It does not culminate in the production of other statesmen, in contrast with the education of the philosophers

[304] The connection of the two virtues with the two alternating ages of the cosmos is noted by, among others, Scodel (1987, 164–165), and Dixsaut (1995, 271).

in the *Republic*; for all his knowledge the true statesman cannot ensure his own reproduction in the city.

We might say that civic virtue appears in the Stranger's argument in relation to genuine virtue as the rule of law appears in relation to the rule of the true statesman: one is rigid and otherwise biased in ways that make it inappropriate to a number of settings; the other is flexible, able to cope with changing circumstances, and never biased. Civic virtue is like "law" in the mind—a somewhat more flexible and complex law than the written law of the city, since it is the product of education, but nevertheless in the final instance only marginally better than the law of the city, since it remains mere (true) opinion, even if it is a deeper, more secure form of opinion.

At any rate, the statesman's education of the city has three stages or components. The first stage (308c–309b) is essentially preparatory, separating those whose character can be "woven" with the character of others from those whose characters cannot be so mixed. This first stage furnishes the statesman with the appropriate "material" for the web of politics. The second stage, which is most properly the statesman's task, binds together the people selected in that way by means of what the Stranger calls a "divine bond" (309c1–2). The third and final stage reinforces the divine bond with what the Stranger calls a "human bond" (310a7–e4). A successful civic education produces a population of citizens whose judgments are not as biased in the direction of their natural dispositions (quick or slow) as they might otherwise be, have "secure true opinion" about "noble, good, and just things" (309c5–8), and can maintain such unbiased dispositions and opinions over the generations.

It should be stressed that the Stranger nowhere suggests that civic education can ever completely erase the original tendencies of human beings towards "quickness" or "slowness" (cf. 311a6–9). It can at best ameliorate them, substituting a lesser sort of rigidity for the natural bias of human beings towards judgments that accord with their own nature, so that people of each tendency can find more plausible the case for alternative policies proposed by people with the contrary tendency. This openness to the other side, so to speak, functions as a kind of substitute for the unattainable wisdom of the statesman, making rational decision-making by the city slightly more likely to occur because decisions would be less likely to be based on irrational attachments to policies that are in tune with each citizen's own disposition. Such education thus makes the rigidity of law somewhat less fatal to the city, allowing the city to react relatively intelligently and virtuously to novel situations without actually having knowledge. In order to see how civic education accomplishes this without necessarily producing any real statesmen, we need to examine each of its stages in greater detail.

The preparatory stage

The first stage in the process of civic education is explicitly likened to the preparatory stages in the process of weaving (308c1ff., especially 308d6–e2), and it is said to separate good from bad. Within this first stage, the Stranger suggests that the statesman first "tests" the nature of children through play (308d3–4), allowing him to determine who has a particular character disposition, that is, who is predominantly "quick" or "slow." Such testing then allows the statesman to separate the good "quick" or "slow" natures from the bad, that is, those capable of tempering their own natural tendencies by education from those incapable of doing so, a process that is compared to carding in weaving (308d4–e2).

Though the Stranger does not say so, such preliminary education is thus likely to consist in activities that expose each nature to the other disposition. For example, the quick and the sharp may be exposed to appropriate music and poetry, and the moderate may be exposed to martial games. Though the actual instruction can be delegated, at this point, to unspecified "educators" and "nurses" (308d5, 308e5), only the statesman has the requisite knowledge of what is to be taught. These educators do not represent a different art that needs to be explicitly separated from statesmanship but seem to merely include all those people that were earlier included with the makers of "ornaments" and "games" (288c1–d1).

This interpretation of the substance of the preliminary education the Stranger proposes is in keeping with well-known ideas in Plato's political thought, though admittedly it is not directly supported by the text. For example, in the *Laws* the Athenian Stranger associates martial and physical games with the development of "courageous" dispositions and music with the development of "moderate" dispositions, and criticizes those states that emphasize only some of these activities at the expense of the others, since such states (like Sparta or Crete) tend to have an unbalanced view of virtue (see especially the Athenian's criticisms of Cretan and Spartan educational institutions in book I of the *Laws*, 631bff.). One may assume that the Eleatic Stranger thinks that participation in martial games or musical exercises will tend to reveal that some characters are more on the "courageous" side, others more on the "moderate" side, but that most characters can participate in and benefit from both kinds of activity.

Note that preparatory education mixes the natural tendencies, but only at the level of dispositions, not of opinion. The Stranger does not suggest that this stage of the educational process produces anything like true opinion in those exposed to it; its primary purpose is to select an appropriate body of citizens, not to instruct them fully or to completely temper their biases. It is thus analogous in weaving both to carding and to warp- and woof- making (cf. 309a8–b7). The "wool" of the statesman consists of the potential citizens, and the separation of good from bad "wool" thus produces a body of citizens. Those cast out are either made into slaves (309a5–6, the incorrigibly "slow" or "soft," who are said to have a tendency towards ignorance and self-abasement) or put to death and exiled (the incorrigibly "quick" or "sharp," who are said to tend to atheism, *hubris*, and injustice).[305] The remaining citizens, though they retain a "bias" towards one extreme or the other (neither tendency is ever fully eliminated), have natures that can be tempered by education: some are warp-like, fundamentally "quick" but mixed a bit with the "slow" disposition, and able to take further mixing at the level of opinion; some, conversely, are woof-like, fundamentally "slow" or "soft" (309a8–b7). What this seems to mean is that the citizens remaining after the selection process takes place are able to perceive reasons for some policies that go against the grain of their natures, and no longer consider all such policies to be contrary to virtue, unlike those who have no mixture of the other nature in their soul.

The divine bond

These two kinds of citizens must be "woven" together so as to complete the work of the statesman, the "web of politics." In weaving the citizens the statesman "binds" together the city, that is, unifies it for the long term, by means of two "bonds," a divine one (which takes precedence both temporally and in other respects) and a human one (309c1ff.). The "divine bond" is characterized by the Stranger as the "secure true opinion about beautiful, just, and good things as well as their opposites" (309c5–8). Exactly what the Stranger has in mind is not clear, though our view of the specific role that a genuine statesman plays in a city depends on how we understand this idea.

It is important to stress, however, that "secure true opinion" of noble, just, and good things is not, on any potential reading of this passage, knowledge of the beautiful, the just, and the good, as the use of the plural forms indicate. Secure

---

305 The difference in treatment suggests that for the city excessive "slowness" is less harmful, and can be put to more profitable use, than excessive "quickness." Cf. Bobonich (1995, 320). The city, as we have already indicated, is an essentially conservative place. Contrast this view with Mill's judgment that the "active disposition" is the most beneficial to mankind (*Considerations on Representative Government*, ch. 4).

true opinion cannot articulate the unity in that plurality; it remains at best inductive and inarticulate, a catalog of propositions rather than a deep understanding of the underlying forms. One important implication of this point is that it seems to be impossible for the statesman to "institutionalize" his knowledge; unlike cobblers and doctors, the statesman cannot train the next generation of statesmen who will be ready to take over the city when he dies, and the Eleatic nowhere hints at the possibility which Socrates indicated in the *Republic*, namely, the idea that the primary task of the statesman is the construction of an educational system to produce the right sorts of rulers (that is, more statesmen). To be sure, the passage provides no direct evidence for the idea that the knowledge of the statesman cannot be properly institutionalized. But the idea that the knowledge of the statesman is not the kind of thing that can be produced "on demand" is supported by a number of indirect considerations. First, and most obviously, the knowledge of the statesman is, as we have already noted, a very difficult one; failure rates in learning statesmanship would be correspondingly high. Second, such knowledge would also seem to depend critically on character: the true statesman is likely to require a "balanced" nature, inclining neither towards the "courageous" nor towards the "moderate" sides of human character. Moreover, the Athenian Stranger in the *Laws* suggests that "divine men" (people with genuine virtue) spring indifferently "in cities with good laws . . . [and] without" (951b), he himself being the paradigm of such men (642c–d). In general, then, there is reason to think that statesmen, unlike other craftsmen, are not part of the self-reproducing network of artisans that produces the city, and indeed, as we shall see, that his long-term presence is disruptive for it. One has at least to wonder why, if Plato thought that it was possible to institutionalize this knowledge, neither the Eleatic nor the Athenian Strangers ever suggest that the best way of ordering a city would be to ensure the self-reproduction of the knowledge of the statesman, even if the Athenian does try to integrate what might be seen as a knowledge-producing institution within the city (the Nocturnal Council).

How, then, should we understand the idea of "secure true opinion" as the divine bond? Though secure true opinion is not knowledge, the Stranger does implicitly distinguish it from mere true opinion (which, after all, can be produced occasionally by the city on its own, as we saw in the previous chapter). Mere true opinion is like law, liable to be falsified by changes in circumstances. "It is raining outside" is true today, but potentially false tomorrow. Thus, presumably "secure" true opinion is not just opinion that is retained (as a prejudice) in a variety of circumstances, whether or not it is true in those circumstances, but opinion that is true in a very large range of circumstances and thus not easily falsified. Let us further assume that an opinion is true in a wider variety of circumstances if it is closer to real knowledge, that is, if it articulates some underlying regularity (a "form" for example) that is expressed in all sorts of situations. Such opinions may concern enduring articulations of the principles of justice or other virtues that are relatively stable over a wide variety of circumstances. The idea that murder is wrong, for example, is a true opinion in a very large variety of circumstances (perhaps all possible human circumstances), though it is also an opinion that in the Stranger's terminology refers to only one of the many things that are just or unjust, not to the underlying unity of the form of justice. "Secure true opinion" about the (many) just, good, and noble things would thus involve a catalog of opinions like the opinion that "murder is wrong." Whether an opinion belongs in this set, however, does not depend on any "subjective" aspects of those holding the opinion, but merely on how well it articulates the underlying regularity that makes it true, that is, on how much it approximates real knowledge of forms (of justice, goodness, and the like). Hence only the genuine statesman, that is, the possessor of genuine political knowledge, can articulate a "secure" true opinion with any degree of certainty. We should nevertheless emphasize again that even secure true opinion is liable to be eventually falsified by changes in circumstances or by cases that do not fall under it: it is only a more refined form of the law, a law in the souls of the citizens, a more perfect image of the knowledge of the statesman than the law but an image nevertheless (cf. 310a1–2).

But the "stability" of an opinion has both subjective and objective aspects, and both aspects are presumably intended by the Stranger. That is, a "secure" true opinion must both remain true in a wide variety of circumstances, and be *considered* to be true by those who profess it in those circumstances. What makes an opinion "secure" in this subjective sense is not explained by the Stranger; but it certainly need not be restricted to rational considerations. The fact that an opinion is widely and stably held to be true does not depend on whether or not the citizens have any grasp at all of the reasons behind the opinion, as Plato consistently reminds us throughout the corpus; no special assumptions about the mental capacities of the citizens need to be made. To be sure, a partial understanding of the regularity underlying an opinion (a partial grasp of the idea of justice, for example, if such a thing is possible in Platonic metaphysics) may help cement a true opinion subjectively, but then again it may not. And various processes of persuasion and social engineering can certainly be imagined that cement an opinion subjectively without necessarily providing the people with any very good grounds for its truth. Pure habituation, censorship, and religious ritual can do the job just as well, perhaps better, though, judging by the procedures used by the Athenian Stranger in the *Laws* to create enduring true opinions, some amount of reason-giving is thought useful, perhaps even just, by Plato. Yet even though the Athenian of the *Laws* emphasizes that the legislator must try to persuade in its attempt to create enduring true opinion, he is not above using extra-rational means to accomplish this, including religious ritual, myth, vague and not entirely valid argument, and censorship.[306]

At any rate, secure true opinion, however produced, constitutes a "bond" among the citizens because it provides them with a background of basic agreement against which their ineradicable disagreements can be mitigated. Thus, as long as the citizens, whatever their natural disposition, agree on basic "values" (to use an anachronistic term) they will be less likely to misjudge the *kairos* of the city's actions by judging solely in accordance with their own tendency, and will be less likely to believe that the contrary tendencies of other citizens are vicious. By sharing such opinions, the courageous, the Stranger suggests, will be "tamed" (309e1) so that they will now become very much willing to partake of justice (309c7–8, e3), whereas the orderly will become truly moderate and prudent, at least insofar as the *polis* is concerned, rather than merely naive (309e5–8), and so the city will be less polarized.

The different tempering of courage by justice and of moderation by a kind of civic prudence (309e6–7) deserves some notice, as it reintroduces the virtues of justice and prudence into the discussion. Earlier the Stranger had silently suggested that the moderate already partook of justice, but not of prudence: they "minded their own business" (307e3–4, echoing *Republic* 433a–434d; cf. also 311a8, where the moderate are expressly said to be naturally just), but failed to prudently check that people in other cities also behaved in the same way (cf. also 311a8–9). Similarly, we might understand the failure of the "courageous" as one of justice but not necessarily prudence: unlike the moderate, the courageous are not naive about the intentions of others

[306] Thus, *pace* Bobonich (1995, 323), and Cooper (1997, 93), I do not think that the endurance of true opinion is necessarily to be accounted for by some process of reason-giving or -accepting, though such a process is not incompatible with it. Such reason-giving or -accepting might be said to be a partial understanding of the underlying regularity that accounts for particular things being just or beautiful. But the mere generality or entanglement of the opinions in question can serve just as well to make them enduring.

outside the *polis*; they are appropriately suspicious (cf. 276e1–2 and the discussion of this passage above, chapter 2, 111–117), but they fail to mind their own business sufficiently and often attack others without sufficient justification (cf. 311b1–2).

Justice and prudence are thus both "limits" on the dispositions of courage and moderation, which left to themselves are "unlimited," to use the terminology of the *Philebus*. Civic courage is limited and brought closer to true virtue by directing energetic action only towards causes that are deemed just, while civic moderation is limited and brought closer to true virtue by a recognition that sometimes *phronēsis* demands that one "meddle" in the affairs of others. The "tempering" of both natures leads to a partial convergence of their judgments of the *kairos* for energetic or gentle action among both types, though we should stress that courageous natures remain more disposed to action, while moderate natures remain less so, as the everyday meanings of justice and prudence indicate: the just are fired by the quest for justice, like the courageous; the prudent are slower to action, pondering the many things that can go wrong in any course of action. Their judgments, informed by true opinion, are correct for the most part, but they may diverge in some cases or as circumstances change. The statesman cannot ensure that the judgments of the courageous and the moderate will always converge, much less that they converge to the appropriate energetic or moderate action; if he were able to do this, he would have succeeded in inculcating not true opinion but knowledge.

The most the statesman can achieve, therefore, is to open a space for persuasion (established and circumscribed by law and true opinion) where the energetic are willing to be convinced that the city can be preserved if their actions are stayed, while the slow and gentle are willing to be convinced that the city can be preserved through energetic action, against a background of commonly held and generally true values. Such agreement can be a bitter pill to swallow, yet in a sense it underpins all stable political systems, including modern democracies. The

Stranger simply presents a very general formulation of the idea that in any enduring political system partial and opposed interests and dispositions to judgment must recognize each other's potential validity; each part of the city must recognize the "burdens of judgment" of the other, in Rawls's phrase. And these burdens of judgment are perhaps highest with respect to the question of whether the city should act quickly or moderately in the face of external threats in a highly competitive political ecology like that of classical Greece.

The statesman's divine bond is thus merely a *pharmakon*, an imperfect drug (310a3), for a situation that has no real solution, given the dissimilarity of the parts of virtue (310a5; cf. 294b2). This dissimilarity is a reflection of the general dissimilarity and sickness of the cosmos left on its own by the god (cf. 273d6, 273e2), and it thus cannot be cured completely except by the god, whose rule eliminates the need for energetic action altogether. The "divine" remedy, which is, after all, designed by a human being, can only arrest the progress of the sickness for a time. Its character as a mere remedy is emphasized by the fact that the true opinion of the citizens must be embedded in law and habits (310a2), that is, unchangeable and firm rules which will eventually cease to be true unless they are continually updated; but they cannot be continually updated except by one with knowledge, that is, the statesman. Yet the statesman cannot ensure the reproduction of his own knowledge in the citizens, or else he would have given them knowledge rather than mere true opinion; and "updating" these opinions would mean destroying habits and laws, something that only a true statesman is in a position to do well, according to the Stranger.[307] The statesman's remedy is better than mere law in that it provides a basis for the inevitable judgments of the citizens which need to go beyond law, but it is still only a remedy that will eventually fail. The (increasing) dissimilarity of the

307 Cf. Miller Jr. (1980, 110).

cosmos in this age seems to imply that for the Stranger there can be no complete solution to the political problem.

We should emphasize that the fact that the divine bond consists of "secure" opinions implies once again that the presence of the true statesman in the city must be strictly limited. If the statesman were to assume the day-to-day management of the affairs of the city beyond framing its laws and opinions, then he would either need to do things that contradicted the stable opinions that he has fixed in the souls of the citizens or not. If he would not need to do so, then his management of the city's affairs would be unnecessary, since the true opinion of the citizens would effectively arrive at the same decisions he himself would make; but if he did need to do things that contradicted the citizens' opinions because these become false in some circumstances (opinions that, we must remember, he himself has given to them) then he would effectively undermine their stability and thus his own authority. The best thing a statesman could do after creating the "divine" bond would thus be to leave the city (or at least retire from politics), since his continuing presence in it would represent a threat to the stability of the citizens' opinions, just as the god must let go of the cosmos after he has put it in order if he does not want it to "unravel" by a complete separation of body from soul (see chapter 3, pp. 139–140). The principle of "*stare decisis*" holds, despite the arguments on the inferiority of the rule of law, for the statesman as well.

This is in fact what the Stranger recommends (311a1–2): the web the statesman creates requires "turning over" (*epitrepein*) the city's offices to the citizens, though in such a way that these offices are shared among both dispositions.[308] The statesman must remain a stranger to his creation, given the limitations of his material; the weaver is not part of the web.

---

[308] See Lane (1995, 283). In her later work (1998), she retreats from this position, in my opinion wrongly. See also Rowe (1995b, note *ad loc*), for a defense of the contrary view.

The human bond

Having discussed the divine bond, the Stranger now turns to the discussion of the "human" bond, the bond of marriage (310a7–e4). Proper marriage is supposed to bind citizens of "courageous" bias (already tempered by justice, to be sure), with citizens of "moderate" bias (tempered by *phronēsis*). True opinion about beautiful, just, and good things will quickly prevent marriages contracted for the sake of money and power, since such things are not true goods (310b7–9). But the citizens will still retain their attraction to their like; and to allow such attraction to proceed unchecked risks undoing the bond of true opinion, as the children of such families will be less likely to be exposed to the moderating or encouraging influence of the opposite tendencies, leading, in the course of the generations, to either madness (in the case of courageous dispositions, 310d6–9) or complete dullness (in the case of moderate dispositions, 310d11–e3).

The Stranger is not proposing some sort of crude eugenic theory. It matters little whether dispositions are transmitted genetically or by means of education. Without exposure to the "other side," however, the bond of true opinion can hardly be expected to endure, and such exposure can only be guaranteed through physical living together. The "human bond," however, is a limited, desperate expedient, which, in going against the grain of *erōs*, is unlikely to last much after the statesman dies or goes away. Like Socratic matchmaking (cf. *Theaetetus* 149d10ff.), the making of such bonds should in theory be a delicate art, requiring the individual attention of the statesman to each citizen. In practice, the marriage bond is merely the rough expedient the statesman uses to compel human beings to become "interbreeding" creatures, when they are not naturally so, and it is unclear how such a bond may be established in law rather than through the personal, and unsustainable, intervention of the statesman on a case by case basis.[309] The

[309] Cf. Dorter (1994, 227).

true statesman, in his concern for the long-run preservation of the city, foresees the consequences of allowing natural likes and dislikes to run their course, and takes (legislative) measures accordingly; but these measures can hardly have much effectiveness if the divine bond is no longer effective, or if he is not physically present in the city.

The web of politics

The creation of the divine and human bonds completes the work of the statesman. These bonds induce the citizens, whose nature is divided, to share in the same opinions, thus considering the same things honorable and dishonorable, and to exchange marriage-pledges with one another while sharing in the various offices of the city (310e7–311a2).[310] In practice, this means that the statesman chooses for those offices where a single individual is required a person who has both courageous and moderate dispositions (311a4–5), and for those bodies that require multiple members he ensures that the courageous and moderate dispositions are more or less evenly distributed (311a5–6). With this initial distribution of people into offices, the web of politics is finally complete, and it protects and "encloses" everybody else in the city (311c3–5), both slave and free: the citizen body properly speaking does not include everybody in the city. Though the Stranger does not further elaborate on the constitutional structure of the regime, he seems to be pointing to the kind of mixed regime described by the Athenian Stranger in the *Laws*.

As we have seen, the statesman prepares the city to survive without him. No hope is offered of a quick return, just as the god does not promise to return until the cosmos is nearly destroyed. He cannot train others to take his place—his knowledge is too

[310] The word *homēreia*, "marriage-pledge," at 310e10 could also mean "hostage"; it is as if the moderate and the courageous give "hostages" to one another in agreeing that sometimes the best policy for the salvation of the city may not be one that they can wholeheartedly approve of. Benardete in fact translates *homēreiōn ekdosesin* as "betrothals of hostages."

scarce and too difficult, too tied to the "seeing" of the *kairos* in its connection to the good, the just, and the beautiful, to be easily taught by the normal means by which knowledge is transmitted. His continued presence would moreover threaten the necessary stability of the citizens' opinions, a stability that will be especially required after he dies.

But this is not to say that his achievement is all for naught. Even after he is gone, the opinions he has implanted in the souls of the citizens will likely continue to be true for some time, and they will be reproduced by the laws and institutions he creates. The rhetoricians and the generals, whose supervision by the statesman I had earlier argued was necessary, would still be able to draw on these opinions to do their work well, since, after all, they too are citizens; and as long as they do not pretend to know the just and the good and the noble when they do not, the city will not revert to lawlessness. With the cloak the statesman creates, the city can survive the stormy times when the statesman is no longer around to help it (cf. 273d5); but it is to be expected that the web of politics, like the cloak of a man, will eventually become quite ragged. The best regime decays into the law-governed *polis* at best.

The ultimate achievement of the statesman is a partial healing of the partiality or incompleteness of human nature at the level of the community.[311] This partiality is most apparent in the split between the courageous and moderate dispositions, but it was also apparent in the dispersal of knowledge among all the forms of expertise in the city. At any rate, this achievement now appears in its most paradoxical light, since the Stranger has implicitly indicated that neither nature nor the city normally produces the knowledge of the statesman. Nature does not normally produce statesmen, since it produces people with a bias towards one or the other disposition, but not the kind of balanced people that would be able to acquire the knowledge of the statesman. This makes naturally occur-

[311] Cf. Strauss (1989, 230), as well as Dixsaut (1995, 253, 270–273).

ring statesmen exceedingly scarce. But this natural scarcity is amplified by the fact that everybody, future statesmen as well as everybody else, is born in cities that are not normally ruled by statesmen, and hence places that are thus devoid of the knowledge of the statesman. Though occasionally such places allow scarce natural talent to develop (as Athens allowed the Athenian Stranger to develop, *Laws* 642c6–d2), in general they provide very little support for the development of the statesman's knowledge. The statesman is a freak accident of both nature and culture, a stranger to both the city and the world.

7. Knowledge and Politics: A Conclusion

THE *STATESMAN* IS A BLEAK and melancholy dialogue, offering few comforts to the reader. Early on the Stranger demeans human beings by comparing them to two-legged pigs and featherless bipeds, and suggests that their possession of reason is insufficient to guarantee them the ability to rule themselves. The great myth that follows this discussion implies that the world tends towards disorder and decay with only a slim hope of rescue by the god at the end of time. In this world, human beings are left to secure their survival on their own with an inadequately distributed and integrated share of intelligence.

Politically, the *Statesman*'s message seems just as bleak. The city, like the cosmos, has a tendency toward disorder, and it has only a slim hope of being rescued by a genuine statesman, since statesmanship is exceedingly rare. Yet even if a genuine statesman were to emerge, against the grain of both nature and nurture, the city would be caught in a seemingly impossible dilemma in deciding whether to accept his claim to knowledge, since it does not have the ability to distinguish genuine statesmen from their imitators. The dialogue's main "positive" recommendation for the city in these circumstances is to err on the side of caution, holding on to its laws insofar as these reflect the city's experience of those things that have helped preserve it in the past. This conservatism of experience is all the more striking in Plato because it seems to close off or at least greatly diminish the possibility that a genuine statesman could eventually come to rule the city. Even if, as I have also argued, the dialogue nowhere closes off the possibility that institutions of inquiry could be incorporated into the city, as in the *Laws*, it must be admitted that the dialogue itself does not raise this possibility, and in general suggests that it would be extremely difficult for the city to determine whether a particular person who proposes change actually has the requisite knowledge.

Moreover, even if a city had the good fortune of being ruled by a genuine statesman, the dialogue suggests that the task of the statesman can at best be to make the city resilient to the conflicts that come from the ineradicable biases of human nature and to prepare the city for his inevitable absence through appropriate laws and forms of education. Just as a weaver cannot make himself part of the cloak, the statesman cannot integrate his knowledge into the fabric of the city. His achievement is thus depicted as both very difficult and very modest; "success" at best means that the city ruled by the statesman will have somewhat better laws than a city that bases its laws entirely on experience, not that it will be able to integrate in a permanent way the knowledge of the statesman into its fundamental institutions.

The essential modesty of the statesman's potential achievement is reflected in the place for the statesman in the hierarchy of knowledge that the dialogue's long divisions uncovers (see figures 5 and 6). Though the statesman is, in a sense, the unmoved mover of the city—the sole possessor of the theoretical insight capable of turning the indeterminate manifold of society into an ordered mixture by imposing limit and measure on it, to use the more abstract language of the *Philebus*—it is clear that human society can nevertheless limp along without him. And though this fact is in a way tragic (since it shows how human beings miss their potential, at the very least), it also shows that genuine statesmanship is to some extent dispensable. The human race does not need statesmanship to go on, even if individual political communities may be more or less in need of such knowledge; and Plato seems acutely aware of this fact in the *Statesman*.

Power or capacity (*dunamis*, *Sophist* 219a6)

0.	Other capacities	Knowledge or expertise	*Statesman* 258b4
1.	Practical	Theoretical or cognitive	258b6-259d6
2.	Critical	Commanding or directive	259d7-260b6
3.	Mediating	Autonomous	260c6-261a1
4.	Concerned with inanimate beings	Concerned with ensouled beings (=care of animals)	261a1-c3; an extra step seems required to separate plants from animals
5.	Of wild animals	Of tame animals	264a1-4; not strictly speaking a division of knowledge
6.	Individual care	Collective care	261c4-e4, 264a5-6
7.	Of water-dwelling animals	Of land-dwelling animals	264b7-e2
8.	Of users of wings for locomotion	Of users of feet for locomotion	264e2-11
9.	Of animals with horns	Of animals lacking horns	265b8-d5
10.	Of interbreeding animals (=smooth hooves)	Of non-interbreeding animals (=split hooves)	265d6-e9
11.	Four-footed (=pig)	Two-footed (=man)	265e10-c7
12.	Divine care	Human care	276c12-d7
13?	Unwilling (=tyranny)	Willing	276d8-276e14; dubious (recapitulated later)

Figure 5: Statesmanship as the care of human beings by human beings

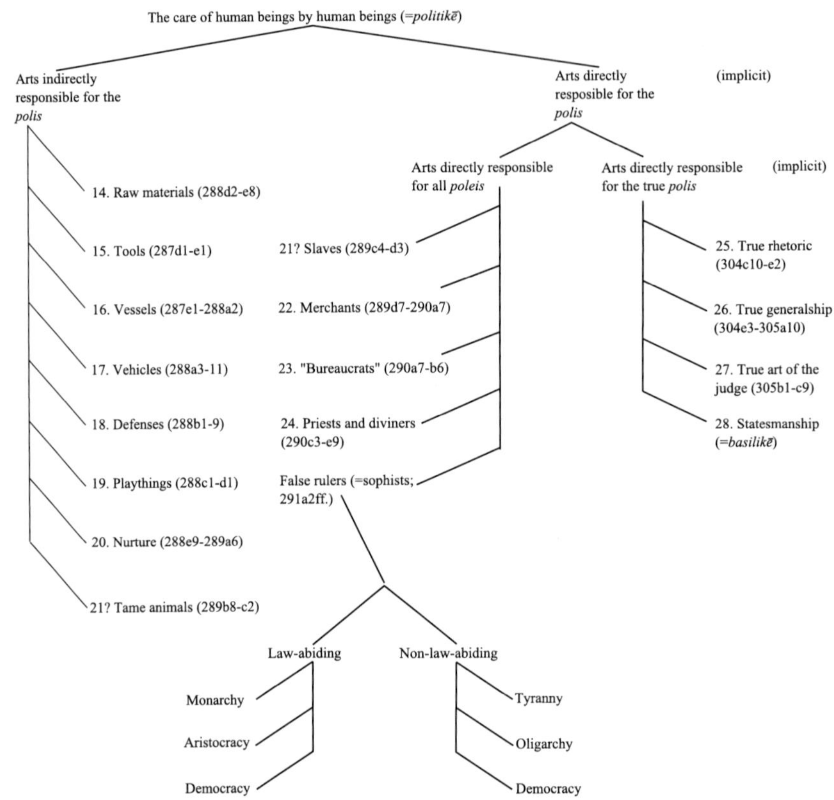

Figure 6: Statesmanship in the network of arts that care for human beings

Finally, the dialogue's modest expectations of statesmanship are also reflected in the subtle separation of the statesman from the philosopher I have argued is visible from the early pages of the *Sophist* and which continues in the *Statesman*. Philosophy remains a vital practice for Plato, of course; as the discussion of the relative value of life in the "Age of Cronos" shows, the Stranger clearly thinks that only the practice of philosophy can make a human being happy. But by the same token, statesmanship cannot; it can at best provide a propitious environment where certain kinds of destructive conflicts are minimized, though whether this environment is then capable of fostering philosophical practices is not clear.

And yet the *Statesman* strongly reasserts Plato's fundamental politico-philosophic project, namely, the project of empowering reason in politics. Even after acknowledging how hard it would be for the knowledge of the statesman to find any purchase in the city, the dialogue still ultimately asserts that the only solution to the fundamental problem of political conflict is knowledge, though given human ignorance and embodiment such knowledge would have to be constrained by mere opinion, that is, ultimately, by law. In this the *Statesman* stands with the rest of the Platonic corpus, including the *Republic*: only knowledge is ultimately sufficient, even if in human affairs such knowledge is exceedingly scarce. What distinguishes the *Statesman* from the *Republic* is less the idea that genuine statesmanship is scarce (an idea that is also given its due in the *Republic*), but that the best response to this scarcity is not the education of new statesmen but the creation of legal constraints and educational and other institutions that prevent the ignorant from gaining power and temper the natural biases of ordinary citizens towards inappropriate responses in common political situations. Statesmanship remains the standard against which political institutions are to be measured.

Is this project still tenable, or even useful, today? Does it make sense to think of the measure of political life as a form of knowledge, indeed a science, that can be potentially embodied in individual persons? Does it make sense to think of legal and constitutional arrangements as imperfect approximations to this knowledge? There is reason to doubt this. The mainstream of political philosophy today tends to understand the measure of political institutions in ways that seem to leave little or no part for genuine political knowledge. The idea of political knowledge in Platonic terms has been plausibly criticized as a denial of politics, as a misunderstanding of the unsystematic and culturally rooted nature of political prudence, and as a dangerous substitution of making for acting, leading inevitably to the justification of violence in pursuit of ideologically determined goals. And the modern rejection of Platonic metaphysics leaves the tenability of the idea of a knowledge based on a transcendent vision of the forms of order—the forms of justice, the good, and the beautiful—in grave doubt. Yet I shall argue that, with suitable modifications, many parts of the Platonic project of the *Statesman*, in particular the idea that political knowledge can provide the measure of political institutions, are still workable and fruitful ideas for political theory.

However, before we evaluate the general value of the Platonic project of the *Statesman*, or its usefulness today as political theory, it is worth examining one important internal critique of the dialogue, that is, a critique that raises doubts about the coherence of the views expressed in the *Statesman* with the political theory of the *Republic* and the *Laws*. The problem is that the picture of statesmanship in the *Statesman*, insofar as it stresses epistemic judgment over character, and the formal characterization of the expertise of the statesman over a substantive discussion of the goals of politics, seems to neglect the dominant concerns of the *Republic* and the *Laws* with the goodness of the ruler and citizens and with the means of promoting virtuous character, and further seems to ignore the basic insight of the *Republic* concerning the need for rulers who do not want to rule.[312] If these two accounts of the requirements of political rulership are in contradiction or even in tension, for whatever reason (maybe they differ because of the different dramatic contexts of the dialogues in question, for example), we would then need to decide which of them, if any, is the stronger account, and which of them, if any, is endorsed by Plato.

Character and expertise

The relative neglect of the moral character of the rulers in the account of statesmanship offered in the *Statesman* has been widely noted. This neglect goes hand in hand with the

[312] See Schofield (2006, 178, 182); Zuckert (2005).

expressly formal character of the discussion in the dialogue: while we get complex discussions of the virtues and their relationships to each other in the *Republic* and the *Laws*, in the *Statesman* we get what appears to be a fairly impoverished set of divisions that capture, at best, the formal structure of the kind of knowledge necessary for politics. One misses, for example, a discussion of the moral dangers of office: would not a statesman of the kind described by the Eleatic Stranger be easily corrupted? What assurance do we have that he would not be so corrupted? And one misses detailed discussions of the goals and means of politics: what are the specific goals of statesmanship? Why these goals and not others? As Schofield puts it, the *Statesman*'s "methods of classificatory definition and controlled use of example do not characteristically involve a reasoned specification of a goal. In fact at no stage in his methodologically self-conscious sequence of discussions of the topic does the Eleatic Visitor explicitly raise and debate the question: what is the goal of statesmanship?"[313]

To be sure, the Stranger expressly emphasizes the interconnection between the character of the statesman and his knowledge, as we have noted; the statesman is said to be both "wise and good" (cf. 296e3). So there is no formal contradiction in anything that the Stranger says with anything said about the virtue of rulers in other dialogues. But though one suspects that the statesman's goodness is identical with his knowledge (or rather, that his knowledge is essentially knowledge of the good), the Stranger does not articulate the relationship between the expertise of the statesman and his virtue, or say anything about how the concept of a union of knowledge and goodness actually plays out in mortal bodies, subject to temptations and corruption. Again Schofield articulates this worry most clearly: while the philosopher-king of the *Republic* is sketched as someone whose insight into the good makes him reluctant to be dragged back into the cave, and whose knowledge is

313 Schofield (2006, 182).

essentially of unchangeable forms, the statesman is someone whose knowledge is essentially focused on human affairs and whose main reason for existing is precisely to order the city, not to engage in philosophical contemplation.[314] And while the *Republic* directly connects the philosopher's reluctance to rule with his suitability for rule (only those who really do not want to rule should rule), the *Statesman* does no such thing.

Yet the neglect of these issues of character in the *Statesman* can only be a problem if the views articulated in the *Statesman* are in actual conflict with the views articulated in other dialogues, and this is less clear. Given that each dialogue has its own specific project and its own dramatic frame, we should not expect Plato to have addressed every important subject at length in every one of his political works. And though there is reason to believe, as I have argued, that the kind of figure that the Stranger describes in the *Statesman* is not identical with the philosopher-king of the *Republic*, it is not necessarily the case that these two accounts of political knowledge are in conflict. The reason is that while the *Statesman* depicts the statesman as a figure external to the *polis*, who shapes its order but is not produced by it, the *Republic* instead depicts the philosopher-king as internal to the *polis*, both the producer and the product of its order. The *Statesman* thus abstracts in important ways from the institutional structure and educational system of the city to which he is related: he is outside of it, and hence cannot be fully integrated into it. The *Republic*, by contrast, integrates the knowledge of the philosopher-king into the institutional structure and educational system of the city. The philosopher-king grows organically from the soil of the city, except perhaps at its foundation, where the philosopher (Socrates) stands outside of it, fully formed, to give shape to it.[315] In other words, a key difference between the *Statesman*,

---

314 Schofield (2006, 137–142).

315 The *Republic* equivocates on this point: sometimes the philosopher-king is depicted as the day-to-day ruler of the city, at other times merely as its

the *Republic*, and the *Laws* has to do with the position of the statesman *vi-à-vis* the city: outside of it in the *Laws* and the *Statesman*, inside of it in the *Republic*.

The difference in the position of the knowledgeable individual *vis-à-vis* the city explains some of the peculiarities of the depiction of the philosopher-king and the statesman in the *Republic* and the *Statesman*. As Schofield has rightly noted, for example, the philosopher-king of the *Republic* does not require a great deal of training in what we might call "empirical" politics precisely because the city of the *Republic* is so structured as to eliminate "politics."[316] But the statesman of the *Statesman* and, in a different way, the *Laws* approaches the city from the outside; he must confront ineliminable political realities on the way to shaping the city. It is in this sense that the knowledge of the statesman in the *Statesman* and the *Laws* is not "continuous" with the Socratic project, as Schofield also notes; it is only in a city like the *kallipolis* where Socrates could be ruler. But it is only a Plato or an Aristotle, that is, an "empirical" researcher into politics, who could become a statesman in the sense of the later dialogues, someone who produces the order of the city and is not also produced by it.

This is the reason why the goals of politics appear in a slightly different light in the *Statesman* than in the *Republic*, and indeed appear to be neglected in the former dialogue. When the statesman remains outside the city, unintegrated with it, the goals of politics must necessarily be reduced to the preservation of the city, subject to the constraint that it also be made as good as possible in the potential absence of the statesman. When the statesman is a philosopher-king, internal to the city, the idea of making the city as good as possible acquires a substance it could not have when he remains outside of it. The

---

legislator and founder, but most people agree that in the final account the *Republic* does depict a city ruled by knowledgeable individuals, and not merely established by them.

[316] Schofield (2006, 159).

city can only be best when knowledge is integrated within it; it can only be second best when knowledge remains external to it, ordering it as a weaver makes a cloth and sending it on its way when the statesman dies or moves away. If there is a real development in Plato's views on politics, one important shift could be said to be the shift from the view that political knowledge can be fully integrated into the city to the view that political knowledge cannot be so integrated, that is, to the view that real politics is always "second best."

We can also see how the externality or "strangeness" of the statesman *vis-à-vis* the city also makes the problem of corruption in the statesman less pressing. If the statesman is not envisioned as a ruler with an enduring line of successors who also have his knowledge and in an enduring position of power, his corruption is less likely and of less importance than if the statesman is envisioned as a philosopher-king who must be continuously produced by the city and who is expected to rule it on a day-to-day basis. Philanthropic legislators who possess real knowledge can exist and have existed; it is philanthropic rulers who are more problematic. Hence the Eleatic Stranger's stress on the idea that the statesman can be merely an "advisor" to those in power, an idea that is curiously absent from the *Republic*. While the reference to the statesman as an "advisor" may reflect, in some complicated way, some twist or turn of Plato's own biography and ill-fated adventures in Sicily, the point remains that corruption in a philosophical advisor is less likely than corruption in a ruler. The corruption of rulers, and their judgment, remains of paramount importance in the *Statesman*; that is the point of the discussion of the parts of virtue at the end of the dialogue. But such a discussion is no longer identical with a discussion of the virtues of the true statesman, whose long-term presence in the city is no longer assumed.

Doubts

The statesman, then, turns out to be the external measure of the city: no longer a product of the city's order, political knowledge appears now as the personal capacity that can access the standards against which the city's institutions must be measured but which they cannot themselves access. Is such an "external" standard for politics—the knowledgeable legislator whose knowledge cannot be integrated into the city—possible or even desirable? Three kinds of doubts about this project, especially as presented in the *Statesman*, can be raised.

The first sort of doubt concerns the possibility of such knowledge. The skeptic need not deny that political decisions can be better or worse, and that some people perhaps are better qualified than others to make such decisions; but he may deny that such competence is or depends on a "science," dependent on ineffable insight into transcendental forms of order, or on the "measurements" that such forms make possible, for, the skeptic might say, no such forms exist, or we cannot know if they do exist, and thus that the measure of political order is ineradicably tied to the contingent desires and interests of the members of the polity.[317] Political competence, on this view, is (in Platonic terms) always a form of sophistry, an inarticulate ability to guess well in those matters that concern the life of the *polis* what will satisfy certain publicly felt needs and wants, but not a science that can be taught or learned, much less a science that is independent of the community's "culture," to use the modern term.[318] Or, to put the point in more neutral terms, political competence is identical with the virtue of prudence, which is not a science, an objection that goes back at least to Aristotle.

The second sort of doubt concerns not so much the possibility of the knowledge of the statesman as the idea that some privileged access to it is possible independent of the decision procedures of the community. The objection is in this case

[317] Something like this argument is to be found in Robert Dahl's democratic response to the advocate of guardianship in Dahl (1989).

[318] Something like this argument underlies Oakeshott's (1991 [1962]) attack on "rationalism in politics," as well as Sheldon Wolin's (1960, ch. 2) criticism of Plato.

primarily epistemological, not ontological, we might say; the problem is that even if there is such a thing as justice or the good of the community, and such a thing is knowable, it may not be possible to know it except by means of certain procedures (e.g., the ideal deliberative situation of Habermas or the "original position" of Rawls). The good of the community is then understood in procedural terms as what the community would agree under certain ideally specified conditions, not as something independent of it and accessible through the insight of especially trained individuals. A variation on this objection, which goes back to Aristotle (*Politics* 1286a25–31, b2–16, 1287b8–35, 1287a7–24) suggests that the expertise of a ruler would not necessarily be better than the aggregated experience or partial know-how of many non-experts; individual expertise need not have more epistemic access to the truth than a well-designed institution where many people (not necessarily experts) participate.

The third sort of doubt concerns the authority of the statesman, that is, what his knowledge could actually license in political terms. On the one hand one may doubt that just because the statesman has a specific kind of knowledge he is therefore entitled to rule. This is what David Estlund calls the "expert/boss" fallacy, the idea that knowledge *per se* gives political authority.[319] But one may put this doubt in more "political" terms, following Hannah Arendt,[320] and argue that Plato's position in the *Statesman* misunderstands the nature of political action as a form of "making," and hence ultimately justifies all kinds of violence.

Let us call the first sort of objection the "ontological" objection, the second the "epistemological" objection, and the third the "political" objection. Each of these objections has been articulated, with varying force and diverse arguments, by

---

[319] See Estlund (2008, 22).

[320] In her critique of the *Statesman* in *The Human Condition* (Arendt [1958, especially 221–227]).

many thinkers, and they apply more broadly than to the specific account of political knowledge developed in the *Statesman*. I do not propose to answer each potential variation on these objections, but only to indicate the resources that the *Statesman* might bring to bear against them, and hence the value that the project of the dialogue might still offer political theory today.

The ontological objection

The *Statesman*, like all Platonic dialogues, understands knowledge in contradistinction to opinion, and indeed to true opinion; yet it also connects them in a very specific way. I have claimed in this study (see especially chapters 4 and 5) that knowledge in Plato is always a direct grasp of the formal and invariant structures of reality, but that (in the *Statesman* at least) such grasp of formal structure can *enable* its possessor to produce reliable correct judgments (to have "true opinion") in some domain of reality where there can be no grasp of invariant form (e.g., in the domain of particular judgments about what actions are just *right now* for the city). In particular, knowledge that secures the reliability of judgments (opinions) in a particular domain of being can be called an *art* or *expertise*. For example, the Plato of the *Statesman* might say that knowledge of letters is a direct grasp of the formal and invariant structures of the manifold of the sound of the human voice in their individual distinctness, that such grasp secures the reliability of our judgments about spelling specific words (whose components "participate" in these formal structures in some particular combination, and are identified by those with knowledge any time someone speaks), and that its possessor can be said to have the *expertise* of spelling. Achieving a grasp of these invariant structures of reality (the "forms" for short) is often difficult, and may on occasion require the use of *models* that do not fully reflect the ways in which the formal elements of a particular complex being are related; but once such grasp is attained, it can be leveraged to correctly *judge* how the elements of arbitrary complex beings (within some domain of reality) are connected, as well as to *produce* images of these beings through two kinds of measurement.

The details of Plato's metaphysics need not detain us here, and I do not claim that Plato presents us with a true and complete account of knowledge. But it is worth noting that his account of knowledge is less foreign to our own intuitions about knowledge than it might seem at first glance. Consider, for example, what we might mean by speaking of the knowledge or science of physics. Physics is the knowledge of the laws of physics, which are assumed to be invariant structures of reality. These structures, moreover, are thought to be representable by explicit mathematical models that specify in a precise way the relationships between different formal elements of reality (e.g., mass and energy); and the knowledge of these fundamental physical structures (the invariant laws of physics) is typically understood to *enable* us to make correct judgments about particular events (e.g., to predict the position and momentum of a body) through the use of some form of measurement. Finally, we learn about the formal elements of physical reality by a process that involves, *inter alia*, leveraging our correct judgments about physical events using simplifying models to discover which of the postulated elements of these models can be understood as formal elements of reality. A broadly "Platonic" account of knowledge is in fact rife among physicists and mathematicians, though it usually goes by names like "structural realism."[321]

---

[321] For a good example, see Tegmark (2008). The story of the development of Quantum Chromodynamics is also instructive for our purposes (Cao [2010]). In 1961, Murray Gell-Mann postulated the existence of quarks on the basis of the abstract symmetries described by a specific mathematical structure, the Lie group called the "special unitary group" of degree three or SU(3). The existence of all the postulated particles was later empirically confirmed and all the predictions based on the theory verified to astonishing degrees of accuracy; but it is not obvious that these often incredibly evanescent particles (which furthermore cannot actually be "separated" from one another, but must always exist as composites) are more real than the "abstract" mathematical structure SU(3) that fully describes them. Moreover, though there are analogies between the "eightfold symmetries"

Analogously, to say that there can be such a thing as political knowledge in the "Platonic" sense would be to say that one can achieve a grasp of certain invariant or at least universal and enduring structures or forms of order, which we might call the principles of morality; that these structures can be represented by explicit models that specify relationships between formal elements (e.g., rights, agents, the good, etc.); that these structures are understood to be *normative* for us in light of their connection to the formal notion of the good; and that they can enable us to make judgments *about* and to *order* our everyday social lives via the mediation of certain forms of "measurement" (e.g., to say that certain *particular* actions fall short of justice or nobility). In order to learn about these forms of moral order we would have to leverage our intuitively "correct" moral judgments to test or construct theories or models of justice and the like, and to subject these models to stringent dialectical examination to discover *which* of their elements should be accepted as genuine parts of the moral order and *how* these elements are truly related. In principle this process need not have anything to do with Plato's dialectical method (the process of arriving at a "reflective equilibrium" via a social-contractarian device in Rawls comes to mind as an alternative), and may end up discovering formal elements that escaped him (e.g., the idea of "rights"), but it is also not especially incompatible with anything that Plato says, so long as we do not insist on making unnecessary metaphysical assumptions about the ontological status of the enduring structures of human morality or imposing spurious methodological constraints on the means by which we may discover them.

On a first approximation, then, to say that there can be no "knowledge" of political matters is thus to say that politics

---

of Quantum Chromodynamics and various processes in the sensible world (such as color changes: hence "chromodynamics"), *understanding* the theory ultimately necessitates a grasp of the mathematical structure itself; analogies based on color changes are at best approximative and need to be discarded eventually to achieve a full grasp of the theory.

cannot be like physics: there is and can be no grasp of the enduring and universal formal structure of justice, because there is no such structure (or no such structure is accessible to human knowledge), and *a fortiori* such a grasp cannot ground any kind of correct judgment about what is good for a political community. There are then perhaps true or false opinions about the goodness of some particular course of action given some assumptions about what people in a community believe is good for them, but no overall and enduring regularity that can be apprehended by human beings and which both clearly distinguishes between good and bad courses of action and is independent of the contingent circumstances of the community and the desires and interests of its current members.

Note that the question of the possibility of political knowledge is not a question of whether anyone can gather the requisite information about the relevant desires and contingent circumstances of the political community. To be sure, if information about relevant desires and circumstances cannot be gathered, that would constitute a practical obstacle to the rule of the statesman, as the Stranger acknowledges; indeed, that is a reason for using laws. But it would not constitute an objection to the possibility of political knowledge, which is of the formal structure of justice and the noble in light of a principle of order that makes us understand these structures in normative terms, namely the good. In other words, the denial of political knowledge is the denial that there can be knowledge of "fact independent" principles of morality or forms of order, to use some contemporary terminology.[322]

At any rate, the argument of the *Statesman* does not require that the statesman have extensive access to correct information about the circumstances and desires of the people of a community in every possible situation, since it does not demand that

[322] The term is from G. A. Cohen. The similarities between Cohen's "fact independent" fundamental principles of justice and Platonic forms are quite striking, though not acknowledged. See Cohen (2008).

the statesman decide for the community on every important policy issue. He needs only two things: first, accurate information about the characters of the people in the city at the moment of founding (which he can gather through an elaborate system of tests that ends in a determination regarding who can be a citizen, and which citizens have courageous or moderate dispositions, a process that serves as a kind of "relative" measurement), and second, the correct grasp of the general forms of order (the good, the just, and the noble). Armed with these two things, the statesman can devise an institutional order, that is, a set of relations and beliefs among the citizens that are "measured" against the true forms of order, and which "works" by mitigating certain fundamental conflicts over the basis of policy in an uncertain and competitive environment over the long run. The knowledge required for this project is essentially legislative, not prudential in the narrow sense of the word; the ideal is Lycurgus or Solon, not Pericles, and the focus is on the foundation of the city, not its day-to-day running.

We might usefully compare Plato's focus in the *Statesman* on the founding of the city with Rawls's focus in *A Theory of Justice* on the "basic structure" of society: the knowledge the philosophical statesman brings to bear, in both cases, is not of every little policy decision, but of the correct principles of justice, which in both cases are determined without reference to purely contingent facts about the political community and its membership (though they do make reference to enduring facts about human nature). To be sure, one could also deny that such "legislative," rather than prudential, knowledge exists by denying that there can be insight into the forms of order; but if by "forms of order" we mean something like the actual structure of justice, the good, and the noble, the skeptic's argument becomes less plausible.

Moreover, we must beware of simply asserting that just because these principles or forms of order are controversial, or subject to "reasonable" disagreement, that no such principles exist. The fact that it is difficult to find and articulate such principles, and hence that it is difficult to say what the right institutional structure for a community would be, does not mean that there can be no knowledge, at least in theory, of such a structure. The difficulty of the task, at any rate, is something that the *Statesman* acknowledges both explicitly and in its dramatic movement, which is full of errors and wrong turns. For one thing, the "forms of order" are not the kinds of thing that can be easily articulated in a simple rule or an easily applicable model; otherwise the rule of law would not necessarily be second best. Here it is worth noting the Plato of the *Republic*, like the Rawls of *A Theory of Justice*, does not claim to have fully grasped the structure of justice or to present a complete image of it; *kallipolis* remains a model of the real structure of justice, just as Rawls's theory of justice remains a theory, an incomplete model or image of the real structure of justice. Moreover, both the Stranger in the section on measure in the *Statesman* and Socrates in the *Philebus* express some doubts about the possibility that in the world of becoming even attaining real knowledge of the forms of order can secure correct judgments that are free of imprecision. Knowledge is ultimately of unchanging order, not of the order mixed with randomness that characterizes human life, and hence any determinations about the proper order of the city (the "measures" of its order that constitute the real contribution of the statesman) will be laced with imperfection, or, to put the point in modern terms, they will be subject to reasonable disagreement. But this does not mean that knowledge of them is impossible in principle.

The epistemological objection

Even if such knowledge is not impossible in principle, we might still raise objections about the privileged epistemic role of the individual statesman in Plato. The objection here is about the *locus* of epistemic access to the forms of order, not a denial of their existence: we might want to say that individuals, however educated, have no better access to the good, the just, and the noble than certain institutional situations in which non-experts participate. At its most comprehensive, the objection says that the standard of justice for a political community is defined by what participants in a certain idealized institutional situation would agree to (e.g., the ideal speech situation in Habermas or the original position in Rawls), and is hence not reliably accessed by individual human beings, however educated; access to the standard of justice increases by better approximating this ideal situation, not by special philosophical instruction.

But one could also argue, less ambitiously, that even if an idealized institutional situation does not define the standard of justice, some potential institutional architectures provide better access to the correct standard than the mind of any given individual, however educated. A team of diverse experts may be better than a single one, as Aristotle argued; and sometimes a team of diverse non-experts is better than a single expert, as we have known since Condorcet.[323]

It may well be the case that epistemic access to the best policy is best secured in particular institutional situations, a possibility that Plato nowhere explores. But the prior question of which social structure best provides the community with access to the truth is not one whose answer is necessarily accessible to these same procedures. Otherwise philosophers like Habermas or Rawls could not claim that the institutional situation they think provides access to justice actually does provide such access! Moreover, as David Estlund has rightly argued, even if we accept that some particular institutional situation defines a standard of justice, it does not follow that epistemic access to that standard of justice increases linearly with successive approximations to the ideal situation.[324] Just because the ideal speech situation defines the standard of justice does not mean that real speech situations provide better epistemic access to this standard than philosophical reflection.

[323] For more on these ideas, see Surowiecki (2004), Page (2007).

[324] See Estlund (2008, especially ch. X).

At any rate, the question of whether experts or groups have better epistemic access to the truth about justice or the good in particular cases is not a question that can be resolved independently of the problem in question. Some problems require merely the aggregation of individually held "private" information, and are therefore easily solved by institutional architectures that promote such aggregation (as in well-designed markets or democratic systems). But the solution to other problems depends not so much on the aggregation of information as on access to the correct model that applies to the situation; and the problem of which institutional situation best provides epistemic access to the common good of a community is one of these. But this is precisely the problem that the statesman of the *Statesman* is expected to consider.

Even if no individual had better access to the forms of order, and hence to the common good of a community, than certain institutional structures, it does not follow that the epistemological objection is devastating to the Platonic project. For the statesman in the end functions more as a regulative ideal than as a live possibility, as I have tried to show in this study. What matters ultimately for Plato is that knowledge is empowered in politics as far as possible; whether such knowledge is an individual possession is, in the end, immaterial. To put the same point in slightly different terms, the fact that "medicine" is not something that any single doctor can now master, or that "mathematics" is not something that any single mathematician can master, does not imply that there is no knowledge of mathematics or medicine, embodied in the practices of the community of doctors and mathematicians, and deserving of authority within its own field; and so similarly with political knowledge. Plato in the *Statesman* does not enjoin us to look for the statesman in our midst, but to cultivate political knowledge in whatever form it may be found. Hence he is open to considering the experience embodied in the laws of the city as an approximation, however incorrect, to real knowledge, an approximation that in the *Laws* appears as something that can be improved through the efforts of ordinary people engaging in study. We may then go beyond Plato and grant that the city may sometimes have some (perhaps small) degree of epistemic access to the true standards of justice and the good; though even then, we might want to say that knowledge about which institutional arrangements best secure such epistemic access is not vouchsafed to the city, but to the genuine statesman, the possessor of political science.

The political objection

There still remains, however, the political objection to the Platonic project. The objection has a number of different forms, though underlying it there is a basic preoccupation with the problem of violence. In its more general form, the problem seems to be that allowing the claims of knowledge in politics opens the way for a violence that we do not believe justified. David Estlund calls this the "boss/expert" fallacy: just because you have knowledge does not give you authority.[325] But the objection also goes beyond traditional concerns with authority. So, in Hannah Arendt's critique of the *Statesman*, the problem is that it misunderstands the nature of political action, which is not about *making* the *polis* (with all its attendant violence) but about preserving the common world where individuals can appear in their plurality.[326] In both cases, the problem is that the political realm is necessarily a realm of conflict, which the appeal to truth and knowledge short-circuits rather than manages.

There is some truth to these concerns, and Arendt is indeed right that Plato tends to understand political action in terms of "making." But it is worth being clear about what the Platonic project does not license. It does not grant authority to mere *claims* to knowledge, mere "subjective certainty" about politics. Plato is extremely concerned, in the *Statesman* as elsewhere,

[325] Estlund (2008, 22).
[326] See Arendt (1958, especially 221–227).

with the problems of false claims of expertise, leading him to apparently propose a radical legal conservatism so long as the people of the city have no way of distinguishing true from false statesmen. And even though the Eleatic Stranger argues that violence that results in justice cannot be called "unjust," and he suggests that on occasion the genuine statesman may need to use drastic measures, he never argues that knowledge grants the statesman a blanket license to use violence. Violent utopianism is alien to the conservative spirit of the *Statesman*.

To be sure, though ideally the rule of the statesman is backed by the consent of the people (as I argued in chapter 2, pp. 111–117: the statesman is not a tyrant), when this consent does *not* exist (despite the statesman's efforts to secure it), the statesman may still have authority to use force. But it is worth stressing that the statesman's expertise is not the expertise of the general, and to the extent that the violence of the statesman is on occasion justified, it is not necessarily clear that it is justified merely *by* knowledge, or that the consent of the ruled counts for nothing (even if it only counts "prudentially"). The statesman's art is neither the art of violence nor the art of persuasion, but it is *closer* (as a theoretical art) to persuasion and teaching than to the violence of the general (who is always very close to the tyrant); and as the Athenian Stranger in the *Laws* argues, persuasion is preferable to compulsion in law, even if compulsion is sometimes unavoidable (*Laws* 720bff.). Nothing the Eleatic Stranger says about the distinction between the tyrant and the statesman in the *Statesman* conflicts with the Athenian's views.

Moreover, given the limited role envisioned for the statesman in the *Statesman*, the idea that Plato intends to eliminate conflict from political life seems misguided. In fact, the making of the well-ordered *polis* is a foundational act that marks the retreat of political knowledge and opens up a space for political doing, that is, activity for the sake of the constant care of human beings through the arts and their regulation, in a context where fundamental but reasonable differences of opinion, rooted in fundamental differences in character disposition, are ineradicable. Politics in the *polis* then becomes the constant struggle to preserve the city and its laws—the image of political knowledge—in a world largely devoid of such knowledge; and this is not an inconsiderable or unimportant task. Such politics do not leave a great deal of room for radical political change (unlike Arendtian politics), but I take it that the Stranger—and Plato—are correct in thinking that change that is not led by knowledge is unlikely to be any good. That radical or nearly-radical change sometimes happens for the good merely testifies to the fact that human beings can achieve something at least like such knowledge from time to time.

It is worth emphasizing that the *Statesman*'s fundamental message is to put less stock in the claims to knowledge of various sophists and more stock in the experience embodied in the laws, to be humble rather than arrogant; hence its consistent humbling of Young Socrates. We might go so far as to say that the *Statesman* argues against utopian violence; for while it may be true that such violence could be justified by knowledge, the *Statesman* shows that the city does not have the resources to distinguish real knowledge from its imitations. This is not to say that the dialogue entirely closes off the possibility of improvements to the law, but that such improvements cannot come about through messianic interventions into politics, except perhaps in moments where founding or refounding the city is necessary, the desperate times when the statesman, like the god in the myth, returns to produce a new lasting political order. As the *Laws* suggests, learning can be integrated into politics, though not necessarily in a way that produces statesmen.

One might nevertheless wish to argue that the understanding of human beings in the *Statesman* as not self-evidently rational animals but rather as "modularly" rational animals (that is, rational only insofar as they have one art or another, and no further) prevents the Stranger (and thus Plato) from understanding the rational basis of consent in the moral autonomy of each individual human being. This results necessarily in an authoritarian politics—whether of law or of men, it hardly matters—for it is only through an understanding of human beings as rational beings that a politics that avoids the twin pitfalls of extreme conservatism and revolutionary messianism can be found, that is, a politics where the care of human beings by human beings is the truly common and progressive task of all (a politics such as presented in the myth of the *Protagoras*, perhaps) rather than the ultimate responsibility of an impossible and hypothetical statesman. There is some truth to this objection, since the statesman's knowledge, as described by the Eleatic, is clearly incompatible with any doctrine of human rights. Yet such a politics would still require the idea of a political knowledge independent of any deliberation or consent, as Protagoras assumes in the *Protagoras*. At any rate actual politics does point to the occasional necessity of statesmen, that is, people who know what is to be done far better than other people.

The vindication of the philosopher-king

The *Statesman* has a twofold "practical" lesson: political knowledge is such that political leaders and citizens should be epistemically humble, conservatively holding on to the law and refusing to let go of it (a particularly timely reminder today, when some advocate that our leaders ignore the law in the face of supposedly existential threats); and inquiry into political matters is necessary (though not sufficient) to the care of the *polis*. Jointly, they amount to a vindication of the philosophical attitude in politics, or, more bluntly, of the "Socratic" philosopher-king.

By now it should be clear that I do not use the term "philosopher-king" to mean "statesman," as the term is sometimes used in the *Republic*. The philosopher-king is precisely the humble king, not the self-confident and brash statesman of legend, in possession of the truth about the world. To be sure, self-confidence and brashness may be essential ingredients of the successful leader, as Machiavelli pointed out, but the

Statesman suggests that though these qualities may occasionally lead to improvements in human life, more often than not they will also lead to disaster. Only the proper mixture of both is adequate to the city, but such mixture is impossible without knowledge. In its default, the dialogue suggests, the political leader should err (for erring it is) on the side of caution, that is, on the side of established law.

But precisely because such "erring on the side of caution" is in fact erring—for caution alone, just as much as brashness alone, is inadequate to political life—political inquiry is also essential to the city, that is, inquiry into what is good and just for the circumstances and the times. Thus kings must be "philosophers," inquirers after the truth of what is good for the *polis*.

Such inquiry looks towards the integrative care of human beings, not towards their "pastoral" care, to use Foucault's term. This means that political inquiry (and, indirectly, political power) should respect the partial autonomy of the many arts by which human beings care for themselves while pointing towards their integration in the care of the city. But it need not take the exact form it takes in the *Statesman*, nor do we need to think of it as necessarily issuing in the mastery by one person of a complete know-how. In fact, given the complexity of the modern political community, such inquiry will necessarily be performed through a division of labor and a great deal of dialogue. The search for statesmanship need not be the search for saviors, but rather, for the kinds of partial and temporary improvements in our condition that the systematic accumulation of experience and its analysis permit.

In the end, the *Statesman* tells us that there is no cessation of evils in human affairs, only a partial mitigation of them through law and inquiry. This mitigation is a great and always-threatened achievement, but nonetheless it remains only an insufficient remedy for an incurable condition in an always changing world. The *Statesman* is the great Platonic reflection on the necessary imperfection of the political world.

Bibliography

Ambuel, David. 2007. *Image and Paradigm in Plato's* Sophist. Las Vegas: Parmenides Publishing.

Annas, Julia. 1992. "Plato the Sceptic." In *Methods of Interpreting Plato and his Dialogues,* edited by J. C. Klagge and N. D. Smith. Oxford: Oxford University Press.

Annas, Julia, and Christopher Rowe, eds. 2002. *New Perspectives on Plato, Modern and Ancient.* Washington, D.C.: Center for Hellenic Studies.

Annas, Julia, and Robin Waterfield. 1995. *Plato:* Statesman. New York: Cambridge University Press.

Arends, J. F. M. 1993. "Survival, War and the Unity of the *Polis* in Plato's *Statesman.*" *Polis* 12 (1–2): 154–187.

_______. 1999. "The Long March to Plato's *Statesman.*" Review of *Plato:* Statesman, ed. with an Introduction, Translation & Commentary by C. J. Rowe. *Polis* 16 (1–2): 93–122.

_______. 2001. "The Long March to Plato's *Statesman* Continued." Review of *Method and Politics in Plato's* Statesman by Melissa S. Lane. *Polis* 18 (1–2): 125–152.

Arendt, Hannah. 1958. *The Human Condition.* Chicago: The University of Chicago Press.

_______. 1963. *On Revolution.* New York: Penguin.

Arieti, James A., and Roger M. Barrus. 2007. *Plato:* Gorgias. Newburyport, MA: Focus.

Ausland, Hayden. 1997. "On Reading Plato Mimetically." *American Journal of Philology* 118 (3): 371–416.

_______. 2000. "Who Speaks for Whom in the *Timaeus-Critias*?" In *Who Speaks for Plato?*, edited by G. A. Press. Lanham, MD: Rowman & Littlefield.

Barker, Ernest. 1918. *Greek Political Theory: Plato and his Predecessors*. London: Methuen.

Baum, Eric. 2004. *What is Thought?* Cambridge, MA: MIT Press.

Benardete, Seth. 1963. "Eidos and Diaeresis in Plato's *Statesman*." *Philologus* 107 (3/4): 193–226.

_______. 1984a. *The Being of the Beautiful*. 3 vols. Vol. II, Plato's *Sophist*. Chicago: University of Chicago Press.

_______. 1984b. *The Being of the Beautiful*. 3 vols. Vol. III, Plato's *Statesman*. Chicago: University of Chicago Press.

_______. 1992. "The Plan of the *Statesman*." *Métis. Anthropologie des mondes Grecs anciens* 7 (1–2): 25–47.

Blondell, Ruby. 2002. *The Play of Character in Plato's Dialogues*. Cambridge: Cambridge University Press.

Bobonich, Christopher. 1995. "The Virtues of Ordinary People in Plato's *Statesman*." In *Reading the Statesman: Proceedings of the III. Symposium Platonicum*, edited by C. Rowe. Sankt Augustin: Academia Verlag.

_______. 2002. *Plato's Utopia Recast: His later Ethics and Politics*. Oxford: Oxford University Press.

Brisson, Luc. 1995. "Interprétation du mythe du *Politique*." In *Reading the Statesman: Proceedings of the III. Symposium Platonicum*, edited by C. Rowe. Sankt Augustin: Academia Verlag.

Burnyeat, Myles. 1990. *The* Theaetetus *of Plato*. Indianapolis: Hackett.

Campbell, Lewis. 1867. *The Sophistes and Politicus of Plato, with a Revised Text and English Notes*. Oxford: Clarendon Press.

Cao, Tian Yu. 2010. *From Current Algebra to Quantum Chromodynamics: A Case for Structural Realism*. Cambridge & New York: Cambridge University Press.

Caplan, Bryan. 2007. *The Myth of The Rational Voter*. Princeton: Princeton University Press.

Carone, Gabriela Roxana. 2005. *Plato's Cosmology and its Ethical Dimensions*. Cambridge: Cambridge University Press.

Castoriadis, Cornelius. 1999. *Sur Le Politique de Platon*. Paris: Seuil.

Chiesa, C. 1995. "De quelques formes primitives de classification." In *Reading the Statesman: Proceedings of the III. Symposium Platonicum*, edited by C. Rowe. Sankt Augustin: Academia Verlag.

Clark, Stephen R. L. 1995. "Herds of Free Bipeds." In *Reading the Statesman: Proceedings of the III. Symposium Platonicum*, edited by C. Rowe. Sankt Augustin: Academia Verlag.

Cohen, G. A. 2008. *Rescuing Justice and Equality*. Cambridge, MA: Harvard University Press.

Cole, Eve Browning. 1991. "Weaving and Practical Politics in Plato's *Statesman*." *Southern Journal of Philosophy* 29 (2): 195–208.

Conroy, Drew. 1999. *Oxen: A Teamster's Guide*. Gainesboro: Rural Heritage.

Cooper, John M. 1997. "Plato's *Statesman* and Politics." In *Proceedings of the Boston Area Colloquium in Ancient Philosophy* 13: 71–103, edited by J. J. Cleary and G. M. Gurtler.

Cornford, Francis Macdonald. 1935. *Plato's Theory of Knowledge: The* Theaetetus *and the* Sophist *of Plato*. London: Routledge and Kegan Paul.

Coulobaritsis, Lambros. 1995. "Le paradigme platonicien du tissage comme modèle politique d'une société complexe." *Revue de Philosophie Ancienne* 13 (2): 107–162.

Cropsey, Joseph. 1995. *Plato's World: Man's Place in the Cosmos*. Chicago & London: University of Chicago Press.

Crosson, Frederick J. 1963. "Plato's *Statesman*: Unity and Pluralism." *New Scholasticism* 37: 28–43.

Dahl, Robert. 1989. *Democracy and its Critics*. New Haven: Yale University Press.

Davis, Morris. 1967. "The Statesman as a Political Dialogue." *American Journal of Philology* 88 (3): 319–331.

de Pinotti, Graciela Marcos. 1995. "Autour de la distinction entre *eidos* et *meros* dans le *Politique* de Platon (262a5–263e1)." In *Reading the Statesman: Proceedings of the III. Symposium Platonicum*, edited by C. Rowe. Sankt Augustin: Academia Verlag.

Delcomminette, Sylvain. 2000. *L'inventivité dialectique dans le Politique de Platon, Cahiers de philosophie ancienne no 16.* Bruxelles & Paris: Ousia.

Denyer, Nicholas. 2007. "Sun and Line: The Role of the Good." In *The Cambridge Companion to Plato's* Republic, edited by G. R. F. Ferrari. Cambridge & New York: Cambridge University Press.

Diamond, Jared. 2005. *Collapse: How Societies Choose to Fail or Succeed.* New York: Viking.

Diès, Auguste. 1935. *Le Politique.* Vol. IX, *Platon Oeuvres Complètes.* Paris: Société d'édition "Les Belles Lettres."

Dixsaut, Monique. 1995. "Une politique vraiment conforme à la nature." In *Reading the Statesman: Proceedings of the III. Symposium Platonicum*, edited by C. Rowe. Sankt Augustin: Academia Verlag.

Dodds, E. R. 1959. *Plato:* Gorgias. Oxford: Oxford University Press.

Dorter, Kenneth. 1994. *Form and Good in Plato's Eleatic Dialogues: the* Parmenides, Theaetetus, Sophist, *and* Statesman. Berkeley: University of California Press.

Erler, Michael. 1995. "Kommentar zu Brisson und Dillon." In *Reading the Statesman: Proceedings of the III. Symposium Platonicum*, edited by C. Rowe. Sankt Augustin: Academia Verlag.

Estlund, David M. 2008. *Democratic Authority: A Philosophical Framework.* Princeton: Princeton University Press.

Ferrari, G. R. F. 1995. "Myth and Conservatism in Plato's *Statesman.*" In *Reading the Statesman: Proceedings of the III. Symposium Platonicum*, edited by C. Rowe. Sankt Augustin: Academia Verlag.

Foucault, Michel. 2000 [1979]. "Omnes et Singulatim: Toward a Critique of Political Reason." In *Power*, edited by J. D. Faubion. New York: The New Press.

Gadamer, Hans Georg. 2003 [1960]. *Truth and Method*. Translated by J. Weinsheimer and D. G. Marshall. 2nd revised ed. New York: Continuum.

Gawande, Atul. 2004. "The Bell Curve: What Happens When Patients Find Out How Good Their Doctors Really Are?" *The New Yorker*, November 29.

Gill, Christopher. 1995. "Rethinking Constitutionalism in *Statesman* 291–303." In *Reading the Statesman: Proceedings of the III. Symposium Platonicum*, edited by C. Rowe. Sankt Augustin: Academia Verlag.

Gill, Mary Louise. 2005. "Method and Metaphysics in Plato's *Sophist* and *Statesman*." In *Stanford Encyclopedia of Philosophy*.

Goldschmidt, Victor. 1947. *Le paradigme dans la dialectique platonicienne*. Paris: Presses Universitaires de France.

Goodin, Robert E. 2003. *Reflective Democracy*. Oxford: Oxford University Press.

Griswold Jr., Charles L. 1989. "Politikê Epistêmê in Plato's *Statesman*." In *Essays in Ancient Greek Philosophy III: Plato*, edited by J. P. Anton and A. Preus. Albany: State University of New York Press.

Grote, George. 1875. *Plato and the other Companions of Sokrates*. 3rd ed. 3 vols. Vol. II. London: John Murray.

Guthrie, W. K. C. 1978. *A History of Greek Philosophy. Vol. V: The Later Plato and the Academy*. Cambridge: Cambridge Univ Press.

Harvey, George. 2009. "Techne and the Good in Plato's *Statesman* and *Philebus*." *Journal of the History of Philosophy* 47 (1): 1–33.

Heidegger, Martin. 1962. *Being and Time*. London: SCM Press.

Hemmenway, Scott R. 1994. "Pedagogy in the Myth of Plato's *Statesman*: Body and Soul in Relation to Philosophy and Politics." *History of Philosophy Quarterly* 11 (3): 253–268.

Hoffmann, Michael. 1993. "The 'Realization of the Due-Measure' as Structural Principle in Plato's *Statesman*." *Polis* 12 (1–2): 77–98.

Horn, Christoph. 2001. "Warum Zwei Epochen der Menschheitsgeschichte? Zum Mythos des *Politikos*." In *Platon als Mythologe: Neue Interpretationen zu den Mythen in Platons Dialogen*, edited by M. Janka and C. Schäfer. Darmstadt: Wissenschaftliche Buchgesellschaft.

Howland, Jacob. 1998. *The Paradox of Political Philosophy: Socrates' Philosophic Trial*. Lanham, MD: Rowman & Littlefield.

Irwin, Terence. 1979. *Plato:* Gorgias. Oxford: Oxford University Press.

______. 1995. *Plato's Ethics*. New York: Oxford University Press.

Kahn, Charles H. 1995. "The Place of the *Statesman* in Plato's Later Work." In *Reading the Statesman: Proceedings of the III. Symposium Platonicum*, edited by C. Rowe. Sankt Augustin: Academia Verlag.

______. 2007. "Why Is the *Sophist* a Sequel to the *Theaetetus*?" *Phronesis: A Journal for Ancient Philosophy* 52: 33–57.

Klein, Jacob. 1977. *Plato's Trilogy:* Theaetetus, *the* Sophist, *and the* Statesman. Chicago: University of Chicago Press.

Klosko, George. 1986. *The Development of Plato's Political Theory*. New York: Methuen.

______. 2006. *The Development of Plato's Political Theory*. 2nd ed. Oxford: Oxford University Press.

Klosko, George. 2008. "Knowledge and Law in Plato's *Laws*." *Political Studies* 56 (2): 456–474.

Kochin, Michael S. 1999. "Plato's Eleatic and Athenian Sciences of Politics." *The Review of Politics* 61 (1): 57–84.

Lafrance, Yvon. 1995. "Métrétique, mathématiques et dialectique en *Politique* 283c–285c." In *Reading the Statesman: Proceedings of the III. Symposium Platonicum*, edited by C. Rowe. Sankt Augustin: Academia Verlag.

Lane, Melissa. 1995. "A New Angle on Utopia: The Political Theory of the *Statesman*." In *Reading the Statesman:*

Proceedings of the III. Symposium Platonicum, edited by C. Rowe. Sankt Augustin: Academia Verlag.

_______. 1998. *Method and Politics in Plato's* Statesman. Cambridge & New York: Cambridge University Press.

Lovejoy, Arthur O., and George Boas. 1935. *Primitivism and Related Ideas in Antiquity*. Baltimore: Johns Hopkins University Press.

Márquez, Xavier. 2006. "Measure and the Arts in Plato's *Statesman*." *Plato: The Internet Journal of the International Plato Society*, http://nd.edu/~plato/plato6issue/Marquez_IPS_paper_Statesman.pdf. Last accessed: 12/7/2011.

_______. 2007. "Theory and Practice in Plato's *Statesman*." *Ancient Philosophy* 27 (1): 31–53.

_______. 2011. "Cicero and the Stability of States." *History of Political Thought* 32 (3): 397-423.

_______. 2011. "Knowledge and Law in Plato's *Statesman* and *Laws*: A Response to Klosko." *Political Studies* 59 (1): 188–203.

Masters, Roger D. 1977. "The Case of Aristotle's Missing Dialogues: Who Wrote the *Sophist*, the *Statesman*, and the *Politics*?" *Political Theory* 5 (1): 31–60.

Mattéi, Jean-François. 1996. *Platon et le miroir du mythe*. Paris: Presses universitaires de France.

McCabe, Mary Margaret. 1997. "Chaos and Control: Reading Plato's *Politicus*." *Phronesis* 42 (1): 94–117.

Miller, Mitchell, Jr. 1980. *The Philosopher in Plato's Statesman*. The Hague: Nijhoff. Reprinted 2004. Las Vegas: Parmenides Publishing.

Miller, Mitchell. 2007. "Beginning the 'Longer Way.'" In *The Cambridge Companion to Plato's* Republic, edited by G. R. F. Ferrari. Cambridge & New York: Cambridge University Press.

Mishima, Teruo. 1995. "Courage and Moderation in the *Statesman*." In *Reading the Statesman: Proceedings of the III. Symposium Platonicum*, edited by C. Rowe. Sankt Augustin: Academia Verlag.

Morrow, Glenn R. 1960a. "The Nocturnal Council in Plato's *Laws*." *Archiv für Geschichte der Philosophie* 42: 229–246.

_______. 1960b. *Plato's Cretan City: A Historical Interpretation of the Laws*. Princeton, N.J.: Princeton University Press.

Nails, Debra. 2000. "Mouthpiece Schmouthpiece." In *Who Speaks for Plato?*, edited by G. A. Press. Lanham, MD: Rowman & Littlefield.

Narcy, Michel. 1995. "La critique de Socrate par l'Etranger dans le *Politique*." In *Reading the Statesman: Proceedings of the III. Symposium Platonicum*, edited by C. Rowe. Sankt Augustin: Academia Verlag.

Neiman, Paul. 2007. "The Practicality of Plato's *Statesman*." *History of Political Thought* 28 (3): 402–418.

Nightingale, Andrea Wilson. 1996. "Plato on the Origins of Evil: The *Statesman* Myth Reconsidered." *Ancient Philosophy* 16 (1): 65–91.

_______. 2002. "Distant Views: 'Realistic' and 'Fantastic' Mimesis in Plato." In *New Perspectives on Plato, Modern and Ancient*, edited by J. Annas and C. Rowe. Washington, D.C.: Center for Hellenic Studies.

Notomi, Noburu. 1999. *The Unity of Plato's* Sophist*: Between the Sophist and the Philosopher*. New York: Cambridge University Press.

Nussbaum, Martha Craven. 1986. *The Fragility of Goodness: Luck and Ethics in Greek Tragedy and Philosophy*. Cambridge & New York: Cambridge University Press.

Oakeshott, Michael. 1991 [1962]. *Rationalism in Politics and Other Essays*. Indianapolis: Liberty Fund.

Ober, Josiah. 2008. *Democracy and Knowledge: Innovation and Learning in Classical Athens*. Princeton: Princeton University Press.

Owen, G. E. L. 1973. "Plato on the Undepictable." *Phronesis* Supplementary Volume 1: 349–361.

Page, Scott. 2007. *The Difference: How the Power of Diversity Creates Better Groups, Firms, Schools, and Societies*. Princeton: Princeton University Press.

Palumbo, Lidia. 1995. "Realtà e apparenza nel Sofista e nel Politico." In *Reading the Statesman: Proceedings of the III. Symposium Platonicum*, edited by C. Rowe. Sankt Augustin: Academia Verlag.

Parfit, Derek. 1984. *Reasons and Persons*. Oxford: Clarendon Press.

Penner, Terry. 2005. "Platonic Justice and What We Mean by 'Justice.'" *Plato: The Internet Journal of the International Plato Society* 5. http://gramata.univ-paris1.fr/Plato/spip.php?article60. Last accessed: 7/12/2011.

Philip, J. A. 1961. "Mimesis in the Sophistes of Plato." *Transactions and Proceedings of the American Philological Association* 92: 453–468.

Polya, George. 1971. *How to Solve It: A New Aspect of Mathematical Method*. 2nd ed. Princeton: Princeton University Press.

Pradeau, Jean-Francois. 2002. *Plato and the City: A New Introduction to Plato's Political Thought*. Exeter: University of Exeter Press.

Rawls, John. 1999. *A Theory of Justice*. Rev. ed. Cambridge, MA: Harvard University Press.

Rawson, Elizabeth. 1975. *Cicero: A Portrait*. Ithaca: Cornell University Press.

Reeve, C. D. C. 1988. *Philosopher-Kings: The Argument of Plato's* Republic. Princeton, N.J.: Princeton University Press.

Robinson, D. B. 1995. *Politicus*. In *Platonis Opera: Tomus I*, edited by E. A. Duke, W. F. Hicken, W. S. M. Nicoll, D. B. Robinson, and J. C. G. Strachan. Oxford: Oxford University Press.

Roochnik, David. 2005. "Residual Ambiguity in Plato's *Statesman*." *Plato: The Internet Journal of the International Plato Society*, http://gramata.univ-paris1.fr/Plato/spip.php?article26. Last accessed: 12/7/2011.

Rosen, Stanley. 1979. "Plato's Myth of the Reversed Cosmos." *Review of Metaphysics* 33 (1): 59–85.

_______. 1995. *Plato's* Statesman*: The Web of Politics*. New Haven: Yale University Press.

Rowe, Christopher. 1995a. "Introduction." In *Reading the Statesman: Proceedings of the III. Symposium Platonicum*, edited by C. Rowe. Sankt Augustin: Academia Verlag.

_______. 1995b. *Plato:* Statesman. Warminster: Aris & Phillips.

_______. 1996. "The *Politicus*: Structure and Form." In *Form and Argument in Late Plato*, edited by C. Gill and M. M. McCabe. Oxford: Clarendon Press.

_______. 1999. *Plato:* Statesman. Indianapolis: Hackett.

_______. 2001a. "Killing Socrates: Plato's Later Thoughts on Democracy." *Journal of Hellenic Studies* (121): 63–76.

_______. 2001b. "Zwei oder Drei Phasen? Der Mythos im *Politikos*." In *Platon als Mythologe: Neue Interpretationen zu den Mythen in Platons Dialogen*, edited by M. Janka and C. Schäfer. Darmstadt: Wissenschaftliche Buchgesellschaft.

_______. 2005. "The Treatment of Non-Ideal Constitutions in the *Politicus*." *Plato: The Internet Journal of the International Plato Society*, http://gramata.univ-paris1.fr/Plato/spip.php?article59. Last accessed: 12/7/2011.

Ruelle, David. 2007. *The Mathematician's Brain*. Princeton: Princeton University Press.

Samaras, Thanassis. 2002. *Plato on Democracy*. New York: P. Lang.

Sayre, Kenneth M. 1969. *Plato's Analytic Method*. Chicago: University of Chicago Press.

_______. 2005. "Excess and Deficiency at *Statesman* 283c–285c." *Plato: The Internet Journal of the International Plato Society*, http://gramata.univ-paris1.fr/Plato/spip.php?page=article&id_article=58. Last accessed: 12/7/2011.

Schäfer, Christian. 2001. "Herrschen und Selbstbeherrschung: Der Mythos des *Politikos*." In *Platon als Mythologe: Neue Interpretationen zu den Mythen in Platons Dialogen*, edited by M. Janka and C. Schäfer. Darmstadt: Wissenschaftliche Buchgesellschaft.

Schofield, Malcolm. 1997. "The Disappearance of the Philosopher-King." In *Proceedings of the Boston Area Colloquium in Ancient Philosophy* 13: 213–241, edited by J. J. Cleary and G. M. Gurtler.

_______. 2006. *Plato: Political Philosophy.* Oxford: Oxford University Press.

Schuhl, Pierre-Maxime. 1968. *La fabulation platonicienne.* 2nd revised and updated ed. Paris: J. Vrin.

Scodel, Harvey Ronald. 1987. *Diaeresis and Myth in Plato's* Statesman. Göttingen: Vandenhoeck & Ruprecht.

Sedley, David. 2002. "Socratic Irony in the Platonist Commentators." In *New Perspectives on Plato, Modern and Ancient*, edited by J. Annas and C. Rowe. Washington, D.C.: Center for Hellenic Studies.

_______. 2004. *The Midwife of Platonism: Text and Subtext in Plato's* Theaetetus. Oxford: Oxford University Press.

Sedley, David. 2007. "Philosophy, the Forms, and the Art of Ruling." In *The Cambridge Companion to Plato's* Republic, edited by G. R. F. Ferrari. Cambridge & New York: Cambridge University Press.

Skemp, J. B. 1987. *Plato's* Statesman. 2nd ed. Bristol: Bristol Classical Press.

Sprague, Rosamond Kent. 1976. *Plato's Philosopher-King: A Study of the Theoretical Background.* Columbia: University of South Carolina Press.

Stalley, Richard F. 1983. *An Introduction to Plato's* Laws. Indiana*polis*: Hackett.

Stern, Paul. 1997. "The Rule of Wisdom and the Rule of Law in Plato's *Statesman*." *American Political Science Review* 91 (2): 264–276.

Strauss, Leo. 1989. "Plato." In *An Introduction to Political Philosophy: Ten Essays by Leo Strauss*, edited by H. Gildin. Detroit: Wayne State University Press.

Surowiecki, James. 2004. *The Wisdom of Crowds: Why the Many are Smarter than the Few and How Collective Wisdom*

Shapes Business, Economies, Societies, and Nations. New York: Doubleday.

Tarrant, Harold. 2000a. *Plato's First Interpreters*. Ithaca, N.Y.: Cornell University Press.

______. 2000b. "Where Plato Speaks: Reflections on an Ancient Debate." In *Who Speaks for Plato?*, edited by G. A. Press. Lanham, MD: Rowman & Littlefield.

Taylor, A. E. 1961. *Plato: The* Sophist *and the* Statesman. Edited by R. Klibansky and E. Anscombe. Thomas Nelson & Sons. Reprinted 1971. New York: Barnes and Noble.

Tegmark, Max. 2008. "The Mathematical Universe." *Foundations of Physics* 38 (2): 101–150.

Teisserenc, Fulcran. 2005. "Il ne faut en rien être plus savant que les lois: Loi et conaissance dans le *Politique*." *Les études philosophiques* 74 (3): 367–383.

Tejera, Victorino. 1999. *Plato's Dialogues One by One: a Dialogical Interpretation*. Lanham: University Press of America.

Tigerstedt, E. N. 1977. *Interpreting Plato*. Stockholm: Almqvist & Wiksell.

Tordesillas, Alonso. 1995. "Le point culminant de la métrétique." In *Reading the Statesman: Proceedings of the III. Symposium Platonicum*, edited by C. Rowe. Sankt Augustin: Academia Verlag.

Turing, A. M. 1950. "Computing Machinery and Intelligence." *Mind, New Series* 59 (236): 433–460.

Vanhoutte, Maurice. 1954. *La Philosophie Politique de Platon dans les "Lois."* Louvain: Publications universitaires de Louvain.

Vidal-Naquet, Pierre. 1978. "Plato's Myth of the *Statesman*, the Ambiguities of the Golden Age and of History." *Journal of Hellenic Studies* 98: 132–141.

Voegelin, Eric. 1987 [1956]. *Order and History. Vol. 3: Plato and Aristotle*. Baton Rouge: Lousiana State University Press.

Waldron, Jeremy. 1995. "The Wisdom of the Multitude: Some Reflections on Book III Chapter 11 of the *Politics*." *Political Theory* 23: 563–584.

Weiss, Roslyn. 1995. "Statesman as EPISTHMWN: Caretaker, Physician, and Weaver." In *Reading the Statesman: Proceedings of the III. Symposium Platonicum*, edited by C. Rowe. Sankt Augustin: Academia Verlag.

White, David A. 2007. *Myth, Metaphysics and Dialectic in Plato's* Statesman. Aldershot, England & Burlington, VT: Ashgate.

Wittgenstein, Ludwig. 1992 [1919]. *Tractatus Logico-Philosophicus*. Translated by C. K. Ogden. London & New York: Routledge.

Wolin, Sheldon S. 1960. *Politics and Vision: Continuity and Innovation in Western Political Thought*. Boston: Little.

Zuckert, Catherine. 2005. The Stranger's Political Science v. Socrates' Political Art. *Plato: The Internet Journal of the International Plato Society*, http://gramata.univ-paris1.fr/Plato/IMG/pdf/Zuckert.pdf. Last accessed: 12/7/2011.

Index Locorum

General Index

• ALSO AVAILABLE FROM PARMENIDES PUBLISHING •

PRE-SOCRATICS

By Being, It Is: *The Thesis of Parmenides* by Néstor-Luis Cordero
To Think Like God: *Pythagoras and Parmenides. The Origins of Philosophy*. Scholarly and fully annotated edition by Arnold Hermann
The Illustrated To Think Like God: *Pythagoras and Parmenides. The Origins of Philosophy* by Arnold Hermann with over 200 full color illustrations.
The Legacy of Parmenides: *Eleatic Monism and Later Presocratic Thought* by Patricia Curd
Parmenides and the History of Dialectic: *Three Essays* by Scott Austin
Parmenides, Venerable and Awesome: *Proceedings of the International Symposium* edited by Néstor-Luis Cordero
The Route of Parmenides: *Revised and Expanded Edition, With a New Introduction, Three Supplemental Essays, and an Essay by Gregory Vlastos* by Alexander P. D. Mourelatos
The Fragments of Parmenides: *A Critical Text with Introduction and Translation, the Ancient Testimonia and a Commentary* by A. H. Coxon. Revised and Expanded Edition edited with new Translations by Richard McKirahan and a new Preface by Malcolm Schofield

PLATO

God and Forms in Plato by Richard D. Mohr
***Image and Paradigm in Plato's* Sophist** by David Ambuel
Interpreting Plato's Dialogues by J. Angelo Corlett
One Book, the Whole Universe: *Plato's* Timaeus *Today* edited by Richard D. Mohr and Barbara M. Sattler
***The Philosopher in Plato's* Statesman** by Mitchell Miller
Platonic Patterns: *A Collection of Studies* by Holger Thesleff
Plato's Late Ontology: *A Riddle Resolved* by Kenneth M. Sayre
***Plato's* Parmenides:** *Text, Translation & Introductory Essay* by Arnold Hermann. Translation in collaboration with Sylvana Chrysakopoulou with a Foreword by Douglas Hedley
Plato's Universe by Gregory Vlastos
***A Stranger's Knowledge: Statesmanship, Philosophy, and Law in Plato's* Statesman** by Xavier Márquez

ARISTOTLE

***One and Many in Aristotle's* Metaphysics**—*Volume I: Books Alpha-Delta* by Edward C. Halper
***One and Many in Aristotle's* Metaphysics**—*Volume 2: The Central Books* by Edward C. Halper
Reading Aristotle:* Physics *VII.3 "What is Alteration?" *Proceedings of the International ESAP-HYELE Conference* edited by Stefano Maso, Carlo Natali, and Gerhard Seel

HELLENISTIC PHILOSOPHY

A Life Worthy of the Gods: *The Materialist Psychology of Epicurus* by David Konstan

THE ENNEADS *OF PLOTINUS*
—WITH PHILOSOPHICAL COMMENTARIES
Series edited by John M. Dillon and Andrew Smith

Plotinus,* Ennead *IV.8: On the Descent of the Soul into Bodies. Translation with an Introduction & Commentary by Barrie Fleet

ETHICS

Sentience and Sensibility: *A Conversation about Moral Philosophy* by Matthew R. Silliman

AUDIOBOOKS

The Iliad (unabridged) by Stanley Lombardo
The Odyssey (unabridged) by Stanley Lombardo
The Essential Homer by Stanley Lombardo
The Essential Iliad by Stanley Lombardo

FORTHCOMING

Presocratics and Plato: *A Festschrift in Honor of Charles Kahn* edited by Arnold Hermann, Vassilis Karasmanis and Richard Patterson
Plotinus,* Ennead *V.5: That the Intelligibles are not outside the Intellectual-Principle; and on the Good. Translation with an Introduction & Commentary by Lloyd Gerson
Plotinus,* Ennead *IV.7: On the Immortality of the Soul. Translation with an Introduction & Commentary by Barrie Fleet
Aristotle's Empiricism: *Experience and Mechanics in the Fourth Century BCE* by Jean De Groot